VICTORIAN FAITH IN CRISIS

D1477730

Also by Richard J. Helmstadter

RELIGION IN VICTORIAN SOCIETY (*editor with Paul Phillips*)

Also by Bernard Lightman

THE ORIGINS OF AGNOSTICISM
VICTORIAN SCIENCE AND RELIGION (*with Sydney Eisen*)

Victorian Faith in Crisis

Essays on Continuity and Change in Nineteenth-Century Religious Belief

Edited by

Richard J. Helmstadter
Professor of History
University of Toronto

and

Bernard Lightman
Associate Professor of Humanities
York University, Canada

THE LIBRARY
COLLEGE OF RIPON AND YORK ST. JOHN
COLLEGE ROAD, RIPON HG4 2QX

MACMILLAN

© Richard J. Helmstadter and Bernard Lightman 1990

All rights reserved. No reproduction, copy or transmission
of this publication may be made without written permission.

No paragraph of this publication may be reproduced, copied or
transmitted save with written permission or in accordance with
the provisions of the Copyright, Designs and Patents Act 1988,
or under the terms of any licence permitting limited copying
issued by the Copyright Licensing Agency, 33–4 Alfred Place,
London WC1E 7DP.

Any person who does any unauthorised act in relation to
this publication may be liable to criminal prosecution and
civil claims for damages.

First published 1990

Published by
MACMILLAN ACADEMIC AND PROFESSIONAL LTD
Houndmills, Basingstoke, Hampshire RG21 2XS
and London
Companies and representatives
throughout the world

Filmset by Wearside Tradespools, Fulwell, Sunderland

Printed in Great Britain by Billing & Sons Ltd, Worcester

British Library Cataloguing in Publication Data
Victorian faith in crisis.
1. Christianity, history
I. Helmstadter, Richard J.   II. Lightman, Bernard
209
ISBN 0–333–49660–4

For Carol and Merle

Contents

Acknowledgements

The editors would like to express their appreciation to the Social Sciences and Humanities Research Council of Canada for their generous support of the conference on 'Victorian Faith in Crisis' from which this collection of essays grew. We are also indebted to Victoria College, University of Toronto, for serving as host institution for the conference. Finally, we acknowledge with gratitude assistance provided by the Ontario Arts Council for help in preparing the manuscript for publication.

RICHARD J. HELMSTADTER
BERNARD LIGHTMAN

Notes on the Contributors

Jeffrey von Arx is Associate Professor of History at Georgetown University. He is the author of *Progress and Pessimism: Religion, Politics and History in Late Nineteenth Century Britain*, and co-author of 'Victorian Ethics of Belief: A Reconsideration', in W.W. Wagar (ed.) *The Secular Mind: Transformations of Faith in Modern Europe*.

Jeffrey Cox is Professor of History at the University of Iowa. He is the author of *The English Churches in a Secular Society: Lambeth, 1870–1930*.

Sydney Eisen is Professor of History and Humanities at York University, Canada. He is the co-author of *Victorian Science and Religion*, and the author of articles on Huxley, Spencer and Positivism.

Richard J. Helmstadter is Professor of History at the University of Toronto. He is the co-author of *Religion and Victorian Society*, and the author of articles and chapters on Victorian religious and intellectual history.

Mark D. Johnson is Assistant Vice Provost at the University of Toronto. He is the author of *The Dissolution of Dissent in Late Victorian England*, and other works on English and Canadian religious history.

George Levine is Professor of English at Rutgers University. He is the author of *One Culture: Essays in Science and Literature*, and *The Realistic Imagination*, and co-editor of *The Art of Victorian Prose*; *The Boundaries of Fiction*; and *The Endurance of Frankenstein*.

Bernard Lightman is Associate Professor of Humanities at York University, Canada. He is the author of *The Origins of Agnosticism*, co-editor of *Victorian Science and Religion*, and author of articles on science and religion in Victorian England.

James R. Moore is Lecturer in the History of Science and Technology at the Open University, UK. He is the author of *The Post-Darwinian Controversies: A Study of the Struggle to Come to Terms With Darwin in Great Britain and America, 1870–1900*, and other works on Victorian science and religion.

John M. Robson is a University Professor at the University of Toronto. He is the General Editor of *The Collected Works of John Stuart Mill*, and editor of several of the volumes. He is the author of *The Improvement of Mankind*, a study of J.S. Mill, and of other works on Victorian literature and intellectual history.

Frank Turner is Professor of History and Provost at Yale University. He is the author of *Between Science and Religion*; *The Greek Heritage in Victorian Britain*, and other works on Victorian intellectual history.

W.R. Ward is Professor of Modern History (retired) at the University of Durham. He is the author of *The English Land Tax in the 18th Century*; *Georgian Oxford*; *Victorian Oxford*; *Religion and Society in England, 1790–1850*; *The Early Correspondence of Jabez Bunting*; *Early Victorian Methodism; Theology, Sociology and Politics – the German Protestant Social Conscience, 1890–1930*; and articles on the religious and political history of England and Germany in the eighteenth and nineteenth centuries.

R.K. Webb is Presidential Research Professor at the University of Maryland, Baltimore County. He was formerly the editor of the *American Historical Review* and before that Professor of History at Columbia University. He is the author of *The British Working Class Reader*; *Harriet Martineau: a Radical Victorian*; *Modern England*, and other works on Victorian history.

Introduction
Sydney Eisen

Until the last two or three decades, historians tended to see the 'crisis of faith' in Victorian England in relatively simple terms. They regarded it as an intellectual and emotional upheaval, stemming from challenges to the historicity of the Bible, discoveries in geology and biology, and concerns about morality, or rather, the apparent lack of it, in nature. Science and religion, more precisely science and theology, were deemed to be 'in conflict', the battle lines clearly drawn, and for some time, the Victorian champions of science and unbelief seemed to carry the day with the historians.

In more recent years, however, scholars with perhaps a deeper sense of the continuity of ideas, or greater sensitivity to the role of religion, have pointed out that Darwinian evolution was rooted in the Christian culture of the day, that science and belief were not inevitably antagonistic, and that advocates of science were not necessarily hostile to religion. They noted as well that doubters often harboured deeply religious yearnings and sometimes found their way back to faith, and they insisted that the 'decline of religion' was neither predetermined nor an automatic consequence of scientific 'progress'. Some have suggested that the great Victorian warriors who fought for 'science and truth' have received more than adequate honours, and that agnosticism, so devastating on the attack, posed disturbing philosophical problems for science as well as faith. On reflection it seemed that the forces of religion were remarkably skilful in parrying the threat from naturalism. Though many Victorians themselves were convinced that they were embattled over questions of science and belief, scholars now argue that not only is it difficult to make sharp distinctions between scientists and theologians in their response to these issues, but that the very notion of a conflict over ideas is itself an oversimplification. They maintain that the antagonisms which arose among intellectuals were less motivated by religious differences than by a mixture of complex, often unselfconscious

1

motives, involving identity, ambition, status, and preferment. They maintain, moreover, that religious tensions were part of a greater struggle between the forces of conservatism and the forces of change, indeed between an old and a new theodicy. Herbert Spencer, whose universal law of development demanded that all things material and mental evolve from the simple to the complex, would have been gratified to find in the historiography of the crisis of faith one more proof to support his grand synthesis.

Perhaps we ought to ask what we mean by 'crisis'. The word itself implies the emergence of a condition of disturbing proportions, one that could be distinguished from both a previous and a later less critical state. A crisis, then, must have both a discernable beginning and end, and the issues which are at stake must be identifiable. Sorting out the evidence for such a crisis in matters of faith in Victorian England is no simple task, as Owen Chadwick suggests in a remark about the reluctance of men, after 1860, to pursue clerical careers in the Anglican Church or the Free Churches: 'Victorian critics were inclined to declare that "many men" were deterred from taking orders by their inability to profess what the Church insisted that they profess. Of course men had always been deterred from taking orders by this inability. It is easier to find general assertions that more men found it difficult during the second half of the reign of Queen Victoria than to find instances of men who found it difficult and told men why'.[1] And one might add that we are only marginally better off when a few men do try to tell us why, for attempts at self-analysis, especially when carried out in the course of reconstructing one's early life for autobiographical purposes, may conceal as much as they reveal. Even if we were to take at face value contemporary cries of spiritual distress, we would still mainly be talking about a small number of articulate middle class intellectuals.

However we define 'crisis', and however we endeavour to interpret the particular sense of crisis in this period, many Victorians did believe that religion was in a perilous state. Disquieting questions involving evidence and faith were the preoccupation of sensitive minds, because religion was not only a matter of belief but also an integral part of personal and public morality, family life, social position, occupation, and friendship, not to mention education and party politics. Convulsions in belief were thus bound to have wide implications, and the accompanying distress found expression in some of the best (and worst) literature of the day.

While the majority of essays in this volume make a compelling case for viewing the crisis of faith as part of a broader social and political context, many articulate Victorians, of course, experienced it and wrote about it in personal terms. They seemed to feel a need to speak out, even to wax poetic, on the pilgrimage of the individual soul, as it passed from what was often (though by no means always) a peaceful childhood, through turmoil, on the way to a new resting place, either within or outside the Christian fold. Relating the whole agonising adventure in somber detail gave a certain aura of legitimacy to the outcome. Those fortunate individuals who left behind traditional religion but were spared such an ordeal (e.g. Frederic Harrison and Herbert Spencer) felt compelled to make us aware of their peculiar good fortune. The struggle, though necessarily an inner experience, did take on a certain ritual quality, and the individual who had suffered through it often emerged with a sense of triumph, over either unbelief, or belief. A happy outcome, however, was not guaranteed, and while some came out of their confusion into the clear sunshine of the old faith renewed, or of a new faith, or of no faith at all, there were others, less fortunate, for whom the clouds never lifted, and who carried the burden of a permanent sense of loss.

As it turned out, neither the fears nor the hopes of Victorians who lived through the period of the crisis of faith were entirely realised. If religion, either in the form of institutional membership or personal belief, 'declined', it certainly did not cease to be a significant social and spiritual force; if the Bible was alleged to be full of errors (not to mention its deficiencies as a guide for proper behaviour), it did not cease to be a source of inspiration or of history; and if the old standard of conduct was undermined by the erosion of traditional values, it did not by any means cease to matter in the larger arena of life. From another perspective, 'the scientific method', as generally perceived by optimistic Victorians, did not always fulfil its promise nor prove to be invulnerable, whether applied to the natural world, humanity, or scripture. Moreover, science, once it established its authority and found its place in education, became less strident, and religion, witnessing its own intellectual and organisational survival, became less fearful. It seems that science and religion, after all the turbulence surrounding their relationship, were able to flourish side by side in an association like that of blood relations, who, whether they like it or not, are permanently linked.

The crisis of faith in Victorian England has called forth its own body of scholarly literature, but as yet there is no single comprehensive study of the subject. The one slender volume specifically devoted to the theme, *The Victorian Crisis of Faith* (1970) edited by Anthony Symondson, consists of a series of six lectures by different authors, delivered in London in November 1968. Five of the contributors focus on different aspects of the turmoil within and around the Church, ranging from the impact of Evangelicalism to the reform of the Prayer Book.[2] The opening address by Robert M. Young, 'The Impact of Darwin on Conventional Thought', while written from a secular perspective, also places Darwin's work and the controversy surrounding it squarely within the framework of the prevailing Christian culture. Without attempting to minimize the initial trauma produced by the *Origin of Species*, Young maintains that 'the evolutionary debate' can be seen as 'merely a demarcation dispute within natural theology', and that the new ideas were in fact accommodated with remarkable ease both by traditional believers as well as those 'who were devoted believers in the secular religion of Progress'.[3] In Young's view, the rapid acceptance of Darwin's ideas in traditional circles can best be understood in terms of the Christian milieu in which evolution emerged. This challenge to the older notion of a sharp break with the past becomes the motif of a number of the essays in the present volume.

This collection is made up of eleven papers by scholars who have explored shifts in religion as they relate to changes taking place in the society as a whole. Most of them have devoted a significant portion of their careers to the study of Victorian belief and unbelief. As these papers advance our understanding of the 'crisis of faith' along several fronts, they leave us with a sense of the persistence of continuity in the midst of significant change.

Simple, more classical notions of the crisis of faith are challenged throughout, and new interpretations unfolded. We learn of the near obliviousness of the English to more radical German biblical criticism, of the logic and rhetoric of the world of Natural Theology in which the crisis germinated, and of the relatively easy manner with which one denomination, the Unitarians, sailed through the spiritual storm that surrounded them. We are invited to understand religious strife in the way it was acted out in the context of the firmly structured Victorian family, as an outward expression of psychological tensions inevitably accompanying the struggles of adolescents for a degree of independence. Several authors maintain that the roots and implications of these conflicts are broadly social, involving not only personal relations, but economic distinctions, professional status, and political action. They argue, moreover, that the battles fought over religion were manifestations of deeper struggles in the course of which a new world view, based on evolution and rationalism, was born, replacing or restructuring the old world view of Natural Theology. Several papers take us into the diverse realm of agnosticism, more than one would suspect, a place of mixed emotions, including sadness, religious longing, as well as elation. And, finally, travelling to distant parts of the empire, we are brought face to face with the 'crisis of faith' in new settings: the missionary activities in the Punjab throw light on the connection between the traditional class attitudes of the Anglican Church at home and abroad towards recruiting among the lower orders and the decline of Church membership in England; and the career of a Canadian Methodist minister points up to the relationship between social action and religious doubt, with the former seen as providing an escape from the predicament of the latter. The essays in this volume explore new ground and apply highly effective tools in that exploration. They promise to be our point of departure for some time to come in the ongoing study of the Victorian crisis of faith.

NOTES

1.   Owen Chadwick, 'The Established Church under Attack', in Anthony Symondson (ed.), *The Victorian Crisis of Faith* (London, 1970) 99.
2.   The lectures and their authors are: 1. 'The Impact of Darwin on Conventional Thought', Robert M. Young; 2. 'Evangelicalism and the Victorians', Geoffrey Best; 3. 'The Church Militant Abroad: Victorian Missionaries', Max Warren; 4. 'Newman and the Oxford Movement', David Newsome; 5. 'The Established Church under Attack', Owen Chadwick; 6. 'The Prayer Book in the Victorian Era', R. C. D. Jasper. A glance at the table of contents of the two volumes will indicate how the field has changed.
3.   Young, in Symondson, 22, 24, 26, 31.

Part I
Continuity and Change

1 The Victorian Crisis of Faith and the Faith That was Lost

Frank M. Turner

In the past scholars have generally regarded Victorian faith in crisis as primarily an intellectual experience. They have tended to point to works of dissolvent literature associated with enlightenment rationalism, the higher criticism of the Bible, or new theories of physical science as the chief causes for particular persons modifying or rejecting the faith of their childhoods. The nineteenth-century documents recording the loss-of-faith experience in no small measure themselves led to that conclusion. In their autobiographies Victorian doubters or unbelievers often recalled the impact of advanced works of science, biblical criticism, or history upon their religious thought and then recounted the manner in which those new ideas had led them to renounce major Christian doctrines, to stop attending church, to change denominations, to leave the Christian ministry, or to embrace atheism, agnosticism, or some other substitute for traditional Christianity. Many of the loss-of-faith novels, such as *Robert Elsmere* (1888) and *The Autobiography of Mark Rutherford* (1881), embodied this same scenario. Furthermore, the earliest histories that examined the rise of religiously dissolvent literature, such as *A Critical History of Free Thought* (1862) by A.A. Farrar, *History of Rationalism* (1867) by J.F. Hurst, and *The History of English Rationalism in the Nineteenth Century* (1906) by A.W. Benn set forth this intellectualist analysis. Twentieth-century historians and literary scholars generally continued this mode of analysis. They rather uncritically assumed that intellectual factors or motivations alone must have moulded actions claimed by the Victorians to have been taken for intellectual reasons.

In recent years, as exemplified by the chapters in this volume, somewhat new outlooks have come to inform the

historical, religious, and literary considerations of Victorian
faith in crisis. Scholars from various fields now regard the
Victorian crisis in faith as a *problematical* occurrence. That is
to say, they no longer regard it as the inevitable and virtually
self-explanatory result of the expansion of progressive historical and scientific knowledge. They have stopped reading
the documents recording and analysing changes in faith at
face value. James Moore's important analysis of the military
metaphor in the debates over the relationship of science and
religion has alerted Victorian scholars to the subtle and
powerful polemic that may reside in what appear to be
non-polemical, rather matter-of-fact figures of speech.[1] Recent literary criticism has awakened a new awareness of the
manner in which setting personal experiences into a narrative format, such as the autobiography, reshapes the experiences so narrated, brings them under control, and provides
outer ordered form to what was a more formless and much
less orderly subjective experience. Narrative may in that
manner render a fearful experience into a more nearly safe
and familiar one. Consequently, the content of a narrative
almost inevitably constitutes only a portion of the experience
narrated and cannot be regarded as an unproblematic record. Finally, even the barest acquaintance with psychology
leads the scholar to understand that behind intellectual and
intellectualised experiences reside non-rational and non-
intellectual forces of feeling and emotion which may both
mask and manifest themselves in rational appearances.

Without intending to deny the power of the printed word
on the mind or the efficacy of ideas on actions, scholars now
feel that it is necessary to think more critically and sensitively
about the social and cultural functions and meanings of that
Victorian behaviour traditionally subsumed under the terms
'loss of faith' or 'crisis of faith' or 'faith in crisis'. Why did loss
of faith as an observable and much discussed cultural phenomenon commence in the 1840s rather than in the immediate wake of the rationalist writings of the eighteenth-century
enlightenment, which would seem to have provided more
than enough critical ideas to shake religious faith if ideas
alone were the crucial motivating factor? Were there elements in the religious life of the nineteenth century rather
than in the dissolvent literature itself that contributed to loss

of faith or determined the course of its occurrence? Why did unorthodox or advanced dissolvent religious ideas find in certain cases a mind or heart prepared to receive them? To what extent were the actions of some persons who experienced a loss of faith related to areas of their lives that were distinct from religion proper? Did their turmoil and apostasy in regard to the Christian supernatural allow them in some manner to deal with natural modes of personal human development that might have been even more painful and traumatic if confronted directly than if mediated through the obviously (indeed necessarily obviously) painful experience of loss or change of faith? In other words, what can be understood about the loss-of-faith phenomena if scholars regard them as something that did occur in the middle and late years of the nineteenth century rather than as something that necessarily had to occur simply as the result of the march of mind? Finally, what new insights into the Victorian crisis of belief can be achieved if scholars regard religious behaviour as a product of social and psychological interaction among human beings rather than as a manifestation of the interaction of human beings with the divine, which has remained the often unstated working assumption of much previous scholarly literature on the subject.

A remarkable and virtually unnoticed irony lies at the very heart of the problem of nineteenth-century religious doubt, unbelief, and scepticism. Victorian faith entered crisis not in the midst of any attack on religion but rather during the period of the most fervent religious crusade that the British nation had known since the seventeenth century, indeed during the last great effort on the part of all denominations to Christianise Britain. The religion that was rejected, modified, and transformed in the lives of generally young intellectuals was not some mode of staid long-established Christianity (whatever that may be) but rather a recently intensified faith associated with militant Christian institutions. In this regard it seems virtually certain that the personal experiences of religious crisis and the public criticism of ecclesiastical institutions arose less from dissolvent, sceptical literature than from a Christian faith that had become overbearingly intense on the personal and vocational levels and shamelessly embittered on the political, educational, and social scenes.

Broady speaking, three basic interrelated factors led to this intensified religious life. First, the political reaction to the French Revolution brought religion to the forefront of public life.[2] Many of the policies of the revolution were anti-clerical and others distinctly anti-Christian. Edmund Burke's counter-revolutionary polemic blamed the turmoil in France on atheistic and materialistic writers. He further linked his criticism of France to the alleged danger of radical domestic political change posed by Protestant Nonconformists in general and the rationalist Unitarians in particular. In Burke's mind and that of others the ongoing resistance to the revolution assumed the character of a crusade to protect religion. As Britain assumed the leadership of the counter-revolutionary coalition against France the protection of religion in turn became increasingly associated with the preservation of the existing social and political structures. For all the propertied classes religion came to have a new importance and became something that required fostering. One manifestation of that public support for the Church of England was the post-Waterloo parliamentary grant for the building of new churches in London.

Also directly related to the anti-revolutionary political polemic was what can only be described as a revival in publications expounding natural religion. The connection between the pursuit of science and natural religion was, of course, a longstanding one, but a new intensity came to that viewpoint at the turn of the century as the religiosity of the anti-revolutionary ideology required British intellectuals working in and near scientific and rational thought to reassert their own orthodox religious commitment. From the publication of Paley's *Natural Theology* (1802) onward one work of natural theology after another fell from British printing presses, with the Bridgewater Treatises being the most famous. Two strategies were in operation. Clergymen appealed to natural theology to refute the alleged materialism, scepticism, and atheism of radical religious, philosophical, or scientific writers. Scientists, who were of course also often clergymen, in turn appropriated a new emphasis on natural theology to demonstrate that science and rational thought correctly understood would lead not to materialism, atheism, and revolution as in France but rather to reverence

for God and support for the existing political and social
order. The leadership of the British Association for the
Advancement of Science (1831) consciously used natural
religion both to protect science from dangerous political
associations, previously embodied by the radical Unitarian
scientist Joseph Priestley, and to advance the cause of science
among the propertied classes during the era of reform.[3]

The second factor leading to an intensified religious life
arose from the attack on, and the demise of, the exclusive
Anglican confessional state. The undermining of the Anglican religious-political monopoly had begun in earnest with
the late-eighteenth-century drive by Protestant Nonconformists to secure broader civil rights and later became most
fully realised in the repeal of the Tests Act, the passage of
Catholic emancipation, the restructuring of the finances of
the Church of England, and eventually in the disestablishment of the Anglican Church in Ireland and Wales. In the
face of these destructive reforms and the unrelenting Nonconformist attacks and institutional growth, the Church of
England found that it must henceforth compete as a denomination in the religious marketplace. Such competition
required Anglicans to define themselves theologically, and
that process in turn, especially as a result of the Tractarian
Movement, generated competing parties within the established church. Consequently, one result of the Anglican loss
of political privilege was a marked resurgence in the religious
activity of the Church of England as well as new political
actions to preserve its surviving advantages or to recapture
lost ones. In addition to this resurgence of Anglican activity
there occurred further new religious activity and denominational competition resulting from the Great Disruption in the
Church of Scotland, the expansion of the Protestant Nonconformist denominations, the Roman Catholic revival in
Ireland led by Paul Cullen, and the restoration of the Roman
Catholic hierarchy in England under Nicholas Wiseman.[4]

The third significant manifestation of new intensity in
British religious life was the late-eighteenth- and early-
nineteenth-century evangelical revival. Evangelical Christianity was an intensely personal religion grounded in subjective religious experience, which could and often did lead to
immense introspection. Evangelical Christians spurned

nominal Christianity that allegedly involved the outward
forms without the inner experience confirming the presence
of real Christian faith. Evangelicals were also Christians of
the Bible as read (by no means always literally) and inter-
preted by individual believers. Evangelicals thus tended to
put much more emphasis on the role of the laity rather than
of the clergy and regarded the visible church as less important than the eternal, invisible church. For evangelicals faith
did come by hearing the preaching of the word and responding to that preaching, but faith also came and received
nurture through reading the word and through reading
devotional works about the Bible and the Christian faith,
many of which were authored by laymen. Finally, evangelicals were quite concerned with the teaching of particular
crucial doctrines, of which the efficacy of Christ's redemptive
atonement was perhaps the most important. The centrality
of the atonement led them to emphasise the Trinity. Thus,
any tendency toward a unitarian view of Christ as a noble,
but less than fully divine person, was theologically no less
pernicious in the eyes of evangelicals than were radical
unitarian political ideas.[5]

Political reaction, denominational rivalry, and evangelicalism expanded the arena of religion in terms of both personal
belief and social behaviour far beyond the normal existential
and tragic dilemmas of life and death that seem always to
arouse religious sentiments. In so doing, these forces of
intensified religiosity sowed the dragon's teeth that generated the soldiers of unbelief. By the end of the third decade
of the century British Christianity was neither institutionally
passive nor spiritually nominal. The sphere of religion
during these years and after touched upon more and more
personal and public concerns. This expansion and intensification of personal religious life transformed religion into
a significant and problematic burden. Increasing numbers of
people for a variety of reasons had to define or redefine their
thinking about the nature and meaning of religious activity.

Paradoxically, a religion that is not oppressive, intrusive,
or demanding of substantial time and attention or that
remains more or less compartmentalised from other social
and intellectual concerns, as would seem to have been the
case with both eighteenth-century Anglicanism and Noncon-

formity, does not generate personal crisis and inner conflict. There exists no fervent faith to be lost or to be rejected or to assert its presence in some other problematical manner. Such times of quiescent or cold faith seem to generate revivals instead of doubt. Rather it is expansive, intensified religion, as in this case fostered theologically first by Methodism and the evangelical revival and later by the Oxford Movement, that establishes a faith to be lost. Only a person with a firm faith can lose it in a problematical fashion, and he or she will lose it in a manner directly related to the character and expectations of the faith itself. In that respect the loss of faith or the modification of faith are inherently religious acts largely conditioned by and channelled through the spiritual categories and social expectations of the original community of faith. To the extent that an intensified religion has attached itself to modes or institutions of normal personality development, it may find itself challenged as individual personalities reach maturation. Finally, to the extent that intensified religion has made extensive cultural or moral claims, those who reject it may do so on the grounds that other sets of beliefs or other ideas appear better to fulfil those goals.

The character of evangelical religion determined many of the forms and categories through which the protagonists of unbelief felt they must explain or give voice to the experience. The key validation of evangelical Christian faith was the subjective experience of conversion, to which the believer afterwards offered witness in terms of actual verbal testimony and through the high moral quality of his or her subsequent personal life. The wrongs, evils, sins, and moral inadequacies of the old life and the shallowness of any previous faith had to be recounted, and the joys, benefits, and sincere moral and spiritual earnestness of the new faith presented. One of the chief vehicles for the presentation of this conversion experience had been the spiritual autobiography that portrayed the passage from one life to another.

From the time of Carlyle's *Sartor Resartus* (1833–4) onward, Victorians who encountered a crisis of faith also often resorted to the literary genre of the autobiography or autobiographical novel.[6] That they adopted this genre is not surprising, since it was the literary vehicle that had long been established to present a change in the direction of one's life and to assert the sincerity of that change. Evangelicals had directed their autobiographies toward former friends in an effort to persuade them of the desirability of the new Christian life. Victorians who lost faith in the Christianity of their childhood or who wished to change religious belief in some substantial manner similarly attempted to demonstrate their former religious orientation to have been morally and intellectually inadequate. Just as the evangelical conversion involved passage from a scene of worldly pleasures and easy friendships to one of spiritual rigour, so also did the loss-of-faith experience. Doubters and unbelievers repeatedly presented their new lives, led without the solace and support of their original faith, as more difficult, rigorous, and in a sense less worldly than their earlier lives as conforming Christians. They had left the way of easy faith for a more arduous path. They had passed from a nominal religious life to a real one and in the process they had moved from an intellectually and morally inadequate position to one that accorded with the real, fundamental truth of morality, history, and nature.

There were other evangelical resonances within those autobiographies or other autobiographical accounts of change in faith. The importance attached by unbelievers to having heard particular secular or scientific lecturers followed the evangelical pattern of emphasising having listened to particularly persuasive preachers. The evangelical emphasis on the benefits of key works of devotional literature found its equivalent in the new emphasis on the power of certain texts of dissolvent scientific or historical scholarship. Most important, the doubters and sceptics upheld the centrality of the Bible for the experience of unbelief. With the unbeliever as with the evangelical the reading of the scriptures led to the seeking of a new life and a real faith. But what the unbelievers encountered in the Bible were moral and intellectual difficulties that transformed the greatest of all evangelical and Christian texts into a dangerous book leading to doubt and scepticism rather than to faith and belief. Finally, doubters of virtually all varieties claimed the moral high ground. They contended that the doctrines of the atonement and hell were immoral and that their abandonment in favour of melioristic, secular moralities was good for all concerned. Furthermore, in the hands of a brilliant polemicist such as W.K. Clifford, the intellectual basis as well as the substance of what could and could not be believed became a moral issue of the highest signficance with the true moral benefits flowing to those who rejected theology.[7]

In their critique of ecclesiastical institutions and doctrines Victorian unbelievers and agnostics pursued a path of lay religious advocacy, criticism, and authorship pioneered two generations earlier by the evangelicals. Evangelicalism in both its criticism of nominal religion and in its devotional and organisational life had been an overwhelmingly lay movement. Its founding text, William Wilberforce's *Practical View of the Prevailing Religious Conceptions of Professed Christians in the Higher and Middle Classes in This Country Contrasted with Real Christianity* (1797) was the work of a layman. In such books and other polemics against the complacency of late-eighteenth-century religion the evangelicals had provided a pattern for sharp criticism of ecclesiastical institutions on the basis of their inadequate moral, intellectual, and spiritual life. The unbelievers repeatedly echoed those changes.[8]

The activities of the advocates of scientific naturalism during the third quarter of the century in particular illustrate the actions of engaged laymen criticising the adequacy of religion in a manner reminiscent of evangelicalism. Their attack pitted what they regarded as real religion, honest in thought and morally beneficent in action, against the nominal religion of the Anglican Church and to a lesser extent of the Church of Scotland. The Church of England had defended its position intellectually as upholding a learned theology that resisted the extremism of religious antinominism on the one hand and the dangers of Roman Catholicism on the other. Anglican clerical scientists and other interested clergy had claimed to resist the inroads of materialism, which was regarded as a political and social as well as a spiritual danger, through their previously mentioned advocacy and support of natural theology. The scientists and scientifically-minded philosophers associated with scientific naturalism sought to beat the Church of England at its own cultural game.

Like the evangelicals of an earlier day, the honest doubters and advocates of scientific naturalism demanded a truer and more genuine religion that was not an intellectual, moral, and political scandal. First, in their metaphysics, despite their rather loose and continuously misunderstood polemical vocabulary, Spencer, Tyndall, Huxley, and others of the camp of scientific naturalism presented themselves as the opponents of any form of reductionist materialism. That is one reason why their adopting the name *agnostic* rather than *atheist* was an important political as well as intellectual move. In works such as Spencer's *First Principles*, and in philosophies such as Tyndall's transcendental materialism, these publicists set forth new versions of generally evolutionary natural religion to replace those associated with the devout Anglican scientists. Second, the scientists attempted to present themselves as advocates of a moderate religious stance in contrast to the revivalism, bibliolatry, superstition, and ritualism rampant within the contemporary Church of England. In the sixties and seventies it was by no means clear whether the ecclesiastical establishment could or even wanted to control extreme religious actions, while it was clear that it wanted to silence advanced learning in the Church and the universities. The ineffectiveness of the attack on Anglo-Catholic ritualism even through parliamentary legislation only served to highlight the success of the vendetta against the authors of *Essays and Reviews*.[9]

Finally, the advocates of scientific naturalism moved to the fore as major public opponents of Roman Catholicism. Indeed, anti-Catholicism marked their polemics in a number of key documents – Huxley's speeches to the London School Board and his attacks on St. George Jackson Mivart, Tyndall's Belfast Address, Spencer's and Edward Taylor's attacks on priestcraft, Clifford's aggressive anti-clericalism, and Leslie Stephen's reviews of English religion in American journals. The significance of their anti-Catholic polemic is that it occurred at the very time when the Anglican Church was becoming increasingly *Anglo-Catholic*. The scientists and agnostics clearly attempted to raise doubt as to whether the Anglican faith could or would remain the certain buttress of the true protestant faith and a firm block against the onrush of Roman Catholics, who had restored the hierarchy in England and led the great revival in Ireland.[10]

In the context of the third quarter of the century, the proponents of scientific naturalism, as well as the spokesmen for other new theologies or new reformations, could in many respects seem to have been claiming the traditional mantle of the Anglican Church. Their cultural claims constituted a virtual mirror image of those of the established church. They were restoring real religion in place of the nominal religion of a divided, strife-torn Anglican Church. The new theologies could now successfully oppose materialism, religious enthusiasm, and the resurgence of Roman Catholicism. Furthermore, they could embrace new learning and knowledge. They alone were the protectors of stability, moderate religion, and protestantism. And in the context of the debates of the 1870s those claims were intended to establish the scientists and secular laymen as the natural successors to the Church of England as the proper educators of the nation.

Just as evangelicalism had at its inception been a faith of social action and reform, so also were the new secular faiths. In numerous cases the scientists and the unbelievers adopted the earlier evangelical role of advocacy for social reform. The fictitious Robert Elsmere pursued that path, as did James Woodsworth in real life, and as did scores of other young men who passed through Toynbee Hall.[11] Often philosophic idealism provided a non-theological ideology for such action, but the advances of science and technology provided new tools for moral reform. Huxley in 1887 used the term 'New Nature' to refer to the nineteenth-century technological infrastructure of powerful inventions, better housing, improved food, novel medicine, and purer water. Huxley also had repeatedly contended that human beings were a part of physical nature.[12] By accepting their role in physical nature, they could command its strength and learn to make themselves safe in its midst. In that regard, Huxley's Romanes Lectures of 1893, in which he called for human progress that would be at odds with cosmic evolution, represented the culmination of his own version of a new natural theology.[13] It suggested a promethean vision of human beings as their own redeemers and as the redeemers of a fallen physical nature. The energies of human beings were not to flow into destructive social discontent or brutal economic competition but into heroically constructive activity.

Thus far, considerations of the affinities of the crisis of faith with the faith that was lost have been drawn from the public sphere of autobiographical publication and scientific polemic. In those areas unbelievers and honest doubters repeatedly mimicked the actions and cultural agendas of believers. But there were other deeper and more intimate ways in which evangelical religion and the general intensification of religious life not only had provided modes of actions and moral expectations for unbelievers but also may actually have unintentionally caused persons to experience loss of faith and to feel the necessity of making changes in personal religious behaviour. Certain of the very successes of evangelical religion contributed directly to unbelief in ways that no evangelical and perhaps no unbeliever really understood.

The most important but neglected private context for those Victorians whose faith entered a time of crisis or change was the family. The primacy of the family setting for nineteenth-century British Christianity was again a direct result of evangelical religion. During the late-eighteenth and early-nineteenth centuries evangelicals seeking to affirm real religion through emphasis on lay activity had discovered the efficacy of numerous institutions outside the church proper for spreading their beliefs and sustaining their faith and values. The most famous of these were the various evangelical societies directed toward reform of manners and morals. But the most powerful of these institutions was the family.

For evangelical religion the family, far more than the church, constituted the centre of Christian nurture. Parents and devout relatives were the chief Christian teachers of their children. The household was the scene of family prayers and devotions. The Bible, along with evangelical devotional literature, provided the text for family-oriented religious training. The image of domestic evangelical Christian piety was frequently associated with the pious mother. It was also generally accepted that women, whether mothers, grandmothers, or aunts, would be very active in the process of Christian education. Indeed, the maintenance of a Christian home, the education of Christian children, and the sustenance of a Christian husband constituted a major part of the gender-defined social role for evangelically reared women. In some cases there also existed a darker side to this family faith. It might involve harsh discipline, personal physical and psychological mortification, and no doubt frequent psychological conflation between God the Father and the father of the household. Many British Christians whose personal theology did not mesh with those of evangelicals nonetheless still embraced the model social expectations of the evangelical family.

By having transformed the family into a major religious institution, the evangelical revival ironically also transformed religion into a vehicle whereby young persons could establish some personal psychological independence through modifying that family religion. In a very real sense the religious character and role of the evangelical family in and of itself fostered spiritual crisis, because the usual familial tensions arising from normal personality development toward the achievement of autonomous adulthood could be and in some cases were mediated through religious categories that had been grafted onto family life. One of the most striking features of both the autobiographical and the fictional accounts of transformation of religious belief or practice is the recognition on the part of the protagonist of the pain and turmoil that his or her action will cause for the family. A person's change or loss of faith inevitably disrupted the family community that was sustained in part on the basis of religion, and provoking such disruption was one of the inner psychological reasons for undertaking the modification of faith. In other words, some people experienced loss of faith and all the pain and anguish accompanying it quite simply because they wished to grow up and consequently and necessarily break out of their original family circle.

Loss of faith almost always occurred in late adolescence or early adulthood. The disruption of family expectations and interpersonal relationships that it involved was part and parcel of the normal and necessary achievement of personal independence and autonomy of a child from a family. Often the change in religious opinion occurred at the university, where not only new intellectual influences impacted on the young man but novel personal loyalties as well. New friends and teachers brought about the acceptance of new ideas.

Furthermore, at the university, then as now, young men of firm religious backgrounds discovered peers who had been reared with different moral and religious expectations. The letters of John Henry Newman and John Ruskin from their university days indicate the kinds of unexpected temptations confronted by the evangelical youth in Oxford colleges.[14] Simply by virtue of growing up and attending the university the young person had begun to disrupt the family community of childhood. So closely related to the family was evangelical religion that virtually any intellectual or moral independence indicating normal maturation of personality was likely to touch some aspect of that faith. The religious and intellectual changes were further indications of that movement toward adult independence and toward the inevitable necessity of choosing which values, expectations, and role models drawn from parents would direct the young man's own life and which of those values would come from other sources.

The frequent reports of the very real emotional pain involved in change of religious belief may indicate the close relationship between loss of faith and the achievement of personal adult autonomy. George John Romanes expressed such despair in *A Candid Examination of Theism* (1878). Having previously written an undergraduate essay on the efficacy of prayer, Romanes, a young scientist becoming warmly embraced by the Darwin circle, completed a second book in which he denied the validity of traditional natural religion that assured the presence of God behind the appearances and operations of nature. At the conclusion he complained:

> I feel it desirable to state that any antecedent bias with regard to Theism which I individually possess is unquestionably on the side of traditional beliefs. It is therefore with the utmost sorrow that I find myself compelled to accept the conclusions here worked out; and nothing would have induced me to publish them, save the strength of my conviction that it is the duty of every member of society to give his fellows the benefit of his labours for whatever they may be worth. . . . And for as much as I am far from being able to agree with those who affirm that the

twilight doctrine of the 'new faith' is a desirable substitute
for the waning splendour of 'the old', I am not ashamed to
confess that with this virtual negation of God the universe
to me has lost its soul of loveliness; and although from
henceforth the precept to 'work while it is day' will doubtless but gain an intensified force from the terribly intensified meaning of the words that 'the night cometh when
no man can work', yet when at times I think, as at times I
must, of the appalling contrast between the hallowed glory
of that creed which once was mine, and the only mystery of
existence as now I find it, – at such times I shall ever feel it
impossible to avoid the sharpest pang of which my nature
is susceptible.[15]

Romanes's voicing of the difficulty he confronted in reaching
this conclusion served in part to manifest his sincerity and to
indicate that he had not undertaken religious change from
base motives. Such statements were common among unbelievers, but they may have served other functions deeper
than that of demonstrating sincerity.

Romanes's pain may well have reflected not only religious
loss but also, through the intellectual and emotional category
of religion, the even more genuine anguish of the psychological process of achieving non-dependent relationships to his
family, part of which involved his movement into a warm
personal relationship with Darwin and other evolutionary
scientists, the desire for whose approval and affection was
displacing that which Romanes felt toward his family. To a
young man of science rejection of traditional natural religion
may have seemed a useful way to bond himself to the
advocates of scientific naturalism in place of previous family
ties and loyalties. His angst over the prospect of a godless
nature may have arisen from both the guilt aroused by
wishing such independence and the simultaneous sorrow of
losing the support and consolation of his first family. The
despair over the disappearance of God indicates at least in
part both the fear of the removal of a parent and the
simultaneous wish for that removal. The manner of the
expression of the sadness similarly suggests both the wish for
and the fear of independence, as well as the desire to reject
the parent without at the same time injuring the parent or

withholding love. In that sense, to some extent – and there is
no desire to reduce the loss of faith only to a familial
dimension – the experience and the recounting of the loss or
change of religious faith and the vanquishment of the
traditional evangelical god served to displace the tensions
and conflicts necessarily involved with the achievement of
normal personal psychological autonomy. Painful and difficult as were the changes in religious belief and practice,
they were less painful than the confrontation that might have
arisen or that the protagonists feared would arise from the
direct manifestation of their deepest residual childhood
feelings toward their families in general and toward their
parents most particularly. Religion could serve such a
mediating role because of the close link established by
evangelical Christianity between religion and family life.

There may well have been another psychological dimension to this sense of loss so commonly voiced by new
unbelievers. The feelings about the inadequacy of the childhood faith, the anguish and suffering experienced, and the
sense of near despair over the prospect of a godless world
may also have arisen in Romanes and other protagonists of
unbelief from the recognition that many of the wishes they
had hoped to achieve as children within their families and
through their parents had not been and would not ever be
fulfilled. To become an adult requires in some measure this
very recognition so that new goals and personal aims may be
developed in place of those of childhood and be fulfilled in a
context other than that of one's original family. To encounter a universe without a God who renders it meaningful was
not unlike confronting life and adulthood without parents
who determine meanings, establish expectations, and assure
safety. The expressed fear or hesitant acceptance of a godless
world suggests the hesitance of a child actually confronted
with undirected or undetermined choices to be made. The
statements of simultaneous wishes to retain faith and to
assert intellectual independence replicate the very kind of
emotional pulls experienced between wishes to retain and
fulfil the hopes of childhood and wishes to establish independent personal goals for one's life.

The close link between family life and religion could serve
to channel several kinds of evangelical child–parent con-

frontations that fostered pain, disappointment, and anxiety as the child attained maturity. Bonds between parents and children and parental goals for their offspring were often profoundly rooted in religious expectations. After all, one of the signs of successful evangelical parenting was the rearing of a child who would experience conversion and acceptance of faith in Christ and then lead a Christian life that would result in a similar nurturing of a succeeding generation. A child in late adolescence or early adulthood might very well decide that he or she entertained other aims in life and might feel that the only way he could achieve sufficient independence to attain those personal goals was to challenge the religious faith of his parents. A challenge to the faith was less fearful than the more direct challenge to parental authority. The process was still painful because the children's rejecting or substantially modifying that parental faith could be viewed as imposing a sense of failure on their parents.

In Edmund Gosse's *Father and Son* (1907), one of the most familiar loss-of-faith texts, the father, upon the death of his first wife, sets an immense personal emotional stake on his very young son's being accepted into the Plymouth Brethren congregation and being admitted to communion at an uncommonly early age. The father was understandably enough seeking to establish a closer bond between himself and his son as well as demonstrating to the religious community his own success as a Christian parent. The son's eventual movement away from the faith of his father clearly meant that he had deeply disappointed and frustrated the father's expectations of his own parenting. The novel also clearly indicates that the son's loss of religious faith involved a simultaneous loss of faith and confidence in his father and a distinct movement toward personal psychological independence, since religious acquiescence was the single way in which the father continued to demand parental obedience and allegiance from the son.[16]

Other children in both fiction and life employed conflict with parents over religion or over expectations of a clerical career to mediate their way to independent adulthood. Change in faith and consequent rejection of the clerical career served to reject parental hopes and expectations. This could be a very painful process for all concerned, because it indicated to the parent less than successful religious nurture and loss of parental control over the child. There was for the child potential guilt for both leaving the faith and causing turmoil in the family fold. Certainly these latter problems emerged in the exchange of letters between young Samuel Butler and his clergyman father over the former's vocational choice. The debate and discussion over the clerical vocation, in which the younger Butler raised questions about theological doctrines relating to free will and which ended in his decision to try his fortune outside the ministry and far away from home in New Zealand, directly mediated and channelled the tensions over personal independence from a very dominant father and from the values that father had fostered in his family.[17]

Even those relatively rare cases of substantial change of faith during early middle age also seem to have involved a rejection of family ties and parental domination. The most memorable example of such late loss of Christian faith is that of John Ruskin. Although his religious opinions had shifted somewhat over the years, he remained a devout moderate evangelical until 1858. In that year, as he later recounted, he visited a Waldensian Church in Italy and upon leaving the service found he was no longer a believer. That experience, which no doubt was the culmination of much more complex inner psychological activity, occurred chronologically very near his completion of the final volume of *Modern Painters*, the great work that from the beginning he had seen himself writing for his father and largely under his father's aegis. Thereafter, becoming much more independent of his father, who died in 1864, Ruskin set out upon his crusade for social reform, much of which he directed at criticism of the commercial middle-class culture that his merchant father had epitomised at its best. Imperfect as was Ruskin's eventual passage to adulthood, his religious crisis and his independence from parental dominance and expectations were closely associated factors in that maturation process.[18]

The relationship between independence in personality development and religious doubt seems to have been especially close in those few cases about which we have significant information in which women experienced modifications in religious faith and practice. Because women did not go to universities and normally remained geographically close to their families even if not necessarily residing in the same household, they tended to confront religious scepticism while still near or within the confines of the family circle. Since relationships to men and most particularly to their fathers determined so much in the lives of women, their personal independence, if achieved at all, almost invariably involved direct confrontations with their fathers and the rejection of the traditional female evangelical social role. Furthermore, since no major religious denomination provided a significant role for women either preaching or administering the sacraments, to engage in serious religious thought leading to modification of faith required women to challenge the limitations set by contemporary religion on their lives and actions.

The personal religious development of the young Marian Evans, later in life to become the novelist George Eliot, provides a well-documented instance of the passage of a woman from faith to doubt and illustrates its ramifications for her family environment. Although Evans once claimed to have entertained doubts near the age of 12 about the tenets of the evangelicalism according to which she had been reared, her real crisis occurred during her late teens and early twenties. She was then living near Coventry, looking after the household of her father Robert Evans, her mother having been dead for several years and her sister and brothers having established their own homes. She had begun to read widely in advanced theology and critical religious history and had become close friends with local Unitarians. Being physically unattractive, she seemed to have little prospect of making a marriage. Consequently, she had failed to fulfil her father's expectations in terms of her religious faith, her social acquaintances, and her eventual role as wife and mother. Early in 1842 Marian Evans, as a result of her reading and conversations among Unitarians, refused to go to church with her father. Normal family interchange came to a virtual halt as each week her father noted in his diary his solitary attendance at the local Anglican services. The silent strife became so considerable that Marian resorted to writing a long letter to her father in an effort to assuage his anger and disapproval.

That letter of 28 February 1842 is a most remarkable Victorian document. Evans brought to her father's attention substantive comments about religion, relationships to men, and money as she made a virtual declaration of independence from paternal domination. Evans explained to her father that she did not, as he apparently had feared, intend to join a Unitarian congregation. However, she also indicated she no longer adhered to important evangelical beliefs. She wrote of the scriptures 'as histories consisting of mingled truth and fiction' and explained that while admiring the moral teaching of Jesus, she considered 'the system of doctrines built upon the facts of his life and drawn as to its materials from Jewish notions to be most dishonourable to God and most pernicious in its influence on individual and social happiness'.[19] One of Marian Evans's biographers has expressed surprise that she had reached the age of 22 before rejecting evangelicalism.[20] That astonishment arises from understanding the process of loss of faith as primarily intellectual when, in point of fact, the renunciation of evangelicalism on the part of a woman involved the rejection of a parent and the rejection of the expected vocations of dutiful, obedient daughter and future pious wife. For both young women and men such intellectual religious scepticism served to establish emotional and psychological detachment from family as they set off into the years of normal sexual activity, which itself invariably involves in some manner upsetting the previous family community.

In her letter of 28 February 1842 Marian Evans made clear that all these associations were very much present in her mind. In the same paragraph in which she had indicated her intellectual difficulties with Christianity, she addressed the issue of the impact of her new beliefs on her personal religious conformity and on her prospects for marriage. She told her father, 'I could not without vile hypocrisy and a miserable truckling to the smile of the world for the sake of my supposed interests, profess to join in worship which I wholly disapprove. This and *this alone* I will not do even for your sake – anything else however painful I would cheerfully brave to give you a moment's joy.'[21] Later in the letter she indicated that she had no hope of convincing her family of the sincerity of her new-found religious opinions and that she clearly recognised the difficulty they might pose to her prospects for marriage.

> From what my Brother more than insinuated and from what you have yourself intimated I perceive that your establishment at Foleshill is regarded as an unnecessary expense – having no other object than to give me a centre in society – that since you now consider me to have placed an insurmountable barrier to my prosperity in life this one object of an expenditure held by the rest of the family to be disadvantageous to them is frustrated – I am glad at any rate this is made clear to me, for I could not be happy to remain as an incubus or an unjust absorber of your hardly earned gains which might be better applied among my Brothers and Sisters with their children.[22]

In effect, Marian Evans, while expressing her change in religious faith, also clearly and expressly declared that she would not depend upon her father for encounters with men. She also not very subtly indicated an awareness of jealousy and rivalry with her sister and brothers as a result of the cost of providing her with a place to meet suitable men. She closed the letter by stating her love for her father, her willingness to continue to care for him, and her willingness to forego any economic provision he might have made for her future.

Shortly after writing this extraordinary letter, Marian Evans went to live for a brief time with her brother. She then returned to her father's household and resumed church attendance but apparently on the grounds that she would think her own thoughts in church. She cared for her father until his death in 1849. However, while dwelling in his household she continued to read widely in philosophy and theology and persevered in her friendships with local theological radicals. In 1846 she published her important translation of David Friedrich Strauss's *Life of Jesus*, then regarded as the most advanced and destructive theological work of the day.[23]

There can be no question that Marian Evans genuinely suffered pain, embarrassment, and humiliation at the hands of her family. Her plight became a public one in the neighbourhood. But it is equally clear that, consciously or

unconsciously, she used her new religious convictions combined with new social relationships to assert and achieve
personal, secular, and vocational independence from her
family. It also seems possible that her later ongoing search
for an acceptable intellectual substitute for Christianity,
which carried her through a number of close relationships
with men associated with particular advanced creeds, manifested in part a desire to achieve once more the closeness to a
man of strong opinions that as a young child she had
experienced with her evangelical father and for which as an
adult she may still have unconsciously yearned, despite her
stronger conscious desire for independence.

Frances Power Cobbe, the Irish-born early British feminist, provides another reasonably well-documented case of a
woman's loss of faith and its relationship to family. In a
passage from her autobiography resonating with the tensions
raised by the attempt to achieve personal independence
within and from the confines of family, Cobbe vividly recalled the occasion of her first inklings of religious doubt in the
evangelical home of her youth.

> The first question which ever arose in my mind was
> concerning the miracle of the Loaves and Fishes. I can
> recall the scene vividly. It was a winter's night; my father
> was reading the Sunday evening sermon in the dining-
> room. The servants, whose attendance was de rigueur,
> were seated in a row down the room. My father faced
> them, and my mother and I and my governess sat round
> the fire near him. I was opposite the beautiful classic black
> marble mantelpiece, surmounted with an antique head of
> Jupiter Serapis (all photographed on my brain even now),
> and listening with all my might, as in duty bound, to the
> sermon which described the miracle of the Loaves and
> Fishes. 'How did it happen exactly?' I began cheerfully to
> think, quite imagining I was doing the right thing to try to
> understand it all. 'Well! first there were the fishes and the
> loaves. But what was done to them? Did the fish grow and
> grow as they were eaten and broken? And the bread the
> same? No! that is nonsense. And then the twelve basketfuls
> taken up at the end, when there was not nearly so much at
> the beginning. It was not possible!' O Heavens! (was the

next thought) *I am doubting the Bible!* God forgive me! I must never think of it again.[24]

Cobbe states that she was 12 at the time of this remembered experience.

What seems so significant about her recollection of first questioning the Bible are the details of the scene she paints rather than the content of her sceptical thoughts. Those details record the memory and consequent associations of a woman in her early seventies. The doubt may or may not have occurred when she was 12, but she remembered and portrayed the experience as a personal subjective disruption, and one recognised as such, of family worship, social hierarchy, and her father's dominant religious role. The image of the dark pagan Jupiter presiding over the scene almost as a rival to her father suggests in addition to the rejection of the Christian dispensation for the pagan a sense of apprehension of the danger to the family circle and its faith posed by awakening sexuality and the spectre of independent personal action.

Although Cobbe indicates that she recoiled from doubting the Bible, she may rather have recoiled from the fear of doubting not the Bible but rather the parents and other figures, such as the governess, who had taught her to trust the Bible. Religious scepticism involved the rejection, either halting or assertive, of parental expectations and values. Frances Power Cobbe's early inner questioning of the miracle of the loaves and fishes presents a child's early attempt at independent thought and the child's almost immediate recognition that such thoughts will bring it into collision with the opinions and authority of its parents and that it may consequently also risk the loss of parental love and an encounter with personal emotional disorientation.

Cobbe also recounts that she later underwent a conversion experience in her mid-teens, as was expected of evangelically reared children. Then in her late teens and early twenties she began four years of soul-searching and religious pilgrimage, at the conclusion of which she no longer believed in the divinity of Christ or the inspiration of the scriptures. While both of her parents still lived, she continued to attend Anglican services but did not take communion. Upon her mother's death she told her father of her new religious opinions. He sent her from home for almost a year, which she spent in the country with her brother. Thereafter she returned to her father's household, where she lived for another eight years, attending neither church nor family prayers. While living in these circumstances, she published with Longmans in 1855 a book on ethics that was deeply informed by the thought of liberal theologians whose opinions she had embraced at such high personal cost. Her father died in 1857, and Cobbe set out on her career in journalism and liberal political and religious causes.[25]

Still other family-related issues came to the fore of the loss-of-faith experience on the part of a man if it took place after his marriage. Should the wife be told? Could a godly Christian woman who had married a then Christian man continue in that intimate relationship when the man was no longer a Christian? Would the children be reared in the faith? Furthermore, the change in the husband's beliefs and vocation could undermine his wife's personal vocational expectations. If she were the wife of a clergyman who lost faith, her prestigious social role in the parish would be almost immediately transformed into a kind of marginal existence. As the spouse of a publicly unbelieving layman, she might experience social discrimination. But whether the wife of a doubting cleric or the wife of an assertive lay unbeliever, her gender-determined role as the religious teacher and model of piety in the family would become problematical. She might in effect stand robbed of her vocation and at the same time appear to be intellectually weaker or more backward than her husband if she persisted in her faith. Similar difficulties of personal vocation and decisions about child-rearing had to be confronted by women who freely entered into marriage with avowed unbelievers. In the past the concerns and difficulties of the wives of doubters, unbelievers, and agnostics have elicited condescension but little or no understanding on the part of scholars, who have assumed that any interference with the attainment and manifestation of a rationalistic and scientific outlook was undesirable and fundamentally contemptible. Such a whiggish intellectualist position has ignored the family dynamic involved in the lives of unbelievers as well as the relatively few resources available to women in asserting a position of influence in family life.

In point of fact, many wives seem not to have reacted passively to being or becoming the spouse of a doubter. Rare was the male unbeliever within the professional classes who actually reared his children with no religious training or no religious sacraments. In many cases wives, the social hopes and expectations that informed their lives, and their determination to set some rules in the family circle seem to have established limits to the expression of their husbands' unbelief. Such family considerations seem to have particularly circumscribed the unbelief of scientists. Thomas Henry Huxley thoroughly disliked the Church of England, but permitted his children to be baptised into the Anglican fold, as did many other agnostics.[26] Joseph Dalton Hooker, distinguished botanist and Keeper of Kew Garden, once complained to Huxley that Alfred Russel Wallace, then unmarried, did not understand the constraints that family considerations set on the expression of one's opinions. 'It is all very well for Wallace to wonder at scientific men being afraid of saying what they think – he has all "the freedom of motion in vacuo" in one sense. Had he as many kind and good relations as I have, who would be grieved and pained to hear me say what I think, and had he children who would be placed in predicaments most detrimental to children's minds by such avowals on my part, he would not wonder so much.'[27] George John Romanes, while still unmarried, had published the aforementioned *Candid Examination of Theism* (1878). He published the work anonymously, but within months of its publication began to back away from that book and its arguments when he decided to marry a woman who was a devout high Anglican. Indeed, the story of Romanes's intellectual movement away from *A Candid Examination of Theism* and toward his posthumous *Thoughts on Religion* (1895), edited by his wife, is in large measure the narrative of loss of faith outside marriage and imposition of faith within marriage.[28]

Scholars have viewed male unbelievers thus constrained as buffeted or wrongly pressured by their devout and insufficiently intellectual wives, but in doing so they have ignored the character of the family dynamic. Wives and the situation of marriage seem to have re-established for the male unbeliever certain familiar religious constraints previously associated with parents. In the relationship of the doubter or agnostic to both parents and wives one of the chief issues was that of family community and family bonds of affection and dependence. With his parents a male doubter's unbelief may have served to establish separation. However, in the case of his wife and children, family considerations limited the husband's unbelief because he wished to establish with them a new family life and community. The very movement to adult psychological independence and autonomy that initially led to unbelief as a mediation of a man's rejection of his parents and original family later led to an acceptance of constraint on unbelief in the effort to establish his marriage and new family.

It is also necessary to note that the challenge to family through the categories of religion did not always lead to a loss of faith but sometimes to a much more moderate religious change within a distinctly Christian setting. For example, William Gladstone moved from evangelicalism to high Anglicanism. Sometimes the modification of religion actually led to more religious conviction rather than less. For example, F.D. Maurice converted from unitarianism to liberal Anglicanism. There were also undoubtedly family dimensions yet to be researched and explored in the numerous conversions from the Chuch of England to Roman Catholicism, as in the case of the children of the evangelical William Wilberforce. Again, in the conversions to Roman Catholicism, the tendency was from less to more religion. In the case of persons who made those conversions, which were perhaps the most frequent mid-century change in religious faith, the departure quite literally led the protagonists to a new mother in the form of the Roman Church or the Virgin, who would intercede with God the Father, and a new father in the form of the priest who possessed the capacity to accept and forgive. Finally, it is important to observe that modification or rejection of the faith of one's childhood was by no means a certain path to personal autonomy, as witnessed by the personal and religious development of Francis Newman and Arthur Hugh Clough. Nor was all religious scepticism necessarily related to family, as with the thought of Herbert Spencer, whose condescension toward ecclesiastical institutions contained much continuity with his nonconformist family's resentment of the established Church of England.[29]

Victorian scholars have had little difficulty accepting family dimensions to John Stuart Mill's 'loss of faith' and mental crisis in regard to the strict utilitarian creed of his childhood and his hesitant movement toward romantic literature and the acceptance of a role for feelings in his personal life. Indeed virtually no historian or literary scholar would examine Mill's intellectual development without consideration of the expectations of his father.[30] Nor would they chart his subsequent intellectual development without attention to the influence of his relationship with Harriet Taylor. Yet scholars of Victorian religious life have tended to limit the analysis of their materials strictly to intellectual and theological categories. The utilitarianism that James Mill imposed on his son was not unlike the total evangelical environment that many Christian parents imposed on their children. Both Mill and evangelical parents dedicated their children to the service of a particular faith or creed and saw their success as parents closely related to the child's fulfilment of that role in life. In both cases the creed and the associated expectations placed on the children were intimately related to parental authority and served as boundaries to the development of the children's personal independence. Just as the achievement of personal autonomy on the part of evangelical children might have been forged in terms other than those of religion had the faith not been so closely grafted onto the family, no doubt so would John Stuart Mill's had his father been less determined to link his utilitarian creed so intimately to the parenting of his eldest child.

About the time that so many English were about to enter a time of religious crisis, Ralph Waldo Emerson confided to his notebook, 'What we say however trifling must have its roots in ourselves or it will not move others. No speech should be separate from our being like a plume or a nosegay, but like a leaf or a flower or a bud though the topmost & remotest, yet joined by a continuous line of life to the trunk & the seed.'[31] Historians of Victorian faith in crisis must begin to take a similar stance to the subject of their research. They must look at the social and psychological as well as the intellectual being of those Victorians who transformed their religious faith.

Scholars must admit that matters of the intellect pertain not to the reason alone, and must become sceptical and curious about why these transformations were and have continued to be so frequently portrayed in strictly rational and intellectualist terms. They must also comprehend that the intensified modes of Christianity that penetrated so deeply into the personalities and social and political milieu of early nineteenth-century Britain may well have been the most important factors leading to change in faith, determining the manner of those changes, and establishing the expectations of the new faiths and theologies. For, to adopt Emerson's metaphor, the trunk and the seed of the Victorian crisis of faith was nurtured and sustained in and by the faith that was lost.

NOTES

1. James R. Moore, *The Post-Darwinian Controversies: A Study of the Protestant Struggle to Come to Terms with Darwin in Great Britain and America, 1870–1900* (New York, 1979) 19–76.
2. Ursula Henriques, *Religious Toleration in England, 1787–1833* (Toronto, 1961) 99–135; Michael R. Watts, *The Dissenters: From the Reformation to the French Revolution* (Oxford, 1978) 478–90; V. Kiernan, 'Evangelicalism and the French Revolution', *Past and Present*, 1 (1952) 44–56.
3. Jack Morrell and Arnold Thackray, *Gentlemen of Science: Early Years of the British Association for the Advancement of Science* (Oxford, 1981) 224–45; Nicolaas A. Rupke, *The Great Chain of History: William Buckland and the English School of Geology (1814–1849)* (Oxford, 1983) 29–34, 209–18, 231–74; Henriques, *Religious Toleration*, 206–59.
4. Owen Chadwick, *The Victorian Church*, 2 vols (New York, 1966) 1: 7–66; P.T. Marsh, *The Victorian Church in Decline* (London, 1969); Kenneth Inglis, *The Churches and the Working Classes in Victorian England* (London, 1964); George Kitson Clark, *The Making of Victorian England* (Cambridge, Mass., 1962) 147–205; J. Edwin Orr, *The Second Evangelical Awakening in Britain* (London, 1949); Olive J. Brose, *Church and Parliament: The Reshaping of the Church of England, 1828–1860* (Stanford, 1959); G.I.T. Machin, *Politics and the Churches in Great Britain, 1832 to 1868* (Oxford, 1977); Henriques, *Religious Toleration*, 1–174; Jeffrey Cox, *The English Churches in a Secular Society: Lambeth, 1870–1930* (New York, 1982) 3–47.
5. Geoffrey Best, 'Evangelicalism and the Victorians', in *The Victorian Crisis of Faith*, ed. Anthony Symondson (London, 1970) 37–56, and his 'The Evangelicals and the Established Church in the Early

Nineteenth Century', *Journal of Theological Studies*, 10 (1959) 63–78; F.K. Brown, *Fathers of the Victorians* (Cambridge, 1961); Ian Bradley, *The Call to Seriousness; The Evangelical Impact on the Victorians* (London, 1976); Elizabeth Jay, *The Religion of the Heart: Anglican Evangelicalism and the Nineteenth-Century Novel* (Oxford, 1979).

6.   M. Maison, *The Victorian Vision: Studies in the Religious Novel* (New York, 1961); R.L. Wolff, *Gains and Losses: Novels of Faith and Doubt in Victorian England* (New York, 1977); Linda Peterson, *Victorian Autobiography: The Tradition of Self-Interpretation* (New Haven, 1986); A.O. Cockshut, *The Art of Autobiography in Nineteenth and Twentieth Century England* (New Haven, 1984).

7.   James C. Livingston, *The Ethics of Belief: An Essay on the Victorian Religious Conscience* (Tallahassee, Fla, 1974).

8.   Howard R. Murphy, 'The Ethical Revolt against Christian Orthodoxy in Early Victorian England', *American Historical Review*, 60 (1955) 800–17.

9.   Bernard Lightman, 'Pope Huxley and the Church Agnostic: The Religion of Science', *Historical Papers* (1983) 150–63, and his 'Scientific Agnosticism and the New Natural Theology', unpublished essay presented to the American Historical Association and the History of Science Society, Chicago, December 1984; Frank M. Turner, *Between Science and Religion: The Reaction to Scientific Naturalism in Late Victorian England* (New Haven, Conn., 1974) 8–37; Turner, 'Victorian Scientific Naturalism and Thomas Carlyle', *Victorian Studies*, 18 (1975) 325–34; Turner, 'Rainfall, Plagues, and the Prince of Wales: A Chapter in the Conflict of Religion and Science', *Journal of British Studies*, 8 (1974) 45–65; Ieuan Ellis, *Seven against Christ: A Study of 'Essays and Reviews'* (Leiden, 1980).

10.   Jeffrey Paul von Arx, *Progress and Pessimism: Religion, Politics, and History in Late Nineteenth Century Britain* (Cambridge, Mass., 1985); Frank M. Turner, 'The Victorian Conflict between Science and Religion: A Professional Dimension', *Isis*, 69 (1978) 372–4.

11.   Melvin Richter, *The Politics of Conscience: T.H. Green and His Age* (Cambridge, Mass., 1964).

12.   T.H. Huxley, *Collected Essays*, 9 vols (New York, 1894) 1: 54.

13.   ibid., 9: 46–116.

14.   *The Letters and Diaries of John Henry Newman*, ed. Ian Ker and Thomas Gornall, vols 1–6 (1978–84), vols 11–31 (1961–77), 1 (Oxford, 1978) 66; V.A. Burd, *The Ruskin Family Letters: The Correspondence of John James Ruskin, His Wife, and Their Son, John, 1801–1843*, 2 vols (Ithaca, 1973) 2: 421–674; Jeffrey L. Spear, *Dreams of an English Eden: Ruskin and His Tradition in Social Criticism* (New York, 1984) 25–9.

15.   George John Romanes, *A Candid Examination of Theism, by Physicus* (Boston, 1878) 113–14. For a fuller discussion of Romanes's religious and intellectual development, see Turner, *Between Science and Religion*, 134–63.

16.   Edmund Gosse, *Father and Son* (1907; New York, 1982) 208–24.

17.   *The Family Letters of Samuel Butler, 1841–1886*, ed. Arnold Silver (Stanford, Calif., 1962) 59–90.

18. Tim Hilton, *John Ruskin: The Early Years, 1819–1859* (New Haven, 1985) 253–79; George P. Landow, *The Aesthetic and Critical Theories of John Ruskin* (Princeton, NJ, 1971) 265–93.

19. *The George Eliot Letters*, ed. Gordon S. Haight, 9 vols (New Haven, Conn., 1954–78) 1: 128.

20. Gordon S. Haight, *George Eliot: A Biography* (New York, 1968) 40.

21. *The George Eliot Letters*, ed. Haight, 1: 129.

22. ibid.

23. For a discussion of the entire incident of Marian Evans's rebellion against her father, see Haight, *George Eliot*, 32–67; *The George Eliot Letters*, ed. Haight, 1: 124–51; and John W. Cross, *George Eliot's Life, as Related in Her Letters and Journals*, 3 vols (1885; New York, n.d.) 1: 61–106.

24. Frances Power Cobbe, *The Life of Frances Power Cobbe, by Herself*, 2 vols (Boston, Mass., 1894) 1: 75–6.

25. ibid., 1: 70–196. Cobbe's account presents an interesting confirmation of the family dimension of loss of faith on the part of women in regard to her comments on Marian Evans. Cobbe had read the Cross biography of George Eliot, which did *not* include the important letter of February 1842 discussed in this chapter. In her autobiography Cobbe indicates her envy and implied puzzlement at Marian Evans's apparently easy and entirely intellectual movement out of evangelicalism (1: 81). Such was the manner in which Cross's narrative and selection of documents portrayed the event, and it was exactly that intellectualist portrayal that disturbed Cobbe when comparing her experience to Evans's.

26. Leonard Huxley, *Life and Letters of Thomas Henry Huxley*, 2 vols (New York, 1900) 1: 240.

27. J.D. Hooker to C. Darwin, 6 October 1865, in Leonard Huxley, *Life and Letters of Sir Joseph Dalton Hooker*, 2 vols (London, 1918) 2: 54.

28. Turner, *Between Science and Religion*, 134–63. This earlier discussion of Romanes on my part does not reflect the family dynamic and would be subject to some revision in light of this chapter.

29. Perry Butler, *Gladstone: Church, State, and Tractarianism: A Study of His Religious Ideas and Attitudes, 1809–1859* (Oxford, 1982); Frederick Maurice, *The Life of Frederick Denison Maurice*, 2 vols (New York, 1884) 1: 22–60; David Newsome, *The Wilberforces and Henry Manning: The Parting of Friends* (Cambridge, Mass., 1966); Evelyn Barish Greenberger, *Arthur Hugh Clough: The Growth of a Poet's Mind* (Cambridge, Mass., 1970).

30. A.W. Levi, 'The "Mental Crisis" of John Stuart Mill', *Psychoanalytic Review*, 32 (1945) 86–101; Michael St. J. Packe, *The Life of John Stuart Mill* (London, 1954); Bruce Mazlish, *James and John Stuart Mill: Father and Son in the Nineteenth Century* (New York, 1975). It should also be noted that scholars have just as often criticised the role of the politically and philosophically radical Harriet Taylor in Mill's intellectual life as they have criticised the role of devout wives in the intellectual lives of Victorian agnostics.

31. *Emerson in His Journals*, ed. Joel Porte (Cambridge, Mass., 1982) 84.

2 Faith and Fallacy: English and German Perspectives in the Nineteenth Century
W.R. Ward

I THE VICTORIAN CRISIS OF FAITH: MYTH OR REALITY?

The agony of faith that failed is one of the familiar echoes of Victorian England, as familiar as the conservative rant against the corrosive scepticism of 'German' professors who would have been better at the bottom of the 'German Ocean'. A crisis of faith, however, is less easy to detect, define, and date, and the hunt for it is much obfuscated by characteristic perceptions of both the mid-nineteenth and the late-twentieth centuries. The *Religious Census* of 1851 seemed more shocking to contemporaries than it does to us because of two assumptions which they shared neither with previous nor with later generations, that there should be a parson in every parish and that everyone free and able to darken the doors of a place of worship should do so weekly. And our own day has blinkers of its own. Is the present religious situation in western Europe an adequate hermeneutic for the whole story? Or is the problem of believing as encountered in Victorian England a chapter in a complicated web of many plots, in which belief finds new social roles as well as losing old ones, not least because of a radical redistribution of Christian belief and practice in the world as a whole. Is there one story, that of secularisation, or are there several?

How uncertain even the best of the current literature is on this question of perspective comes out in the work of that eminent scholar, Owen Chadwick. His history of the Victorian church[1] contains chapters entitled 'Unsettlement of Faith', 'Science and Religion', 'History and the Bible', and

'Doubt', but the general effect is flattening, and secularisation is treated as a vague word for a non-subject. Certainly no church suffered very much from secessions or disciplinary actions based on intellectual appraisals of the content of its teaching, any more than in the golden age of secession and expulsion between 1790 and 1850. But the second volume of this great work was scarcely off the press when he took the opposite line in his Gifford Lectures.[2] Secularisation was now not merely the truth, but the peculiarly stark truth. Insisting that 'if it were proved by historians, for example, that whole societies spent untold centuries believing in a god or gods and then within a hundred years suffered such an intellectual *bouleversement* that they no longer believed in any such person or things, it would have momentous consequences for those whose business is not history but a study of the nature of religious experience.'[3] Chadwick asked the reader to believe that some such change took place in the twenty or thirty years after 1860. The only balm to the wounded spirits of the believer was the silent (and absolutely implausible) implication that secularisation was a transformation of the context within which the Christian faith was held or proclaimed, and did not involve failures in the proclamation itself.

Some light may be cast on this dark matter by both lengthening and broadening the historical perspective in which it is discussed. Neither the pessimistic sociologists who try to persuade us by statistics that hardly anyone has been to church in England since the Reformation,[4] nor those modest Anglicans who are prepared to settle for religious practice in the establishment at no more than 10 per cent of the population even in 1660, have left any room for the supposition that there could be a popular crisis of faith after 1860. The religious census, moreover, confirmed other evidence that the churches were now of limited use either as vehicles of social policy or as devices of social control, and in the next generation this discovery doubtless cost them the loyalty of members of the political classes who had valued them chiefly in this respect. Should this loss of confidence be described as a crisis of faith? Moreover, in the early years of the present century, there was sufficient evidence of recent and present good performance by the churches to convince many

churchmen as well as historians that all was well.[5] Certainly
the English churches as a whole made a much bigger splash
in the world than they had ever done before, and had
created the situation in which, in the next half-century, it was
natural for English to become the sacred language of the
ecumenical movement. All the churches had contributed to a
great effort to take religion to the people, and Roman
Catholics and Dissenters might (perhaps with justice) persuade themselves that England was becoming non-Anglican
much faster than she was becoming non-Christian.

Moreover, after 1850, once the older social tensions had
been dissipated, the churches were spared one potent source
of religious disenchantment. The 1830s and early 1840s had
been the great age of the religious (as well as the political)
doctrinaire. The great spur to total commitment against the
bogey of the moment, be it establishment or disestablishment, revolution or new poor law, ungodliness or liquor, had
been the conviction that nothing could be worse than the
present state of affairs, a façade behind which one evil
interest or another manipulated the nation's affairs; Newman at Littlemore may stand for the army of revivalists,
teetotallers, ecclesiastical disciplinarians like Bunting, who
could screw up courage and induce exaltation to levels
absolutely impossible to sustain.[6] Froude's title, the *Nemesis of
Faith*, was but too apt. Balleine, implausibly, suggested that
the millennarian issue was wound up for Anglican evangelicals by Bishop Waldegrave's Bamptons in 1853,[7] but the end
of the world as an issue in polite society unquestionably came
to an end when the strains which had involved even Arnold's
obsession with it[8] themselves eased. The two political heroes
of the fifties embodied the religious ideals of the age before
the doctrinaires took over. There was the ghost of Peel,
whose religious rationalism had elicited shakings of the head
even from Bishop Charles Lloyd; and there was the very
unghostly Palmerston who had actually been a pupil of
Dugald Stewart. Things looked up for Enlightenment, and,
certainly, none of the political and religious issues of the next
two decades was fought to a finish. Even Dwight L. Moody's
fatal heart attack owed more to his twenty stone of modish
corpulence than to the stress of attempting the conversion of
the world in his generation.

Social and economic developments often deal more harshly with the churches' competitors than with the churches themselves. The great age of the Man of Letters is that of early Victorian years. From Carlyle to Macaulay they were great synthesisers, presenting and interpreting the world of knowledge to their contemporaries and assisting a compact and opulent middle-class public to understand itself in the light of that knowledge; they produced their own body of scriptures in the heavyweight reviews, and set the tone for all those novelists who believed in the necessity (and compatibility) of realism and moral elevation. The menace of Carlyle to organised religion was not his low estimate of the churches, still less his affectation of greater familiarity with German idealism than he had, but the fact that he was a commercially successful Ranter, usurping one of the churches' functions with such effect that long after his death he could be regarded by certain nonconformists as a true prophet against humbug. Yet the men of letters could not long keep up with either the *Natur-* or the *Geisteswissenschaften*, the development of which came to turn on specialised publications and institutions. And they were outflanked on the opposite side by publishers who learned how to tap a mass market at a lower level of literacy.[9] The developments that took the wind out of the sails of the men of letters were not so inimical to the churches. They could obtain a theology school in Oxford and develop journals to match; and they (especially the Dissenters and Roman Catholics) had always drawn at least some preachers who retained the ear of their fellows from the milieu now catered for by the popular press.

In a more fundamental sense, not all was well. As the men of letters transformed themselves into dons, they paid the price of ceasing to interest a public of commercial proportions, and laid hands on university endowments which had long been used to give budding lawyers and parsons a start in life. The clergy found the transition from the crass amateurism of their past to the professional amateurism of their new status particularly difficult. Nothing has ever produced a theologically-minded ministry in England; but clergy put a fair amount of work into the Bible, only to find, as the Germans had found before, that the scriptures were becoming harder to preach from. This might not have mattered had the Social Gospel ever really materialised. When, during the Great Depression, the dominant economic ethic was partially repudiated by sections of the hitherto economically influential classes, it was partially repudiated also by sections of the clergy, particularly of the establishment, and particularly by liberal Catholics whose fortunes had been closely linked with Gladstone.[10] The Social Gospel, however, which in Germany, despite massive intellectual input, was neither an intellectual nor a practical success,[11] was in England little more than a well-meaning sleight of hand;[12] English workingmen knew what they were about in putting their trust in uncontrived improvements in the terms of trade, in Lib-Labism, and in a State of limited ambience. Moreover, although the disappearance of revolutionary tension after 1850 had in the short run made life easier for the churches as for other social institutions, other social developments were much to their disadvantage. Between the middle of the eighteenth century and the middle of the nineteenth, the commercialisation of all sectors of the economy had weakened old forms of deference and given entirely new scope for fresh religious appeals, Protestant and Catholic. Social strains had broken through old habits and broken up the ground for the revivalists in a way they conspicuously failed to do in the second half of the century. The geographical redistribution of resources that underlay the revolt of the fringes of the country against the centre had turned the evangelical awakening into something like a mass movement. The second half of the century, however, sprang the unpleasant surprise that the rise of the provinces had in no way impeded the relentless growth of London, a Great Wen beyond the power of any organisation, religious or political, to organise; a metropolis situated (like Paris) in the old heartland of the establishment, a heartland itself of low religious practice; a metropolis which increasingly attracted the provincial élites who had done so much for the religious as well as the public life of provincial towns,[13] and took control of the economic assets which had supported them. One of the unmentionable calamities of modern British history was allowing London to continue as both a commercial capital and a centre of government spending; and this was calamitous for religion even before the twentieth-century development of the media thrust the ethos of London into every home. None of these developments, however, could be described as a crisis, still less a crisis of faith; and the erosion, though real, was slow.

Cox's famous quip, that the obsessive speculation of young men in Oxford about the marks of the one true church was transformed in the forties into speculation in railway shares,[14] does not disguise the agony sometimes occasioned by loss of faith, nor discount the damage suffered by those as sensitive as Clough and J.A. Froude.

Among those most seriously at risk from the new developments were men of evangelical upbringing within the Church of England. Their immediate forbears had been clear that an inherited *Kulturprotestantismus* would never pull the established institutions of England (not to say Ireland) through the strains of the Revolutionary and Napoleonic Wars. International threats then meshed perilously with domestic discords, and social discontent was sharpened by a popular political programme given actuality by sympathy with the struggles of the Convention in France. In a society in which (to use the modern jargon) the private sector overwhelmingly outweighed the public, survival depended on inculcating an interior discipline. This, it seemed, could spring only from a much more intense religious commitment than had sufficed in the recent past. Indeed, one of the reasons for the perplexing resemblances and continuities between the new evangelicalism and the Puritanism of the seventeenth century was that the latter had aimed (among other things) to plant out Protestantism as a popular faith in the dark corners of the country for the first time, a work resumed by evangelicals on a great scale. Evangelicalism had prospered (as had quite different forms of religious appeal, native Roman Catholicism, for example) on the widening freedom of choice in English society, but it had always sought to set voluntary bounds to the freedom of choice on which it throve; and for many it had been made into a social policy by the stresses of the Revolutionary era, however broad the gap between the details of their faith and the concrete reality of social questions. Before the middle of the nineteenth century the two great connectionally-organised communions, the English Wesleyans and the Church of Scotland, had, nevertheless, been brought to spectacular schism by the need to reappraise inherited policies. The English Church, almost as much an Independent denomination as the Baptists, had only the ructions in the annual meeting of the National Society to set beside the upheavals in Conference and Assembly, but the evangelical party could not escape the pressure created by the doctrinaires; indeed that pressure was compounded by the family. The great discovery of Protestant religious revival in the later years of the seventeenth century and the early years of the eighteenth had been that in the Habsburg lands where the Protestants had lost their church structure the family could, on its own, be an effective means of transmitting and reviving the faith; and that the devotions prescribed by Spencer to supplement the parish round were capable of bearing the whole weight of Christianising successive generations. Anglican evangelicalism was by no means a copy of the revivalism of central Europe, but the family was one of the forms of unecclesiastical action it had sought most energetically to use; and at the very moment when churches were most perplexed by unavoidable changes of course, family pressure produced the paradox that religious 'deviance' or changes of denominational allegiance became more painful to individuals than they had been a century before. Whether what hurt was the inadequacy of the church to fill the role assigned to it by Wilberforce and his friends, or whether the problem was to cope with doctrinal difficulties created by science and history, some evangelicals were in trouble.

Now (as always in the past) there were *moral* difficulties in believing, some of them sharpened by the clerical dispute over the eternity of infernal punishment; but laymen were notably nimble in evading them. When they concluded that their offspring were innocents needing neither baptismal grace nor converting power, they soon found professionals to tailor doctrines of baptism accordingly.[15] Between 1860 and the end of the century, however, there emerged scientific or historical reasons for believing that some things the churches had taught with confidence or even authority were not true, even that some things the Bible had taught or had been thought to teach, were not true. But because the issue fundamentally was one about church teaching, those affected were primarily clergy and prospective ordinands, very scrupulous laymen of intellectual bent, and less scrupulous laymen whose confidence in the church (though not perhaps in God or Jesus)[16] had suffered, and who were not averse to finding the church in difficulties of its own. Science was no great problem except in so far as it impinged on the Bible.[17] In any case, science was English enough; laymen had partly ignored, partly absorbed, Newtonian cosmology; they had done the same with geology; in the Bridgewater treatises they had recently found traditional arguments from natural theology acceptable; even evolution might be harnessed to the argument from design. For those with inadequate flexibility there was some choice of shelter at hand. Liddon was arguing that one must accept the entire Catholic system or watch Christianity crumble piece by piece; and the Plymouth Brethren offered millennialism and an inerrant Bible in an evangelical framework.

History was more difficult because it involved a shift of attitude towards the scriptures, and perhaps towards Jesus himself. Moreover, it was known that more advanced and shocking things were being said about scripture and Christology in Germany than in England; and this knowledge inflamed durable prejudices going right back to the beginning of the eighteenth century, prejudices which distinguished those who thought England should go it alone in religion and diplomacy, and those who held that this was neither desirable nor possible. The role of German scholarship in the Victorian 'crisis of faith' raises the difficult question of the intellectual traffic between two nations, whose fates and religious circumstances moved apart in the nineteenth century as the whole Protestant world fragmented into mutually incomprehending regional enterprises.

II POLITICS AND THE ORIGINS OF MODERN GERMAN THEOLOGY

The wars of Queen Anne's reign and the alarums of the following decade had occasioned bitter disagreements. Those of Whiggish and latitudinarian mind held that the

United Kingdom could not be indifferent to the tottering Protestant interest in the Holy Roman Empire; and those of Tory and high church bent not merely wished their country well out of such entanglements, but were hot for those peculiarities of the English church that distinguished it both from English dissenting communities and from the non-episcopal Protestant churches of the continent.[18] To their chagrin the United Kingdom fetched up with a German dynasty, and drew closer not merely to the internal disputes of the Holy Roman Empire, but to the terrors and the consolations of the German religious mind, than it had ever been before. For the first time Luther, in the guise of the archetype of evangelical conversion, became an English religious hero.

Differences of English attitudes towards continental Protestants were fully matched by differences among German Protestants towards England. At the official church level the Orthodox Lutheranism of the Saxon Church and its friends (especially in the Imperial cities) was sharply separated from virtually all the movements for religious change and adaptation. These movements, which had an anti-Saxon slant, might well enjoy the patronage of the Hohenzollern dynasty, who, as the Reformed rulers of an overwhelmingly Lutheran state, had domestic as well as anti-Saxon reasons for wishing to get round the entrenched religious divisions of the past. So also, in a complicated way, had the Hanoverians after they had succeeded to the English throne. They eased the domestic problem in Hanover by agreeing to accept only local ordinands into the ministry of their church,[19] thus conceding a permanent monopoly to a party of peculiarly dead orthodoxy. But they would not let Prussia seize the leadership of the Protestant interest in the Empire without a contest. When they founded the university of Göttingen in 1734 they adopted the Prussian recipe of an alliance of enlightenment and Pietism exempt from church control, and, in Hanoverian England, the Pietist interest was publicly kept up by a succession of distingished German court chaplains and the open patronage of the thinner of George I's two mistresses, the Duchess of Kendal.[20]

The Lutheran Orthodox, the pro-Saxon party, shared the same sense of confessional isolationism as English high churchmen, and, from the time the Saxon dynasty turned Catholic, shared also their embarrassment in dealing with a monarch of alien faith. All the more reason, it seemed, to insist that Luther was, in effect, the normative doctor of the church, and was a Saxon possession. The Orthodox were prepared to entertain almost unlimited fantasies as to the unsoundness of English religion. The Protestant states of the Empire had been much troubled in the late seventeenth century by anti-institutional movements of a Quakerish kind, as well as actual Quaker missions; 'Quakerism' became the shorthand abuse for radical pietist movements of any sort, the natural product of 'overheated English blood'.[21] England had foisted several varieties of Fifth Monarchy men upon the Lutheran world,[22] had spawned the comic doctrines of Eva von Buttlar and her gang,[23] and was well known to be the source of damaging literature.[24] The Orthodox press retailed politically inspired reports of scandalous hell-fire clubs in England,[25] and could believe that the American colonies were the 'outer darkness' of Matt. 8:12, where the lost were cast with weeping and gnashing of teeth.[26] A steady stream of German ordinands seeking education in England set in late in the seventeenth century, but they could only be defended by the superintendent of the church in Brunswick by the backhanded argument that Socinianism was no more rampant in England than in Germany, and that England was not especially morally corrupting except to those who were already susceptible to corruption.[27] And although some of the enthusiasts thought that 'English' or 'psychic spirits' were good angels,[28] many of them reproduced the prejudices of the Orthodox. Even the Inspired were inclined to describe their physical symptoms as 'English movements' and suspect them of satanic origin;[29] and to Moravians an appropriate title for anti-Christ was 'Englischer Lichtes-Schein'.[30]

No one, however, doubted that England mattered. English theology of all kinds was reviewed in quantities in the journals, much was translated, and large stocks, both in translation and in the original tongue, were brought in for libraries like that of the Stift at Tübingen.[31] Indeed, the very breadth of German exposure to English theological output makes English influence hard to profile with precision. There is no question, however, as to who the Anglophiles were; they were Pietists with a respect for English Puritanism[32] and for an English Bible exegesis unencumbered by Lutheran Orthodoxy or Moravian fantasy;[33] and the *Aufklärer* who, in the field of secular letters, were also devotees of the English moral weeklies.[34] J.R. Schlegel, rector of the Gymnasium at Heilbronn, whose *Kirchengeschichte* is a model of enlightened scholarship, beat the drum about the English inspiration to research abroad, and its especial importance in the fields of the philosophy of religion and Old Testament studies.[35] In other words, exactly as the English latitudinarians had political as well as intellectual and theological reasons for wishing to outflank the isolationist high church party, the Anglophile groups in Germany consisted of precisely those anti-Saxon parties rallied by Prussia and used by Hanover, which had political, as well as intellectual, theological, and religious reasons for wishing to outflank Lutheran Orthodoxy. Like spoke to like. And a bridge was built between the two from the German side.

Sigmund Jacob Baumgarten, the most significant of the transitional theologians, in his final, historical, phase, produced a series of works on foreign religious movements, translating English authors by the dozen, especially the historians, and rhapsodising about the *Biographia Britannica*:

> England and the lands connected with it are more fruitful in noteworthy people of all conditions who attract and hold the attention of their rational fellow creatures, or can yield more notable examples of the most glorious virtues or most shameful vices, of the exceptional use and misuse of unusual capabilities and advantageous opportunities, as well as the most audacious and unsuccessful enterprises, and of the most rapid and unexpected changes of good and ill fortune, than other nations [who lack the exaggerated political liberties of England]. . . . For this reason they have not attained the levels which corporately developed scholarship, wit, shrewdness, industriousness, bravery, arts, science, business, riches, extravagance, boldness, folly, enthusiasm and evil have reached there.[36]

Baumgarten might well respect English liberty, for he would have been ejected from Halle with Spangenberg (with whom he shared a single appointment) but for the personal protection of the Queen of Prussia. Baumgarten, in the current manner, had combined orthodox theology with practical ideals of piety; his offence was to have subjected his propositions to Wolffian logic, as the most rigorous test available. His turning from Wolff to history marked his conviction that what was now required was the rigour of history (regarded by Wolff as factual knowledge and pre-scientific), especially in apologetics and exegesis.[37] It was liberty that made England so rich a field of historical study, and an historical character was firmly impressed on the theological side of the German Enlightenment after 1750 by Baumgarten's greatest and most affectionate pupil, Johannes Salomo Semler.

With Semler the history of modern Protestant theology begins. In a vast series of works, written in what Hirsch described as 'the worst [German] ever written by a German of intellectual standing',[38] Semler contributed to every part of the theological field. In one sense he limited that field by stressing the human element in the reception of revelation; in another sense he broadened it by his very emphasis on the historical and variable element in it. Private and public (or theologically organised) religion were indeed two different things, and the latter bore all the marks of time, place, and circumstance. The same was true of scripture, and Semler plunged boldly into the historical criticism of the New Testament, even of the canon itself. Semler's impact on German thought was not, however, as great as that of Lessing, who bridged two important gaps. For Lessing was a successful man of letters before he became a theologian,[39] and his struggle against the dead hand of a biblical literalism was so much part of a struggle for literary freedom and creativity that it could not be simply repudiated when the German Romantics turned against the Enlightenment. Lessing beat the drum about Providence and the *Education of the Human Race*: he re-established Leibniz's metaphysical determinism and did not despise the 'positive' religions (including Christianity), which he certainly did not hold, because he viewed them as part of the development of mankind, a growth towards a more perfect moral and religious rationality. And he used his right as librarian of the famous ducal library at Wolfenbüttel to publish posthumous *Fragments* of

Hermann Samuel Reimarus (1694–1768). Reimarus was a Hamburg Wolffian and an adherent of English deism. He had made his assault on Orthodoxy on general rational grounds, designed to demonstrate the impossibility of the Christian reading of either Testament, and the frailty of the proofs from miracle and the fulfilment of prophecy. Nor did Reimarus spare the New Testament testimony to Jesus. The scripture writers, he held, embodied the apostolic system of Christianity, which deviated from that of Jesus, who intended neither to set up new articles of faith (like the mystery of the Trinity) nor to free his followers from Jewish religious practice.[40] By showing that the New Testament could be made to yield a portrait of Christ quite different from that favoured by Orthodoxy, Reimarus opened the door to that long series of *Lives* of Christ, some of which so alarmed the Victorians.

From Lessing, German thought could proceed in either of two directions, Kant, who was bred in mathematics and Wolffian logic, pressed beyond it to a universal human *Bildung* that included studies in human and natural sciences. He sought also to lay the foundations of a rational knowledge that should be proof against the confusion of opinions. This object and the synthetic work that was to crown his critical studies proved to be beyond him, but in the last dozen years of his life he produced a series of important works to which German theologians and philosophers would return when the need to get rid of metaphysics became urgent, and which ended in *Religion within the Limits of Mere Reason* (1793). The other line was to take up the theme of history, and especially of the history of cultural creativity, and find in it a revelation or a substitute for one. If Lessing had been a man of letters turned theologian, Herder was one of the few theologians to have earned an important place in the general intellectual and literary history of his people, fetching up appropriately in 1776 as General Superintendent in Weimar. Behind the events of everyday, Herder saw a divine force, and sought to awaken his fellows to a sense of beauty and harmony, a poetic perception of humanity. For Herder, indeed, there was no difference of nature and spirit that was not embraced by the deeper unity of a creative original force. Creation was the self-expression of a living and active God. The documents of

religious history could be made to yield a message in terms of
religious psychology. Psychology and history went together,
for revelation was constituted not by the ideas and concepts it
contained, but by the movement of the heart towards a
humanity devoted to God.

Herder's most powerful impact was upon the young
Goethe. After being raised in a cool and reasonable Christianity, Goethe had come under Moravian influence, but
never quite to the point of conversion. Goethe's obstacle was
not rational objection to points of doctrine, which concerned
him little, but the power of his poetic imagination, the feeling
(as one of his biographers later put it)[41] that he must choose
between being an author and a Christian. At the crucial point
in 1770/1 he met Herder, who opened his eyes to
Shakespeare, Ossian, Homer, and folk-poetry, and led him
to his first great poetic achievements.[42] Goethe's poetic
liberation involved a separation from Christianity of a sort
that seemed to require no decision, and he left it to his
readers to make up their minds how much Christian piety
they would combine with the inward awakening brought
about by his poetry. He found it impossible to make any
person the centre of his thought and life as his friend Lavater
made Jesus. Lavater, he maintained, plucked feathers from
all the world's birds to adorn the bird of paradise. In the
same way it was untrue that God spoke to men only through
the Bible; this was a denial of the whole world of literature,
of which Goethe had come to drink so deeply. The biblical
miracles, the virgin birth and resurrection, also left Goethe
cold; if there was a revelation it was in the unity that underlay
the manifold forms of creative activity. The Bible, indeed,
included images of the three different kinds of religion that
Goethe thought inculcated the proper respect for man as the
highest of the works of God. Ethnic religion (as in the Old
Testament) taught a proper respect for the power above
embodied in the pages of world history. Philosophic religion
taught the relations of man to mankind, and respect for his
equals. The Christian religion taught men to recognise the
divine in poverty, suffering, and death; it inculcated respect
for what is below us, and was only indispensable to those in
adversity. But ultimately religion, the true awakening, was
respect for man in his full humanity.

By the end of the Napoleonic Wars the cultural relations of theology in England and Germany were the reverse of what they had been three-quarters of a century before. Then radical English criticism in the field of the philosophy of religion had given a lead to German theologians, a lead enhanced by an English reputation for being libertarian and larger-than-life, a reputation justified to the extent that deist literature could actually appear in print. After the Seven Years' War German literary creativity, assisted by the fact that no major state was now prepared to put its weight behind Lutheran Orthodoxy, and that even in the Imperial cities brittle Orthodoxy was crumbling to decay, had 'taken off' on a scale which defies simple analysis. In part at least this rise was due to the fact that German nationalism had no political focus and gathered round a set of cultural traditions defined with new historical precision, and freshly developed. If this process enabled Pietists, for example, to mistake the ploys of patriotism for their inherited soteriology,[43] it enabled Goethe to slip out of Christianity altogether. But on the Protestant side, the legacy of Lutheran Orthodoxy, a highly articulated system of doctrine, guaranteed true upon the basis of an infallible Bible, was simply too tough to be ignored by intelligent men who had been bruised by it. For this reason the German Enlightenment, bolstered by the confidence and sense of moral outrage of the English deists, tackled the problem of applying reason to religion with much greater thoroughness than was ever attempted in England, and found, in particular, that history was a better way of overturning the Orthodox exegesis of scripture than 'reason' in the deist sense of the word. History, which did so much to uncover traditions round which national sentiment was gathering, might deal a knock-out blow to one divisive tradition, that of Lutheran Orthodoxy.

When the war was over, and Weimar classicism was spent, when there were religious revivals on both the Catholic and Protestant side, when the Orthodox and Pietists made an unholy alliance with each other and the conservative forces in political possession, when the political atmosphere again became bitterly intolerant, even Prussia, hitherto the most unconfessional of entities, proclaimed itself a Christian state in the narrowest of senses. There being no political activity to hand, and the life of the nation being focused upon a culture rather than a state, the work of ideological demolition must begin all over again.[44] And the aggressiveness on the radical side was justified by the fact that the conservative forces in possession were not merely as isolationist as their Orthodox predecessors, but had proved of even less intellectual interest.

It was this situation that gave such explosive power to the *Life of Jesus* first published by David Friedrich Strauss in 1835, notwithstanding that criticism since Reimarus had approached no consensus of a *Life* without presuppositions to replace the image of Orthodoxy, and notwithstanding that Strauss could only deploy the old weapons with more ruthlessness than his predecessors. What made Strauss a man commemorated by a plaque in the Stift at Tübingen as a bitter offence to the church was that his renewed assault on Christology had political implications. Old English deism had found little room for an incarnation, but the German criticism of the previous generation had grappled with the question in its own way. Kant had seen the moral perfection of humanity in the harmonious community of free individuals, of which the archetype might be the perfect person willing to die for others. Schleiermacher, understanding religion as the feeling of absolute dependence on God, could conceive Kant's archetype as actualised in Jesus, the religious genius, unique in his consciousness of God. Hegel, holding that the content of his philosophy was that of Christianity in another form, and that its built-in understanding of contradiction fitted it to embrace the contradictions in the idea of the God-man, concluded that the real was the rational and vice-versa, and that the incarnation was both real and rational. Strauss was not a stable politician. As recently as 1830 he had been telling his congregation that it was 'better to perish from a lack of earthly bread than suffer a lack of heavenly manna'. The *Life of Jesus*, by contrast, was 'democratic' in the sense that the properties the church (contradictorily) ascribed to Christ were united in humanity; *pace* Hegel, Absolute Spirit was actualised not in a man, but in the human species. This egalitarian message was dangerous both to Christian orthodoxy and traditional political hierarchies. Strauss could not keep up this radicalism for long. The third

edition (1838) of the *Life* was 'aristocratic', in the sense that
Strauss admitted the historicity of the Fourth Gospel, took
up the category of genius, and saw in Jesus a genius who gave
shape to the inner life. He was the genius who of all the
geniuses on offer in the late thirties was the least likely to
realise the outer ideals of the liberal, the rationalist, or the
social critic. Strauss had sold the pass (there were reversions
later).[45] And though this may have helped him to a chair at
Zurich, it did not save him from dismissal as the result of a
revolution. It was entirely in order that his fourth edition
should be put into English by George Eliot in 1846. Heine
could sum up the matter in the phrase that in Germany
philosophy had fought the same victorious fight against
Christianity as in ancient Greece it had fought against
mythology.[46]

III   THE VICTORIAN ENCOUNTER WITH GERMAN SCHOLARSHIP

It is convenient to resume the English side of the story with
the translation of Strauss's *Life of Jesus*, more than fifty years
after the outbreak of the Revolutionary Wars. During that
time Britain and Prussia had been political allies, there had
been a good deal of economic interaction between the two
sides,[47] the evangelical world had had its own go-betweens in
men like K.F.A. Steinkopf,[48] but the English world of
intellect, and especially of theology, had lost contact with the
great developments in German theology, and, encouraged
by the celebrated revulsions against Germany of H.J. Rose
and E.B. Pusey, did not want to know what had been going
on. The 'pro-German' and the isolationist parties were as
they had always been, but the balance between them had
changed completely (as in America it notably had not).[49] The
universities and the clergy of the church had, under the
pressures of the late eighteenth century, been much more
fully incorporated into the new establishment created in
those years than their predecessors had ever been, and, in
their revulsion against enlightenment, were more completely
isolationist in their defence of English ways and institutions
than were their predecessors. This did not harm the German

establishments; even without the sympathies of the English church they did better out of the Vienna settlement of 1815 than they had done from any settlement under the Empire. Nor did isolationism solve the domestic problems of the English church. The Whig triumph of 1830 was far more menacing than that of 1715; it was met, especially at Oxford, by a passionate resistance which parodied that of the early Hanoverian era. Then there had been heads who were latitudinarian and Whig; now they were solidly Protestant high churchmen, and the only way the Oxford juniors could twist their arms to last-ditch resistance was themselves to advance from Protestant high churchmanship to a Catholicism intense equally against Protestant dissenters and Romanists. This artificial construct represented an extreme of isolationism.[50] It was only too clear what a church of low achievement, intellectual and otherwise, the Church of England was,[51] and so, when English divines lost touch with the German developments in an obsession with their own traditions and peculiarities, the Germans, even liberal Germans, avid consumers of the English output in the first half of the eighteenth century, stopped reading English work on the irreproachable ground that it was not worth reading and certainly no longer bore on the progress of German idealism.

Emanuel Hirsch, old, blind, and dismissed from his chair by the victorious Allies, atoned after the Second World War for a lifetime of nationalism by writing his immense *Geschichte der neueren evangelischen Theologie* against the whole history of the West. He cannot, I think, be faulted in the proportion of space allocated to English theology: more than two-fifths of the first of his five volumes (devoted to the late-seventeenth and early-eighteenth century), but of the three volumes extending from the mid-eighteenth to the mid-nineteenth century (and totalling 1536 pages) a mere 82 pages. There were, of course, perils in the isolation of superiority as well as in the very second-rate *Sonderweg* favoured in England. By the 1940s Thomas Mann was writing savagely that it was 'nothing but German provincial conceitedness to deny depth to the world'; and castigating his native land 'where the word "international" has long been a reproach, and a smug provincialism has made the air spoilt and stuffy'.[52] And Rudolf von Thadden has lately spoken of the 'catalogue of ghosts which alienated the [Wilhelmine] intellectual world from the realities of modern life'.[53] Still, if it took exile in America to open the eyes of Thomas Mann to latter-day German isolation, it took exile in Natal to save Colenso from English isolation and make a scholar of him. It happened that the curator of the museum and library in Cape Town was the son of the notable German Old Testament scholar, Friedrich Bleek, and he kept Colenso supplied with good German work in the field that he would probably not have obtained in England.[54] As often happened in England, nonconformists took their cue from the Church. When the Congregationalists created the *British Quarterly Review* in the 1840s, it contained valuable bibliographies of the current German output; but when Samuel Davidson, professor of biblical literature and ecclesiastical history at Lancashire Independent College, 1843–57, a friend of various German theologians of relatively conservative views, contributed to the second volume of the tenth edition of Horne's *Introduction to the Sacred Scriptures* (1856), the college committee made him resign his chair. The very last extant letter of Jabez Bunting, the so-called 'last Wesleyan', was to forbid the teaching of German to voluntary classes in the Didsbury College seminary;[55] the 'first Wesleyan', John Wesley himself, it is noteworthy, had been a principal channel of the influence in England of Bengel, Buddeus, and the Pietists, and translated no fewer than 34 German hymns, much to the advantage of his flock. Most conservative of all were the atheists, who organised themselves publicly in the Secular Society in 1851, still firmly wedded to the doctrines of Tom Paine and the deists of the eighteenth century.[56] Nor were the men of letters more open than the theologians. The German contacts made by letter or by visit of Wordsworth, Crabb Robinson, and the rest, do not amount to much, nor were they greatly enhanced by reading in the literature.[57]

It was outsiders who responded positively to the German achievement: Unitarians, by this time so much outsiders as to be of small general influence, liberal Anglicans interested in German historiography,[58] a learned recluse like Connop Thirlwall (Melbourne had his translation of Schleiermacher's *Critical Essay on the Gospel of St. Luke* vetted by two bishops and the Primate before he felt able to raise him to the least desirable of all episcopal sees),[59] literary men like Carlyle who found in Goethe a painless exit from Christian profession, and one literary in-man, in the shape of Coleridge, who had indeed been a Unitarian for a time. Carlyle's understanding of Goethe is not now regarded as profound, but he corresponded with him, regarded him in 'the hero as Man of Letters' as 'by far the notablest of all Literary Men', and helped Sterling out of the Church of England with him. It was a fitting memorial to this succession that George Eliot, despite her association with Positivists, had much of the Goethean about her, and that her association with G.H. Lewes began when she joined him in Germany, where he was completing his *Life of Goethe* (1856). And with that association George Eliot discovered herself as a novelist. Curiously enough, there was something in this for Germany. Carlyle translated one of Goethe's poems in *Past and Present*.[60] He filled up the metre at the end with an admonition of his own: 'Work and despair not.' This somewhat Calvinist exhortation summed up what Carlyle thought he had learned from Goethe, and, translated into German, it became in the present century one of the mottoes of the Weimar system.[61] Coleridge, a layman with a message for the Church who evoked a succession of his own to preach it, was a curious case. Neither he nor his disciples made any bones that his Platonism took the form it did as a result of his application to Kant, Fichte, and Schelling, even if 'the matured theory of the clerisy which one finds in the *Church and State* arose from the accommodation of his development of German idealist philosophy to English cultural traditions [and] as such ... is specifically English, and Coleridgean'.[62] What Coleridge valued in the Germans, in other words, was not the critical achievement, but the possibilities of metaphysical construction he perceived in them; and given that this perception was open and legitimate, it is extraordinary that he should have proceeded to the extent he did by way of unacknowledged plagiarism.[63] The one 'in-man' who found a conservative message in Germany took great care not to reveal the sources of all he had poached.

The other group of outsiders seeking to be insiders who took up the German cause were the university reformers, and they were quite as selective as Coleridge. After the murder of Kotzebue in 1819, the German liberal students were praised because they had 'adopted the universal wish of the nation, and the professors, so unlike the generality of their brethren in other places, [were] almost without exception the strenuous supporters of national liberty and inalienable rights of mankind'. The excellence of their scholarship matched the excellence of their politics.[64] Thomas Hodgskin was more cautious, but thought that, even at the lowest, 'without placing much confidence in [German] sovereigns, it may at least be supposed that ... they are as capable of organising a university as the same class of men were three or four centuries ago'.[65] This view of the matter was implicitly conceded by conservative opinion, which professed no surprise at the subversiveness of German institutions in which professors offered novelties for fees, instead of expounding approved books in the manner of the English tutors.[66] And for most of the century the issue between men of conservative bent, and liberal (often Unitarian) reformers, over the planting-out of new German universities in London and the provinces was discussed largely in these terms; the real fact was, of course, that German state patronage secured professors who on major issues regarded themselves as lions under the throne, and who, where technological studies were concerned, were as opposed to novelties as the *Quarterly Review*. It was religious and scholarly orthodoxy which was corroded by the critical power of professorial liberalism. Appropriately enough, the broadest critique of the English university system came from the man most seriously engaged with the German philosophical challenge, Sir William Hamilton. He maintained that the universities' defence of chartered liberties was misplaced since the colleges had illegally swallowed up the universities, and that religious tests to enter the arts faculties could hardly be warranted, when they were unknown in universities outside England.[67] Certainly the absence of tests would not explain German scepticism. When Hamilton visited Germany for the first time in 1817 to buy books for the Advocates' Library in Edinburgh, he knew no German, but he speedily put this right, and employed his new knowledge to combine the commonsense philosophy on which he had been raised with the transcendental philosophy of Kant. In Hamilton there was a genuine reception of Kant, hitherto barely known in Scotland, together with an attempt to take the argument further. From Kant Hamilton derived the view that the existence of a God conceived as a being absolute in himself was as undemonstrable as the ground of our freedom. The evidence of our consciousness for God's moral goverment of the world and for our responsibility did not extend to a speculative proof of how God exists and how our freedom is possible. A recent German inquiry maintained that he was the only one of the Victorian agnostics to have made a genuine encounter with German philosophy.[68]

We come finally to what is conventionally treated as the main part of the subject, the topics treated by Professor Chadwick under the headings of 'History and the Bible' and 'Doubt'. Once university teachers found German texts in classical, historical, and theological studies indispensable, they could not avoid some kind of encounter with German scholarship. The furore over *Essays and Reviews* was sufficient to put Jowett and Stanley off their projected reconstruction of New Testament criticism; and, though a somewhat dated Hegelianism became modish among philosophers,[69] there were deep-rooted habits of mind among theologians which discouraged genuine engagement. Locke had regarded knowledge as something external to man, perceived by sense impressions. Revelation was in the nature of the case external to man, though it was recognisable by supporting evidences. Among these were miracles and the fulfilment of prophesies, that is, principally biblical evidences, and all was well as long as the Bible was secure. The boldness of German historical criticism owed, as we have seen, much to the need to dislodge a peculiarly tough doctrinal system; but it was also encouraged by the turn taken by German philosophy. This philosophy had gone inward rather than outward, and encouraged a view of religion as the experience of a liberating God, to be perceived in history as well as within, and confirmed and sustained in scripture. The evidences that mattered were those within. De Wette, the great Old Testament critic of the early nineteenth century, wrote that the supernaturalists 'believe in miracles, and conceive them in a natural and material manner. They consider that the laws of nature are temporarily suspended, that Nature's machine is differently set. With all their exaltation of Faith they are unable to believe without seeing. And if they had lived in the days of Christ, they would indeed have beheld no marvellous works, for, like the Pharisees, they would have asked for a sign from heaven.' On this view, the English theologians were Pharisees. The philosophical stress on 'inner truth' eased the critic's way to recognising the importance in antiquity of myth, and encouraged him, perhaps too readily, to think that the truth could be restated in contemporary terms through speculative philosophy. At the beginning of the nineteenth century there was no English counterpart to the body of Old Testament criticism already available in Germany, and the later practice of T. & T. Clark and others in publishing translations of predominantly conservative German authors encouraged the view that there was no critical case to answer.[70] Eventually the German Old Testament work was summed up and presented in English dress by S.R. Driver, whose *Introduction to the Literature of the Old Testament* (1883) still earns high marks from Old Testament specialists.[71] But Driver's frame of mind had not changed much from that of his Lockean predecessors of the eighteenth century. He accepted a double theory of the truth of the Bible, according to which its inner or spiritual truths could be distinguished from its outward expression. Thus if, on scientific grounds, it became impossible to hold with Genesis 1 that the world was created within seven days, it was permissible to regard this statement as the disposable outer husk of some spiritual truth conveyed by the narrative. That is to say that the Bible was still, in the old manner, to be regarded as conveying external truths. Driver, moreover, did actually believe that the narrative of the Fall was a picturesque description of an event, of man's failure when he had developed to the point of being conscious of the moral law, and breaking it; indeed he thought that if the human race had arisen in several independent quarters of the world, each group would have gone through this event. Real (and otherwise unknown) history lay behind the image. Compare this with Schleiermacher. He maintained that even if the Mosaic narrative were acceptable as 'an historical account communicated in an extraordinary way, the particular pieces of information would never be articles of faith in our sense of the phrase, for our feeling of absolute dependence does not gain thereby either a new content, a new form, or clearer definition.'[72] No comment is needed as to which of these views was more likely to lead to a 'crisis of faith' in an age when historical studies were in the full flood of progress.

It was a similar story with the key issue of Christology. Though Strauss's *Life* was followed up by bestselling successors in England, France, and Germany, what was made available in English was not the German critical work on the New Testament which had Christological implications, but church history and the like. Anglicans in particular took comfort from the fact that Lightfoot was now addressing himself to the whole question of gospel criticism; Lightfoot said (or at any rate implied, for he was economical of words, in both speech and writing) that accepted views of the Incarnation were all right, and wrote that the critical views of the Tübingen school were too extravagant to last. It is not now thought that Lightfoot engaged with the Tübingen school in any fundamental degree,[73] and where the shoe pinched was made clear in his anxiety to defend the historicity of the Fourth Gospel. The Fourth Gospel presented a clearly Christian view of Jesus, and if the historical accuracy of the gospel were basically reliable, then Christian claims about the Incarnation could be held to be rooted in historical reality. The information would have been conveyed in the Lockean manner. Yet in the main Lightfoot stuck closely to his exegetical last, creating the impression that all would come out all right if historical criticism were honestly pursued, and avoided wider issues. The degree of reassurance his fellows required may be measured by the abundant veneration he received.

This need for reassurance is in itself evidence for the sense of unease that marked so many during the long Victorian crisis of faith. With that unease no longer with us, it is interesting to observe that in our own time a much fuller exposure to nineteenth-century German scholarship is taking place. A great deal of important German work on gospel criticism nearly a century old has recently been translated into English, some of it for the first time. In 1973, after almost 140 years, the English version of Strauss's *Life of Jesus* reappeared, and was well received;[74] in comparison with other weapons, this particular hand grenade now seemed benign.

NOTES

1. Owen Chadwick, *The Victorian Church* (London, 1966–70).
2. Owen Chadwick, *The Secularization of the European Mind in the Nineteenth Century: The Gifford Lectures in the University of Edinburgh for 1973–4* (Cambridge, 1975).
3. ibid., 2.
4. Clive Field in an unpublished paper on 'Religious Practice in England: 17th and 18th Centuries'.
5. On the 'golden age of the Church of England' see Desmond Bowen, *The Idea of the Victorian Church: A Study of the Church of England, 1833–1889* (Montreal, 1968).
6. Owen Chadwick, *The Mind of the Oxford Movement* (London, 1960) 50.
7. G.R. Balleine, *A History of the Evangelical Party in the Church of England* (London, 1957) 164–5.
8. W.R. Ward, *Religion and Society in England, 1790–1850* (London, 1972) 287.
9. T.W. Heyck, *The Transformation of Intellectual Life in Victorian England* (London, 1982) 24–49.
10. W.R. Ward, 'Oxford and the Origins of Liberal Catholicism in the Church of England', *Studies in Church History*, 1 (1962) 233–52.
11. W.R. Ward, *Theology, Sociology and Politics: The German Protestant Social Conscience, 1890–1930* (Bern, 1979).
12. W.R. Ward, 'The Protestant Churches, Especially in Britain, and the Social Problems of the Industrial Revolution', in *Religion und Kirchen im industriellen Zeitalter*, Schriftenreihe des Georg-Eckert-Instituts für internationale Schulbuchforschung, Bd I.23 (Braunschweig, 1977) 63–72.
13. For the case of Reading see S. Yeo, *Religion and Voluntary Organisations in Crisis* (London, 1976). Cf. G.E. Milburn, 'Piety, Profit and Paternalism: Methodists in Business in the North-East of England, c. 1760–1920', *Proceedings of the Wesley Historical Society*, 44 (1982) 45–92.
14. C.V. Cox, *Recollections of Oxford*, 2nd edn (London, 1870) 355.
15. For a Canadian study of this which could be paralleled in contemporary England see Neil Semple, '"The Nurture and Admonition of the Lord": Nineteenth-century Canadian Methodism's Response to "Childhood",' *Histoire Sociale – Social History*, 14 (1981) 157–75.
16. In a famous book, *Dreimonate als Fabrikarbeiter und Handwerksbursche* (Leipzig, 1891; Eng. tr. *Three Months in a Workshop* [London, 1895]), Paul Göhre reported that Jesus had not gone downhill in the esteem of the Chemnitz textile workers, among whom he had spent three months incognito, as had the Church. He proposed therefore to take

them the historical Jesus. A similar situation obtained in England.

17. The best study of this subject is by James R. Moore, *The Post-Darwinian Controversies: A Study of the Protestant Struggle to Come to Terms with Darwin in Great Britain and America, 1870–1900* (Cambridge, 1979). For an earlier period there is a suggestive American study that makes use of German material: H. Hoverkamp, *Science and Religion in America, 1800–1860* (Philadelphia, 1978). See also T.D. Bozeman, *Protestants in an Age of Science* (Chapel Hill, NC, 1977).

18. On all this and on continuing alarm for the Protestant interest on the continent see my paper, 'Orthodoxy, Enlightenment and Religious Revival', *Studies in Church History*, 17 (1980) 275–96.

19. *Unschuldige Nachrichten*, (1735) 52, 235–7; (1741) 57. Cf. the ordinances of 1744 forbidding foreigners to preach in Hanover (*Acta Historico-Ecclesiastica*, 9: 264–5).

20. *Zeitschrift der Gesellschaft für nieder-sächsische Kirchengeschichte*, 39 (1934) 185, n. 54. The Duchess of Kendal was also a contact of Zinzendorf. Another Pietist at the Hanoverian court in London, 1714–28, was the Countess Johanna Sophie of Schaumburg-Lippe (ibid., 63 [1965] 187).

21. J.G. Walch, *Historische und theologische Einleitung in die Religions-Streitigkeiten ausser der Evangelisch-Lutherischen Kirche*, 5 vols (Jena, 1733–6; repr. Stuttgart, 1972) 1: 606.

22. Johannes Reiskius, *Commentario de Monarchia Quinta* (Wolfenbüttel, 1692).

23. F.W. Barthold, *Die Erweckten im protestantischen Deutschland während des Ausgangs des 17. und der ersten Hälfte des 18. Jahrhunderts besonders die frommen Grafenhöfe* (repr. from *Historisches Taschenbuch 1852–3* [Darmstadt, 1968]) 1: 166. Eva von Buttlar gave it out that her lover (a theologian called Winter) and a medical student from Jena were God the Father and God the Son, while she was no less than the Holy Spirit.

24. *Acta Historico-Ecclesiastica*, 9: 298.

25. *Unschuldige Nachrichten* (1721) 493. Cf. ibid. (1726) 841–3; (1727) 437.

26. For Löscher's assault upon the alleged unorthodoxy of the English church see M. Greschat, *Zwischen Tradition und neuem Anfang* (Witten, 1971) 236.

27. H.L. Benthem, *Neu-eröffneter Engländischer Kirch- und Schulenstaat*, 2nd edn (Leipzig, 1732) preface, paras 9–10.

28. Dr Kayser, 'Hannoversche Enthusiasten des siebzehnten Jahrhunderts', *Zeitschrift der Gesellschaft für niedersächsische Kirchengeschichte*, 15 (1905) 59.

29. Max Goebel, 'Geschichte der wahren Inspirations-Gemeinden von 1688 bis 1850', pt III, *Zeitschrift für die historische Theologie*, N.F. 19 (1855) 98.

30. Andreas Gross, *Vernunftiger und unpartheyische Bericht über die neuaufkommende Herrnhütische Gemeinde*, 3rd edn (Frankfurt/Leipzig, 1740) 21.

31. M. Brecht, 'Die Entwicklung der alten Bibliothek des Tübinger Stift

in ihren theologie- und geistesgeschichtlichen Zusammenhang', *Blätter für Württembergische Kirchengeschichte*, 63 (1963) 59, 63. The holdings of the library at the Stift are a marvellous continuous record of what was thought worth buying. Whitefield and Watts, for example, were thought more important than Wesley.

32. There was strong English representation in J.H. Reitz, *Historie der Wiedergebohrnen*, 5th edn (Berleburg, 1724).

33. Carl Heinrich von Bogatsky, *Aufrichtige und an aller Kinder Gottes gerichtete Declaration über eine gegen ihn herausgekommene Herrnhütische Schrift* (Halle, 1751) 10.

34. Wolfgang Martens, *Die Botschaft der Tugend: Die Aufklärung im Spiegel der deutschen moralischen Wochenschriften* (Stuttgart, 1971).

35. Johann Rudolf Schlegel, *Kirchengeschichte des achtzehnten Jahrhunderts* (Heilbronn, 1784–96) esp. 2: 814.

36. Siegmund Jacob Baumgarten, *Sammlung von merkwurdigen Lebensbeschreibungen grossten Teils aus der britannischen Biographen übersetzt* . . . (Halle, 1754–7), unpaginated preface. As late as 1798 it could be reported that 'the English imperial constitution . . . without doubt one of the best in the world . . . opens to all foreigners without distinction access to this blessed island. . . . English freedom causes the land . . . to blossom'; but it was already noticeable that 'the Briton is not himself inventive, but . . . follows the track pointed out to him by the foreigner' (*Kirchengeschichte der deutschen Gemeinden in London* [Tübingen, 1798] 9–13).

37. Martin Schloemann, *Siegmund Jacob Baumgarten: System und Geschichte in der Theologie des Überganges zum Neuprotestantismus* (Göttingen, 1974). Among the English authors whom Baumgarten had gone out of his way to introduce to German readers were the deists and their critics.

38. Emanuel Hirsch, *Geschichte der neuern evangelischen Theologie*, 5th edn, 5 vols (Gütersloh, 1975) 4: 50.

39. A substantial East German Lessing-reader (*Lessing für unser Zeit: Ein Lesebuch*, 25th edn [Berlin/Weimar, 1984]) almost excludes Lessing the theologian. This imbalance may be rectified by *Lessing's Theological Writings*, ed. H. Chadwick (London, 1956).

40. *Reimarus: Fragments*, ed. C.H. Talbert (London, 1971).

41. H. von Schubert, quoted in Hirsch, 4: 248.

42. *The Autobiography of Johann Wolfgang von Goethe*, ed. K.J. Weintraub, 2 vols (Chicago, 1974) 2: 8–23.

43. Gerhard Kaiser, *Pietismus und Patriotismus in literarischen Deutschland* (Wiesbaden, 1961).

44. The political parallel was explicitly drawn by Heine in his *Zur Geschichte der Religion und Philosophie in Deutschland* (1834), *Sämmtliche Werke*, 13 vols, Bibliothek Ausgabe (Hamburg, n.d.) 7: 126.

45. For a fuller development of this argument, see Marilyn Chapin Massey, *Christ Unmasked: The Meaning of 'The Life of Jesus' in German Politics* (Chapel Hill, NC, 1983).

46. Heine, *Sämmtliche Werke*, 7: 147.

47. Hans-Joachim Braun, *Technologische Beziehungen zwischen Deutschland*

und England von der Mitte des 17. bis zum Augang des 18. Jahrhunderts (Dusseldorf, 1974).

48. Ward, *Religion and Society in England*, 45.

49. Carl Diehl, *Americans and German Scholarship, 1770–1870* (New Haven, 1978) esp. 1.

50. W.R. Ward, *Victorian Oxford* (London, 1965) chs 5 and 6. Walter Harley Conser, Jr, shows indeed that the confessional frame of mind was an international phenomenon, but does not admit that confessionalism could only become international by following migrations of population ('Church and Confession: Conservative Theologians in Germany, England and America, 1815–66', Ph.D. diss., Brown University, 1981. Published under the same title, Macon, Ga. 1984).

51. Writing in 1890, Otto Pfleiderer ascribed the difficulty to the fact that no English counterpart of German idealism was to hand when popular Lockeanism, 'that barren view of things which binds man to the world of the senses', ceased to satisfy. But he did not mince the 'fact that the church life of England ... has remained almost completely untouched by the vast progress of ... scientific thought ... and that whenever the two come into contact, such a violent collision is the consequence that popular feeling is shocked' (*The Development of Theology in Germany since Kant, and Its Progress in Britain since 1828* [London, 1890] 307).

52. Thomas Mann, *Doctor Faustus* (London, 1978) 175, 174.

53. *Troeltsch Studien*, Bd 3, eds Horst Renz and Friedrich Wilhelm Graf (Gütersloh, 1984) 119.

54. John Rogerson, *Old Testament Criticism in the Nineteenth Century: England and Germany* (London, 1984) 221.

55. W.R. Ward, *Early Victorian Methodism* (Oxford, 1976) 420–1. More information of this kind, mostly of a later date, is to be found in Willis B. Glover, Jr, *Evangelical Nonconformists and Higher Criticism in the Nineteenth Century* (London, 1954).

56. S. Budd, *Varieties of Unbelief: Atheists and Agnostics in English Society* (London, 1977) 10.

57. R. Wellek, *Confrontations: Studies in the Intellectual and Literary Relations between Germany, England and the United States during the Nineteenth Century* (Princeton, NJ, 1965) 6–11.

58. Duncan Forbes, *The Liberal Anglican Idea of History* (Cambridge, 1952).

59. *Letters Literary and Theological of Connop Thirlwall*, eds J.J.S. Perowne and L. Stokes (London, 1881).

60. 'Mason Lodge' (Thomas Carlyle, *Past and Present*, in *Works*, 30 vols [1897; repr. London, 1969, 1974] 10: 237–8).

61. On the 'Goethe Gemeinde' see W.H. Bruford, 'Goethe and Some Victorian Humanists', *Publications of the English Goethe Society*, NS 18 (1949) 34–67. On Carlyle see R. Wellek, 'Carlyle and German Romanticism', and 'Carlyle and the Philosophy of History', ibid., 34–113; and C.F. Harrold, *Carlyle and German Thought, 1819–34* (New Haven, Conn., 1934).

62. Ben Knights, *The Idea of the Clerisy in the Nineteenth Century* (Cambridge, 1978) 65.
63. On the plagiarism see N. Fruman, *Coleridge, the Damaged Archangel* (London, 1972) e.g. 31–4, 80–3. On Coleridge as a philosopher, see J.H. Muirhead, *Coleridge as a Philosopher* (London, 1930); R. Wellek, *Immanuel Kant in England, 1793–1838* (London, 1931); T.B. McFarland, *Coleridge and the Pantheist Tradition* (Oxford, 1969); Donald MacKinnon, 'Coleridge and Kant', in *Coleridge's Variety*, ed. John B. Beer (London, 1975) 183–203.
64. *A Memoir of Charles Louis Sand: Including a Narrative of the Circumstances Attending the Death of Augustus von Kotzebue; also A Defence of the German Universities* (London, 1819).
65. T. Hodgskin, *Travels in the North of Germany*, 2 vols (Edinburgh, 1820) 2: 265–9.
66. *Quarterly Review*, 23 (1821) 446–8.
67. Ward, *Victorian Oxford*, 82–3, 92.
68. Karl-Dieter Ulke, *Agnostisches Denken im Victorianischen England* (Freiburg/München, 1980).
69. The study being commended in a book which delighted Emerson and Carlyle, J.H. Sterling, *The Secret of Hegel* (Edinburgh, 1865).
70. On this whole subject see Rogerson, *Old Testament Criticism, passim*.
71. J.W. Rogerson, 'Philosophy and the Rise of Biblical Criticism: England and Germany', in *England and Germany: Studies in Theological Diplomacy*, ed. S.W. Sykes (Frankfurt, 1982) 22–3. Cf. *The Cambridge History of the Bible*, 3: 274–95.
72. Quoted in Rogerson, *Old Testament Criticism*, 73. Strauss likewise pleaded that he had cut across old divisions in the interests of truth. 'Orthodox and rationalists alike proceed from the false assumption that we have always in the gospels testimony, sometimes even that of eye witnesses, to fact. They are, therefore, reduced to asking themselves what can have been the real and natural fact which is here witnessed to in such extraordinary ways. We have to realize that the narrators testify sometimes not to outward facts but to ideas, often most practical and beautiful ideas.... [This] results in narrative, legendary, mythical in nature, illustrative often of spiritual truth in a manner more perfect than any hard prosaic statement could achieve' (*Life of Jesus*, Preface).
73. R. Morgan, 'Historical Criticism and Christology: England and Germany', in *England and Germany*, 87.
74. e.g., *Theology*, 76 (1983) 602–3. Even Reimarus appeared in English translation in 1971.

Part II
Natural Religion and the Heritage of the Eighteenth Century

3 The Fiat and Finger of God: The Bridgewater Treatises

John M. Robson

'Science was not generally seen as in opposition to religion before the publication of the *Origin of Species*, but as part of a widely accepted natural theology.' This judgment by T.W. Heyck is well based,[1] though it is not correct to see 1859 as the end of natural theology for scientists. An examination of evidence that might be used to support such a judgment, however, suggests an excitement not completely compatible with complacency about the effect on religious belief of scientific facts and theories, especially on the untutored mind. In particular, the series of Bridgewater Treatises, published initially from 1833 to 1836, invites conclusions and speculations about the perceived relations between science and religion.[2]

I ORIGINS

The Right Honourable and Reverend Francis Henry Egerton, FRS, FSA, 8th Earl of Bridgewater, bequeathed £8000, with the interest accruing, to be devoted to securing

> a person or persons ... to write, print, and publish one thousand copies of a work *On the Power, Wisdom, and Goodness of God, as manifested in the Creation; illustrating such work by all reasonable arguments, as for instance the variety and formation of God's creatures in the animal, vegetable, and mineral kingdoms; the effect of digestion, and thereby of conversion; the construction of the hand of man, and an infinite variety of other arguments; as also by discoveries ancient and modern, in arts, sciences, and the whole extent of literature.*[3]

The terms of the bequest were to be carried out by the

President of the Royal Society of London. This office, when the Earl died in February 1829, was held by Davies Gilbert, who, feeling inadequate to the task, decided to take the advice – and to use the good offices – of William Howley, Archbishop of Canterbury, and Charles James Blomfield, Bishop of London. With the concurrence of Bridgewater's brother-in-law, Charles Long, Lord Farnborough – whose advice they little heeded – they proceeded to the task in a fashion that the record suggests, perhaps unfairly, was not the less dilatory for being sincere. By mid-May Howley and Blomfield had agreed to advise, but the plans then lay fallow for a year.

Then, in June 1830, Howley gave Gilbert a push, clearly intended to be self-disengaging, that got the process started (if not properly), by saying Gilbert should select 'a certain number of eminent persons', and ask them 'to form outlines of a plan, the several parts of which might be filled up by them respectively, as they might agree among themselves'.[4] This proposal would appear to have led Gilbert back into consultation with Howley and Blomfield to make the crucial decision that no one author should undertake the work, and that it should extend to more than one volume. That, at least, is the account he gave when, making the first committed move in a piecemeal process, he wrote to John Herschel saying, 'We have resolved on dividing the Work into eight Treatises by separate Authors under their respective names; the whole should perhaps occupy two 8vo. vols., and if you will favour us by accepting Astronomy we offer it to you.' Herschel, whose *Discourse* was to be one of the major authorities cited by the Bridgewater authors, showed a fine and rare punctiliousness in his reply of 1 July, declining the offer, much as he was impressed by the truths of Natural Theology, because he felt repugnance at the thought of weakening 'the weight of [his] testimony in their favour by promulgating them under the direct and avowed influence of a pecuniary reward'.[5]

At or about this time, presumably after consultation, Gilbert approached P.M. Roget who, as Secretary of the Royal Society, was the most accessible candidate, and William Buckland, perhaps the most obvious.[6] On 23 August, Gilbert wrote to Howley laying out his understanding of their compact: Charles Bell should be given 'Human Anatomy including of course Lord Bridgewater's favourite topic the Human Hand'; Roget should be offered 'the department of Physiological or Comparative Anatomy'; William Whewell should have Astronomy proposed to him; and 'Geology should be given to Dr. Buckland.'[7] The assigning of subjects by now revealed the lack of a concerted plan, and the nominators exchanged irresolute ideas about the allocating of such topics as Light and 'the other imponderable Fluids' including Heat.[8] But on 2 September, Gilbert produced a formal scheme for the project as a whole.[9]

From this point affairs moved quickly, though still in a fashion not likely to support the design argument. Mayo, Brewster, and Knapp were rejected; Prout was approached, probably by Gilbert, Kidd by Howley, and Chalmers by Blomfield.[10] The final author, William Kirby, was approached on Blomfield's part by John George Children of the British Museum on 16 November, and agreed almost immediately.[11] Then in December the 'final arrangements with respect to the publication of these works were made at a meeting ... of the majority of the selected writers', Bell, Roget, Buckland, Kirby, and Prout, 'and were sent for their approval to Dr Chalmers, Dr Kidd, and Professor Whewell, who had not been present'.[12]

The chosen authors were well qualified. All but Chalmers (who was to become a Fellow of the Royal Society of Edinburgh in 1834, an honour that Bell already held) were Fellows of the Royal Society of London. All eight are included in the *DNB*, and five in the modern *Dictionary of Scientific Biography*. All but Kirby were in the full course of their careers, and continued after the Bridgewater Treatises to increase their reputations; in several cases these works are still judged to be among their most significant as well as popular.

The prominence of the nominees, as well as the amount of money involved and Bridgewater's notoriety, made it inevitable that the scheme would become news. And so, in garbled form, it did, at a meeting of the Linnaean Society reported in the *Literary Gazette* on 5 February 1831.[13] Buckland was understandably agitated by the reference in that report to 'competitors for the legacy', and accusations of 'jobbery' that appeared in other journals, and on 8 February asked Gilbert to issue a correct statement of the arrangements.[14] Gilbert responded with a notice in the *Philosophical Magazine* and a statement read to the Royal Society.[15]

The precise activities of the next months are unclear, but at some point the authors seem to have taken over the arrangements, and to have chosen Roget as their spokesman. They concluded a publishing agreement with Murray, but in September 1832 he asked to be released from the contract because of the decline in trade. On 11 October 1832, the nominees met and agreed with Pickering 'for the publication of the work, which is to be completed before the end of next June (1833)'. The first two treatises, those of Whewell and Kidd, were published at the end of April 1833, at which time the other six were said to be 'in great forwardness', and would 'shortly appear'.[16]

The series sold very well through the middle 1830s, and then less well in the original format, except for revised editions of Roget in 1840 and Prout in 1845. But the story does not end there, for starting in 1852 the treatises began to appear in Bohn's Scientific Library in London (with US editions), and continued with reissues and 'new editions' even into the 1880s – that is, well after the crisis caused by Darwinism.[17] This format and longevity help establish three points: (1) the concern and argument about Natural Religion to some extent continued into the latter part of the century; (2) the works were seen as scientific, and not merely homiletic or apologetic; and (3) not only Gilbert, Howley, and Blomfield accepted the Bridgewater authors as authorities.

Further evidence of the significance of the Bridgewater Treatises and their themes is found in the response to them and in the other cognate works that appeared in the 1830s. Of the periodicals included in the first three volumes of the *Wellesley Index*, *Fraser's* was the most assiduous in noticing the Bridgewater Treatises, and prided itself on being the only major review to consider all of them. The *Edinburgh* had three full reviews, the *Quarterly* two, and the *Westminster* one. All except the *Westminster* (which dealt only with Chalmers) treated the authors and themes with respect, though there was much adverse criticism (especially in *Fraser's*) of the carrying out of the bequest's terms. Of the many other works of the 1830s on or pertaining to Natural Theology (omitting the great number bearing directly on Genesis and Geology), the most intriguing is Henry, Lord Brougham's edition, with massive commentary and notes, of Paley's *Natural Theology*. Begun in 1830, and pursued in the short intervals of comparative quiet in the Lord Chancellor's hectic life, it eventually appeared in five volumes.[18] As a final indication of how much more detailed work might be done to establish the centrality of Natural Theology in the practical scientific work of the period, here is a passage from a very popular work, Sir Henry Steuart's *The Planter's Guide*, concerning trees:

> If we take a survey of Nature, in all the forms, under which existence is manifested, we shall perceive, with admiration, the wisdom of the Creator, in accommodating every animate and inanimate being to the economy of a universal and connected plan. By his incomprehensible power, every organized production is adapted to the place, which it is destined to occupy in the world of life; and every organ of every living whole is curiously modified to the circumstances, which affect the exercise of its functions, and to the conditions, which regulate the development of its energies.[19]

II ARGUMENTS

How best can one use the Bridgewater Treatises as revealing the relation of science to religion in these years? What little modern comment there is on them concentrates, as one would expect, on the status of their authors and of their scientific facts and theories, with special emphasis on matters that proved central in the later evolutionary controversy, i.e., geology, paleontology, biology, and related sciences.[20] Indeed, like other works of the period, they are seen as 'pre-Darwinian', with all that such a label implies about our ways of examining or estimating them. Such an approach has its uses, but others – which too have limitations – are possible. One that has not been taken centres on the means of persuasion, in a large sense the kinds of argument, the rhetorical devices, that characterise the works.[21]

These means are not merely the 'rhetorician's tools', used for decoration and embellishment and as covers for weak or offensive rationalisations; they are the results of the meeting of belief and language on the road to persuasion. Choosing them may be a conscious or merely habitual response to the particular needs of an author, and, because the range of choice is not immense, no means is special to any author, though the combination and relative frequencies are.

In the Bridgewater Treatises one would expect to find argumentative forms typical of apologetic, homiletic, and sacred and secular exegetic works. And one does. But a study of the particular uses of these forms, especially as they indicate the perceived relations between the author and audience and between purpose and theme, enables us to see something of the assumptions, perceptions, and beliefs of an age not always revealed by other studies.

The first consideration is the context of the Bridgewater Treatises. The task facing each of the authors was distinctly odd in some respects, for they were engaging collectively but separately in writing a single work, with a preconceived single end, made up of units whose scope had virtually been prescribed before the authors had been chosen, and with no guidance or supervision, and apparently trivial consultation. The result, as reviewers were quick to point out, was confusion – but only for someone looking beyond the common purpose and method for a unified, unrepetitive, and exhaustive treatment. Would the intended audience for the Bridgewater Treatises find such faults? The volumes were sold separately, and it seems likely (because the library sets are so mixed) that few individuals bought all the volumes, fewer still read them all, and probably no one looked for coherent unity in the series.

The context for each was initially identical in respect of the bequest's terms: the treatises were to be demonstrations of 'the Power, Wisdom, and Goodness of God, as manifested in the Creation'; that is, they were to be works of Natural Theology, with specific reference to three of God's attributes. The authors saw themselves as writing works in a well-established genre, at a particular time in the history of that genre. Recognition of this element is important, for to the student of nineteenth-century history the Bridgewater Treatises may seem unusually untimely. The contractual arrangements for the Bridgewater Treatises is not what most of us remember 1832 for, yet there is no mention in any of them of the specific and social issues of the time. What is more, the title of the chapter on this period in Owen Chadwick's magisterial *Victorian Church*, 'Church in Danger', seems quite inappropriate to the Bridgewater Treatises; none of the themes Chadwick there discusses, as central to the religious and ecclesiastical life of the times, appears in them.[22]

It may seem, then, that the Bridgewater Treatises were anachronistic, not representative of the spirit of the age, which seemed to many to be presiding over a world about to be turned upside down. But the spirit was moving in other ways not foreign to the Bridgewater Treatises: in the broadening and deepening of scientific knowledge, both theoretical and practical, and in the increasingly avid public appetite for natural science, part of the surging interest in education (for which 'march of mind' is too measured and controlled an image). The Bridgewater authors did not see themselves as merely reworking Paley's *Natural Theology*, or as performing the relatively insignificant task of making Paley's thought available thirty years on. They were quite aware that neither Paley nor the Bridgewater Treatises marked the beginning or the end of Natural Theology, and that an active market continued, for some of them had already written works of or bearing on Natural Theology, and some contributed later works to the genre. Their attitude is caught most concisely (not a tough test in the Bridgewater Treatises) by William Prout's concluding words: 'the tendency of knowledge, and of its due application, is to abstract the attention from inferior things, and to fix the mind on the source of all knowledge and of all power – the GREAT FIRST CAUSE; who exists and acts throughout the universe; whom we can approach only, by studying His works; and whose works, an eternity, will be inadequate to explore.'[23]

The circumstances of their appointment ensured, of course, that the authors were both Christians and scientists;[24] their acceptance of the commission signalled their beliefs that Natural Theology was itself a science, and that it had a place within Christian Theology. They did not agree exactly on its placing with reference to Revelation, but they agreed on its force and utility in bolstering belief. And that, at bottom, was their brief.

How did they go about their task? In strict terms, they should have ignored certain traditional issues in Natural Theology. The bequest assumed – and in so doing matched the authors' and the intended audiences' beliefs – that the Creation is of divine origin, that the divine origin is *one* Creator, and that the Creator is the Christian God. But these issues, especially the first two, are hard to ignore, and so they enter into the treatises. Also, on a strict interpretation, there was no need to look beyond the three specified attributes, Power, Wisdom, and Goodness, but normally Natural Theology is used to show that Nature reveals the God of one's own theology, and – to choose the strongest case – Chalmers' God was not to be so limited. There was, further, no requirement that Revelation be discussed; however, the very strength of some authors' orthodoxy would not let them stay quiet on the matter. Finally, the belief in immortality was – perhaps by oversight – not mentioned by Bridgewater, but it also was too important and too traditional a topic to be ignored completely. In short, then, the authors collectively saw their task as covering the main issues in Natural Theology, but occasionally and explicitly they fell back within the limits suggested by the bequest.

And they advanced the 'science' in two ways: (1) by covering new sets of topics, and (2) by introducing massive amounts of novel evidence. The most obviously new topics were those initiated in the proposal that the series include an 'Essay on the adaptation of the *Physical constitution* of man to his intellectual and moral faculties, his social propensities, and the provision made for his wants in the works of nature', with the intellectual and moral going to Chalmers and the physical to Kidd.[25] Within areas at least touched on in earlier works on Natural Theology, the authors generally introduced instances that were new, the main intent being not to emphasise their novelty, but their number and extent.

Here, in fact, lies the main argumentative force of the Bridgewater Treatises. Owen Chadwick's words are appropriate: 'In the Bridgewater treatises the reader roamed enchanted from barnacles to migrating swallows, from the habits of worms to the mouths of whales, from the duodenal tube to electrical galvanism, and marvelled at the beautiful machinery of God.'[26] Description equates with argument: 'enchanted' and 'marvelled' catch the mood of the actual authors as well as of the putative audience, and point to the means of argument. 'Wherefore did nature pour her bounties forth?' as Kidd asks (169n) through Milton's *Comus*. The device may be compared to that of the catalogue (say in epic),[27] where the mere listing, with appropriate epithets, overwhelms judgment in wonder. An example is Buckland's Chapter xiv, 'Proofs of Design in the Structure of Fossil Vertebrated Animals', with its thirteen sections, on Fossil Mammalia – Dinotherium, Megatherium, Fossil Saurians, Ichthyosaurus, and so on, concluding with Fossil Tortoises, and Fossil Fishes. Compare Prout's Book I, Chapter iv, Section 1, 'Of Chemical Elementary Principles', which has subsections on the Supporters of Combustion, the Acidifiable Bases, the Alkalifiable Bases, the Alkaline Bases, and so on to the Noble Metals (which, like the others, are individually treated).

The effect is that of a complete iteration; nothing seems omitted, and the potential query 'What about . . . ?' remains unasked. Logically this method is that of simple enumeration, a listing of all observed cases, a method of considerable rhetorical force, whatever its shortcomings as a tool of induction. (It needs at least the complement of the method of difference, used by the Bridgewater authors only occasionally,[28] and then usually to explain the existence of apparent evil and suffering, on which see below.) In this respect it is worth noting that the distinction between matters permitting of demonstrative proof and those admitting only of probable proof was alive in the minds of the Bridgewater authors. The latter were seen as the ground on which most of, and the most important of, human issues dwelt. Probability ruled in moral, political, and social discussions, and in those of Natural Religion as well. And inductive methods are the tools of probability.[29]

Nor is this the end of the matter, for in the context simple enumeration has special force in calling repeated attention to the sheer wealth, the bounty, the fecundity of creation. Calmness and deliberateness are inappropriate responses even in a scientist to the 'exuberance of material', to 'lavish', 'inexhaustible', and 'prolific' nature, with its 'endless perpetuity'; to the 'endless succession of life and happiness', instances so numerous as to 'embarrass our choice', and a globe that 'teems with endless examples'. The first set of phrases is from Roget, the second from Buckland; like them, I am faced with only too much evidence for citation. The overwhelming effect is that of the simple hymn: 'Count your blessings, name them one by one, and it will surprise you what the Lord hath done.'

Of the three relevant attributes of the Creator, the one most closely associated with this plenitude is Power, though the Bridgewater Treatises also refer it on occasion to Goodness[30] and Wisdom. Here, for them, is God's plenty, and a tour through it, with a merely expository guide and lecturer, is enough to persuade all but the dullest, nothing more being needed to clinch the case than an exclamation point.

Bound into sheer quantity is variety, of surprising and marvellous diversity, again pointing principally to Power. Whewell explicitly cites 'this *variety* as *itself*' an argument for a Creator, serving 'to produce and confirm a reverential wonder' at the 'apparently inexhaustible stores of new forms of being and modes of existence' (73–4). Roget refers to organic beings as showing 'boundless variety, . . . inscrutable complexity, . . . perpetual mutation' (8), Kirby to their 'infinite diversity' (1: 1), and Prout to their 'infinite variety' (364). The proper responses are wonder and humility, as the contrast grows between what surrounds humankind and what its feeble powers are. And the revelation of this wealth and diversity meets the avid craving of people for information, as we survey it 'with curious and delighted eyes' (Kirby, 1: 230); in fact one of the adaptations cited is that 'there is a boundless field in all the objects of all the sciences for the exercise of curiosity' (Chalmers, 2: 125).

'Wonder' and its cognates, common in the Bridgewater Treatises, are still inadequate to express the proper reaction to 'one stupendously grand, and consistent, and harmonious *Whole*' (Buckland, 1: 413). Indeed the final degree is inexpressible for Whewell and Roget except as an unspecified further term of a series: the former says that a general contemplation of the universe gives a 'lofty and magnificent conception of the Author of so vast a work', but with 'a more exact view . . . the impression is incalculably increased' (269); while the latter asserts that a study of 'the finished state' of organic structures inspires 'the most sublime conceptions of the Great Creator', and observing their development is calculated 'to exalt our ideas of the transcendent attributes of the Almighty' (2: 537–8).

The genuinely scientific mind seeks the wealth of varied

information in a curious and wondering way, but what truly delights it, guides its hypotheses, and serves as a standard of truth, is the belief in an underlying, controlling unity. For Christian scientists like the Bridgewater authors the task is to demonstrate that a study of natural phenomena shows the uniform law of an almighty lawgiver (Bell, xi; Roget, 2: 560; Whewell, 251).

Chance is thus ruled out in no uncertain terms. The 'idea of chance seems too monstrous to be entertained for a moment by an rational being' (Prout, 89); 'It must be borne in mind that nothing really happens by chance, or is the result of an accidental concourse of fortuitous events' (Kirby, 1: 54); 'To say that [effects] are the results of chance conveys no information; and is equivalent to the assertion that they are wholly without a cause' (Roget, 1: 20). Or, as Einstein said not so very long ago, 'God does not play at dice'. (That some modern theologians are anxious to adapt the uncertainty principle to their needs indicates that the world has been turned upside down.)

'Simplicity', emphasised by Whewell,[31] points to another element in this concept, the acceptance of Occam's razor; in Chalmers' words: 'it is commonly received, and has indeed been raised into a sort of universal maxim, that the highest property of wisdom is to achieve the most desirable end, or the greatest amount of good, by the fewest possible means, or by the simplest machinery' (1: 49). Again one is struck by the perdurability of the concept, and the impression is strengthened when it is associated with those quietly asserted but powerful criteria beloved of philosophers and scientists alike, 'elegance' and 'beauty'. For instance, Kidd refers to 'metaphysical elegance' as giving force to an idea that otherwise lacks argumentative power (142), and Whewell assents that 'simplicity . . . is a mark of beauty to us in our contemplation' of the universe (236).[32] Yet another attached notion is that of 'economy' in its older sense of 'good housekeeping', with its corollary 'nothing wasted, nothing in vain'. Whewell, after referring to the 'new and striking views of the animal economy' that lead 'us to admire the design and care of the Creator' (283), praises 'the admirable order and consistency, the subordination and proportion of parts', 'the harmonious relations', the 'completeness of detail', the 'beauty and perfection in the arrangements' (288–9).[33] God, says Kirby, 'created nothing in vain' (2: 524), and Prout gives an example of the argumentative use of the belief that may be taken as typical in its kind if extreme in its degree: God certainly could have created this marvellous world without including a being to marvel at it, but to do so would leave an incompleteness. 'In the beautiful world which he had created, He would have wished to see *one* being at least, capable of appreciating to a certain extent his design and his objects' (402).

The argumentative centre for all these statements lies in the doctrine of 'adaptations' that binds together the Bridgewater Treatises. In the event, the term contained a worm that aided in weakening Natural Theology. For the Bridgewater authors and their contemporaries, its main implication for the creation was passive. That is, if one sees a relation of utility between *a* and *b*, it does not signify whether one says that *a* is adapted to *b*, or that *b* is adapted to *a*; in fact, the relation is a *pre*adaptation, a piece of design. 'As the eye is made for light, so light must have been made ... for the eye' (Whewell, 128–9).[34] The force of the geological and biological discoveries and theories was eventually to alter the primary meaning of 'adaptation' so that the term implied activity and process. Something *became* adapted: the emphasis then fell on the living individual or species that adapted to an environment, and it did not make obvious sense to say that the environment 'adapted to' the living thing. It could be accommodating, be a comfortable or capacious station or niche, and so on, but it did not show, in the old sense, 'adaptation'. (I speak in simplified terms, not meaning to indicate, for instance, that ecological interaction and balance are passive.) This alteration is part of the substitution of organic for mechanistic models, which was not sudden. But it is just to see the Bridgewater authors as holding to preordained adaptation, for when discussing the past changes the geologists and paleontologists were recording, they found evidence either that the environment and organism were changed together by divine fiat, or else that the Deity had built characteristics into either organism or environment that would become available when the appropriate (divinely ordered) change came to one or the other.

The search for ever more adaptation was not merely the result of facts made available by 'natural history' (which even in pre-professional days was seen as a lesser study), but of a scientific passion. The ancient, seemingly perennial urges operated then as now: anomalies, irregularities, *lusus naturae*,[35] are not to be endured: there are no gaps in nature, only as yet unexplained phenomena. So of each living being, organ, chemical, geological stratum, the question is asked, not just what, where, when, but *how*? And the 'how' of secondary causes moves inexorably, for the Bridgewater authors, towards the 'why' of first causes. The goals of science include uniformity, regularity, elegance, simplicity: these are the conditions of order, of law. So each entity and process must be explained not as a singularity, but as a component, fitting into and contributing to a patterned, regular movement – with, for the believer, an end.

It will not do to be scornful about the smuggled implications of 'why' questions, or their liability to infinite regress. 'How' questions imply relations, and engender 'because' clauses; very often a 'why' is answered without being directly asked. And if one believes that there must be 'a reason' for everything, then the transition is so smooth as to be unremarkable. Unless 'explanation' is, in modern philosophic jargon, 'unpacked', the different kinds of explanation easily (if fallaciously) blend. In any case, the Bridgewater authors were not greatly concerned with this problem in considering adaptations. Their problem was the more basic one of proving that all phenomena can be seen as adapted; indeed that was their commission.

In this light, the challenges are direct: show that (1) phenomenon *a* is adapted to phenomenon *b*, and that (2) the adaptation of *a* to *b* illustrates one or more of the Deity's Power, Wisdom, and Goodness. How does one answer the first challenge? To begin, by showing what the phenomenon, the thing or process, is, and what its properties are. In so doing, one achieves the rhetorically important intermediary goal of attracting the audience by instruction, satisfying the curiosity (to use Chadwick's examples) about barnacles and sparrows, worms and whales, duodenal tubes and galvanism. The audience's curiosity is not merely idle; as argued above, in its higher sense it partakes in the primal itch that prompts the scientist's incessant scratching away of surfaces. As Chalmers says, there is a parallel between the savant's curiosity and love of novelty, and 'the love of news' in the 'ordinary citizen' (2: 205).

The desired response, which includes wonder, is aided by magnitude – the multiplying instances provided by telescope and microscope fill many pages of the Bridgewater Treatises. One of the minor means of persuasion in this regard is the humble exclamation mark: humble not only as a mere typographical rendering of inflection, but more significantly, as is implied by its alternate name, 'mark of admiration', because it shows beyond surprise an awareness of a gap between normal human expectations and admirable fact. Two uses are typical. The first is to express wonder, most commonly at a particular instance of omnipotence, shown in profusion or magnitude (small as well as large), though sometimes at a manifestation of benevolence shown in a surprising adaptation. Bell, for instance, pointing out that the soft texture of the tongue prevents our using it to take the pulse (he's right – try it!), to which function 'the form and elastic pad of the finger' is suited, says: 'Is it not interesting to find that we should positively lose one of our inlets to knowledge of matter, were the organs of touch formed as delicately as the tongue!' (203–4) That the lens of the codfish's eye 'is composed of upwards of five millions of fibres', locking together by 'more than sixty-two thousand five hundred millions of teeth', prompts Roget to a series of three successive exclamatory sentences, their type indicated by their structures: 'If such be ... how intricate! What exquisite elaboration must...! What marvellous workmanship must...!' (1: 51) Prout wonders at the speed of light: 'nearly 200 000 miles in a second!'; a cannonball 'would scarcely move in a year, as far as light moves in a second!' (70) The young of the opossum, Kirby reports, at birth 'do not weigh more than a *grain* each!' and, maturing in the maternal pouch, they do not wholly leave it 'till they are as big as a rat!!' (2: 490) Kirby is most addicted to this device, especially in its doubled intensity, two exclamation points being called for by the possibility of a female cyclops being 'progenitrix' of 4 500 000 offspring, by a pike 267 years old and weighing 350 lbs, by a shark 'extending to the enormous length of more than *forty* feet', and by a 'sea-devil' ray that required '*seven pairs* of oxen to draw it on shore' (2: 28, 383, 385, 386).

The second typical use is seen even in the rhetorically calmer Whewell, who employs the device as the others do when applying the natural evidence to religious inferences in the conclusions of chapters or of the treatises as a whole: 'How strongly then does science represent God to us as incomprehensible! his attributes as unfathomable! ... How entirely lost and bewildered do we find ourselves...! At what an immeasurable interval is [God] thus placed above...; and how far must he transcend...!' (372–3) It will be noted that these tend to come in series: Prout has six on the final two pages of his first book, three of them in succession to close it (181–2). Compare Kirby: 'What power...! what Wisdom...! and what Goodness and stupendous Love...!' as part of the climax of his second chapter (1: 137). And Prout again, in ending Chapter iv, uses two exclamatory sentences, separated by three rhetorical questions (33). There can be little doubt that the Bridgewater authors had not heeded one part of Jonathan Swift's *Advice to Young Clergymen*: 'To skip over all sentences where he spied a note of admiration at the end.'[36]

What might be called the argument *ab majuscule* is seen in the Bridgewater Treatises' liberal display of large and small capitals as clinching a case. The simplest examples are those where the Creator, and His Attributes (Power, Wisdom, and Goodness) are given initial capitals; the reverence implied in this practice can be spread to what might be called Sub-attributes or Characteristics, such as 'Connexion', 'Unity', 'Whole', 'Foresight', and 'Design', to choose almost at random from Buckland (1: 523, 525).[37] Kirby once again is most given to this loud device; the substantive part of his extraordinary and extraordinarily long introduction concludes: 'WITHOUT HIM THEY CAN DO NOTHING.' (ciii; 'THEY' are the Cherubim, who figure as second causes in Kirby's argument.) One further example shows the device again with concluding force:

Is it probable, nay is it possible, that what can thus comprehend the operations of an immortal Agent, *is not itself immortal*?
Thus has reasoned man in all ages; and his desires and his feelings, his hopes and his fears, have all conspired with his reason, to strengthen the conviction, that there is something within him which *cannot die*. That he is destined,

in short, for a future state of existence, where his nature will be exalted, and his knowledge perfected; and where the GREAT DESIGN of his Creator, commenced and left imperfect here, WILL BE COMPLETED. (Prout, conclusion of bk II, 412)

The heightening devices in this passage are multiple, as is normal in perorations. For example, the argument by typography includes italicisation, to cite other representative examples of which would be tedious. Suffice it to say that, unsurprisingly, italics tend to build up in concluding passages where the truths of Natural Theology are stated with homiletic intent. Another device used in the passage last quoted from Prout merits at least a few examples, however: the rhetorical question.

Once again, while there are many examples of single questions, they are more impressive when running in packs, no matter what the quarry. For instance, softening nostalgia: 'Who does not look back with feelings, which he would in vain attempt to describe, to the delightful rambles which his native fields and meadows afforded to his earliest years? Who does not remember . . . the eager activity with which he was used to strip nature's carpet of its embroidery . . . ? Who, . . . in catching the breeze that has passed over the blossom of the bean or of the woodbine, does not again enjoy the very delights of his early childhood?' (Kidd, 202) Or to induce analysis of a phenomenon, such as the limits to periodic oscillations in weather: 'Now, why should this be so? Why should . . . ? Would it be so . . . ? Is it a matter . . . ?' (Whewell, 107) The strongest cases are those in which only one answer seems appropriate; these resemble argument by limiting or counter hypotheses, to which I shall return. One example, in much condensed form, also from Whewell:

Now is it not impossible to avoid asking, whence was this light, this heat, this diffusion? How came the laws . . . ? . . . When and how . . . ? Whence too . . . ? And if, . . . whence . . . ? how came there to be . . . ? Do we not . . . require an origin of this origin? an explanation of this explanation? Whatever may be the merits of the . . . hypothesis can it for a moment prevent our looking beyond . . . to a First Cause . . . ?

> But . . . let us suppose the nebulosity diffused through-
> out all space. . . . How are we to suppose . . . ? Is it . . . ?
> clearly not, . . . for if it were, what should cause . . . ? . . .
> Whence were these circumstances? this inequality? . . .
> Why must . . . ? Why should not . . . ? why should . . . ?
> why should . . . ? If . . . , what . . . ? Into what . . . ?

'Innumerable questions of the same kind might be asked',
says Whewell, having asked twenty (with only three assertive
sentences intermixed), and then indicates that the answers all
lie in seeing 'the universe as the work of a wise and good
Creator'; he closes the chapter: 'God said, let there be light'
(188–91). The interrogatives are frequently used in conjunction with exclamatory sentences that serve as self-evident
conclusions; see Whewell (184–5) where ten questions are
topped off with 'Except we allow . . . , how irreconcilable is it
with the evidence which crowds in upon us from every
side!'[38]
Even this tautness is exceeded, in my view, by Kirby who
uses the 'who can believe . . . ?' formula not only in the
normal way (1: xxxi), but also in a hybrid assertive form, as at
1: xxvii, where the sentence (a full paragraph) begins, 'Can
any one in his rational senses believe for a moment', and ends
with a full stop; and at 1: 39, where 'who can think' is so
obviously answered 'no one' that no mark of interrogation is
needed. Kirby may also be cited for an instance of the strong
negative form: 'Who can say that the All-wise Creator did
not . . . ?' (1: 211) Presumption is here challenged at its
height, and one is reminded all the more that the question
will lead the ideal audience to feel exhilarated by a fellow-
feeling of assurance, and will not challenge them to think.
One other, quite different use of rhetorical questions by a
generation aware of the classical demands for clear *dispositio*
and *divisio* can be illustrated by Whewell and Prout. The
former, at the beginning of Chapter ix, asks four questions:
'how came . . . ? Are there also . . . ? And if so, can we . . . ? We
have already attempted. . . . Can we in the same manner . . . ?'
(210–11) Here is the outline of the argument, moving from
what has already been shown, through the present staging-
point, to the steps that will follow. That is, the arrangement
(*dispositio*) is laid out, and the separation of topics (*divisio*)

hinted at. An even neater *divisio* is found in Prout (3rd edn, 47–8), who begins with, 'The question then is, in what agencies is this intelligence immediately vested?', and goes on to put proposed answers by two groups ('as some contend') and by himself ('as *we* contend') in question form, thus attempting to bring the reader along in the effort, coherently laid out, to resolve the initial question.

It is highly appropriate to the rhetorical surround of the Bridgewater Treatises that the reader should comfortably accept that questions will be dealt with by the author in satisfactory form. It is also appropriate in terms of the main focus of the argument, for once a natural phenomenon has been described – and much of the Bridgewater Treatises is given to such description – one or more of its properties can be isolated and put to the test of the predetermined question in one form or another. Can this be seen (to choose the most common relation) as useful to human beings in any way? The softness of the question is shown in the concluding phrase: any use, even the most peripheral and inessential, will qualify. The challenge is thus an invitation to ingenuity, one not to be refused. Because the major part of each of the Bridgewater Treatises is given to one stage or another of the adaptation argument, the best way of quickly appreciating the ingenuity is to glance down the Tables of Contents, remembering that each class there mentioned will contain many specific examples, and that for each example an adaptation will be found.

Let me give just one list, to save the trouble of even that glance. Whewell's Book I contains chapters discussing the length of the year and of the day, the mass of the earth, the magnitude of the ocean and of the atmosphere, the constancy and variety of climates, the constituents of climate (including the laws of heat with respect to the earth, water, and air), electricity, magnetism, light in respect to vegetation, sound, the atmosphere generally, light in general, and the ether. In recapitulating all this (and giving a rather clearer list), he says that to all the inorganic data 'the constitution of the organic world is adapted in innumerable points. . . . Thus, the vital functions of vegetables have periods which correspond to the length of the year, and of the day . . .' (143) – and so on and on. Finally (but perhaps only to one who reads all eight treatises – or to a sceptic) the performance seems itself an adaptation of another kind: the Creator has made the Bridgewater authors ingenious to solve the multitude of puzzles (and vice versa). We are all the Lord's examinees. I do not wish to give the impression that all the arguments are outlandish or forced; most of them are of the powerful kind (the eye, as a prime example) that have impressed even such unorthodox minds as that of J.S. Mill. But, as the section below on theodicy indicates, some arguments are, at the least, not obvious.[39]

As is appropriate in scientific texts, the main rhetorical elements are description and exposition, which neither need nor permit summary illustration. As Brewster comments in reviewing Buckland: 'The extraordinary and inestimable facts which he has brought under the grasp of the general reader, have been illustrated by numerous and splendid embellishments; and while his descriptions of them are clothed in simple and perspicuous language, the general views to which they lead have been presented to us in the highest tone of a lofty and expressive language.'[40] To this should be added recognition of the plates illustrating the treatises of Bell, Buckland, Roget, and Kirby. Bell, a particularly fine artist, made his own, and it was generally believed that the whole of Buckland's £1000 was spent on his engravings.[41]

Having said this, however, one can still identify the common pattern in the Bridgewater Treatises as a movement from one example to another (whether or not the implications for Natural Theology are brought out each time), without argumentative transitions other than 'and', 'similarly', etc., and without worry about more rigorous standards of proof than single explanations afford. (For instance, an exhaustive examination of the consequences of other, non-accidental properties might reveal that beneficial uses are cancelled by harms, or that a property useful in one respect is at least neutral if not harmful in another.) The method might be described as using the 'best-available' argument: in its crudest form the argument from exhaustion, 'I can't think of anything better, so it must be so'. A more sophisticated version is that of Stephen Jay Gould, who asserts that in science 'fact' can only mean 'confirmed to such a degree that it would be perverse to withhold provisional assent'.[42] Discordant facts do not, on this understanding, disconfirm theories, but appear as anomalies, and the Bridgewater authors knew that such appearances were that and no more. The prevalence of rhetorical questions is indication of the 'best-available' approach, for questions that evidently permit of but one predetermined answer make 'best' seem 'only'.[43] Another interesting device is that of the counter, or alternative hypothesis, or negative imagining, which tends to make 'this' explanation the 'best'. An example is seen in Chalmers (2: 52–3), who imagines (though it is 'difficult' to do so) an omnipotent God who loved falsehood, and so arranged the world that vices would lead to esteem and enjoyment. Such an imagining is ruled out by 'the actual economy of things, the whole experience of life'; so much so that an 'induction of particular cases' is unnecessary, for following the hypothesis (deductively, though Chalmers does not say so) one finds the inevitable result would be anarchy or stagnation, neither of which is or should be. Ergo, the original assertion, that God loves truth, is the correct one.

This procedure is related to the inductive method of difference, though it is loose rather than stringent: a negating hypothesis is introduced apparently to test, but really to strengthen; all exceptions 'test' the rule in the traditional sense, that is, they 'prove' it by removing absurd alternative explanations, and finally form into additional buttresses. Kidd, who is fond of this device, provides an explicit statement of the method:

> As in mathematical reasoning the truth of a proposition is sometimes indirectly proved by shewing that every process of proof but the one proposed would lead to an absurd conclusion: so, though the supposition of a general and total privation of light is on all probable grounds of reasoning inadmissible, it may yet serve to shew us indirectly the value of the good we enjoy. But it is sufficient to have given a few instances of the necessary effects of such a privation: and it will be a more grateful task to enumerate the actual benefits which we derive from the agency of light (92; see also Bell, 166).

Because these methods are not by any measure exhaustive,

this stage of the argument is open to the charge of biased selection. But the process of growing assent is not allowed to be checked, for the massive accumulation of instances is vital to persuasion, probability increasing in force as the examples converge and substantiate one another. The intended result is an overwhelming sense of design in nature.

Once this is felt, the second challenge may be faced: that of showing that adaptation illustrates the Deity's Power, Wisdom, and Love. In fact, the two demonstrations are not strictly separated by the Bridgewater authors, for any one adaptation, once established, can be taken to show a divine attribute; it is useful, however, to separate the means of demonstration for discussion, particularly because the authors organise their arguments differently. At issue in this demonstration is the use of analogy. Analogies, weak as is their logical status,[44] continue to be used, and to persuade: to forfeit their use in the empirical realm is, *inter alia*, to cripple hypothesis, the great engine of discovery; to forfeit their use in attempting to cope with non-empirical questions is (to describe the modes of thought of an earlier age in our terms) to say that a right to know does not go with a need to know. The Bridgewater authors, one must constantly recall, were Christians: they were convinced of the existence and attributes of God through revelation, and so the task for them was not as insurmountable as for Deists. Natural Theology helped bolster religious truths, but did not establish them; the convergence of different kinds of evidence was a safeguard and comfort, but the convergence was on a pathway laid down before the facts of nature were marshalled onto it. For this reason the challenge facing the Bridgewater authors is best seen as 'showing', not 'proving'; while the language of the Bridgewater bequest is casual, even careless, it is significant that what is required of the authors is 'illustrating' the work 'by all reasonable arguments', with 'arguments' used in a weak sense ('as for instance the variety and formation of God's creatures; the effect of digestion . . . ; the construction of the hand of man, and an infinite variety of other arguments'), and as coordinate with 'discoveries ancient and modern' – that is, with facts. In that formulation, if one assumes that *proof* is at issue, there is *petitio principii*, for the Earl asserts that the 'creatures' are 'God's'. Granting the authors their donné, then, one should not expect them to face the problem of the truth-status of analogy.

Still the 'showing' was required.[45] One mode of argument was to present the basic analogy in new as well as traditional forms. An extended example will illustrate. Asserting that a full exposition of the design argument is inappropriate in his treatise, Prout says that he will confine himself to such statement of the argument as is 'deducible from a simple instance of the adaptation of means to an end, among the objects of nature: we shall then enquire into the validity of the argument of design; and shall show the conclusions to which that argument leads'. The instance chosen is that of fur-clad animals in cold climates; men in such climates cover themselves with that fur. In both cases, whatever

> the end or intention; no one can deny that the *effect*, at least, is precisely the same: the animal and the man alike protected from the cold. Now, since the animal did not clothe itself, but must have been clothed by another; it follows, that whoever clothed the animal must have known what the man knows, and must have reasoned like the man: that is to say, the clother of the animal must have known that the climate in which the animal is placed, is a cold climate; and that a covering of fur, is one of the best means of warding off the cold: he therefore clothed his creature in this very appropriate material.
>
> The man who clothes himself in fur to keep off the cold, performs an act directed to a certain end; in short, an act of *design*. So, whoever, directly or indirectly, caused the animal to be clothed with fur to keep off the cold, must likewise have performed an act of *design*.
>
> But, under the circumstances, the clother of the animal, must be admitted to have been also the *Creator* of the animal: and, by extending the argument, the Creator of man himself – of the universe. Moreover, the reasoning the Creator has displayed in clothing the animal, He has designed to impart to man; who is thus enabled to recognize his Creator's design.
>
> Such is an instance of those varied adaptations of means to ends which he beholds in the world around him; and which man by his reasoning, appreciates; and which de-

monstrate to him, the existence of an intelligent Creator (xxv–xxvi).

In the Bridgewater Treatises traditional elements of the argument by analogy appear, for instance the Creator is seen as Watchmaker and as artificer (architect, 'Mighty fabricator', etc.).[46] Also one delights in the familiar terms (especially in Chalmers): 'vestiges', 'signatures', 'veil', and the nice version in Chalmers (1: 27) from which I have taken my title, 'the fiat and finger' of God. Here analogy is revealed as metonomy, effect standing for cause. One set of images is specially favoured, that arising from the analogy between God's word and God's world. The basic notion is that Nature is a book, sometimes difficult to read, often in need of interpretation, but always and forever revealing to the persistent and pious reader not only the message but its Divine source. Some of the terms used are 'transcript', 'documents', 'representation', 'tablet', 'table', 'characters', 'sentence', 'inscription', 'handwriting', 'narrative', and 'decypher'. The evidence of the Deity's existence is immediate. Once one sees that there is pattern, design, confidence grows that the figure in the natural carpet can be made out, the mundane scripture read.

The authors are in this respect (as half of them were in fact) priests, guides and interpreters for the laity. They were not, however, apostles to the Gentiles. In the foregoing, I have hinted at the ideal reader of the Bridgewater Treatises, and it is impossible to understand the authors' arguments properly without inferring their intended target. Little is said directly,[47] but much is implied, all of which suggests a pastoral care. The assumed audience, as already indicated, is Christian but not clerical (the Bridgewater Treatises are not guides for preachers, though certainly they provide apt materials for sermons); it is avid for information about all aspects of science, but is lay in this respect also; it is not in a state of doubt, but needs a demonstration of the growing certainty of God's providential care provided by scientific discoveries and applications; it is not sceptical, but should be bolstered in faith by witnesses and protected against error. It should be assured that scientific discoveries serve only to strengthen faith, not, as some wicked men had argued, to weaken it.

The best evidence of assumed agreement, beyond the sly use of 'we' (the first-person hegemonous), is seen in the declarations that proof is easy and immediate, and that those who refuse to accept it are stupid or blind. Not often do the authors go so far as Kirby's dismissive 'But enough of this' (xxv) when dealing with an opponent (compare the modern philosophers' repellant 'This will not do'), but very commonly they employ some such formulation as 'It will at once be seen' (Chalmers, 1: 35).[48] Or, more fully: 'That the parent cause of intelligent beings shall be itself intelligent is an aphorism, which, if not demonstrable in the forms of logic, carries in the very announcement of it a challenging power over the acquiescence of almost all spirits. It is a thing of instant conviction, as if seen in the light of its own evidence, more than a thing of lengthened and laborious proof' (ibid., 36). This and one of Whewell's formulations indicate the background of Newman's later distinction between certainty as a property of propositions and certitude as a property of mind. In Whewell's words: 'The various trains of thought and reasoning' leading from 'a consideration of the natural world to the conviction of the existence, the power, the providence of God, do not require, for the most part, any long or laboured deduction, to give them their effect on the mind' (293–4).

Whewell supports this statement by citing the 'universality' of such a belief, employing another appeal to the common reader. The negative form of the declaration of incontrovertibility embodies the claim to universality: 'No one can for a moment doubt. . . . No one can doubt. . . . No one will maintain. . . . In short, it is manifest . . .' (Prout, 478). Thus opponents can be dismissed. Those, for instance, with minds 'so obtuse, or so singularly constituted', that they see the evidences of design as 'unreal', and deny a First Cause, 'need no other refutation, than the facts detailed throughout these Treatises'; if someone is not persuaded by them, 'his mind must be most singularly constituted, and apparently beyond the reach of conviction' (Prout, 3rd edn, 5, 20, the latter ending the chapter).[49] The supposition of 'intellectual atheism' indeed 'involves an intellectual absurdity' (Kidd, ix).

Further evidence of the adaptation of the Bridgewater authors to their sought audience lies in their use of authorities. Arguments from authority are not all of the same kind. The most frequent in the Bridgewater Treatises, not surprisingly, is that relating to fact, the Classical kind of 'extrinsic' proof. But 'fact' implies authentication. The proper way to get you to believe something depends on my assessment not only of evidence in general, but also on my assessment of your openness to conviction. In an elementary textbook or a general summary, where the unstated contract includes a clause that the reader has suspended disbelief, a mere assertion suffices, and some passages in the Bridgewater Treatises are of this kind. In a more advanced work, or one where many specific details are given and the reader is assumed to be familiar with the background, a reference to an acknowledged expert will be more effective. So one finds in the Bridgewater Treatises (though not equally in all of them) a procession of famous scientific witnesses: Newton, Cuvier, Herschel, Bacon, Linnaeus, Galileo, Kepler, Copernicus, Sedgwick, Thompson, Decandolle, St Hilaire, Davy, Owen, Lyell, as well as a host of specialised authorities on specific points, including Brewster (himself, as noted, an assiduous reviewer of the Bridgewater Treatises), and Dr Robert Darwin. That the authors were up-to-date, if not prescient, is indicated startlingly at one point, when Buckland (whose treatise, it will be recalled, first appeared in 1836) says in a note added in 1837: 'Mr. C. Darwin has deposited in the Museum of the Royal College of Surgeons, London, a most interesting series of fossil bones of extinct Mammalia, discovered by him in South America' (1: 603). (The stage direction, for anyone odd enough to dramatise the Bridgewater Treatises, would be: 'Enter the devil, bearing fair-seeming gifts.')[50]

Normally, especially if the witness is not so well known, more than a name is needed, for example the title of a journal that can be assumed to be authoritative (in our terms, 'refereed'), the *Philosophical Transactions*, the *Zoological Journal*, etc., etc., or a certificate of reliability ('MD', 'FRS', etc.). One is reminded that a great age of exploration and observation was in progress by the frequent mention of reports by travellers, scientific, technical, military, naval, native and foreign (see especially Kidd, Kirby, and Prout).

The author may deem himself an authority for his own

authority: at least five of them cite writings of their own, Buckland being most persistent. In one place he cites a 'Letter from J. Taylor, Esq. to Dr. Buckland', and nine pages later another 'Letter from Mr. John Buddle, an eminent Engineer and experienced Coal Viewer at Newcastle, to Prof. Buckland' (1: 535n, 544n). These examples show the authentication by the author of a friend or acquaintance, as though to say, 'Anyone I can trust, you can trust'; note that Buddle is not 'one Buddle' or 'a certain Mr. Buddle', but 'Mr. John Buddle, *an eminent Engineer*' and also (though the impression Buckland was after is now hard to capture) 'an experienced Coal Viewer'. Elsewhere Buckland refers to 'my friend, Count Sternberg' (1: 406; cf. 492n). In all these respects Buckland is typical of the Bridgewater authors, as he also is in using personal experience and knowledge: 'This genus was established by the Author' (1: 234); 'In September, 1834, I saw' (1: 470n); 'There is in the Oxford Museum' (1: 489n); 'In September, 1835, I found' (1: 528n).

The authors' friends include the other Bridgewater authors. Only Kirby and Buckland published late enough to cite other Bridgewater Treatises, and the latter uses Kidd's, Whewell's, and Prout's, while the former uses Roget's, but there are many references to earlier works: Kidd, Bell, Roget, and Kirby all cite Buckland; Roget cites Kidd, Bell, Kirby, and Prout; Bell cites Kirby; Buckland cites Chalmers; and Kirby, Kidd.

One set of authorities thought appropriate in the 1830s has diminished so sadly in weight since then as to make their appearance in the Bridgewater Treatises somewhat surprising: the Classics. There are not just, as might be expected, illustrative commonplaces and tags from Horace, Virgil, Ovid, and Cicero (all of whom appear), but scientific citations, especially of Aristotle: Kidd devotes about one-twelfth of his treatise to comparing Aristotle with Cuvier, passage against passage, on physiology and classification, concluding that 'the descriptions of Aristotle are hardly inferior in accuracy to those of Cuvier' (375). Others include Galen (used by Kidd and Bell), Pliny, Thales, Vitruvius, Philo, Dodorus, Epicurus.[51]

Authorities are of course used by the Bridgewater authors not only for facts but for generalisations, from simple opinions to elaborate theories. Most of these are purely scientific, but some – fewer perhaps than anticipated – are to writers on Natural Theology, especially Paley, who is mentioned by all. Some of the scientists, of course, especially Newton and Bacon, are cited both for their science and their religion. Butler, Ray, Burnet, Sumner, Derham, Tucker, Cudworth, More: each is mentioned, but not used extensively. Of contemporaries (in addition to those scientists who are also dual authorities, such as Herschel and Owen), Brougham is mentioned by Buckland (the only one who wrote after Brougham's *Natural Theology* appeared in 1835), as is Blomfield, who is also cited by Whewell. There are few important citations of philosophers, except by Chalmers. The general avoidance of this kind of authority is indicative of the approach and tenor of mind of the Bridgewater authors: they are not here concerned with metaphysics or 'speculation', where indeed dangers lie; logic is not relevant; and ethics is covered by writers on Natural Theology and the Bible.

One kind of authority is mainly illustrative, though on a receptive audience, a line from Milton (who is cited by Kidd, Whewell, Buckland, and Kirby) can be subtly persuasive beyond its ostensible purpose of adding clarity or variety of expression to an idea, for the name brings with it the power of cultural acceptance, of a general acclaim that serves as vehicle for the argumentative theme. One should not make too much of this, for the Bridgewater authors are in this respect, as in their citations of the Classics, typical of their times. But recovering the times is important in understanding the rhetoric, and so it is worth noting the references to Coleridge, Shakespeare, Rogers, Byron, Boswell's *Johnson*, Spenser, Addison, Pope, and that competitor with 'Anon.' for popularity, 'the poet'.

The final authority is the Bible. As mentioned earlier, there are differences of a ticklish sort among the Bridgewater authors about the exact relation between the two revelations, natural and scriptural, and about the degree to which the latter should be excluded from the treatises. But given their backgrounds, their beliefs, and the temptation, they did not hold a firm line – indeed one, Kirby, brushed away all trace of a line. The commonest form of citation is alike in kind to the quotation of great poetry that epitomises and energises affective perception, but of course the effect on the Christian reader is heightened by the sacredness of the words. In this category also fall the familiar scriptural allusions that, while having the sacred dimension, are not in their use and effect special to the Bridgewater Treatises, and indeed are not common in them, except in Kirby's and to a much lesser extent in Kidd's. Given the piety of all the authors (and the priestly calling of four), and indeed the homelitic tone ('-eth' in the third person in key passages, and constant reference to God, or the Creator),[52] one would be surprised at this paucity, were it not that the authors generally accepted the limitations imposed by the terms of the Bridgewater bequest. Whewell, who is compunctious, states the position in his Dedication to Blomfield:

> ... I feel most deeply, what I would take this occasion to express, that this [work] and all that the speculator concerning Natural Theology can do, is utterly insufficient for the great ends of Religion: namely, for the purpose of reforming men's lives, of purifying and elevating their characters, of preparing them for a more exalted state of being. It is the need of something fitted to do this, which gives to Religion its vast and incomparable importance; and this can, I well know, be achieved only by that Revealed Religion of which we are ministers, but on which the plan of the present work did not allow me to dwell (vi–vii).[53]

Typical and understandable, however, is a tendency to make it clear by giving at least a hint near the beginning and more than a hint at the close that Natural Theology is not free-standing, but is dependent on the context and meaning given by the revealed word. Whewell, for instance, after the statement in his dedication, makes almost no reference to revealed truth until his concluding chapter, where he indicates in its title that 'the Progress of our Knowledge' can never enable us 'to comprehend the Nature of the Deity', and, as the italics, rhetorical questions, and marks of admiration build up, he quotes Bacon's 'Confession of Faith' on the inadequacy of natural knowledge (pointing out that Bacon's vocabulary there is drawn from the Bible), and in his closing paragraph quotes Psalm 48:14: 'This God is our God, for ever and ever' (366–81, esp. 377–8 and 380).[54]

Buckland is equally instructive. On his half-title page we have: 'Thou Lord in the beginning has laid the foundation of the earth' (Psalm 102:25), and the volume concludes:

> The Earth from her deep foundations unites with the celestial orbs that roll through boundless space, to declare the glory and shew forth the praise of their common Author and Preserver; and the voice of Natural Theology accords harmoniously with the testimonies of Revelation, in ascribing the origin of the Universe to the will of One eternal, and dominant Intelligence, the Almighty Lord and supreme first cause of all things that subsist – 'the same yesterday, to-day and for ever' – 'before the Mountains were brought forth, or even the Earth and the World were made, God from everlasting and world without End' (1: 596).[55]

Consideration of the perceived opponents contributes in a rather unusual way to appreciation of the Bridgewater authors' attitudes collectively and individually. The initial observation is the abiding one: there is no great fear of informed scientific opposition. For the most part the sceptics are not named in connection with arguments against Natural Theology, and those arguments are distanced by anonymity or by their presentation as more possible than actual or even likely. These are part of the classical repertory of devices of *refutatio*, but the full range is not employed. There are quite a few instances of argument against a particular point, inductive and deductive weight being used to bear down a mistaken view, but these include many cases where the opponent on that point is an ally overall.[56] Occasionally there is a detailed account of mistaken views, laid out as a *divisio*, with summaries of the case to be made; the best example is in Bell's second chapter (28–44).

The real villains seldom are allowed to appear in *propria persona*, and never are given full voice. Laplace is specifically mentioned by Chalmers, Whewell, and Kirby; Lamarck by Kidd, Whewell, Buckland, and Kirby; but Hume, Hobbes, and Mandeville are dealt with only by Chalmers (and not at length), and no others are given more than passing reference. The overall impression is of premonitary care, the authors saying in effect: 'If you find a sign labelled "Here be dragons", fear not. When they do thus and so, your reply is so and thus.' Broadly speaking, the threat is from those who see no order, those who see no end (or none beyond an intrinsic one), and those who deny the existence or validity of a search for first causes. These are identified collectively, usually as 'philosophers' (sometimes 'speculative'), or atheists (in a sense close to the later 'agnostic'), and sometimes as antitheists, deists, and polytheists; more commonly they are given no collective name at all, perhaps to reduce their apparent threat to what the authors believe – given this audience – is its very limited scope.

Whewell's explanation of the opposition (323–37) is not found in the other Bridgewater authors, but it seems commensurate in its conclusion, if not in its subtlety, with their positions. He notes that there have been complaints, especially recently, that piety does not grow in proportion to the growth of knowledge.[57] There is a belief that 'men of considerable eminence and celebrity for their attainments in science' frequently hold irreligious views; this belief, 'extensively diffused', has produced 'inquietude and grief in the breasts of pious and benevolent men'. Whewell thinks the belief goes beyond the fact,[58] but if there are 'strong cases' they should be explained. (There may not be a crisis of faith – at least as yet – but who needs 'inquietude and grief'?) The problem lies in one of the two ways in which science works, and in the mental habits it encourages. The 'discoverers' of truth, such as Newton, are inductivists; they are safe and sure: 'The inscription is decyphered; the enigma is guessed; the principle is understood; the truth is enunciated.' After them come the 'developers and appliers', who work by deduction, and who (like d'Alembert, Clairault, Euler, Lagrange, and Laplace) have great powers of mind, but are more liable to the error of attributing all to mechanical causes than is the inductivist: the mind of 'a mere mathematician or logician' is not forced to face reality as is that of 'one who studies the facts of the natural world and detects their laws'. The latter, knowing by experience that his light is imperfect, realises that 'there must be a source of clearer illumination at a distance from him'; the former is likely to 'rest in the mechanical laws of the universe as ultimate and all-sufficient principles', and substitute 'certain axioms and first principles, as the cause of all', for the Deity. This danger being understood, and its explanation given, the errors of these 'mechanical philosophers and mathematicians' need concern us no more 'than those of common men'. Thus, 'with the greatest propriety' their supposed 'authority' may be denied on the matters of supreme importance beyond their special competence.[59] Laplace, Whewell quotes Napoleon as saying, disastrously 'carried into his official employments the spirit of the method of infinitely small quantities [l'esprit des infiniment petits]'.

A less subtle explanation and attack – defence is not really the issue – is found in Prout (173–7), whose introductory argument includes the illustration of adaptation and design by fur-bearing animals. He divides the incredulous[60] into (1) those who deny a First Cause, 'Atheists, or rather Pantheists, "to whom the laws of nature are as gods"', and 'affect to believe, that all the beautiful adaptations and arrangements we witness in creation, arise from what they term "the necessary and eternal laws of nature"'; and (2) 'those who, without denying the existence of a First Cause, contend, that the adaptations among the objects of nature, cannot be *proved* to be the effect of design; that these objects appear to us well adapted to each other, because we have nothing, besides our own intellects, with which we can compare them; and that the limited powers of the human mind, are a standard altogether inapplicable to the Deity'. The first class are, as we have seen, repudiated simply by the recital of facts in the Bridgewater Treatises. The answer to the second class has been adumbrated above, but, as it is so important in understanding the approach and level of argument in the Bridgewater Treatises, it merits brief recapitulation. We are 'gifted with' (again the *petitio* is embedded) mental faculties that 'recognize certain abstract truths, or necessary existences', that we cannot doubt 'without doubting the existence of ourselves'.[61] Other faculties we are gifted with enable us to recognise external entities and their properties, but we cannot know them as necessary. So we cannot prove design by necessary or *a priori* reasoning. How then do we proceed? Prout refers back to his illustration of fur-bearing animals, and says that our belief in 'the agency of an intelligent Creator' is founded on our recognising an identity of external effects with our internal ones, leading to an inference of 'identity of purpose, – the *existence of design*, without reference to a designer'. But immediately, looking within, we see our designs as fulfilment of our role as designers, and so infer a designer of the external world. Then, recognising in the design of nature 'the creation of the objects designed', one is 'led to infer the existence of a *Creator*'. And reason enables us to recognise that Creator as our own. Though 'conscious that he is reasoning from the finite to the Infinite, from weakness to Almighty Power', still 'man *feels assured* [italics added] that his own reasoning, when it coincides with the reasoning evinced by his Creator, *can be no other than the same*'. To think otherwise is to impugn God, the constitutor of our reason. So the argument, though not necessary in a strict sense, '*is of a validity equal to that of our knowledge, of the existence of, and of our connexion with, an external world*', and 'speculative men' only reveal insincerity when, professing doubt about the existence of the external world or of themselves, 'they continue to act like other men'. Therefore we 'discard such speculations, as worthless fallacies, and contend for the *common-sense* view of the existence and origin of things', a view 'which has all the probabilities on its side; and which alone, of all others, points out to man his true and natural position, among created beings'.

The logical weaknesses of this argument are as open to view as are its philosophic antecedents, but it is foolish to think of it as lacking force. Parity of reasoning, piety, the *ad populam* appeal of commonsense as against sophistication and sophistry, the familiar and accessible diction, even the economy of statement: all these work well on an audience disposed to agree; they are the marks of preachings to the converted.

Only one of the Bridgewater Treatises is somewhat suspect on these grounds, that of Chalmers, for whom pastoral duties include strenuous goal control. He was a convert to Evangelicalism who remained (*pro tem.*) in the Church of Scotland, and who was aware of a full range of opponents. He saw the main threat continuously arising from inadequate conceptions of God's attributes, from those who, 'in the mere force of their own wishfulness, would resolve the whole character of the Deity into but one attribute – that of a placid undistinguishing tenderness' (2: 61). Such, with 'tasteless or sentimental but withal meagre imagination . . . despoil Him of all sovereignty and of all sacredness', forgetting that 'the affectionate' is also 'the great moral Teacher, the Lawgiver, and moral Governor of man . . .' (ibid.). These 'patrons of a mild and easy religion' (2: 62), 'poetical religionists' (2: 100), pose less an intellectual than a moral threat, appealing to the soft and tender emotions in the human breast, but leading to perdition. And they corrupt also by leaving the individual with a perpetually recurring apparent paradox that results in intellectual paralysis or disbelief: the existence of pain and evil in a world created by a benevolent and omnipotent God.

This, the central problem for Natural Theology, is an appropriate theme on which to conclude a consideration of the argument in the Bridgewater Treatises. Pain, evil, death will not allow themselves to be ignored. In one classic formulation: God's beneficence allows us to be the compleat anglers – but isn't it a little hard on the fish? Prout's reply (at least out of context) seems narrow and unreflective, but typical in arising from an enthusiastic account of adaptations (see 3rd edn, 341–3). The tropical climates show, he says, a special demonstration of the Creator's power and wisdom, and he cites 'the implacable ferocity of the Tiger, and of the larger beasts of prey', the 'fangs of the serpent' with 'the most malignant venom',[62] and insects 'as formidable as they are numerous'. But 'this intensity of . . . destroying power' is 'in perfect harmony with the rest of creation, and with the design of the Creator'. The 'wonderful productiveness' of tropical animals requires checks, which reveal the wisdom and no less the benevolence of 'the great Author of Nature'; the destructiveness of tigers and serpents is needed only in the parts of the world where they exist, and since '*All must die*' (Prout's italics), death in the tropics must be seen in perspective, as probably no more painful than the unheeded slaughter around us of mice by cats and flies by spiders. 'The question, therefore, is simply' one of degree; 'viewing the existence and the destruction of animals, as they ought to be viewed, on the great scale, we find that the whole is perfectly in unison. While as checks on over-productiveness in temperate climates, we have cats and spiders; amidst the grandeur and the luxurious development of the Tropics, the same wise purpose is executed by the Tiger and by the Rattlesnake.' The discussion – Malthus with relish – may illustrate the connection between sanguine and sanguinary.

Roget (2: 60–2) is more explicit about the difficulties. After a vivid account of predator and prey, he says we cannot but question the consistency of this carnage with 'the wisdom and benevolence so conspicuously manifested' elsewhere, and refers the reader to the classic discussion in Paley's Chapter xxvi. The 'only plausible solution', all the 'best theologians' (including Paley) agree, 'is to consider the pain and suffering thus created, as one of the necessary consequences of those general laws which secure, on the whole, the greatest and most permanent good.' Roget's development of the case again seems unreflective: that one animal is the food of another 'leads to the extension of the benefits of existence to an infinitely greater number of beings than could otherwise have enjoyed them'. Also, the 'scheme', the 'system', is 'the spring of motion and activity in every part of nature'. So, while one part is occupied in, and takes pleasure from, pursuing prey, the other part is occupied with defence, flight, and precaution, using the powers of sagacity and ingenuity with which they are gifted. Prout, not noting that virtually the whole of the animal world is both predator and prey, then cites some of the marvellous defences, and without returning to the problem, concludes the section with another celebration: 'Thus does the animated present a busy scene of activity and employment: thus are a variety of powers called forth, and an infinite diversity of pleasures derived from their exercise; and existence is on the whole rendered the source of incomparably higher degrees, as well as of a larger amount of enjoyment than appears to have been compatible with any other imaginable system' (3rd edn, 343). This is one of the more express instances of Panglossianism, as the best of all possible worlds is asserted to be without any examination of counter-hypotheses: the method of elimination persuades merely by the assertion that alternatives are unimaginable.

Buckland devotes a short chapter (1: 129–34) to the same proposition under a rubric that few debaters would find attractive in the affirmative: 'Aggregate of Animal Enjoyment increased, and that of Pain diminished, by the existence of Carnivorous Races.' He mentions the apparent inconsistency with divine benevolence of the capturing and killing organs, but then, pointing out as Prout had that there is a 'law of universal mortality', asserts that 'it is a dispensation of kindness to make the end of life to each individual as easy as possible'. The easiest is the 'least expected', and though our species is peculiarly liable 'to deprecate the *sudden* termination of our mortal life', for all inferior animals such is 'obviously the most desirable', avoiding the 'pains of sickness, and decrepitude of age' that can be 'alleviated' only in humankind with its unique 'internal sources of hope and consolation' and duties of charity and sympathy. In the rest of the animal world 'the feeble and disabled are speedily relieved from suffering, and the world is at all times crowded with myriads of sentient and happy beings . . .'. The 'scene of perpetual warfare, and incessant carnage' is but the reading of those with limited views; properly seen, 'each apparent case of individual evil' is 'an example of subserviency to universal good', the predators acting as the 'police of Nature', removing 'the sick, the lame, the aged, and the supernumaries', to leave 'more room for the comfortable existence of the healthy survivors of its own species'. Carnivorous death, in short, is 'a dispensation of benevolence', acting as angel to a permanent repertory company performing the divine comedy: 'the great drama of universal life is perpetually sustained; and though the individual actors undergo continual change, the same parts are ever filled by another and another generation; renewing the face of the earth, and the bosom of the deep, with endless successions of life and happiness.' Again plenitude, plenty, fecundity are prime values; the ever moving stage is ever filled. (Malthus – typecast as a drama critic? – is not on Buckland's programme, as he was not explicitly on Prout's or Roget's.)

Human pain is dealt with by Bell (175–90) and Roget (2: 331–3) in similar ways. Without pain sensors we should be destroyed by incessant unsignalled dangers; pleasure (the rule) would be meaningless without its opposite (the exception); and the variation in susceptibility to pain between external and internal organs is a marvellous instance of beneficient design. In Bell's words: 'Pain is the necessary

contrast to pleasure: it ushers us into existence of consciousness: it alone is capable of exciting the organs into activity: it
is the companion and guardian of human life' (190). Actually
that summary omits one part of his discussion where he
moves for a moment from pains associated with 'the neutral
functions' of the body to those that 'result from disease'.
While it is foreign to his subject to deal with the latter, or 'to
reconcile those who suffer in an extraordinary degree' with
the providential dispensation, he offers a few words 'as a
witness' much experienced in hospital wards for the termi-
nally ill. In spite of the ideas of 'insufferable pain and certain
death' associated with these wards, they 'are not the least
remarkable for the composure and cheerfulness of their
inmates', who have 'a mysterious counterbalance to that
condition, which to us who look upon her [*sic*] appears to be
attended with no alleviating circumstance' (188).

A few specific cases are offered that point to unexpected or
delayed instances of design. Kidd, for example, discussing
adaptations in atmospheric conditions, mentions their dreadful effects, but before the sentence is concluded has introduced the necessary qualification that we may rest 'assured
on general principles of reasoning that in the main they are
beneficial', and has also gone back to specific experience as to
their sometimes 'remedying a greater evil' (136). The case is
that of a destructive infestation of ants on Grenada, proof
against poison, fire, and a £20 000 reward for a method of
eradication, but ended by a providential hurricane.[63] Chalmers also mentions inclement weather, including hurricanes,
in a far more elaborate demonstration of the real good of
apparent evil (2: 39–48). First, what harms one benefits
another, and harvests occur at different times. Even so, there
are years when food supplies are short; however, second, the
price depends on what is brought to market, not on what is
produced, so the surplus-and-shortage cycle leads to 'wholesome restraint' on families, and to prudence as farmers
reduce consumption (their own and their animals'), thus
bringing more to the market and increasing exports. Here
the Creator's foresight is explicitly embodied in the laws of
political economy, which recognise 'self-regulating interests'
and promote proper adaptations; there is an 'inseparable
connexion between the moral worth and the economic

comfort of a people', that would prevent the 'dreary [periodic] intervals of suspended work or miserable wages' caused by 'gluts' if people would but apply the lessons.

None of these amounts to anything like a full theodicy, and for good reason: as emphasised above, the authors are generally playing by the rules of the game, which preclude the use of arguments from Revelation. As one would expect, however, when the authors come to their concluding remarks there may be room for at least tentatively fuller answers to the dilemma. Bell's concluding paragraphs will illustrate: reasons 'accumulate at every step' for assurance that the 'condition' of the 'living soul' is 'the final object and end of all this machinery'. 'To this', he says in his last sentence, 'must be referred the weakness of the frame, and its liability to injury, the helplessness of infancy, the infirmities of age, the pains, diseases, distresses and afflictions of life – for by such means is man to be disciplined – his faculties and virtues unfolded, and his affections drawn to a spiritual Protector' (256–7). The notion of moral discipline appears also in Kidd's peroration (340–1), which emphasises the test of faith, and the promise of rectification in another world. Prout (360–1) makes the case implied at least by all the others, that, properly understood, physical properties that appear harmful must be seen as existing 'less on their own account, than as ... the inevitable results of general laws established for a higher purpose'; not that they could not have been 'avoided or removed', but that, in Paley's words, 'the Deity has been pleased to prescribe limits to his own power, and to work his ends within these means'. The uncomfortable deistic implications of this position are not allowed to develop, as Prout immediately refers to the limitations of human understanding and reason, which leave us properly prostrate before the 'unsearchable ways' of the Almighty, who 'sits on the whirlwind, and directs the storm', but (Job being too demanding a witness) brings good as the general result. Even (somewhat anticlimactically) the 'deadly malaria' serves one apparent good, the stimulation of 'the reasoning powers, and the industry of man' to produce an antidote, with the result that malaria has been stripped of 'half its terrors, ... the marsh has been converted into fertile land, and disease has given place to salubrity'.

Here the discussion remains on the natural level except for the scriptural quotations. The level of grace is essential to Chalmers' position, however, for like Kidd he introduces the argument from immortality, a postponed but certain justification (2: 118–25). His argument is stronger (and therefore, in a work of Natural Theology, less justifiable) as his full wrath falls on those sentimentalists excoriated by him elsewhere in his volumes, who forget that the Lord of Creation is just. He in no way plays down the suffering, especially from injustice and cruelty (he includes a short but powerful denunciation of slavery, in one of the few non-scientific contemporary allusions in the Bridgewater Treatises), but lays all to human 'moral perversity'. Such an explanation does not of itself lead to satisfaction and reassurance; they can come solely from the belief that in the afterlife not only will mundanely uncompensated virtue be rewarded but, and far more significantly, seemingly triumphant vice will be crushed.

For Kirby there is no real problem, for the word explains the works: sin, evil, and death came into the world with the Fall (1: 12–13). The other Bridgewater authors of course held in strong or weak forms this orthodox view, which can be seen in the metaphoric terms especially common in geology and paleontology whose origin is evident enough. Kirby gives the clue in 'our race in ruin': compare 'the ruins of a former economy'; 'the wreck of old' systems, and 'the wreck of animal life'; the 'Organic Remains of a former World' and 'the relics of a former world'.[64] And there are many other hints, such as the human 'moral depravity' just cited from Chalmers. Kirby is, however, as usual worth quoting for the detail, which centres on the appalling damage to the body's economy by worms. Having begun his list of their ravages, he says: 'Such are the ills that flesh is heir to from these our internal assailants and devourers. – The recital is really enough to cause our hair to stand on end. No one can believe that all these instruments of punishment were at work in the first pair when they came from the hands of their Maker, and nothing, except *death*, can prove with a greater strength of evidence, that he is fallen from his original state of integrity and favour with God, than such an army of scourges set in array against him' (1: 325). He goes on to a fuller account of the havoc, and then concludes the discussion:

> Though at first view the animals of which I have in the present chapter given some account seem to be altogether punitive, and intended as scourges of sinful man both in his own person and in his property, and their great object is hastening the execution of the sublapsarian sentence of death, yet this evil is not unmixed with good. Though fearful and hurtful to individuals, yet it promotes the general welfare by helping to reduce within due limits the numbers of man and beast. Besides, with regard to the Lord of the Creation, these things are trials that exercise his patience and other virtues, or tend to produce his reformation, and finally to secure to him an entrance into an immutable and eternal state of felicity, when that of probation is at an end, so that the gates of Death may be to him the gates of PEACE and REST (1: 330–1).

So Parson Kirby, with the aid of Parson Malthus – to which the only proper response seems to be 'Amen!'

But though he would undoubtedly be pleased to find us in the congregation, his message was not primarily intended for us. What conclusions can properly be drawn from this account? I hope that it is evident that the Bridgewater Treatises should be read in their own context, including their audience, those 'to whom', Kidd says, his treatise 'is principally addressed', who 'are conscious that some ulterior cause exists for the adaptation of the external world to the nature of man, beyond the transient supply of his physical wants, or even the exercise of his intellectual faculties . . .' (343).

Aimed as they were 'to explain and recommend to general readers the proofs of the being and providence of God as shown in the arrangement of the world',[65] and it being understood that the general reader in those years was seen to be a Christian curious about God's world, the Bridgewater Treatises must be judged a success. Scrope's words praising Buckland's treatise on the grounds of 'the quantity of information contained in it', and 'the judgment with which that information has been applied to the case to be proved', can be appropriated to the series as a whole: 'Even as a *repertorium palaeontologicum*, it will be eagerly sought for; and when we find that the subject is made an appeal to the better and nobler sentiments of our nature, in plain language, unencumbered as much as possible by the technical terms that deter too many from entering this most pleasant field of inquiry,' its success is certain.[66] Charles Bell who was (at least in his private correspondence) not overawed by his task, chided his brother for suggestions that would lead to 'a large and consequently tedious volume, which nobody would read, however good. It must be a slight and, if possible, an elegant *sketch*, a thing of easy digestion.'[67] 'Sketch' is not the word for some of the other treatises, of course, but the notion is a healthy corrective to the view that the series is one of heavy argumentation. In accordance with an attitude much more prevalent than acknowledged, the Bridgewater authors saw proof as pragmatic. Joseph Napier expresses the maxim succinctly: 'A practical proof . . . is that which is sufficient for men to act upon.'[68] That which is insufficient for proof is sufficient for belief; as Newman argued, certainty is a property of propositions, of notional assent; certitude of minds, of real assent.[69] Napier makes his remark in relation to a quotation of Butler's guiding principle, which underlies the Bridgewater Treatises as a whole: 'probability is the very guide of life.'[70] Brougham must indeed have been annoyed when his *Natural Theology* was judged inappropriate for publication by the Society for the Diffusion of Useful Knowledge because it was a work of religious controversy; for him (the schoolmaster abroad) it was preeminently 'useful'.

The argument, it will have been noted, in ignoring the mission to the Gentiles, largely avoids the appeal to personal interest (*ad crumenam*) and to threats (*ad baculum*). There are hints, as we have seen, of immortality, and the merest whiff of sulphur, but these devices are not typical of or suitable to Natural Theology, which proceeds with a calm assurance infuriating to the non-believer. George Jacob Holyoake, for example, on Paley: 'The argument of design is unquestionably the *most popular* developed, and the *most seductive* ever displayed. It has the rare merit of making the existence of god, which is the most subtle of all problems, appear a *mere truism* – and the proofs of such existence, which have puzzled "the wisest of human heads", *seem self-evident*. It has given

dogmatical confidence to the learned, and encouraged inso-
lence in the ignorant.'[71]

Until recently, the history of science has tended to Whig-
gism, and so it is not surprising that the Bridgewater
Treatises have been seen merely as irrelevant, a late hectic
blossoming of a dying species, or as providing (especially in
Buckland) some slight evidence of spreading evolutionary
doctrines. I have tried to avoid such judgments, in an
attempt to understand the works in their own terms. It is not
unfair, however, to touch briefly, in concluding, on some
aspects of the argument that may not (given our preservation
techniques) have shortened their shelf life, but have made
their shelf an unvisited one.

As is obvious in the quotation from Holyoake, the argument did not touch sceptics any more than had the traditional works on which it built. 'Up and down the walk of design',
says Holyoake, 'which Paley made, and gravelled, and rolled,
Professor Whewell, and all the writers of Bridgewater Treatises, promenade. In fine, the whole eight of the Bridgewater
Treatises adduce many new illustrations, but add no principles.' And concerning Paley's rejection of the view that God's
existence cannot be inferred from natural design, Holyoake
stands firm: Paley says it is a 'doctrine to which, I conceive, no
sound mind can assent'; Holyoake replies: 'But to this
doctrine I do assent.'[72] Assertion meets counter-assertion,
and no ground is gained or given. More evidence, no matter
how amassed, is not of itself persuasive; in uncontrolled
induction a multitude of facts will support a multitude of
hypotheses – and beliefs.

This weakness is curiously perceived by the true believer as
well as the sceptic. Pursuing a theme that runs through all
their reviews of the Bridgewater Treatises, Heraud and
Maginn say in their concluding one: 'the natural theologian . . . , in one (not offensive) sense, is a mere empiric, a
collator of facts, not an investigator of truths or principles;
and . . . , taking these for granted, is always, necessarily, a
very defective logician, though pretending to much logical
arrangement. . . .'[73] For the principles, one must go to revelation.

Such reference is particularly necessary because what to

the logician is merely a failure to deal with counter-examples is to the Christian (and not only she or he) a great boulder on the road to salvation. As Richard Whately said about the problems in unsupported Natural Theology: 'In every part the universe we see marks of wise and benevolent design; and yet we see in many instances apparent frustration of this design,' productiveness destroyed by unfavourable seasons, animal vigour by disease, suffering and destruction; wars and civil dissension; and so we cannot on natural grounds 'explain the great *difficulty*, which, in proportion as we reflect attentively, we shall more and more perceive to be the *only* difficulty in theology, the *existence of evil* in the Universe'.[74] So when calmly stated; when more fervently, as by Heraud and Maginn in attacking Chalmers (not the most obvious target):

> Indeed, one would think, from the doctor's book, and, verily, from all these treatises, that evil had no existence in nature – human, or purely physical – that in nature there was no oppugnancy to our physical, moral, and intellectual constitution. Such optimism is absurd; it is at variance with every man's experience, and with the express declarations of Scripture. The writers, one and all, so far as they go, are demonstrating 'a happy *life* in the regions of *death*,' for what is all nature but a 'body of death' – a great body of corruption, tending, however, to a new generation – a death unto life, but still a death – a new birth into righteousness, but still a birth, and accompanied with birth-throes? 'For we know that the whole creation groaneth and travaileth in pain together until now.'[75]

The Bridgewater authors would presumably reply that they too are orthodox, and rely on revelation, but were not appointed to deal with it (Kirby dissenting), but this reply begs the question of the relation between natural and re-vealed truth, and the Bridgewater Treatises as a whole do not resolve that blurred issue. To say two truths cannot conflict is little help if they apparently do, and to say that natural depends on revealed is not only to undercut the Bridgewater enterprise but to run headlong into the oppo-site view, expressed succinctly by Brougham, 'revelation cannot be true if natural religion is false', words eagerly picked up by Holyoake as support for his view that 'revelation itself is based upon natural theology'.[76] Holyoake is eager, of course, because he sees the vulnerability of that position; the general confusion over the issue proved, I believe, eventually more disabling.

Another intractable problem not clarified by the Bridgewater Treatises is that of analogy. Bishop Butler's celebrated demonstration that there are as many anomalies in nature as in revelation was explicitly anti-Deist; its continued use, however, had unexpected results, leading James Mill into agnosticism as surely as it reinforced Newman's orthodoxy. The Bridgewater approach, traditional as it was in taking analogy for granted, left a great opening for opponents by the close and dependent relation it developed between answers to 'how' questions (second causes) and 'why' questions (first causes). Leaving aside the growth in positivism, which rejected first causes more thoroughly than had its eighteenth-century antecedents, the increased spread and penetration of scientific inquiry, which provided new and better (more satisfying) answers to the 'how' questions, led to problems of credence. New dependent relations can be developed in argument, but the substitution of these for the old is no more pervasive than the 'new and improved' labelling of soap powders. 'What was wrong with the old?' one is entitled to ask, and 'If you knew it wasn't the "best", why did you tell us it was?' In this respect the very specificity of the Bridgewater Treatises, engaging and (*pro tem.*) elegant as it was, could not be enduring as an argumentative force. Though his expression is almost as obscure as Kirby's account of the Cherubim as second causes, the comment of Southam (apparently an Owenite) is prescient:

Even the Bridgewater Treatises, now so much read and so well worth reading, are but the unconscious sacrifice of decrepit '*revelation*,' at the shrine of the physical sciences to implore the youthful vigour of REALITY; and the reverent authors of those treatises may perhaps live to see the day when the omnipotence of the auxiliary forces they so fondly enlisted in the *holy* cause of *blind faith*, shall turn around upon them to enthrone THOUGHT, INDUSTRY, and SCIENCE, on the decayed altars of mysticism, as a useful *trinity* for the human brain, when educed and developed.[77]

When the basic assumption is gone, the *petitio principii* that coloured the whole argument becomes vivid.

Related to this weakness is that of saying 'Nature, a.k.a. God'. The divine cause, of course, does not have only effects: it is purposive; the effects are intended. This view is essential to the design argument, for one reads back (inductively) from the effects so that all phenomena can be included. Chance being (necessarily) excluded, if the identities of God and Nature have been imaginatively melded, the Deistic road is well paved for the evolutionist's purposive Nature. (Once more the logic is not impressive, but virtually all popular presentations of 'nature' – e.g. the splendid television programmes of David Attenborough – smuggle in purposive change.)

Of other latent weaknesses,[78] including the problem arising from the shift in meaning of adaptation, the most unsettling (and unfair) is the unintended effect of particularity. The danger is seen by Brewster who, in praising Brougham's method, says: 'The process of the theologian lays the argument open, by its pretension to minuteness, to fresh devices of the enemy: That of the statesman repels them by its boldness and its breadth. The one exhibits the flower of his syllogism in a corolla of a hundred leaves, affording food and shelter to the devouring insect. The other presents it in the freshness and condensation of the kind coiled up against the resistance of aggression.'[79] The words 'theologian' and 'syllogism' may suggest that Brewster was not making a Bridgewater flower arrangement, but in another place he directly attacks Whewell for binding conviction to particular scientific findings, specifically for uniting praise of God's creating a luminiferous ether with the assertion that 'if the world had no ether, all must be inert and dead!' Suppose science disproves the theory? 'The enemies of natural religion will [in such a case] doubtless obtain a temporary ascendancy; and what is more mortifying still, they will enter at the very embrasures of the stronghold which have been opened up for its defence.'[80] Paley had tried to anticipate this attack,[81] and Whewell dealt with it in his own fashion. His reply illustrated so well the intractibility of the problem, and the way in which the Bridgewater authors saw the issues, that he should have the last of this very long say. The degrees of conviction appropriate to different matters vary, he admits, but writers on Natural Theology must not avoid topics 'while there is any shade of uncertainty or difficulty concerning a theory'. In the first place, 'religious men *will* endeavour to connect with their views of the Creator what they *believe* about the creation, even if their belief do not amount to demonstration'. It is vain to stand in their way, and wrong as well: 'religion should claim her share in these treasures as fast as they are discovered, and endeavour to perceive in every new truth the stamp of the author of all things.' In the second place, one cannot make a genuine distinction between 'certain truths and highly probable theories. *No* scientific truth is demonstrated so as to possess a proof different *in kind* from that of a good theory.' But it may be said, Whewell admits, that if you found arguments on 'transitory theories', when the theory falls, 'the cause you have pretended to support with such buttresses is shaken'. Without attempting a full answer, he says that when a theory, 'received on good evidence, appears to fall, the really essential and valuable part of it survives the fall; which has once been discovered continues to be true'.[82]

The rest is history – or historicism.

NOTES

1. 'From Men of Letters to Intellectuals: The Transformation of Intellectual Life in Nineteenth-Century England', *Journal of British Studies*, 20 (Autumn 1980) 162.

2. Nothing about these Treatises lacks complexity, including their titles. On the half-title page of each volume appears the series title: *The Bridgewater Treatises On the Power Wisdom and Goodness of God As Manifested in the Creation*, followed by the treatise number and title. The titles on the half-title pages, however, sometimes differ from those on the title pages, and the listing of the titles of the full series in the prefatory 'Notice' sometimes has one, and sometimes the other, and sometimes neither. A sorting out therefore seems appropriate:

    Treatise I, 2 vols, by Thomas Chalmers. [Title page and series list:] *On the Power Wisdom and Goodness of God As Manifested in the Adaptation of External Nature to the Moral and Intellectual Constitution of Man.* [Half-title page:] *The Adaptation of External Nature to the Moral and Intellectual Constitution of Man.*

    Treatise II, by John Kidd. [Title page:] *On the Adaptation of*

External Nature to the Physical Condition of Man Principally with Reference to the Supply of His Wants and the Exercise of His Intellectual Faculties. [Half-title page and series list:] *On the Adaptation of External Nature to the Physical Condition of Man.*

Treatise III, by William Whewell. [Title page and series list:] *Astronomy and General Physics Considered with Reference to Natural Theology.* [Half-title page:] *On Astronomy and General Physics.*

Treatise IV, by Charles Bell. [All three:] *The Hand: Its Mechanism and Vital Endowments as Evincing Design.*

Treatise V, 2 vols, by Peter Mark Roget. [Title and half-title pages:] *Animal and Vegetable Physiology Considered with Reference to Natural Theology.* [Series list:] *On Animal and Vegetable Physiology, Considered with Reference to Natural Theology.*

Treatise VI, 2 vols, by William Buckland. [Title and half-title pages:] *Geology and Mineralogy Considered with Reference to Natural Theology.* [Series list:] *On Geology and Mineralogy.*

Treatise VII, 2 vols, by William Kirby. [Title page:] *On the Power Wisdom and Goodness of God as Manifested in the Creation of Animals and in their History Habits and Instincts,* [Half-title and series list:] *On the History Habits and Instincts of Animals.*

Treatise VIII, by William Prout. [Title page and series list:] *Chemistry, Meteorology, and the Function of Digestion, Considered with Reference to Natural Theology.* [Half-title:] *Chemistry, Meteorology, and the Function of Digestion.*

3. This passage appears in the prefatory 'Notice' in each of the Treatises.

4. Pages 5–6 in the principal source on these matters, *Correspondence Regarding the Appointment of the Writers of the Bridgewater Treatises between Davies Gilbert and Others* (Penryn, [1877]), prepared (but not very well) by Gilbert's nephew, John D. Enys, for private circulation only.

5. ibid.

6. Enys does not give these parts of the correspondence, and in any event the first approach at least to Roget would have been informal; Roget, however, must have been tentatively asked – and he must have agreed – before 17 August, as his letter of that date in Enys clearly implies.

7. Enys, p. 9.

8. See Enys, pp. 9–11.

9. The list (Enys, pp. 12–13) reads:

1. – Human Anatomy with special reference to Lord Bridgewater's peculiar topic, the Hand	Mr. C. Bell
2. – Comparative Anatomy with Physiology	Dr. Roget
3. – Geology	Dr. Buckland
4. – Astronomy	Mr. Whewell
5 and 6. – The Adaptation of the Physical Condition of Man to his intellectual and moral Functions, his social propensities,	

and the provision made for his wants in the
works of nature

The Intellectual and Moral	Dr. Chalmers
The Physical	Dr. Kidd
	Dr. Mayo

7. – Chemistry Chiefly in reference to the
Etherial or Imponderable Fluids or   Dr. Prout
especially to Light, including Optics   Dr. Brewster
with the recent discoveries of
Polarization

8. – Natural History particularly with   Mr. Knapp
reference to its Physiology as evincing
the Beneficence of the Deity'

10. Kidd's letter of 15 October indicating acceptance is in Enys, pp. 18–19. The letter from Blomfield to Chalmers of 1 October is in William Hanna, *Memoirs of the Life and Writings of Thomas Chalmers*, 4 vols (Edinburgh, 1849–52) 3: 308–9; Enys gives his affirmative response, dated 15 December; the date must be mistaken, as all but Kirby had been enlisted by mid-November, or else his agreement had been signalled by other means earlier. I have not found letters covering Prout's accession.

11. John Freeman, *Life of the Rev. William Kirby* (London, 1852) 435–7.

12. I. Todhunter, *William Whewell*, 2 vols (London, 1876) 1: 42.

13. 'Linnaean Society', *Literary Gazette, and Journal of Belles Lettres, Arts, Sciences, &c.*, 5 February 1831, 88.

14. Enys, 20–1.

15. Enys, 17.

16. Advertisement by Pickering, e.g., in *Morning Chronicle*, 25 and 27 April 1833, 1.

17. Bohn's business was sold in 1864, so after that date 'Bohn's Scientific Library' was published by Bell and Daldy (after 1872, Bell alone). One instance of its popularity: Buckland's treatise, edited by his son Frank, in 1858 sold 5000 copies in three days (Lynn Barker, *The Heyday of Natural History, 1820–1870* [London, 1980] 144).

18. The astonishing Brougham included a discussion of the cells of bees that takes up 119 pages, and an account of Newton's *Principia* that stretches for 237. The major reviews took serious notice of the work. Other relevant works of the period include: Alexander Crombie, *Natural Theology*, 2 vols (London, 1829, but reviewed in *Quaterly Review*, 51 [March 1834] 213–28, in relation to the Bridgewater Treatises); [John Minter Morgan,] *The Critics Criticized: with Remarks on a Passage in Dr. Chalmers's Bridgewater Treatise* (London, 1834); Thomas Wallace, *Observations on Lord Brougham's Discourse* (London, 1835); A.C.G. Jobert, *Two Words on Lord Brougham's and Dr. Paley's Natural Theology* (London, 1835; the two words were not short); William J. Irons, *On the Whole Doctrine of Final Causes* (London, 1836); Nicholas Wiseman, *Lectures on the Connexion between Science and Revealed Religion* (London, 1836); 'A Student in Realities', *Serious*

Thoughts, Generated by Perusing Lord Brougham's Discourse, 4 pts (London, 1836, 1837); Charles Mountford Burnett, *The Power, Wisdom, and Goodness of God, as Displayed in the Animal Creation* (London, 1838); Fowler De Johnstone, *Truth, in Defence of the Word of God . . . Addressed to the Rev. William Buckland* (London, 1838); and Baden Powell, *The Connexion of Natural and Divine Truth* (London, 1838). And, of course, Charles Babbage's *The Ninth Bridgewater Treatise: A Fragment* (London, 1837), which went into an enlarged second edition in 1838. Its description as 'A Fragment' should not be taken very seriously; the second edition has 440 pages. In dissociating himself from the official series, Babbage says he thinks it permissible to 'connect with' his 'reflections . . . a title which has now become familiarly associated in the public mind, with the evidences in favour of Natural Religion' (vi).

19. (Edinburgh and London, 1828) 75–6.
20. The fullest account I have seen is in Charles Coulson Gillispie's valuable *Genesis and Geology* (Cambridge, Mass., 1951), 209–16; his attitude is perhaps not fairly caught in his characterisation of the Bridgewater Treatises as a 'strange and, to the modern reader, deadly series' (209). See also Chadwick, *The Victorian Church* (cited in n. 22 below); D.W. Gundry, 'Historical Revision No. CX: The Bridgewater Treatises and Their Authors', *History*, n.s. 31 (September 1946) 140–52; and 'Sir Charles Bell and the Bridgewater Treatises', *Bulletin of the History of Medicine*, 12 (July 1942) 314–22. A judgment nearly mid-way between their times and ours may be seen in Andrew Dickson White, *A History of the Warfare of Science with Theology in Christendom*, 2 vols (New York, 1896) 1: 43–4.
21. A full examination should cover such matters as the author (including *persona*), audience, occasion (including provenance), materials, and genre, as well as purpose, theme, and thesis. When all are considered, analysis can easily outstrip its text in length, and since the Bridgewater Treatises run (in the original edition) to twelve volumes, any normal reader (as a Bridgewater author would say) can reach the conclusion that the following comments will not be exhaustive. Two implications of that conclusion should be explicitly mentioned, however: (1) in concentrating on modes of persuasion, I shall be slighting the kind of evidence cited; that is, I shall say very little about the actual scientific detail in the volumes. (2) In treating the Bridgewater treatises as one work, I conflate the arguments of the separate volumes, and so blur the very real differences in method and ability among the authors; however, the examples are identified by author, and interspersed comments on their special characteristics should indicate where further analysis would lead.
22. Chadwick does not ignore the Bridgewater Treatises, but discusses them briefly in his chapter on 'Unsettlement of Faith', under the heading 'Genesis and Geology', where they are described as 'the late flowering of the physico-theology of the previous century' (*The Victorian Church*, 2 vols, 2nd edn [London, 1970] 1: 560–1). The placing of the discussion illustrates my judgment above about the

usual context in which the Bridgewater Treatises are considered.

23. Prout, 551. Henceforth volume and page numbers for the 1st editions of all the Bridgewater Treatises are given in the text except as cited.

24. Chalmers might be thought an exception on the latter ground, though he had written on scientific subjects and was well informed, but in any case his subject was a 'moral science' well within his purview.

25. Enys, pp. 12–13.

26. Chadwick, 1: 561.

27. Other epic devices are not absent. 'When, after a dark and tempestuous night, the mariner first perceives the dawn of returning day; although that dawn discover to his view the evil plight to which the storm has reduced his vessel, why does he still hail day's harbinger as his greatest relief . . . ?' (Kidd, 84.)

28. See, e.g., Kidd, 184; Whewell, 112; and Bell, 34–5. A complex instance, best illustrative of the demonstrative 'The cake is eaten, yet, lo, it stayeth in my hand', is seen in Buckland (114), where he argues that the 'non-discovery' of the remains of organic links may indicate the 'existence of intervals' that are part of the original design; on the other hand, these may just be 'apparent voids' resulting from our necessarily imperfect knowledge. When links are found, they of course demonstrate 'an unity of design which proves the unity of [originating] intelligence'.

29. On the doctrine and force of probability, see e.g., Chalmers, 1: 35; 2: 385; Kidd, 75; and Prout, 7.

30. e.g., Chalmers, 2: 204: 'the teeming, the profuse benevolence of the Deity'. One is unfortunately reminded of Haldane's reported response when asked what nature suggested about the Deity's attributes: 'an inordinate fondness for beetles'.

31. See, e.g., 236: The first law of motion 'is the *simplest* conceivable of such laws' (Whewell's italics).

32. See, for a variety of ways in which such criteria are applied: Kidd, 132; Bell, 177; Buckland, 1: 140, 214; Kirby, 1: 1, 69.

33. Cf. Buckland on 'the economy of our Planet' (1: 481).

34. One latent problem here was not a stumbling-block for the Bridgewater authors. A passage from Chalmers will serve as suggestive: 'the constitution of the mind, and the adaptation of that constitution to the external world', provide pre-eminent evidence in demonstrating God's attributes (1: 38). The problem would arise only if, following the account in Genesis of the sequence of Creation, one interpreted this as a one-way adaptation: the world being such-and-such, then the human mind had to be so-and-so. *Pre-adaptation* is the orthodox solution (and one might say that the Bridgewater authors' minds were so well pre-adapted for this problem that it did not arise for them). And everything is not yet unfolded. The notion of 'prospective contrivances' to which Paley devoted a chapter, would merit a separate paper. Chalmers, e.g., after referring to Paley, says: 'Nature abounds, not merely in present

expedients for an immediate use, but in providential expedients for a future one' (2: 127), and he instances foetal characteristics. Kidd, also referring to Paley, cites the laying down of coal (104), as does Buckland (1: 481), who also uses salt as an example (1: 71), while Roget refers generally to 'provident anticipation' (2: 139). One might, in this mood, see an unstated assumption in places (such as Whewell's discussion of the polarisation of light, 134) where a confession of human ignorance as to use is part of the argument for humility, but might equally serve as an example of as yet unneeded and so unrevealed adaptation.

35. Explaining these freaks as only apparently exceptional is a theme in several of the Bridgewater Treatises, because their uncontested strangeness stood as counter-proof to the central belief in uniformity, harmony, etc. See, for instance, Kidd, 51–2 (on *lusus naturae* and species' intermixture, citing Horace on the offence to 'correct taste' of the 'unnatural'); Whewell, 91–2 (on the density inversion of water near the freezing point) and 111–12 (thunder and lightning); Kidd, 151 (an explicit discussion of the problem and its solution); Roget, 2: 560 and 568n (*lusus naturae*, the result of defective embryos, are in 'perfect harmony with the established laws of organic development' and 'afford . . . striking confirmations'); Buckland, 1: 233 (dinosaurs are only apparently 'monstrosities'), and 1: 539 (the geological evidence of 'disturbing forces' properly understood does not support the view that the forces are random and fortuitous); and Kirby, 2: 407 ('the seeming defects . . . incident to almost every animal form' really testify to the Creator's 'fertility of expedient').

One spectacular instance that raises more questions than it settles deserves quotation at greater length. Concentrating on the argument for adaptation, and apparently forgetting that for uniformity, Prout argues that the density inversion of water and the composition of air (then not well understood) are exceptions to so-called 'laws of nature'. Why? Because '*laws must be infringed* – and THEY ARE INFRINGED . . . precisely when their infringement, both in kind and degree, is indispensably necessary to organic existence.' These facts must convince sceptics: 'Of the sophistry by which the evasion of the plain question may be attempted, we are quite ignorant. But we cannot resist the conviction, that one purpose of the arrangement has been that of confounding the presumptuous sceptic; who is thus perpetually reminded of the infringement of his boasted "laws of nature," by the very water he drinks, and by the very air he breathes' (360).

36. *Works* (1755) 2: ii, 8.

37. Early-nineteenth-century practice is different from ours, of course, and the authors themselves are somewhat different in their use of initial capitals; however, the tendency to induce reverence by capitalisation is demonstrably part of the rhetoric of the Bridgewater Treatises, as of other religious writings in the period.

38. Cf. in Whewell, 301–2, three successive 'Can . . .' questions, answered by 'This appears to be altogether inconceivable . . .'; ibid.; 343–4, and

two questions followed by four on 345, with the next sentence beginning 'No doubt . . .'. See also the champion, Prout, 168–9, 198, 341, for sets of five questions, 351 for four, and 180, 192, 238, 329 (with an exclamation mark), 334, 336, 400 (here and on 401 combined with frequent italics) for three, as well as the colossal sequence of thirteen on 357–8 that introduces the passage quoted on pp. 35–6 above.

39. One interesting if ambiguous example only. Kidd, evidently with humorous intent, but without evident awareness of the ironical application to all the Bridgewater Treatises, cites the case of the canal proprietor (presumably not the 3rd Duke of Bridgewater) who, asked for what purpose rivers had been made, replied, 'no doubt, they were intended to feed canals' (118n).

40. *Edinburgh Review*, 65 (April 1837) 38.

41. See the reviews by Brewster, ibid., 15, and Scrope, *Quarterly Review*, 56 (April 1836) 62n.

42. 'Evolution as Fact and Theory', *Hen's Teeth and Horses' Toes* (New York and London, 1983) 255. I am indebted for the reference to J.S.P. Robson.

43. Prout employs the rhetorical question in a variant form that imbeds inadequate alternative answers: Who can tell that 'these poisonous matters have not been left with such subdued properties, as scarcely to interfere with His great design, – not because they could not have been prevented – not because they could not have been removed – but on purpose, and designedly, to display His power?' (155).

44. For indication that some of the Bridgewater authors were aware of the problems in analogy, see Chalmers, 1: 34 ff., and Whewell, 5–6. The latter attempts to cope with them in his chapter on Final Causes, where he admits that while with human beings one can argue from effects to causes, because experience tells us of their designs and purposes, in the case of God there is no 'analogy with known examples' (343). Nonetheless, he uses the analogy with human works, saying that conviction comes not by reasoning, but by 'consciousness of what thought, purpose, will are' (345).

45. For examples of specific uses of analogy in establishing the main point, see Chalmers, 1: 52–3 and 2: 123; and Roget, 24–5. Of course analogies used as evidence for subsidiary cases also abound: see, e.g., Chalmers, 1: 19 and 2: 254–7; Roget, 2: 2–3; Bell, 86; Kirby, 1: 42–3 and 2: 474, 524–5.

46. For the former, see e.g., Chalmers, 1: 23–4 (cf. 50–1), and Whewell, 29–30 and 206; for the latter, Chalmers, 1: 27, 49, and 2: 268; Roget, 2: 3; and Kirby, 2: 91.

47. Kidd (vii) refers to the need for a 'popular' exposition of facts, and Prout, admitting that his remarks on the Laws of Heterogeneous and Homogeneous Chemical Union 'can scarcely be so given as to prove a source of interest to the general reader', advises passing them over and turning to the Book's final chapter, 'General Reflections and Arguments' (132). Both Prout and Bell, in their solicitude, use variants of *occupatio*, the device of saying that something does not

need to be said while saying it, and so both flattering and insulting while informing (Prout, 209, cf. 161; Bell, 163).

48. Cf. 'instant transition' (ibid., 78); 'we cannot refuse to admit' (Kidd, 330); 'believing, as we conceive we cannot but believe' (Whewell, 250); 'we cannot but perceive' (Roget, 2: 560); 'No reasonable man can doubt' (Buckland, 1: 9); 'surely no one can reasonably doubt' (Prout, 13). Other examples occur in rhetorical questions, such as the 'who can think . . . ?' already cited (Kirby, 39); indeed the pure rhetorical question, permitting only one answer, can be viewed as a variant of this mode of argument.

49. Later Prout says such minds are 'warped' – but offers them some exclusive arguments from meteorology in a last attempt at straightening (316). Kidd dismisses that 'class of speculatists whose minds are too weak to apprehend any truth' (44).

50. Buckland also (in 1836 and 1837) cites Charles Darwin's findings at 1: 549 and 2: 20.

51. An indication of the general acceptance of such citations by scientists is seen in Charles Lyell's response to a charge by William Daniel Conybeare (a priest and geologist, FRS, who was himself cited as an authority by the Bridgewater authors) that in his *Principles of Geology* he had plagiarised from Conybeare's *Outlines of the Geology of England and Wales*. Lyell's able defence is that the citations in question – which are Classical – are used by so many other (including such writers on Natural Theology as Hooke, Ray, and Burnet) as to be commonplaces, and that in particular they had both drawn them secondhand from Pritchard's *Egyptian Mythology*. What now seems odd did not then even merit comment: that geologists should depend on Classical authorities. See Charles Lyell, 'Reply to a Note in the Rev. Mr Conybeare's Paper Entitled "An Examination of those Phenomena of Geology, which Seem to Bear Most Directly on Theoretical Speculations"', *Philosophical Magazine*, NS 9 (January 1831) 1–3.

52. Roget tries to keep his text clean. 'In order to avoid the too frequent and consequently irreverent, introduction of the Great Name of the SUPREME BEING into familiar discourse on the operations of his power, I have, throughout this Treatise, followed the common usage of employing the term *Nature* as a synonym, expressive of the same power, but veiling from our feeble sight the too dazzling splendour of its glory' (11n). His claim breaks down very quickly; see e.g., 28 ('God'), 71n ('Creator'), and *passim*.

53. Cf. Roget, 1: 23n.

54. There are some telling comments by Whewell about the convergence of the two truths on 254–5, and a complicated manoeuvre by which he brings in Pascal, an opponent of Natural Theology though a fervent Christian, both to refute him by the counter-authority of Boyle, Black, and Dalton, and to use him and them not 'as *authorities* merely' (because they may like all men be mistaken) but because on this particular issue 'their teaching must be looked to with a peculiar attention and respect' (317–22).

55. It is pity (or an act of grace) to commit Kirby's attitude to a footnote;
     my excuse is that he is indeed anomalous. In discussing the wording
     of the Bridgewater will, he points out that it states that the divine
     attributes should be proved not only 'by all reasonable arguments
     derived from physical objects, but also by discoveries ancient and
     modern, and' – he italicises the concluding words – *'the whole extent of
     literature'*. The Holy Scriptures are contained within that category,
     and indeed are its 'most interesting portion, in every respect', and
     since his own habit is ever 'to unite the study of the *word* of God with
     that of his *works*' he will do so here, though the 'main tenor' of his
     argument will be 'in accordance with the brief put into his hands'
     (xvii–xviii). Perhaps he felt that by confining his discussion of the
     Cherubim as second causes in Nature to his 100-page introduction
     he was safe from criticism, but in the text itself there is a far richer
     mixture of word and works than in any other Bridgewater Treatise.
     It is only fair to note that Kirby (whose treatise, it will be recalled, did
     not appear until 1835) may well have been responding to the direct
     call for just this sort of treatment in the reviews of the Bridgewater
     Treatises in *Fraser's Magazine*; but it is also fair to say that the call
     continued *after* Kirby's work appeared (see *Fraser's*, 16 [December
     1837] 728).
         On the issue generally, see also Chalmers, 2: 248n, 303, and Kidd,
     ix–x and 341–2; on the religious limits of natural knowledge and
     reason, see Chalmers, 2: 262; Whewell, 213–14; Bell, 169; Roget,
     2: 5; Buckland, 1: 14.

56. For example, Kidd, after taking 'pleasure in recording the well-
     earned fame of a friend', Buckland, with whom he had 'lived in
     habits of intimacy for more than twenty years', differs from him on
     the interpretation of animal remains in gravel deposits (180 ff.).
     Whewell identifies Aristotle's erroneous view of motion (309); Bell
     takes issue with 'the eloquent Buffon' and 'even' Cuvier on supposed
     imperfections in animal structures (29 ff.); and Kirby reluctantly
     disputes on instinct with Spence, co-author with him of the massive
     Introduction to Entomology (2: 222).

57. A subtle contemporary example is Newman's 'Tamworth Reading
     Room', where he attacks those who think the diffusion of knowledge
     is *per se* a religious good.

58. Babbage in his *Ninth Bridgewater Treatise* refers to 'The prejudice . . .
     that the pursuits of science are unfavourable to religion' (x), which he fears
     Whewell's Bridgewater Treatise has revived from its moribund state.
     Rereading Whewell did not remove this fear (2nd edn, iv), though
     Babbage's general agreement is signalled by his including an epi-
     graph from Whewell's Bridgewater Treatise in both editions. The
     other epigraph in the first edition, which disappeared in the second,
     clearly bears on the title and urges quotation: 'The ninth pedestal
     redoubled his amazement, for it was covered with a piece of white
     satin, on which were written these words: – "It cost me much toil to
     get these eight statues; but there is a ninth in the world, which
     surpasses them all: that alone is worth more than a thousand such as

these"' (*Arabian Nights*, Story of Zeyn Alasnam).

59. Whewell's position provides an example of the danger of precise argument; he can offer no good counsel against the sceptical inductivists who lurked in the wings.

60. It may be noted that if such qualities as incredulity are their only cited characteristics, they pose no active threat.

61. The method, of course, resembles that of Descartes as well as of Newman, who was formulating his views in these same years.

62. On the 'serpent's tooth' see also Chalmers, 1: 38–9, where it evidences God's power and wisdom but not (typically in Chalmers) benevolence.

63. At this point Kidd's attention flags, for he introduces, as a negative illustration of the beneficial effects of air circulation, the harmful results of stagnant air in valleys, but forgets to assert any compensations.

64. Kirby, 2: 11; Chalmers, 1: 27 and ibid.; Buckland, 1: 113, ibid., vii and 61 (cf. 525).

65. Whewell, 'Preface to the Seventh Edition', *Astronomy and General Physics*, new edn (Cambridge and London, 1864) ix. (Note that Whewell, at this distance from the beginning of the plan, includes 'the being' of God, which was not part of the original charge.) Brewster chides Buckland for forgetting 'the general reader' in one description (*Edinburgh Review*, 60 [October 1834] 161); he asks (ibid., 179) for 'a popular abridgement', but his emphasis is on 'abridgement'.

66. *Quarterly Review*, 56 (April 1836) 62.

67. *Letters*, 320 (3 September 1831).

68. *Lectures on Butler's Analogy of Religion to the Constitution and Course of Nature* (Dublin, 1864) 15. In an almost perverse way this case is paralleled by Holyoake in a Podsnappian dismissal of all religious arguments: 'Clarke and Paley – *a priori* and *a posteriori* – arguments of intelligence and design, and the whole progeny of "Bridgewater Treatises," are to us as though they were not. We dispute nothing and are moved by nothing which does not bring with it practical efficiency' ('Influence of the Pulpit in the Nineteenth Century', *Reasoner*, 2 [23 June 1847] 346).

69. See his *Grammar of Assent* (1870), esp. ch. iv, 'Notional and Real Assent'.

70. *Lectures*, 15.

71. *Paley Refuted in His Own Words* (London, [1847]) v (my italics).

72. ibid., 9, 10.

73. *Fraser's Magazine*, 16: 727. Cf. 'All books of natural theology seem to us very much to resemble what an Euclid would be with the propositions only, without the definitions, the axioms, and the postulates' (ibid., 723).

74. *Introductory Lectures on Political Economy* (London, 1831) 114–15.

75. *Fraser's Magazine*, 8 (September 1833) 79–80. Interestingly, Heraud and Maginn thought Samuel Taylor Coleridge would have been ideal to fulfil the terms of the Bridgewater bequest, 'if he could have been got to work' (ibid., 77).

76. Holyoake, *Paley Refuted*, 34.
77. *Serious Thoughts*, pt 2, 96–7.
78. One that is perhaps ambivalent I shall only mention. A multiplicity of instances calls urgently for classification, and classification mirrors an assumed regulated, related plenum. It may well be that the Great Chain of Being had lost its metaphoric force in the early-nineteenth century, and that Cannon is right in arguing that there was an anti-classificatory feeling in the English tradition (*Science in Culture*, 19), but I see in the Bridgewater Treatises an excitement about the elements of classification that implies adherence to a hierarchical ordering. Such a view made trouble for the evolutionists, of course (the search for the 'missing link' – of what chain?), but it also presented difficulties for traditional natural theologians by focusing attention on development and insisting on accommodation into a fixed pattern of new and discordant elements.
79. 'Lord Brougham, *Discourse*', *Edinburgh Review*, 64 (January 1837) 275.
80. *Edinburgh Review*, 58 (January 1834) 429.
81. 'The proof is not a conclusion which lies at the end of a chain of reasoning, of which chain each instance of contrivance is only a link, and of which, if one link fail, the whole fails; but it is an argument separately supplied by every separate example. An error in stating an example affects only that example. The argument is cumulative, in the fullest sense of that term' (in *Paley's Natural Theology*, ed. Brougham, 1: 97–8; end of ch. vi).
82. Whewell, 'Bridgewater Treatises. Mr. Whewell's Reply to the Edinburgh Review', *British Magazine*, 5 (March 1834) 266.

4 The Faith of Nineteenth-Century Unitarians: A Curious Incident

R.K. Webb

'Is there anything to which you would wish to draw my attention?'
'To the curious incident of the dog in the night-time.'
'The dog did nothing in the night-time.'
'That is the curious incident,' remarked Sherlock Holmes.
  (Sir Arthur Conan Doyle, 'Silver Blaze', in *The Complete Sherlock Holmes*, 1: 347)

I

Firmly established at the liberal end of the spectrum of English society and able significantly to influence the formation and implementation of advanced opinion, Victorian Unitarians – from wealthy, broad-minded patricians to liberated, self-consciously intellectual workingmen – were prepared to welcome almost any advances the scientists might make.* But to understand the distinctive way in which they accommodated science to religion, one must first understand their inheritance from the man who stands at the beginning of English Unitarianism as a continuous movement – the scientist and theologian Joseph Priestley.

At least from 1729, when Philip Doddridge opened his academy at Northampton, some Dissenting students had been exposed to all sides of a question and encouraged to make up their own minds, and, in the end, a couple of generations later, the resolute pursuit of truth led to some surprising resting-places. Bit for thirty or forty years from the 1780s, Priestley's ideas proved startlingly persuasive to students even in orthodox academies and as well to many other Dissenters marked by that healthy-mindedness that readers of William James will recognise. It was said, for

* The research on which this essay is based was done with the help of the John Simon Guggenheim Memorial Foundation and the American Council of Learned Societies. To both I am deeply indebted, as I am to the librarians of Manchester College Oxford, Dr Williams's Library, and the John Rylands University of Manchester Library.

example, of the Birmingham minister John Kentish that he demanded clear and definite ideas about everything, a characteristic echoed a generation later in the 'prepared completeness' that Thomas Carlyle saw in the young Harriet Martineau.[1] The new Priestleyans were severely tested almost at once, on the one hand by extremists in their own ranks, on the other by the pervasive anti-radicalism that swiftly arose in response to the French Revolution and its admirers in Britain. The Unitarianism that came out of this crucible was not scepticism or a revived Deism but a committed, articulated *Christian* religion, buttressed by sweeping metaphysical views and genuine piety.

The system that Priestley bequeathed to his followers rested on two foundations, natural religion and Revelation. Natural religion gave assurances that all creation flowed from an omniscient, benevolent God, working through agents in accordance with law. As it was God's manifest intention to bring all His creatures to happiness, the study of nature would make His purpose and means increasingly plain, and, as much apparent evil came to be understood, men would learn how to work with God's purpose and not against it. But the study of nature must be critical, taking full precaution against too precipitous judgments and too dogmatic and inclusive a certainty that putative law was actual: hence – contrary to the caricature of Priestley the scientist as an inspired putterer wedded to a discredited theory – there can be found beneath the constant, brilliant (and sometimes hasty) controversy a sophisticated and cautious mind, concerned with the indispensable role of hypothesis and remarkably attuned to history as an explanatory method.

While a student at Daventry Academy in the early 1750s, Priestley read and was utterly convinced by the *Observations on Man*, which David Hartley had published in 1749. Drawing on a suggestion thrown out in Newton's *Opticks*, Hartley had advanced a theory of vibrations in the nerves to explain how sense impressions were transmitted to and implanted in the brain, where complex ideas were formed from simple ideas by repeated association. Associationist psychology, with its polarities of pleasure and pain and in fundamental opposition to the faculty psychology of the Scottish philosophers, was regnant for more than a century in England, filtered through sensibilities as different as Jeremy Bentham's and the Romantic poets'. For Priestley, as for Hartley, associationism provided the mechanism to support and explain a determinism uneasily commonplace in the eighteenth century and to reconcile it with God's postulated foreknowledge and benevolence. Every human action, the argument ran, had to follow from a motive, the outcome of the state of mind, including prior experience, at a given moment. Repeatedly, Priestley and his followers insisted that they denied only *philosophical* liberty: an individual might feel himself free to choose, but unless the state of his mind had changed, confronting the same alternatives he would always make the same choice. The state of mind could be changed, however, and the system accordingly put great emphasis on education and its possibilities. Moreover, they maintained, only on this hypothesis could any rational system of rewards and punishments be constructed. If a person were truly free to choose arbitrarily, what became of God's foreknowledge or of man's responsibility for error? How could the ultimate destiny of happiness (in this world or the next) be encompassed without a certain mechanism for improvement?

What nature taught about God, the world, and man was also taught by Revelation. Here, too, Priestley insisted on the full exercise of the critical faculty and on the test of reason. The Bible was inspired, to be sure, but not all parts of it were equally so: how could they be, as the work of fallible men? While Priestley worked hard, as had so many writers before him, to establish the 'harmony of the gospels' and what, suitably construed, they might reveal about the ministry of Jesus, he was also concerned to eliminate unreliable reporting, linguistic misunderstandings, inconsistencies, and time-bound settings for the divine message. As in his experimental science, the greater task was disproof, not proof, and Priestley worried the texts and discarded what he believed could no longer be maintained. Bishop Butler had argued that revelation was as hard to read in the Bible as in nature, but Priestley and the Priestleyans took up Butler's challenge with a different outcome – not faith, now, but more reason. Some miracles could be explained away, some were convincing as proofs needed in a rude age of the divinity of Jesus's mission.

Beyond the surviving miracles, the Resurrection was the other claim of Priestleyan Unitarians to Christianity. Priestley looked hard and sceptically at the gospel narratives; as a materialist, he looked equally critically at our resurrection – certainly our bodies disintegrate after death, and he denied the existence of a separate soul. But in the end, at great retrospective risk, he stood by the biblical promise that, through some unknown means, our resurrection would take place.

The generation following Priestley's death in 1804 was a time of consolidation for Unitarianism. By 1820 few Arians – those, that is, who maintained some measure of divinity for Jesus – were left in English pulpits, and the transition of Presbyterians and the Old Connexion of the General Baptists to Unitarianism was virtually complete. But within that broad rubric there were wide differences of opinion. They disagreed over the propriety of sectarian advocacy and propaganda, though in general it was an age of dashing public advocacy. There was complete agreement about the importance of pursuing and avowing truth, as a multitude of surviving sermons attest; but this was no credal truth: rather, Unitarians were encouraged to make up their own minds by an unprejudiced examination of the evidence. Enthusiastic materialists were balanced by those who found the doctrine repellent. There were equally enthusiastic necessarians, while others rejected determinism or were only reluctantly persuaded into acknowledging its power, never losing their doubts. What needs to be appreciated is that these metaphysical questions were widely canvassed, not only among ministers but among laymen. To take but one instance, even the philosophically disinclined could not have missed the decisions taken again and again during and after the war years against observing fast days or thanksgivings decreed by the government. Sometimes services would be held, but to hear a sermon denouncing the fast, not only because it represented government interference in spiritual matters, but because it was useless to appeal for divine intervention in a system determined from the beginning of time. Letters and diaries confirm the extent of discussion of such religious and metaphysical questions in schools, in study groups, in family gatherings, and in casual conversation among the like-minded, and high-minded, Unitarians so prominent in the society of provincial towns and, increasingly, in radical London.

II

Nineteenth-century Unitarians, then, came naturally, as it were, by their fascination with science. Unitarian ministers were well-trained in natural philosophy. Scientific apparatus had been much in evidence in the better Dissenting academies (both orthodox and heterodox) in the eighteenth century, and scientific instruction at Manchester College – the principal source of Unitarian ministers for much of the nineteenth century – was a major part of the curriculum. Some ministers enthusiastically pursued science as an avocation or lectured on it to their congregations and a wider public. By the same token, some scientists were drawn to Unitarianism. The most famous of them was Charles Lyell, who regularly attended services at Little Portland Street chapel in London, convenient to his house in Harley Street, convenient too to his assumptions. Augustus De Morgan, professor of mathematics at University College London, though he never joined a church, most respected the Unitarians, 'as being most honest in their expression of opinion, and having most critical learning'; most Trinitarians, he thought, kept the doctrine 'caged in a creed' and were in all practical applications of religion 'except pelting Unitarians, as truly Unitarian as Mr. Martineau himself'. De Morgan's deep friendship with the great mathematician and logician George Boole was based in part on their shared moral and religious values; and, as professor of mathematics at Queen's College Cork from 1849, Boole had as his colleague in natural history the Reverend William Hincks, who had been tutor in natural philosophy at Manchester College from 1827 to 1839 and the founding editor of the *Inquirer*, the principal Unitarian newspaper from 1842 to 1847, later going to Toronto as professor of natural history, beating T.H. Huxley for the post. Hincks was speaking a common faith when he insisted that if the facts were correctly observed and the generalisations carefully done, Science could not possibly be in opposition to Revelation. Should there be an apparent contradiction after the most careful weighing and balancing, 'the only remaining question is, whether we have more reason to doubt the evidence on which we believe in Revelation, or that by which we obtain the scientific conclusions'. Revelation must be judged by the evidence as much as science, and to assume the infallibility of one side of the equation alone is to exclude ourselves from the light to be gained elsewhere.[2]

As early as 1821 Thomas Belsham, the principal transmitter of Priestley's doctrine to the next generation, had already rejected the Mosaic account of creation as incompatible with science as it was then known, so thoughtful Unitarians were prepared to see Genesis revised and to welcome the newly fashionable science of geology. John Kenrick, for forty years a tutor and then professor in classics and history at Manchester College, wrote in the preface to his *Primeval History* (1846) that the uneasy truce between theology and science established in the wake of the Copernican theory – an agreement on both sides that scripture did not teach astronomy – had been shattered by the geologists: what the Hebrew writer of Genesis clearly intended to teach about the age of the earth was beyond reconciliation; and modern physiology and ethnography had similarly forced the issue. Although Robert Chambers's anonymous *Vestiges of the Natural History of Creation*, published two years earlier, had brought down some Unitarian criticism – for atheistic implications as well as for his reliance on phrenology and spontaneous generation – Unitarians raised in the Priestleyan tradition, with its emphasis on history and progressive development, found evolution an appealing mode of thought, whatever caution might be needed about the specific mechanism of natural selection.[3]

Harriet Martineau had by 1859 dissolved even nominal ties to her inherited Unitarianism, but her necessarianism remained quite intact and was indeed reinforced by her engagement with Positivism. It was hardly surprising that she welcomed Darwin's *Origin of Species* warmly. Regretting Darwin's occasional invocation of the 'Creator', she felt 'that one might say "thank you" all one's life without giving any idea of one's sense of obligation' for the simple earnestness, industry, and patient power by which he had collected 'such a mass of facts, to transmute them . . . into such portentous knowledge'. What is particularly noteworthy is a similar enthusiasm among those who had most resolutely abandoned Priestley's purposes and axioms. John James Tayler, one of the leaders of the 'new Unitarianism', wrote to Lyell that he believed profoundly that creation was 'a progressive and continuous work of God', with questions such as Darwin's theory resolved into 'the simple question – which is one of *fact* – of the actual *order* of the Divine agency'. 'I cannot comprehend *growth* and *development*, especially if orderly and progressive, apart from *mind*, apart from *God*. Therefore my faith is not disturbed by the possibility of such a theory as Darwin's being shewn ultimately to be true. A mighty mystery which religion only can solve, still remains behind . . .'. That was just the opening that Harriet Martineau regretted that Darwin had given.[4]

We can see the accommodation in a series of lectures by a mid-Victorian Unitarian minister – the more revealing for his own modesty about his capacities and accomplishments – confronting science, and in the life work of a distinguished Unitarian scientist who continued to draw intellectual strength from his religion. Edward Higginson – a brother-in-law of James Martineau – came out of Manchester College in the late twenties and served successively as minister at Hull, Wakefield, and Swansea. A consistent adherent of the older Priestleyan dispensation and a firm believer in miracles, in Christ's resurrection and ours (though not in present bodily form), and in a future life, he delivered and published in 1855 four lectures on *Astro-Theology, or the Religion of Astronomy*. Starting from the debate between Sir David Brewster and (anonymously) William Whewell on the startling question, rich in theological implications, of the plurality of worlds, Higginson deplored the separation of religion and science, prudentially adopted by many on either side, for the religious yield of the vast advances in science could lead the theist, concentrating on nature, to grasp the immensity of the prospect thus opened, while the Unitarian, confronting the same prospect, could 'feel the happier for even the vaguest thought thus gained of the diffusiveness of Divine love'. The orthodox believer, however, was left behind with his limited assumptions of incarnation and expiatory sacrifice for human beings in this world alone.[5]

William Benjamin Carpenter was the eldest son of Lant Carpenter, the distinguished Bristol minister; two of his brothers became ministers, and his sister Mary was one of the most notable social reformers of the century. Carpenter was a physician, a pioneer in forensic medicine, a marine zoologist of immense distinction, and a physiologist of international renown. His sympathetic but critical reading of Chambers led him to publish a long series of articles in the *Inquirer* on the harmony of science and religion and in particular on the dovetailing of natural and revealed religion. Holding to the notion that distinct species were non-convertible, he nevertheless advanced the probable analogy of evolution of any given species and of the whole organic world to the evolution of the solar system, just as he insisted that mental and moral phenomena too originated with God, though tracing that evolution was beyond the capacities that allowed us to perceive the development of simpler, physical existence. To a Priestleyan theodicy he added a defence of Revelation and miracles, occurrences 'not so *unreasonable* in themselves as to require that different rules of evidence should be applied, when we are weighing the testimony of the phenomena commonly termed supernatural from those which we employ in other cases, in which there are various degrees of probability'. Carpenter's reaction to Darwin was admiring but cautious, and Darwin himself set great store by even this partial adherence from so eminent an authority. Over the years, Carpenter was willing to concede more and more weight to the Darwinian hypothesis, but toward the end of his life he remained as convinced as ever that the undoubted facts of astronomical and geological evolution and of organic and human evolution, both physical and psychical, in their very obedience to law, bespoke intelligent creation.[6]

Carpenter specifically acknowledged his obligation to James Martineau, the most important theologian of the 'new school' and of Unitarianism in general in the nineteenth century. Here is perhaps the most surprising development in the Unitarian response to nineteenth-century science. In the mid-thirties, Martineau had begun his long disengagement from the Priestleyanism that had been so strong a bond between him and his sister, and he punctuated that apostasy with startling verbal blows, creating, if not a crisis of faith, a major battle among Unitarians, as we shall see. In the sixties, Philip Henry Wicksteed recalled,

> Dr. Martineau had not only departed from the orthodox theological position, but in his lectures he used to attack a great part of what was called natural theology. He was most contemptuous of the argument from design ... and referr[ed] to those people who 'walked through the mysterious glades of nature with the elastic step of the connoisseur, and patronised the ingenuity of the Almighty.' But when the Darwinian theory of evolution was advanced, he deliberately turned around, and at the very moment when the argument from design seemed to have completely gone, he started and built it up into one of the most striking parts of his great book on religion.

Martineau was engaged in the problem of reconciling the new science and religion at least as early as the mid-forties. He alluded to the *Vestiges* and its challenges in his essay of 1846 on Theodore Parker, asking what was to be done if the forces of nature proved an adequate explanation of how our world came to be as it is, and was already toying with the notion that order itself presupposes mind. He continued to develop this line of thought in an essay in 1852 on the work of the Danish physicist Hans Christian Oersted: the need to bring science and religion together without endangering either; the interrelations of law, cause, and force; the will as 'the fulcrum ... the true balance-point' of a moral theism standing between atheism and pantheism. In 1870 he read a paper on causation at the Metaphysical Society, where he expected T.H. Huxley to be his principal critic; to his surprise, Huxley agreed with his main philosophical argument – 'that *physically* we have no cognisance of causation; that *intellectually* we are obliged to think it; and that in thinking it we necessarily identify it with *Will* ...'. Huxley ventured that as he saw Personality, it was unequal to the immensity of the product; but Martineau thought that a physiologist's bias, the habit of looking at human personal attributes as emerging from 'the simply vital phenomena at their culminating point; and that this Naturalist's estimate of

them rose up to damp and quench his inward reading of
them from the consciousness of intellectual light and moral
freedom'. Martineau's final summation appeared in *A Study
of Religion, Its Sources and Contents,* published in 1888, where
in a long section on 'The Place of Teleology' – a *tour de force*
drawing on extensive reading in biology – he argues for the
realisation of all creation as an act of will. It is a synthesis of
literally cosmic proportions: nothing less would counter the
atheistic tendency he saw among the leading scientists of his
later years.[7]

   J. Estlin Carpenter saw Martineau's thought as the product
of two early influences: his training as an engineer, which
gave him conceptions of matter and motion and of mathematical relations as a part of necessary truth, and from his
having been taught to live under a persistently high moral
tension. But there is another element from his upbringing
that may lend further consistency to his career – the very
Priestleyanism he had been at such pains to reject. In 1857
Edward Tagart – a fellow-student at Manchester College
York (Manchester College moved several times before set-
tling in Oxford in 1889) and in time one of the leaders of the
traditional wing of Unitarianism in opposition to Martineau's
innovations – retired as secretary of the British and Foreign
Unitarian Association; on that occasion, Martineau wrote a
fascinating letter to Tagart's wife Helen, who had once been
married to Martineau's elder brother. Attempting to play
down the 'poor antipathies' so evident in the battle between
the old and the new Unitarianism, Martineau offered a
revealing bit of self-analysis: 'For myself I feel that I am still
what I was at York; – the same in whole essence of every
taste, affection, and conviction; – different only ... by a
process of slow & steady change needful to bring opinions
instilled from without into harmony with the nature given
me within.' We thus confront once more the old question of
substance and accidents in the history of ideas, of what is
truly novel and what survives unaltered in the passing of
generations. It seems incontestable that the twin pillars of
natural religion and Revelation that had supported Priestley's thought continued to support Martineau's in much the
same way, just as they had borne up all those intervening
Unitarians who were forced to take account of a world and a

universe changed in every proportion. The Unitarians of Martineau's later years were, no doubt, as convinced as he, though in a somewhat vaguer way, of the vastly expanded conception of the Deity that was imposed by the almost inconceivable conclusions of the scientists: still the piety of the late nineteenth century confronting evolution was not very different from the piety of the late eighteenth century confronting Newtonian mechanics. What one must ask, however, is whether the late Victorians either knew so much about the issues or cared so deeply about them as had those Unitarians, ministerial and lay, of the generations that bore the immediate stamp of Priestley's passionate advocacy.[8]

III

If the persistence of a powerful mode of thought over more than a century is a plausible explanation of the accommodations Unitarians made between science and religion, how well does that, or a similar, hypothesis work in considering the storms that buffeted the pillar of Revelation? Priestley and his successors insisted on the application of canons of rational criticism to the Bible and to churchly tradition, and early Victorian Unitarians repeatedly declared that religion was no more proof against evidence than were speculations about the natural world. But did the accumulation of historical evidence become so great as to carry the burden of criticism beyond degree to kind?

We need pause only briefly with the impact from Germany. As on so many other things, Belsham was utterly confident. A biblical critic himself, he wrote in 1820 that he loved German criticism and would have given much to have have heard Eichhorn lecture; but he could not abide German theology: at least, Belsham said, when Hume disbelieved miracles, he also said he disbelieved Christianity, whereas the Germans were attempting to deny one and maintain the other. Belsham knew of only two English disciples of German theology, thought that no one was willing to advance the anti-supernaturalist argument, and was certain that, if anyone were, it could not stand an hour against the scorn and ridicule it would receive. Nor did German philosophy fare much better: Kant, said a reviewer in the *Inquirer* in 1845, was 'the perfection of a London fog in the regions of intellect'. Strauss set off a series of alarm bells, particularly once cheap and suspect translations began to be circulated by Chartist booksellers as polemical companions of Paine and Richard Carlile. Indeed, John Relly Beard, minister at Salford and indefatigable Unitarian publicist, proposed an anti-Strauss publication, though one correspondent in the *Inquirer* feared that such a work would only call attention to the malign influence. When he moved from Manchester to London in the late fifties, J.J. Tayler found the general tone of London Unitarian theology almost stationary: not very studious and mouthing all the old phrases, the ministers seemed hardly aware of what was happening in Germany, or even in France and America.[9]

Tayler was a prejudiced witness, and he was certainly misleading if he meant his indictment to include the striking impact made throughout English Unitarianism by the American William Ellery Channing and by his friend Joseph Tuckerman, whose example and encouragement were directly responsible for the extensive setting up of domestic missions around the country from the early thirties. Channing's influence reflects a profound change in sensibility, conveniently summed up in the invocation of romanticism, though among Unitarians the shift also included a broadening of social sympathies. From all parts of the spectrum came praise for Channing's moral fervour and 'resistless language'. For Harriet Martineau, as for many, Channing merited particular praise for his courageous denunciation of slavery, but it was his appeal to the emotions that counted for more in the long run. And nothing could have delighted him more. American Unitarianism had been relatively little affected by Priestleyanism, but Channing was determined to root out what residuum there was. The old Unitarianism, he told James Martineau, whatever its virtues, 'does not work deeply . . . does not strike living springs in the soul . . . cannot quicken and regenerate the world', and though he professed sympathy with the new, rebellious 'transcendentalist' Unitarians in his own country who were dallying with Victor Cousin and the Germans, his certainty of 'the needs of the soul & the conditions of growth' made him fear for the foundations of Christianity and led him to greater sympathy with what he saw (under Martineau's instruction) was happening in England. There were severely practical as well as doctrinal results – extensive efforts to give congregations a greater sense of community, to make strangers feel welcome, and, portentously, to transform the role of the minister: the old Presbyterian ideal of a learned ministry was seriously qualified by demands for greater participation in congregational life and for more 'popular' qualities of style and personality. There was, however, at least one defender of the old attitude: 'The very sympathy and firmness of our belief produces coldness; not coldness of heart, of religion, of love, far from it; but the calmness which a man feels when he knows his house to be built upon a rock. . . .'

In 1842, the year of Channing's death, Theodore Parker published *A Discourse of Religion*. Mediating the conclusions of Strauss and other continental critics to his American audience and attempting to distinguish, in the words of a later sermon, the transient from the permanent in Christianity, Parker brought home to many in the English Unitarian world the extent to which anti-supernaturalism and the sweeping denial of miracles had gone. In a startling confession of denominational bankruptcy – or was it merely his own calculated diffidence? – James Martineau wrote to John Gordon to say that, with Channing dead, 'we must watch the horizon for some rising light by which to live'. He thought Parker was not that source: he was, for all his strength of mind and greatness of heart, too rash, dogmatical, and exaggerated. But the debate over anti-supernaturalism lasted in Unitarian circles for more than a generation, continuing long after Parker's death in 1860. The debate was fuelled by a succession of theological publications in England and by the rapid progress of some Unitarians into free thought (or near it) and Positivism. In 1840, Thomas Wood, minister at Stamford Street in London, preached a sermon rejecting biblical evidence and the divinity of Christ's mission, bringing William Hincks and Joseph Hutton, then minister at Little Carter Lane in London, into the lists against him. Philip Harwood, the son of a wealthy Bristol wholesale grocer, a product of Lewin's Mead Chapel, and for a time a protégé of W.J. Fox, ended up lecturing at the Beaumont

Institution, in Mile End, London, a secular church, before moving on to a distinguished journalistic career.[11]

A particularly revealing move outward from Unitarianism was that of Charles Christian Hennell, from an old Presbyterian family that had naturally grown into Unitarianism, a position reinforced by Robert Aspland, whose services the Hennells regularly attended at the Gravel-pit Chapel, Hackney. Hennell's faith was challenged by his necessarian but agnostic brother-in-law, the Coventry ribbon manufacturer and newspaper proprietor Charles Bray. Together with his sister and his wife, Hennell worked out his *Inquiry into the Origin of Christianity* (1838), a piece of home-grown higher criticism that Strauss was sufficiently enthusiastic about to have translated into German. The Hennells's sweeping critique of the Bible was done, as a High Church reviewer eagerly pointed out, by applying the methods of Priestley and Belsham, merely rejecting more. Yet Hennell still hankered after the notion of a future life and thought it probable that it could be derived from imputing goodness and perpetual superintendence to the intelligent first cause he posited as the basis of his Christian theism.[12] It was, of course, in this circle that George Eliot underwent the first steps of her religious emancipation.

Another Unitarian, of an even more distinguished family, who made a similar pilgrimage, was W.R. Greg, whose *Creed of Christendom; Its Foundations and Superstructure* appeared in 1851; while a far greater influence than any of these was exercised by Francis W. Newman, who went through a Unitarian period and who was for a time in close connection with Unitarians in his association with University College London and with University Hall, a London residence for Unitarian students. Newman's curious essay on *The Soul, Its Sorrows and Its Aspirations* (1849) and his autobiographical *Phases of Faith* the next year had a deep effect on his Unitarian admirers, so much so that, despite his advance into an exiguous theism, he held a vice-presidency in the British and Foreign Unitarian Association in 1879 and remained a life-long friend and confidant of James Martineau. The odyssey chronicled in *Phases of Faith* was certainly more arduous, even traumatic, than were any of the leftward moves of those of Unitarian background: to start from

Evangelicalism was a far greater burden and, as the diverging careers of the Newman brothers shows, far more incalculable in its results than a commitment to pursuing truth by critical and scientific means. It is probable, though, that more troubling than any of these free-thinkers were two earlier deserters from the Unitarian cause to the Church of England, Samuel Taylor Coleridge and Frederick Denison Maurice.

The centre held, however, though it was divided. And to understand that division, we must look at two of the principal revisionists in some detail.[13] John James Tayler, thoroughly imbued with necessarianism as a young man at Manchester College York, had some reservations about his direction as early as 1822, concerned whether his essentially literary interests could bear him up in a neighbourhood of cotton-spinners, dyers, and printers, where mechanics and chemistry were all the rage. A self-confessed Wordsworthian, he made his way to Germany in 1834–5 on a leave granted by his Manchester congregation so that he might recover from a mental crisis. His letters to his congregation and to his friends reveal the greatly expanding horizons that came with the German visit, though he did not at first go all the way with the corrosive conclusions of German theology. On his return, his detachment from the old moorings continued. By 1839 he was calling for the abandonment of 'hard, defined, metaphysical systems of divinity' in favour of a loving, believing spirit of Christianity, 'living and breathing and speaking to the inmost heart – realized and embodied in all the great unchanging relations of humanity to God and man and eternity – in the life and character of the pure and blessed Jesus'. Unitarians should give up their posture of intellectual superiority and return to the principles of the old Puritans without their excesses, be tolerant of diversity of opinion, and offer an example of how the middle ranks of society could provide the means of transition to a 'more just, equal, and rational institution of things'. Tayler's theology may have strained the elastic capacities of a cloudy rhetoric, but his prescriptions for his fellow Unitarians were pointedly plain: Priestleyanism had come to the end of a road. Evidences never tell, he wrote to his friend Thom in 1858, 'till the inner man is previously touched and already won by a

deep feeling of spiritual want' – a statement he said Unitarians found incomprehensible mysticism, 'while to my mind
it flashes with all the conclusiveness of the clearest light'. The
next year he was denying the resurrection of the body, and in
1864 he was not at all troubled by evidence that the gospels
were written at a much later date than had been thought:
'Happily the spiritual side of Xtian^y, of which I daily feel
more deeply the assertive [power?] and self-evincing truth, is
quite independent of all such theories.'[14]

James Martineau, almost from the moment of his leaving
Manchester College York in 1827, was regarded as the most
promising of the younger ministers, and whatever difficulties
ensued, everyone conceded that the promise was abundantly
fulfilled. He was a reviewer of immense range and startling
insights and a teacher of surpassing power, and the succession of large books he wrote at the end of his life testify to the
care and imagination he had brought to the lectures out of
which they grew. He was a preacher of uncommon, though
lapidary, eloquence. And the complex movement of his mind
is as fascinating to watch as it is difficult to unravel. His
commitment to Priestleyanism was, apparently, more intense
than Tayler's, yet his dissatisfaction with it began early,
proclaimed in a brilliant pair of articles on Priestley and
Channing. His evolution as a thinker was, however, more
tortuous than Tayler's, marked by hesitations and drawing
back, even though it is equally possible to find the basic
contentions of his treatises at the end of his life present in
germ, sometimes even in language, in those writings of the
thirties and forties that later came to seem so unsatisfactory
to him. The teaching that he began at Manchester College in
1840 – it was now back in Manchester – made everything he
had done to that point unsatisfactory, 'and every subject had
to be melted down again in my own mind, and be recast in
other moulds'. He did not go abroad until 1848–9 – by that
time a period of residence in Germany was obligatory for
advanced Unitarians – but, interesting though he found his
stay, it had nothing like the effect of Tayler's earlier sojourn,
coming as it did at a time of great mental malleability.
Indeed, after Martineau's return from the Continent, he
dismayed Crabb Robinson by his strong adverse opinion
(later softened in conversation) of Germany, where, he said,

religion was nearly extinct, a judgment he compounded by telling his Dissenting audience that he preferred the religious tendency of education at Oxford and Cambridge.[15]

That little vignette is revealing of a trait. Martineau could not resist bold and disquieting, even offensive, statements, in print or in public. In 1838, at a meeting of ministers in London to plot strategy for repelling orthodox attacks, he created a furore by his slashing refusal to go along with a strengthening of the British and Foreign Unitarian Association. This was the first salvo in his lifelong campaign against the Unitarian name – he preferred the historical redolence of 'Presbyterian' and in the sixties came up with the term Free Christian – and against what he saw as the evolution of a sect rather than a church; this insistence was a major factor in the hostility he evoked among so many of his fellow-Unitarians and that helped to defeat most of his proposals to reform the denomination. Along with the outspokenness went (at least in his opponents' eyes) a tendency to deviousness; the accusation that he constantly worked through confederates is given point by the scarcity of his contributions to the *Inquirer*, even though, after Hincks gave up the editorship, the newspaper tilted markedly to the new school.[16]

There was, however, a more touching side to this unpleasant strategy of direct and indirect assault. He found it necessary to keep his contacts with old associates and to explain himself to them, with whatever difficulty. Take, for example, his position on miracles. In *The Rationale of Religious Enquiry*, his first book, published in 1836, retention of miracles appeared as a test of Christianity, a position he abandoned in the third edition of 1845. Four years earlier, in 1841, in a letter to Mary Carpenter, the daughter of his old teacher Lant Carpenter, he had tried to define the problem of miracles apart from Priestleyan preoccupations, though the underlinings suggest, by their very vehemence, the tentativeness and unease with which he approached the question. In his article on Theodore Parker in the *Prospective Review* in 1846, he reiterated his argument that a religion centrally concerned with causality is vulnerable; and his sceptical view on miracles and their uses deeply offended his

old Norwich minister, Thomas Madge, long since trans-
planted to Essex Street in London. Yet Martineau felt it
appropriate, even necessary, to ask Madge to take part in the
opening of the Hope Street Church in Liverpool, an invitation that Madge, with uneasy gratitude, accepted. In a letter
to Tagart in 1857, Martineau was concerned to rebut allega-
tions among the various schools that he was misty and cloudy
or not objective. He thought, he said, his conception of
evidences and of natural religion was as distinct and un-
wavering as those of the old school, whatever their differences. 'And though 30 years have certainly changed some
estimates which I brought from College, they have not
abated the reverence in which I hold the old names or
impaired the justice with which I love to exhibit the old
doctrines, of Locke & Hartley, Priestley & Paley.' The
modern reader, puzzled by this brilliant and defensive man,
must share the concern of Sara Sophia Hennell about 'his
shiftingness', a notion that seemed to have a particular
appropriateness in the wake of Darwin's book. Perhaps, she
thought, he signalled the emergence of a new species of
religion: 'it seems to me that his mind (so to speak, without
irreverence), is wriggling itself forward in a true straight
forward direction.'[17]
Congregations accustomed to the clarity and balance of
eighteenth-century pulpit style or to the thrilling calls of a
preacher like George Harris to do Unitarian battle faced a
difficult adjustment to the mode of discourse of the new
school, with its elaborate sentences, its idiosyncratic use of
words to carry significance other than their plain meaning,
the direct appeal to deep and only partially uncoverable
emotions. Early in his long pastorate at Renshaw Street in
Liverpool, J.H. Thom boldly resigned when congregational
leaders ventured to suggest changes in 'stile and manner';
backed by a majority of the congregation, Thom withdrew
his resignation, but not before reading the congregation a
lesson on the duties of minister and flock. Robert Brook
Aspland eagerly repeated gossip about Martineau's incom-
prehensibility at Little Portland Street or the utterly inappropriate sermon he preached on the relations of doctrine
to high art – in Rochdale, of all places. But both men became
figures of awe to their congregations, and visitors to London

were told that hearing Martineau was something they should do.[18]

Still, the war of thrust and counter-thrust went on. When Tayler and Martineau consolidated their hold on Manchester College, which moved to London in the fifties and to Oxford at the end of the eighties, a new college – at first the Unitarian Home Missionary Board – was founded in Manchester, and disgruntled supporters of the older college considered withdrawing all support from it. Tagart wrote a book to defend Locke against his Scottish enemies and against the accusation that his philosophy led to the scepticism of Hume. When Tayler and Martineau denied that Jesus was the Messiah, Samuel Bache (another brother-in-law of Martineau) not only wrote a pamphlet to reassert the claim but in 1862 persuaded his congregation – Priestley's, in Birmingham – to name its new church the Church of the Messiah. But three years later the old school overreached itself when Bache tried unsuccessfully to persuade the British and Foreign Unitarian association to adopt a definition of Unitarian principles – a creed, it was unkindly pointed out, for a denomination that prided itself on being creedless. But again and again Martineau failed to impose his stamp on Unitarianism: the Free Christian movement of the sixties left only its name attached to some churches built (or re-christened) in the period and in a subordinate place in the full title of the General Assembly that governs Unitarianism in Britain today; the triennial National Conference, founded in the eighties on an American example, proved not to be a replacement for the British and Foreign Unitarian Association but a supplement, until the two were merged in 1928; and Martineau's scheme of 1887 to reform the denomination – by providing more financial support, requiring a better-educated ministry, and returning to a quasi-Presbyterian structure – was voted down in congregation after congregation under cover of profound expressions of respect for its author.

Yet Martineau was right to say that younger men would be with them. The new school had attracted them from the start, as with Richard Holt Hutton, the eminent intellectual journalist, or Thomas Hincks, of Exeter, who boasted in 1848 that he had been involved in every deviation in the West of England from what George Armstrong, the veteran minister at Bristol, thought was the true path. And in 1868, Bache's church passed into the hands of Henry W. Crosskey, the very model of the new-school political minister. The victory was, however, a temporary one, for still younger ministers went chasing after a number of competing enthusiasms, went farther and farther in anti-supernaturalism, and became political in a sense that earlier generations of Unitarians had not known, political even to the point of socialism. Martineau remained wedded to his mature beliefs in the power of personal example, as against social reconstruction, and was aware not only that he had been passed by, but that 'the future of English Religion is not with us. Whatever aspects of truth we may have saved from neglect, whatever spiritual resources we may have rendered more accessible, pass into other keeping and need another administration, before they lay hold of the minds and hearts of men.'[19]

The *locus classicus* of faith in crisis is in the middle of the century, and there were some who came then, to borrow the medical definition of crisis, to that decisive juncture when the disease must become better or worse. W.R. Greg's description of the agitation of mind that could accompany such a crisis of faith might have been somewhat heightened, but Francis Newman did suffer, the more so as the revelations that came to him were so unexpected and shocking. Joseph Henry Hutton, who in the fifties became Minister at Upper Brook Street in Manchester, found himself agonizingly torn between F.D. Maurice and F.W. Newman; in 1859 he resigned his pulpit, to become, in effect, an Arian and to take up, not very successfully, a career as a schoolmaster; at last in 1870 he conformed. Joseph Hunter, minister at Bath until 1833, distinguished antiquarian and archivist, shed layer after layer of his once sunny Priestleyanism as disappointment in his church was compounded by personal troubles. In the end he even abandoned his conviction in the importance of pursuing truth; how much better were 'the sweeter pleasures of Safety, Hope, Joy, which the religious man has, though he may not be able to prove his title to them'. Yet that process was nearly twenty years in working itself out – less a crisis, it seems, than a kind of growth.[20]

Most of the Unitarians we have touched on here, though they were embattled, tended to find in the scientific and critical cataclysms of mid-century reinforcement of the particular outlines of their faith than a need, compelled at last, to abandon it. Those who moved out of Unitarianism into some variety of free thought seem to have done so without great trauma and almost with a joyous sense of discovery, whatever skirmishes there may have been along the way. The capacity to absorb and adjust, to make the strange seem familiar, to alter accidents without greatly altering substance was all but ineradicably set by the intellectual premises of the faith that descended from Joseph Priestley. This perception of unity in what the nineteenth-century actors, primary and secondary, had seen as profound division is confirmed in a remarkable lecture given by L.P. Jacks, principal of Manchester college, in 1920, on 'The Old Unitarianism and the New'. He defined the Old Unitarianism − which he saw as embracing the Priestleyans and the revisionists − as a religion of vision, to which teaching was secondary, and the new Unitarianism of his own time as having reversed the order. The vision of the old rested on the idea of a complete or perfect personality we call God, of whom men are but imperfect images; the vision of the new rested on the idea of a perfect world, without sin, suffering, or death, of which our own world is a mutilated fragment. The work of the Old Unitarianism remained incomplete, bypassed by 'philosophies of life of many types, teaching equipment derived from many sources, ethical flowers culled from all the religions, social theories of every conceivable variety', all of them interesting but without the power or capacity to move. Despite its imperfections, the old offered Jacks greater satisfaction. 'Its insights did not always go very deep, − but it went in the right direction. Its grasp was often feeble − but it grasped the big things, the essentials of the Christian vision. The advances it made from Priestley to James Drummond were immense. It absorbed all that was of permanent value in the work of James Martineau, but it absorbed this and much else without losing its own distinctive character as a ministry of vision. It held within it immense but undeveloped resources of evangelical power.'[21] Despite all the quarrels, hesitations, changes of front, and soul-searchings of nineteenth-century Unitarians, crisis, in any meaningful sense in either faith or the institutional church, must be found in our own century and not among the Victorians.

NOTES

1. John Kenrick, *Memoir of the Rev. John Kentish* (London, 1854) 46–7. Thomas Carlyle to Richard Monckton Milnes, 19 July 1841, in T. Wemyss Reid, *The Life, Letters, and Friendships of Richard Monckton Milnes*, 2 vols (London, 1891) 1: 265–6.

2. K.M. Lyell, *Life, Letters, and Journals of Sir Charles Lyell, Bart.*, 2 vols (London, 1881), contains many letters touching on Unitarianism, but the long philosophical letter written to Lyell by J.J. Tayler, 23 February 1862, suggests that more on Lyell's religious interests must exist in unpublished manuscripts (J.H. Thom, *Letters Embracing His Life of John James Tayler, B.A.*, 2 vols [London, 1872] 2: 186–92); S.E. De Morgan, *Memoir of Augustus De Morgan* (London, 1882) 86–7, 168, 342–3; cf. George Boole, *The Claims of Science, Especially As Founded on Its Relations to Human Nature* (London, 1851) 8; William Hincks, *Illustrations of Unitarian Christianity* (London, 1845) 34–5.

3. Thomas Belsham, *Reflections upon the History of the Creation in the Book of Genesis* (London, 1821); John Kenrick, *An Essay on Primeval History* (London, 1846).

4. Harriet Martineau to Erasmus Darwin, 2 February 1860, and to Fanny Wedgwood, 13 March 1860 (*Harriet Martineau's Letters to Fanny Wedgwood*, ed. Elizabeth Sanders Arbuckle [Stanford, 1983] 185–93); John James Tayler to John Kenrick, 18 February 1863 (Thom, *Tayler*, 2: 223–4).

5. Higginson's brief, detailed, and diffident autobiographical sketch is in a manuscript collection of such sketches in Dr Williams's Library, MS 38.64.

6. Published in the *Inquirer*, 22 March and 16 August 1845. See the biographical essay by J. Estlin Carpenter prefacing W.B. Carpenter, *Nature and Man: Essays Scientific and Philosopical* (London, 1888), for a discussion of reviews of Chambers and Darwin; his matured views on Darwin appear in two essays reprinted in *Nature and Man*, 384–408, 409–63.

7. The quotation from Wicksteed appears in C.B. Upton, *Dr. Martineau's Philosophy: A Survey*, rev. ed. (London, 1905) 181–2; the description of the debate with Huxley is taken from a letter to Charles Wicksteed, 26 August 1870 (ibid., 120); Martineau's essay on Parker appears in *Essays, Reviews, and Addresses*, 4 vols (London, 1891) 1: 149–89, the essay on Oersted, ibid., 3: 83–116.

8. J. Estlin Carpenter, *James Martineau, Theologian and Teacher: A Study of His Life and Thought* (London, 1905) 547; in the possession of James Martineau to Helen Tagart, 15 May 1857 (Dr R.S. Speck Collection, Bancroft Library, University of California, Berkeley).

9. John Williams, *Memoirs of the Late Rev. Thomas Belsham* (London, 1833) 702–5; *Inquirer*, 22 February 1845, on Kant; ibid., 20 and 27 April, 4 and 11 May, on Strauss; Beard's answer was *Voices of the Church, in Reply to Dr. D.F. Strauss* (London, 1845); Tayler to Martineau, 1 August 1858 (Thom, *Tayler*, 2: 104–5).

10. Channing to James Martineau, 13 September 1841 (Manchester College Library); Buriensis (*Inquirer*, 19 November 1842).

11. Martineau to John Gordon, 20 January 1843 (Unitarian College MS B 1.22, John Rylands University of Manchester Library); *Inquirer*, 3 February 1844, for a sweeping attack on anti-supernaturalism; Thomas Wood before and after is displayed in *Four Lectures on the Evidences and Doctrines of the Christian Religion* (London, 1836) and *The Mission of Jesus Christ* (London, 1840); William Hincks, *Anti-Supernaturalism Considered* (London, 1841); Joseph Hutton, *Jesus Christ Our Teacher and Lord by Divine, Not by Self, Appointment* (London, 1841).

12. Sara Sophia Hennell, *Memoir of Charles Christian Hennell* (London, 1899) 3–69. The *Inquiry* went through three editions in Hennell's lifetime; the first edition was followed the next year by his *Christian Theism*. The article in *Christian Remembrancer*, NS, 11 (1846) 355–6, is an admirable, passionate survey of anti-supernaturalism and its evils.

13. Besides Tayler and Martineau, two other ministers were particularly associated with the change in direction – Charles Wicksteed and J.H. Thom. On Thom, see R.K. Webb, 'John Hamilton Thom: Intellect and Conscience in Liverpool', in *The View from the Pulpit*, ed. P.T. Phillips (London, 1978) 211–43, where there is much information on the domestic mission movement, passed over in the present chapter. Wicksteed remains a more shadowy figure and was certainly less important than his three friends.

14. On Tayler's conversion to necessarianism, J.J. Tayler to Richard Tayler, 28 February 1818 (Dr Williams's Library, MS 24.102). On his uncertainty, JJT to John Kenrick, 19 September and 6 December 1822 (Thom, *Tayler*, 1: 50, 52); on his Wordsworthianism, to his wife, 16 July 1830 (ibid., 1: 86). His mental crisis is alluded to in a letter to his congregation, 14 October 1834 (ibid., 1: 111–13), and in a letter to Richard Tayler, 14 June 1835 (Dr Williams's Library, MS 24.102), a date that suggests his recovery was not easy. The letters for the German stay (Thom, *Tayler*, 1: 105–73) are of great interest. Tayler, *The Present Position, Prospects, and Duties of Unitarian Christians* (London, 1839) 15–16, 21–7; *Retrospect of the Religious Life of England* (London, 1845) 197, 300, 312. His denial of the resurrection of the body is reported by Robert Brook Aspland (no friend) to John Gordon, 29 April 1859 (Unitarian College MS B 1.15, John Rylands University of Manchester Library). The letter touching on evidences is to Thom, 6 September 1858 (*Tayler*, 2: 142–3). On the peripheral evidence of gospel criticism, JJT to John Kenrick, 20 March 1864 (Dr Williams's Library, MS 24.81).

15. Martineau's autobiographical memoranda are in the Manchester College Library; Crabb Robinson's account of the Hope Street meeting is in his travel journal, 18 October 1849 (Dr Williams's Library).

16. The intervention in 1838 is recounted in H.L. Short, 'Presbyterians under a New Name', in C.G. Bolam, *et al.*, *The English Presbyterians*, (London, 1968) 256; Martineau's 'Church Life? or Sect-Life?' appears in *Essays, Reviews, and Addresses*, 2: 381–420.

17. James Martineau to Mary Carpenter, February 1841 (Manchester

College Library); the relevant passage in the article on Parker is in *Essays, Reviews, and Addresses*, 1: 165–8; Crabb Robinson Diary, 5 February 1846 (Dr Williams's Library); Madge to JM, 14 August 1849 (Manchester College Library); JM to Tagart, 22 April 1857 (Dr R.S. Speck Collection, Bancroft Library, University of California, Berkeley); S.S. Hennell to Harriet Martineau, 13 April 1860 (Birmingham University Library, HM 428).

18.   Webb, 'Thom', 217–19, 221–3; Aspland to John Gordon, 5 April 1859, 13 June 1857 (Unitarian College MS B 1.15, John Rylands University of Manchester Library); on George Eliot's eagerly anticipated visit, frustrated by a substitute preacher apparently of the old school, see her letters to Sara Sophia Hennell, 2 and 30 July 1861 (*The George Eliot Letters*, ed. Gordon Haight, 9 vols [New Haven, 1957] 3: 433, 442).

19.   Hincks made his boast in the *Inquirer*, 18 November 1848; James Martineau to R.L. Carpenter, 25 April 1885 (Manchester College Library).

20.   J.J. Tayler to J.H. Hutton, 22 February 1858 and Tayler to J.H. Thom, 6 September 1859, in Thom, *Tayler*, 2: 88–91, 129–44. Hunter's shifts are recorded in his 'thought books' in the British Library, Add. MSS 39818–20, and in his correspondence in Add. MSS 35161–2.

21.   *Inquirer*, 24 April 1920.

Part III
Industrial Society and the New Theodicy

5 Theodicy and Society: The Crisis of the Intelligentsia

James R. Moore

... Is this an hour
   For private sorrow's barren song,
   When more and more the people throng
The chairs and thrones of civil power?

A time to sicken and to swoon
   When science reaches forth her arms
   To feel from world to world, and charms
Her secret from the latest moon?

(Alfred Tennyson, *In Memoriam*, xxi, 13–20)

The Victorian crisis of faith has been regarded conventionally as a spiritual condition endemic among bourgeois thinkers infected by religious doubt after 1859. This chapter takes for granted a broader perspective, which I have adumbrated elsewhere.[1] To put this view concisely: if there was a 'Victorian crisis' – and I think there was – it was not merely a crisis 'of faith'. For faith (which I take here to be synonymous with belief) was, as always, the corollary of action, and action based on faith embodied social purpose. Spiritual equipoise, *balance* moral rectitude, intellectual integrity – not merely these were at stake, but the very order and progress of society. The Victorian crisis was a crisis of legitimation.

Thus, in my view, the crisis among the Victorian intelligentsia arose from the necessity laid upon them of prescribing purposive action, or practical measures, for dealing with social conflict in a manner consistent with securing their own status and emoluments in a diversifying economy.[2] The crisis for the rest of society lay in the social conflicts themselves, arising chiefly from economic change, or in the flux of bourgeois opinion, which tended to undermine personal meaning and coherence. Bourgeois opinion was convulsed by the intelligentsia as they offered competing social prescriptions, or competing *raisons d'être* for closely similar prescriptions, before the general public. These internecine conflicts may be seen as ideological struggles in so far as the points at issue were the ultimate beliefs from which social prescriptions were held to flow. The same internecine conflicts may be seen equally as political struggles in so far as the authority of the respective parties was at stake, and thus the power of each to shape opinion and events. 'Professionalisation', the institutionalising and canonising of independent expertise, was the high road to power and authority among bourgeois intellectuals. 'Secularisation', the marginalising and usurping of power and authority, was the back door for sectors of the intelligentsia who lost out in the political and ideological debate. The Victorian crisis – I shall cease referring to a crisis 'of faith' *per se* – culminated in the professionalisation of science, in this sense, and in the secularisation of religion. But the relationship was not one of cause and effect, as the juxtaposition might suggest. For religious faith was almost never attacked for its own sake by the adherents of scientific naturalism. Rather, in the words of Maurice Mandelbaum, these intellectuals saw their struggles with established authority 'as a means of freeing that faith for what were regarded as being nobler and more adequate forms in which it could find expression'.[3]

This broader view of the so-called Victorian crisis of faith requires a fresh analysis of the spiritual experience featured in conventional accounts of the subject. The crisis of the intelligentsia did not consist solely of personal spiritual angst; nor, as Mandelbaum suggests, was it so simple as a 'conflict of religion and science'. Whatever its manifestations may have been – personal or institutional, political or ideological – the crisis must be referred to the wider struggle to negotiate new doctrines, new beliefs, new vehicles of consent that would be seen to maintain continuity with and fulfil the best aspirations of older creeds but, at the same time, would serve to order and stabilise class relations more effectively by allowing for new patterns of expectation in a liberalising and 'improving' society. In this chapter I shall call these new vehicles of consent a 'theodicy'. I shall view the process of negotiating a new theodicy as part of the 'naturalisation' of religion. If secularisation was the removing of certain religious ideas, religious values, and religious institutions with their professional representatives from positions of power and authority in national life, then naturalisation meant the transforming of these ideas, values, and institutions so that the equivalent religious power and authority became vested in natural ideas, naturalistic values, and institutions led by professional interpreters of nature. In this process the locus of the sacral moved from the noumenal towards the phenomenal, from the eternal towards the temporal, from another world towards this world. Naturalisation may thus be seen as the actual expression of 'meliorism', the contemporary term that perhaps best indicates the real dimensions of the Victorian crisis.[4]

Taken together, 'professionalisation', 'secularisation', and 'naturalisation' form a notional tripod that could well support a full-scale survey of the Victorian crisis from the broader perspective sketched above. In this chapter, however, I must undertake a less ambitious task. As an adjunct to better political understanding, past and present, I propose to show that the ideological aspect of naturalisation, the making of a new naturalistic theodicy, was central to that wider social experience of the Victorian intelligentsia which has been referred to narrowly and misleadingly as a 'crisis of faith'.

I

It would be obliging of the Victorians if they used our own terminology to express their sense of crisis. Then we could simply decide whether to believe them or not, instead of labouring to devise explanations a century later for what we think was really happening in their lives. Now 'theodicy' was not among the Victorians' favourite terms. No one, so far as I am aware, came out and said in so many words that the birth pangs of a new theodicy were the crisis of the Victorian intelligentsia. Ever since Leibniz had incurred Voltaire's savage ridicule by arguing that ours was the 'best of all possible worlds', only preachers to the converted set out to square the vicious ·circle of natural and moral evil. And

Voltaire, despite his calumnies, was making a come-back in late-Victorian Britain. Theodicies *per se* remained abhorrent to most progressive thinkers. Froude in his *Nemesis of Faith* in 1849, blasting the last 'few monstrous efforts from Calvin to Leibnitz to reconcile contradictions and form a theodice', and Huxley remarking coolly in 1892 that agnostic principles were 'irreconcilable with the biblical cosmogony, anthropology, and theodicy', bracketed the Victorian crisis with contempt for the traditional enterprise of justifying the ways of God to humankind.[5]

Yet in other forms, in other phrases, the enterprise was not abandoned, nor could it be. For example, generations of middle-class Victorians whose youthful companions died early, like Tennyson's Hallam, or whose children died young – 'tragically young – like all the others', felt their deepest sentiments affirmed in the anguished epic written under inspiration of Hallam's *Theodicaea Novissima* (1831). Though ravenous nature might shriek of mortality against the 'creed' of those 'Who trusted God was love indeed / And love Creation's final law', Tennyson left no doubt, in his Prologue to *In Memoriam* (1850), that 'thou has made him: thou art just' (12; lvi, 13–16). God had purposed 'one far-off event', the advent of 'the crowning race', which in the Epilogue makes all the interim pain worthwhile: 'For all we thought and loved and did, / And hoped, and suffered, is but seed / Of what in them is flower and fruit' (134–6). These lines, it must be said, also echo the explicitly developmental theodicy that Tennyson had read in Robert Chambers's anonymous *Vestiges of the Natural History of Creation* (1844). The popularity – indeed notoriety – of this book, with its theistic assurance that the present is merely 'a stage in a Great Progress, and . . . the Redress is in reserve', reminds us again, if it were needed, how earnestly the Victorian intelligentsia pondered questions about the nature and purpose of evil.[6] 'These questions . . . are answered in some way by all men, even by those who consider themselves to have no theology at all', wrote the historian J.R. Seeley, a prime advocate of naturalistic religion. 'They have a theology as much as Christians; they must even have a faith of some sort, otherwise they would renounce human life.' For Leslie Stephen, the most evangelical of agnostics, the 'horror' of evil lay 'at the root of every vigorous religious creed'; the great 'insoluble doubt' as to its meaning and purpose had haunted every school of philosophy since human thought began. 'The question', he said, 'is not which system excludes the doubt, but how it expresses the doubt.'[7]

Victorians like Stephen were not just morbidly preoccupied with evil. While theirs was a society noted for moral earnestness, it was also a society that routinely exposed its members to the worst effects of error, misfortune, and greed. If we are to appreciate the Victorian concern for theodicy it is necessary to be reminded briefly of 'the good old days' that never were. Stephen himself, brought up in the polite parlours of Kensington and Cambridge, believed that the 'most appalling' manifestation of the problem of evil in his age was 'that which meets us at the corner of every street. Look at the children growing up amidst moral poison; see the brothel and the public-house . . .', and so forth and so on. Living in the East End of London as I do, one hundred years later, it is still easy to understand how Stephen may have got the wrong impression from things he witnessed on a street-corner. And yet all was not well in the courtyards of Bermondsey, the rookeries of Shoreditch, and the teeming back alleys of every metropolis in the land. Workhouses were penitentiaries. Mothers threw their infants, and sometimes themselves, into rivers for want of food and self-respect. The cholera mowed through neighbourhoods, corpses rotted in garrets, and in pleasant times a gentle reforming breeze blew the smoke and fumes, with their faint aroma of revolution, away from the better parts of town. There, of course, people still died horrible lingering deaths – the Prince Consort himself was not immune – and the terrors of surgical intervention before chloroform came into use at mid-century scarcely abated at the prospect of lying septically insensible under the surgeon's knife. The cut and thrust of industry, by contrast, did not take an immediate toll among the owning and managing class, who usually lived a salubrious distance from the din, the stench, and the fallout. But as space and time contracted with the coming of the railways, all classes became exposed to the unprecedented danger of technology gone awry.

Sudden, violent, indiscriminate slaughter, it was said, had

made 'the carnage of peace more appalling than that of war': 'carriage piled upon carriage, tearing in pieces or crushing to atoms the precious life which they bear – the mother with the infant at her breast – the father taking his children to school – the bridal pair hastening to their honeymoon – the long lost pilgrim in sight of his home – the soldier, the sailor, the civilian, speeding to their duties or their pleasures, – all in the flush of life and hope, – swept to a cruel grave, unwarned and unprepared for the change.'[8] These phrases by a leading naturalist, hurtling like engines to their doom, only surveyed the railway wreckage of the later 1850s, when about 300 people lost their lives each year and some 500 were injured. By 1875 the railways carried between three and four times as many passengers; the length of the lines had nearly doubled. And the average annual death rate had soared above 1300. Five railway employees were being killed for every member of the public – twenty-five in all, each week. A Royal Commission was appointed to investigate why speculative investment, competitive enterprise, and the incentive of private profit had not led to greater happiness for a greater number in the absence of government interference. In 1877, when the Commission reported, Lord Beaconsfield declared in the Upper House that railway accidents were still 'perhaps our greatest domestic question'.[9]

Faced with everyday threats and cataclysms like these, events that made evil not just an intellectual problem but an urgent practical concern, how far, you may well ask, did the Victorian intelligentsia express their hopes and apprehensions through the making of theodices? The traditional enterprise, I have suggested, fell out of favour as a new naturalistic theodicy was being formed. This occurred, however, through continuous emendation and transformation – 'naturalisation', I have called it – of a conceptual system that was articulated in various ways by members of the intelligentsia throughout the nineteenth century. From their writings, and writings about them, this older theodicy can be generalised roughly as follows:

God works all things together for good. His providence in nature and history is orderly and harmonious; nothing is without purpose, nothing is done in vain. In physical nature, in organic matter, and in political society the divine principle is *economy*: motion is distributed, balance is maintained, labour and leisure are apportioned, all in accordance with laws discoverable by man. Happiness results from adherence to these laws, pain and misery from disregarding them. These evils are divinely appointed for our good; they are beneficence in disguise. Evils resulting from accident or misfortune are also appointed for beneficent ends. They keep us humble; they remind us of the fleetingness of life. Indeed, the entire world has been arranged as a vast system of means and ends so that we may come to know and revere the Creator. His gifts to use through that system, the improvement of arts and manufacture and commerce, the very progress of society, are themselves a sublime justification for the existence of those evils which spur mankind's attainments. Such imbalances of recompense as may occur in individual cases will be put right in the hereafter.[10]

The apologetic, reconciling, and ideological character of this theodicy is almost too obvious for words. It is worth recalling, though, that Malthus made his major contribution to the enterprise in order to scotch inordinate hopes for social change, while political economists and phrenologists later studied the laws of human life with a view towards abetting industrial progress. The basic tendency in any case was the same: to maintain the status quo.[11]

Consider the railways again. A Scottish minister, John Blakely, travelled to the Great Exhibition at London shortly after it opened in 1851. On touring the Crystal Palace it occurred to him that the motto of the exhibition – 'The earth is the Lord's and the fullness thereof' – might be applied instructively to the exhibits. He returned home – no doubt by train – and wrote a book entitled *The Theology of Inventions* (1856). It contains the essence of the old theodicy in Blakely's view of the awful 'railway mania' of the 1840s, which hit the country in the wake of famine and Chartist insurrection:

At this very period, the construction of railways lessened at once the misery and the social danger, by giving employment to those very parties who were nearest the point of starvation, and most likely to be roused in physical force demonstrations. By being scattered over Britain, their power was diminished, and their local ranks thinned, so that by the time the Railways had been completed, they were transferred beyond the Atlantic by emigration, or absorbed in the social community. Is there nothing in all this, but fortuitous coincidences falling out at random? They must be blind indeed, and verily ungrateful, who do not see and adore that God who is 'the moral Governor among the nations'.[12]

So enamoured was Blakely of God's providence that throughout his *Theology of Inventions* he remained almost blind even to the 'accidental' evils resulting from technological change. Not so John Herschel, a decade later, in addressing a village audience on the subject of natural disasters.

Herschel, the great astronomer, wished to show that 'the volcano and the earthquake, dreadful as they are, as local and temporary visitations, are in fact unavoidable (I had almost said necessary) incidents in a vast system of action' without which people would not be blessed with the earth to stand upon. He therefore drew an analogy: 'A ship sometimes strikes on a rock, and all on board perish; a railway train runs into another, or breaks down, and then wounds and contusions are the order of the day; but nobody doubts that navigation and railway communication are great blessings. None of the great natural provisions for producing good are exempt in their workings from producing occasional mischief.'[13] One implication that may be drawn from Herschel's analogy is that it is unreasonable to expect our technologies to be any safer than God himself makes the world. Blessings are always accompanied by buffetings. It was precisely this complacent view of the providential working of things that informed certain railway directors who tried to evade responsibility for the carnage on their lines by adopting 'the theory of a necessary percentage of accidents'. By 1877 a critic could dismiss this theory as an 'arbitrary irrational . . . species of fatalism'. The world to him was no longer a place where 'pecuniary self-interest' automatically sufficed to induce railway companies to fulfil their duty under the law of providing for the safety of passengers. Improved technology and tougher legislation alone would avert catastrophe. The old theodicy was being overthrown.[14]

II

But what of a new theodicy? Faced with the flagrant evils of the day, how far did the Victorian intelligentsia express their hopes and apprehension along other lines? Or to what extent were they concerned that a practical scheme of reconciliation be produced? I should be a good deal more diffident in this chapter were it not for a series of lectures by an 'intellectual of the industrial bourgeoisie',[15] which met these questions head-on. To 'hear' these lectures, as it were, we must board a train – if we dare – at London's Victoria Station and travel to the leafy suburb of Brixton in the borough of Lambeth.

It is 1870. Lambeth is not the dilapidated poverty-trap that it has become today. Brixton is not the scene of race riots as it was at the beginning of the 1980s. Shady lanes and tidy villas and lofty spires of newly-opened churches proclaim that here each weekday the nation's wealthy retire for domestic sustenance. On Sundays they attend the churches – churches that they themselves have built. Ensconced across South London, as Jeffrey Cox has shown, were the rich patrons of Lambeth's churches and chapels. 'The list of companies they owned, managed, or directed (and their successor companies) reads like a catalog of Britain's current economic giants: Guest, Keen and Nettlefold; Courtauld's; Tate and Lyle; Higgs and Hill; Barclay's Bank; Courage breweries; the Doulton potteries.'[16] It is Henry Doulton with whom we have to deal, or rather the man he installed at Claylands Congregational Chapel in 1845, J. Baldwin Brown. For twenty-four years Baldwin Brown has ministered there, on Brixton's borders, filling to capacity the modest side-street building (today a trendy office complex full of 'city planners'). Now the congregation has erected a new preaching station for him. They call this imposing neo-Gothic edifice, squatting portentously along a major thoroughfare, the Brixton Independent Church. Baldwin Brown is inaugurating his new up-market ministry by delivering a series of four lectures that take stock of the period in which the congregation has prospered under his leadership. He entitles the series, 'The Revolution of the Last Quarter of a Century'.

The subject of the first lecture is 'The Intellectual Revolution'. 'Measure the growth of the great centres of commerce',

Baldwin Brown urges. 'Think of the size of our ships, the tonnage of our ports, the scale and weight of our armaments, the magnitude and destructive energy of our wars. Count the mills, vast and wonderful in their complicated and perfect machinery, ... the forges and foundries that stain with smoke and deafen with their roar the choicest nooks and loveliest glens of our land. Realize, in a word, the vastness and rapidity of our progress.' Then consider that in this nation, which gave the world the steam engine, the spinning jenny, the steam boat, the electric telegraph, the penny post, and Free Trade – consider that here 'the ignorance seems denser, the penury more dire, the vice more rampant, the misery more utter, than when we commenced our work a quarter of a century ago'. Science may be the 'true author' of the agencies extending 'our material civilization', but it has also raised the fundamental question: 'Is there, or is there not, a moral order of the world?' To some it seems that 'society is transferring itself to a new basis; ... laying deep down new fundamental principles of order, ... new ideas of human relationship, new principles of political and social constitution.' If this be so, ours is not to 'play the censor' but to 'enlarge our borders'. We must take 'wider and deeper views of God, of Man, of the Bible, and of the Creation' so that we may find 'common ground' with 'the leaders of ... intellectual progress' and address the problem of a moral order in our times.[17]

In his second lecture, 'The Social Revolution', Baldwin Brown recalls the crisis of the Roman Empire in the fourth century AD, which gave birth to modern philosophy in the attempt to 'construct theodicies', justifying the ways of God to man. The events of the nineteenth century are not dissimilar. We have seen the progressive overthrow of feudalism through the instrumentality of 'commerce and war'. The French revolution was the 'death-wound', the advent of Free Trade in 1846 the *coup de grâce*, to a system whose weakness was its resistance to the world's 'inevitable progress' but whose great strength was 'the definite order which it established in society'. For 'the social sorrow of our times is that men do not know their places. . . . All things are in constant flux' and men are filled with 'distress and apprehension'.[18]

During these twenty-five years, the growth of a commercial civilization has widened the breaches and embittered the jealousies and enmities of society. So far from a new order springing up under the aegis of commerce, the world has seen, sadly enough, deepening disorder; stern struggle and fierce hatred of classes; gigantic armaments, tremendous wars, and universal distrust. The knowledge and intercourse which have attended the progress of our commerce, by means of cheap papers, cheap postage, railways, and telegraphs, have stimulated rather than allayed the internal discords and miseries of the great European nations.[19]

And yet 'men have in them a deep instinct for social order'. We may be sure that popular democracy through universal manhood suffrage will not achieve a well-ordered society, let alone the 'universal confiscation' proposed by 'the extreme Reds', whose doctrine must be studied earnestly and met fairly lest it 'grind us to powder before many years have passed over the world'. Nay, we shall only 'escape revolution' as we come to understand those who, by fomenting class hatred, seek a new social order, and as we pursue this end, instead, 'through the rearrangement of the thoughts, feelings, and principles of individual human hearts. It is always the Divine method.'[20]

Baldwin Brown's third lecture, 'The Ecclesiastical Revolution', contains a familiar nonconformist attack on 'the worldly, wealthy, creed-bound, disjointed system of the Establishment', followed by a call for free trade in religion, or laissez-faire, as the prerequisite of a new social order.[21] Then, in the fourth lecture, 'The Theological Revolution', Baldwin Brown returns to that 'remarkable crisis' of the fourth century, when the Augustinian theology was born. 'Man's ... ideas of the Divine order will always be some counterpart of the human order which he sees around him, and which contents him in his day.' The Augustinian theology was suited to the circumstances of its time: the poor and wretched of society stood apart from the circle of the elect, while over all ruled an absolute feudal lord. In our day the 'decline and fall' of the Augustinian theology has accompanied the final collapse of feudalism. With the rise of middle-class civilisation the conviction has grown that 'the relation of God to the world is less fairly set forth by the relation of a king to his subjects, than by that of a father to his household'. 'The transformation is the inevitable result of those new and wonderful phases of development through which, as we have seen, society has passed' since the French Revolution. Now it remains to reconcile the pain and distress present in this 'sad world' with the 'fatherly heart and the fatherly reign of God'. 'The world as well as the Bible is full of dark, sad difficulties,' Baldwin Brown concluded his final lecture; 'theodicies under any conditions are hard.' But the task of reconciliation is 'the problem of the Church of the future'.[22]

The candour, the timeliness, and the scope of Baldwin Brown's lectures clearly suggest that the crisis of the Victorian intelligentsia lay in the making of a new theodicy. But you may well object that I have hardly proved my point. 'Granted that Baldwin Brown was a nonconformist, a liberal, and a representative of the industrial bourgeoisie: he was also a Christian and a prominent divine. What else would you expect but a theodicy from a theist? And what kind of theodicy did you get? A "Church" theodicy of course, not a new naturalistic reconciliation of humanity and the world. Anyway, the theodicy is never spelled out; it appears as a task for the future. Baldwin Brown may have been a member of the intelligentsia but he surely was no alienated intellectual, no professional scientist, no naturalistic thinker.'

In self-defence I might reply: 'Baldwin Brown was in fact a minimal supernaturalist – he stuck at the Resurrection – who sought to make common cause with scientific professionals, naturalistic thinkers, and others now regarded as Victorian intellectuals.[23] During the 1870s his liberal message attracted the young Havelock Ellis, who attended Brixton Independent Church. No fully fledged theodicy emerges from the four lectures, to be sure, but a recognition of the enterprise is surely the first step towards undertaking it. And, in any event, I have only proposed in this chapter to show that the *making* of a new theodicy was central to the crisis-experience of the Victorian intelligentsia. What this theodicy turned out to be in its several shifting dimensions is another matter, although in due course we may receive some general indications. Ideology is always argued out and negotiated among different interest groups within the ruling class, and Baldwin Brown was clearly a member in good standing of that sector of Victorian society.'

I say, I might defend myself in this manner, but I would still not answer the objection that theodices pertain only to theists. Here I require the analysis of Richard Kennington in an essay on the origins of 'modern technological humanitarianism'. Kennington traces modern technological humanitarianism back to the syncretic union of philosophy and politics in the writings of Bacon and Descartes. There knowledge and power join hands to master nature for the amelioration of human existence. The syncretic doctrine, put crudely, comes to this: what's good for science is good for humanity, and politicians can make capital out of it provided they let science get on with the job. That job is mastery of nature. But the problem arises that mastery of nature is never complete, nor does it always appear to conduce towards human good. Therefore Kennington goes on to explain that

> syncretic philosophy cannot take responsibility for the material and spiritual well-being of society without confronting the necessity of society for the over-arching framework of belief which is always, if in varying degree and form, a 'theodicy'. This responsibility is more clearly recognized if we divorce it from the classic theological formulations it received in the biblical tradition. 'Theodicy' in the broad sense here employed means accounting for the relation between goodness and the expectation of happiness, and of evil and misfortune, in terms of human activity and the suprahuman whole, be it nature or history, in which man finds himself.[24]

Kennington states that philosophies of the syncretic type, associated with Leibniz, Kant, Hegel, Marx, and Nietzsche, all 'acknowledge, if in varying forms, the responsibility for theodicy'.[25] I only wish to add that the same responsibility is also acknowledged in Victorian intellectual discourse, although here, as in seventeenth-century philosophy, it is often difficult to distinguish an emerging naturalistic theodicy from the Christian apologetic theodicy it was intended to replace. But when a spokesman such as Baldwin Brown seeks – in his own words – to cultivate 'the leaders of . . . intellectual progress', to find a bulwark against revolution in 'the large number of able men in the foremost ranks of the political and the literary life of our times',[26] we at least know where to look for a new 'over-arching framework of belief' suitable for reconciling social expectations to the realities of a liberalising industrial and imperial social order. It is therefore to the intellectuals who constructed this new theodicy, or 'creed', that I now turn.

III

Judging from the titles of literature dealing with the conventional 'crisis of faith', one would think that Victorian intellectuals lost their faith as the rest of us lose umbrellas. As if faith were some 'thing' that could be lost. As if there were some Victorians who ended up without beliefs. Susan Budd's important article on 'reasons for unbelief' among English secularists, entitled 'The Loss of Faith', is incorporated in her book *Varieties of Unbelief* (1977); Anthony Cockshut's graceful study of English agnostic thought is entitled *The Unbelievers* (1964); and two older essays, 'The Strands of Unbelief' by Noel Annan, and 'Unbelief and Science' by Jacob Bronowski, appear incongruously in a book entitled *Ideas and Beliefs of the Victorians* (1949). The partisan character of this emphasis on non-faith, or unbelief, should be evident from the fact that historically it has represented the viewpoint of the faithful – those who still believe. Vintage titles such as *The Battle of Unbelief* (1878) by Gavin Carlyle and *Unbelief in the Nineteenth Century: A Critical History* (1907) by Henry Sheldon were controversial in tone and apologetic in aim. Contemporary works by so-called 'unbelievers', on the other hand, advertised their authors' positive commitments. Consider just a single theme in titles by late-Victorian intellectuals: *The Foundations of a Creed* (1875) by George Lewes; *The Creed of a Layman* (1907; first used 1881) by Frederic Harrison; and *The Creed of Science* (1881) by William Graham (a title proposed by William Clifford for an edition of his essays that he did not live to prepare[27]). There is of course a sense in which people, like these authors, gradually 'lost their faith' because certain Christian doctrines had ceased to shape their lives.

But in the process, as one fair-minded commentator has observed, 'a faith was slowly forged by which men did shape their lives – the ideals of a humanist, secular, progressive, and scientific age. . . . It was in terms of this newer and confident faith . . . that the truth of revelation was judged.'[28]

Let me pursue the theme of a 'creed' – that 'newer and confident faith' – a little farther. Creeds, we must remember, were in dire straits during the middle decades of the nineteenth century (a period beginning, say, with the publication of Newman's Tract 90 in 1841 and culminating in the Universities Tests Act thirty years later). The basis of Established ideology was being undermined at the same time, and for many of the same reasons, that the institutions in which that ideology had become a material force – an inertial force, I might add – were being pressed to reform. Thus members of the Universities of Oxford and Cambridge were officially obliged to subscribe the Thirty-nine Articles of the Church of England; in 1853 F.D. Maurice, a prominent theologian, lost his job teaching Anglican ordinands at Kings' College, London, because he had publicised his doubts about the morality of eternal punishment, doubts that had driven from the Church morally sensitive persons within his acquaintance, such as John Sterling and Francis Newman. The damnatory clauses of the Athanasian Creed, Maurice declared, 'could not be repeated by any honest or Christian man' unless, in effect, they did not mean what they had always been understood to say.[29] Here, as in most matters, Maurice was before his time. A decade later, not meaning what you said, or not saying what you meant, or just plain trimming, had achieved the sanction of law. The recent flap over the consecration of Professor David Jenkins as Bishop of Durham in York Minster Cathedral, which later inexplicably caught fire, was as nothing compared to the outcry in the early 1860s over the moderate unorthodoxies of the authors of *Essays and Reviews* (1860). Then as now, however, massive petitions and letters to *The Times* failed to stem the tide of events; and successive attempts to defend the Establishment through litigation proved futile. In 1864 'hell was dismissed with costs' by the Judicial Committee of the Privy Council in the appeal of one of the essayists, who had denied the doctrine of eternal punishment, and a Royal Commission was appointed to look into the terms of clerical subscription. The Clerical Subscription Act of 1865 allowed for 'general', rather than 'unfeigned' particular assent to the Thirty-nine Articles. But if one still had scruples, a Clerical Disabilities Bill was in preparation which, on becoming law in 1870, made it possible for the first time for an Anglican clergyman to relieve himself of holy orders. In the same year the Royal Commission on Ritual issued its fourth report, stating that the damnatory clauses of the Athanasian Creed did not, in fact, mean what they said, or what most people had always thought they meant. This gave rise to a controversy that chuntered on in Convocation for several years, an arcane and unedifying dispute, it would seem, until we understand what was at stake.

For the threat of eternal incineration had been a credible deterrent in Victorian Britain. Those who stood in the flickering shadow of hell-fire felt constrained to order and measure their lives in accordance with established moral norms. Hell was also an integral part of a creed or creeds that sanctioned the power and authority of the Establishment.[30] Those who found the deterrent *in*credible – that is, immoral – or who for other reasons could not subscribe the Thirty-nine Articles were officially barred from taking Oxbridge degrees and thus, in effect, deprived of access to certain professions and to positions of social influence. The Universities Tests Act of 1871 relieved everyone in the English universities except ordinands and ordained appointees from the obligation to subscribe. But the problem of collective belief did not end there for dissident intellectuals. Whence public and private morality with the decline of hell? If the creeds could not be upheld by force of law – if, on the contrary, the law were seen to be weakening the basis of official ideology – then what hope for the Establishment? Clearly, the door was open to those who said what they meant and meant what they said, who thought freely and spoke plainly. Their new 'post-Christian intellectual synthesis' would have good claim to furnish the basis of public and private morality. It might become the new creed by which society, under their leadership, should be reformed.[31]

Who were the dissident intellectuals to whom I have referred? How far are we justified in thinking of them not only as reformers, but as specifically religious reformers, constructing a new creed? To what extent may their emerging creed be identified as a new theodicy in the sense established above, an 'over-arching framework of belief' suitable for reconciling social expectations with social realities on the premise that mastery of nature leads to human good?

The intellectuals who sought a new creed in mid-Victorian Britain were mainly the men – especially the young men – to whom Maurice felt a special mission after the untimely death of his intimate friend, Sterling, in 1844. Their increasingly unsuccessful 'struggle' to accept a 'system' of belief that had failed to underwrite real improvements in 'the condition of England' was, according to Maurice, 'more tremendous than any of us know'. Sterling had foreseen in 1840 a 'necessity for a great crisis in the belief in England'.[32] Twenty years later his words had come true. The fears and travails of the hungry forties, followed by the hopes and certainties of a decade set, as it were, in a Crystal Palace, spurred numerous conversions from the other-worldliness of Tractarians and Evangelicals. Froude and Francis Newman, intellectual refugees from Oxford, had searched High and Low for a viable creed. They marked their conversions with spiritual autobiographies published at mid-century. Froude's *Nemesis of Faith* expounded the fundamental perception that society was unjust and the clergy were worse than irrelevant. Religious belief had to give real help to the poor and the suffering; true knowledge had to be 'linked on to humanity', to 'elucidate . . . some of our hard moral mysteries'. Newman, in his *Phases of Faith* (1850), stressed that the clergy were worse than irrelevant because of the immorality of their beliefs. Those who preached that 'the Lord is at hand' and stigmatised politics as a 'worldly' concern thereby 'cut the sinews of all earthly progress'. They declared 'war against Intellect and Imagination, against Industrial and Social Advancement'.[33]

While Froude and Newman, as well as William Rathbone Greg and other allies, remained professing theists, young men who read Carlyle's searing indictments of industrial society passed through what Stephen later called an 'intellectual crisis', akin to a 'religious conversion', that left them without a recognisable belief in God.[34] Inspired to boldness, however, by the heroic spirit of Carlyle's 'natural supernaturalism', convinced that the universe was on their side, they set out to remake society through plain-speaking and righteous deeds. The careers of T.H. Huxley and John Tyndall were cases in point. Other young intellectuals underwent a similar though less dramatic conversion-experience. Frederic Harrison drew inspiration not only from Carlyle, but from Maurice's and Newman's indictment of Christian creeds. 'As the supernatural died out of my view', he wrote of his years as an Oxford undergraduate in the early 1850s, 'the natural took its place and amply covered the same ground. The change was so gradual, and the growth of one phase of thought out of another was with me so perfectly regular, that I have never been able to fix any definite period of change, nor indeed have I ever been conscious of any real change of mind at all.'[35] Harrison's organic metaphor of death and 'growth' was characteristic of the way the dissident intellectuals described their conversion to a fundamental belief in gradualism *per se*, the uniformity and continuity of nature. Stephen, again, whose personal crisis is well known, put it like this: 'The old husk drops off because it has long been withered, and you discover that beneath is a sound and vigorous growth of genuine conviction.'[36]

Years later W.K. Clifford observed that the movement of dissident intellectuals, of which he was by then a leading member, seemed to be 'not mainly an intellectual movement', spurred by destructive new ideas, but a movement that had 'grown out of the strong impulse given to the moral sense by political freedom'.[37] Whatever truth there may be in this organically inspired remark – I am inclined to think there is rather a lot – it is beyond dispute that liberalism, first as an ideology and latterly also as a party political commitment, was the bulwark of the dissident intellectuals in their struggle with Established religious authority. We can trace their skein of associations and alliances, influences and intrigues, from the early 1850s, when the wonders of the Great Exhibition lured them up to London to meet in the home of John Chapman at 142 The Strand. Chapman, a parvenu among publishers, had brought out their latest books: Froude's *Nemesis of Faith*, Newman's *Lectures on Political Economy*

(1851), Greg's *The Creed of Christendom* (1851), and Herbert Spencer's *Social Statics* (1850). His catalogue was a sort of 'index to liberal studies in religion and philosophy'; it had been compiled by a young woman named Marian Evans, now better known as George Eliot. With Eliot as his assistant editor, Chapman undertook to refurbish the old *Westminster Review*, which he had purchased, as a platform for his friends. The journal would advocate progressive 'organic change', wrote Eliot in the Prospectus. It would be 'an exponent of growing thought'. For the editors believed 'that the same fundamental truths are apprehended under a variety of forms, and that, therefore, opposing systems may in the end prove complements of each other'. 'Religion has its foundations in man's nature, and will only discard an old form to assume and vitalize one more expressive of its essence.'[38] The first number of the new *Westminster Review* appeared in 1852. Besides Chapman and Eliot, Froude, Newman, Greg, and Spencer, the contributors that year included George Lewes, George Combe, John Stuart Mill, and James and Harriet Martineau. In 1854 Huxley and Tyndall took charge of the scientific section of the journal. Here were the cream of the 'honest doubters', free-thinking Anglicans and progressive nonconformists, the preachers and the publicists of evolutionary naturalism in Victorian Britain. 'They are amongst the world's vanguard, though not all in the foremost line', Eliot declared. She also used a word, perhaps for the first time, in the sense we understand it today: in 1852 she called Chapman's circle of Westminster Reviewers an 'assemblage of intellectuals'.[39]

The same names crop up repeatedly during the 1850s and 1860s in the controversies now associated most memorably with the so-called Victorian crisis of faith: liberal-minded men and women who supported Darwin, the author of *Essays and Reviews*, Bishop Colenso, the second Reform Bill, disestablishment, and national education. New names also appear beside them in surviving lists of subscribers, petitioners, and members of institutions, lists that bear witness to the networks of power and influence among the Victorian intelligentsia. In 1860 it was a young man on the periphery of the Chapman circle, Frederic Harrison, who electrified the establishment with his analysis of *Essays and Reviews* in the

Westminster Review.[40] Meanwhile an older member, Herbert Spencer, circulated the prospectus for his *System of Synthetic Philosophy*, the leading ideas of which had been canvassed in a series of essays in Chapman's journal. Among the subscribers to Spencer's *opus* were scientists such as W.B. Carpenter, J.D. Hooker, and Edward Frankland.[41] Hooker and Frankland joined Huxley, Tyndall, Spencer, and the younger John Lubbock in 1864 to form the most powerful coterie in late-Victorian science, known to its members as the 'X Club'. One of their first dinner guests was a bishop deposed for mocking Moses with mathematics, John William Colenso. Earlier in the same year Colenso and Huxley had attached their names to an impressive petition in support of the bills to abolish religious tests in the universities. Other signatories were Maurice, James Martineau, Dean Stanley of Westminster, and 'university liberals' such as Stephen, Harrison, Goldwin Smith, and Benjamin Jowett of *Essays and Reviews*. Stephen and Harrison, as well as Smith, who had subscribed to Spencer's *Synthetic Philosophy*, contributed to the famous liberal manifestos published in 1867, *Essays on Reform* and *Questions for a Reformed Parliament*.[42] Two years later they joined another of the contributors, R.H. Hutton, editor of the liberal *Spectator*, in a last-ditch attempt to patch up a consensus among the intelligentsia. Hutton described their organisation as 'a sort of Royal Society of Psychology and Metaphysics, — to contain men of all theologies and schools, — in the hope of leading to some fixed science at last'. The Metaphysical Society, as it became known, met monthly during the parliamentary season, from 1869 to 1880. It enrolled nearly all the dissident intellectuals I have mentioned in this chapter. Maurice, James Martineau, and Dean Stanley were among the earliest members. Rising lights of Liberalism such as Walter Bagehot and John Morley also joined in the polite but fruitless debates with bishops, archbishops, and other Establishment figures.[43] Many of these individuals participated in more strictly political forums: The Century Club, founded in 1866, and its offspring in 1870, the Radical Club, which together eventually expanded into the National Liberal Club in 1882. Elsewhere in clubland the Athenaeum became a safe-house for dissident intellectuals, the internal workings of which, I believe, will one day be shown to have abetted their political intrigues.[44]

IV

If liberal reforms loomed large in the thoughts of those who had renounced the creed of Established Christianity, what evidence is there that they sought to underwrite these reforms with a religious creed of their own? We have already seen that the dissident intellectuals frankly regarded themselves as religious individuals. Religion to them was the living kernel, theology the dying husk that it inevitably outgrew. Husk and kernel, accidents and essence – the root of religion, they believed, lay in the 'deeps of man's nature', in 'enduring instincts which will find expression in one form or another'.[45] The question, therefore, was not whether Victorian Britain would have a religion, but merely how it would be expressed. Religion, after all, was socially respectable; religious people held power that in other hands might be used for greater good. Religion had also been meat and drink to the dissident intellectuals. It had shaped their values, fired their ambitions, and inspired the supreme self-confidence with which they set out to change the world. Now, to use their own word, it would simply take a new 'form'. Most of those who called themselves 'agnostics' had an evangelical background. The X Club was a sort of Clapham Sect *redivivus*. Men such as Harrison and Morley, who lived by Comte's *Catechism of Positive Religion* (1858), had come to intellectual maturity among Oxford Anglo-Catholics. Later these differences in denominational filiation among the dissident intellectuals would lead to open conflicts over the mode in which a new religion should be commended to the nation. But in the fifties and sixties, and into the seventies at least, everyone agreed with Francis Newman that 'the age is ripe for . . . a religion', a religion that would combine the best of Christian ethics with the intellectual rigour of 'the schools of modern science'.[46]

The essential religiosity of the dissident intellectuals can scarcely be over-stressed. Froude believed that God had 'written the tables of His commandments' in natural laws, which clergymen should study 'in the cornfield, in the meadow, in the workshop, at the weaver's loom, in the market-places and the warehouses'. Spencer, whose *Synthetic Philosophy* began with a 'reconciliation' of religion and science, agreed with Froude to this extent, that 'the precepts of the current religion embody that which Biology . . . dictates', and thus 'the inherited and theologically-enforced code . . . has transcendent authority on its side'.[47] Mill called attention to the 'religious duty' of amending the material world, while Stephen urged that the motive for doing so must be shifted to the material world as well. His aim was to 'transform the whole theory' of Christianity 'consistently', to substitute a 'development of natural forces for a Second Advent'. Here Stephen revealed the centrality of evolution to the intellectuals' religious beliefs.[48] 'Trust me,' Tyndall assured the British Association at Liverpool in 1870, 'its existence as a hypothesis is quite compatible with the simultaneous existence of all those virtues to which the term "Christian" has been applied.' Indeed, as a basis of morals, according to Harrison, it came to 'precisely the same thing, whether we say that human nature is adapted to a certain life, or that it was designed by a particular maker to follow that life.' But, unlike conventional theology, evolution held out a real hope for human nature, both individually and at large: adaptation will naturally and inevitably improve. 'The *baneful strife* which *lurketh inborn in us and goeth on the way with us to hurt us*,' wrote Clifford, is a relic of savage life that must surely pass away. Meanwhile, 'by supplying us with a general conception of a good action, in a wider sense than the ethical one,' evolution 'may be made to compensate us for the loss of the immutable and eternal verities.'[49]

Thus ethics and eschatology were transferred to an organic, evolutionary basis, just as the notion of religious truth had been. The religion of science was to be founded on a science of religion. This 'naturalisation' of religious beliefs, as I have called it, which promised material salvation through moral achievement in history, formed the ideological resolution of the Victorian crisis and, as such, marked a profound transformation not only in intellectual culture, but throughout British society. 'Secularisation' is the word now usually applied to this transformation, and I have no objection to the term provided that it is understood as the continuous displacement of one religion, both ideologically and institutionally, with another. For this is precisely how the dissident intellectuals themselves understood the movement of their times. 'New doctrines' based on 'new revelations' were creating a 'new faith' that would proclaim a 'new gospel' for a new social order.[50] To them the process was nothing less than a 'New Reformation'.

The slogan, a 'new Reformation', contained both a taunt and a truth. As controversialists, the dissident intellectuals took every opportunity to point up the ironies of the churches' position in relation to their own. Spencer argued that the dependence of sociology on biology was evident from the First Book of Richard Hooker's *Laws of Ecclesiastical Polity*, the great Elizabethan apologia of the English Church. Hooker's view of individuals in society, he stated, 'needs but better definition and further development to make it truly scientific'.[51] Huxley stressed on various occasions that his own objectionable views were consistent with, or at least theologically no more controversial than, the teachings of Augustine, Erasmus, Calvin, and Bishop Butler. Moreover, Huxley did not begrudge that the Anglican Church as an institution was 'a great and powerful instrument for good or evil'. So engagingly, indeed, did he once describe 'an Established Church which should be a blessing to the community', one which 'no one would seek to disestablish', that his X Club colleague, Lubbock, was pleased to remark that the Church of Huxley did not differ greatly from 'the Church of Arnold and Maurice, Kingsley and Jowett'.[52] It was this ambivalence about the Established Church especially – a coveting of its power and authority coupled with a loathing for its creed, an inclination to reform the institution tempered by an impulse to abolish it – that made the Protestant Reformation a potent metaphor for the dissident intellectuals. For the truth in their slogan, a New Reformation, was that they saw their new religion maintaining continuity with the old; the taunt was that they believed the new religion must be born by means of an intellectual and social transformation not unlike the one in which the Anglican Church had emerged from the Church of Rome.

The proximate source of the slogan may have been the phrenologist George Combe, one of the Chapman circle, who had written as early as 1847 of a 'Second Reformation' to be brought about in Britain through public education in the principles of naturalistic morality.[53] In 1853 Froude adumbrated the slogan in a *Westminster Review* article on the Book of Job. 'The whole question of life and its obligations', he said, 'must again be opened' as it was 'some three centuries' ago in the Protestant struggle with immorality and superstition. To Froude the Reformation was the hinge of modern history; the first four volumes of his *History of England*, completed by 1858, contained an impassioned plea for its principles in the context of an argument for English liberty and freedom of thought.[54] In 1863 Newman took up the argument in the case of Bishop Colenso with an article in the *Westminster Review* entitled 'The Reformation Arrested'. 'Bibliolatry' was 'the critical mistake of the first Reformers', the 'evil legacy' they had left the Church of England. 'A religious Reformation, in the very direction to which Colenso points, is demanded', Newman declared, 'by the most intelligent part of the nation.' Colenso, speaking for himself while under threat of deposition, pointed out coolly that Cranmer, Ridley, and Latimer, although consecrated as bishops of the Roman Church, 'did not *resign* their sees as soon as they became *Protestant* bishops'. Anglicans, having based their church structure on one reformation, had no right to declare *a priori* that there should never be another.[55]

The risk attendant on justifying oneself by appeal to the example of three bishops who, in the event, were burned as heretics, was negligible by the mid-sixties. The 'Church of the Future', as Newman called it, had been born. A new faith was rising, phoenix-like, from the ashes of the old faith that had spent itself pursuing the likes of Colenso and the authors of *Essays and Reviews*.[56] Within the Establishment, the Church of the Future and its new faith were weakly represented by clergymen such as Maurice and Stanley. In 1865 Maurice looked to 'a reformation more complete by far than that of the sixteenth century'; Stanley likewise had no doubt at the time that a 'new' or 'second Reformation' was being prepared by 'the various tendencies of the age'.[57] But it remained for their colleague in the Metaphysical Society, whose notion of a viable Establishment, according to Lubbock, fairly resembled their own – it remained for that preacher of 'lay sermons' and self-consecrated 'bishop' of the 'Church scientific', T.H. Huxley, to press the cause of a New Reformation throughout a public career of more than thirty years. From his announcement of the theme in 1860 at the Royal Institution to his extended analysis of Protestant principles in his 'Prologue' to *Essays on Some Controverted Questions* in 1892, Huxley maintained that 'a reformation ... is waiting to come', a 'wider and deeper change than that effected three centuries ago', or rather, he explained, 'a continuation of that movement'. If only people would live in accordance with 'that agnostic confession' that makes it immoral to profess knowledge of what cannot be known, this 'approximation to the millennium' would arrive.[58]

Huxley's 'agnostic confession' never amounted to a 'creed' after the manner of the Thirty-nine Articles. Mindful of Carlyle's sardonic verse,

> The Builder of this universe was wise
>   He formed all souls, all systems, planets, particles;
> The plan he formed his worlds and Aenons by,
>   Was – Heavens! – was thy small nine-and-thirty-articles![59]

his followers were perhaps disinclined to enumerate their beliefs. When Samuel Laing, the agnostic railway entrepreneur, set down eight agnostic articles to oblige Gladstone, Huxley denied publicly that agnosticism was a creed. If a creed were to be compulsory, he preferred that of St Athanasius, of the meaning of which, he said, 'I have on the whole a clearer conception'.[60] Yet Froude, the devoted biographer of Carlyle, spoke repeatedly of Carlyle's 'Creed' and its influence upon himself and his contemporaries, such as Huxley. And little wonder. These young men and women, who by upbringing had been habituated to a creed as a vigorous summary of collective belief, who had once recited a creed as an 'act of intellectual adoration', could scarcely have used a better word for those 'other forms' of collective belief arising, as Froude put it, from where the 'roots' of the old creed were 'cut away'.[61] To call one's new convictions a creed was to pay them a compliment. A creed united its adherents;

it represented their most deeply felt convictions. To some, *pace* Huxley, it was a moral necessity. Besides, according to the dissident intellectuals, their old and new convictions were organically linked. To call the new convictions a creed signified that the religious instinct underlying them remained unchanged. For just as the 'old creed' was 'adapted ... to the wants of its believers', so, it was said, a 'new creed' would be adapted to 'new social and individual requirements'. The old was 'decaying', the new 'growing' in its place. Society must decide, wrote Stephen, recalling to us his own personal crisis, 'which creed ... favours the faith which is the other side of energetic conduct'? Which gives the 'clearest rules' by which to 'regulate our lives'?[62] For rigour and candour of reply, none excelled the high churchmen among the dissident intellectuals, the followers of Auguste Comte. In the five dropsical volumes of his *Problems of Life and Mind* (1874–9) Lewes laid the 'foundations of a creed' that would 'condense our knowledge, guide our researches, and shape our lives', a creed based on the principles of scientific method. Morley, in his famous essay *On Compromise* (1874), foresaw that 'a new creed by which men can live, ... an expansion, a development, a re-adaptation, of all the moral and spiritual truth that lay hidden under the worn-out forms', would one day be built by 'science'. 'Nothing but such a basis', wrote Harrison, 'can satisfy the mind of the inquirer or give coherence to the social body.'[63]

V

Stripped of its magisterium and its liturgy, its catechism and its saints, the 'creed' of the Positivists was fundamentally the creed of the dissident intellectuals at large. A low church or nonconformist formulary would impart 'coherence to the social body' just as well. In Catholic France, Comte had proposed to 'recommence on a better intellectual and social basis the great effort of Catholicism, to bring Western Europe to a social system of peaceful activity and intellectual culture, in which Thought and Action should be subordinated to universal Love'.[64] In Protestant Britain the dissident intellectuals proposed, more simply, to recommence on a better intellectual and social basis the great effort of the Protestant Reformation to bring about a social system of personal morality and intellectual freedom. In France the chief inspiration of Comte's proposal had been the revolution of 1848, which ushered in history's 'positive' phase with the proclamation of a Republic. In Britain the dissident intellectuals were similarly inspired by the liberalising tendencies evoked by Chartism and the Anti Corn Law League, which commenced in 1846 with the advent of Free Trade. On either hand, in France and in Britain, among Positivists and dissident intellectuals alike, the emphasis in their social prescriptions fell on continuity, moral authority, and progress. The best aspirations of an earlier religious tradition, they believed, would be better fulfilled by a new 'priesthood' – the term was Francis Galton's as well as Comte's – who would place progress on a 'better intellectual and social basis' with the creed of scientific naturalism.[65]

The Positivist motto, 'order and progress', summed up the theodicy inherent in the naturalistic creed better than the indigenous British slogan, a 'New Reformation'. Progress, according to the dissident intellectuals, was merely the natural order at work – witness the technological triumphs that impressed Baldwin Brown – and the natural order throughout the living world, of which society was a part, maintained itself through uniform continuous growth. In reality, therefore, social relations were neither contractual nor conflictive, but vital and organic. 'The whole complex frame of society', Froude declared, 'is a meshwork of duty woven of living fibre, and the condition of its remaining sound is, that every thread of its own free energy shall do what it ought.' Spencer, whose article, 'The Social Organism', in the *Westminster Review* for 1860 spelled out the organic doctrine in minute detail, spent the rest of his life developing its ethical implications. This doctrine, which lay at the basis of Comte's sociology, also furnished the premise of the dissident intellectuals' commitment to liberal reform.[66] *Natura non facit saltum* – Nature makes no leaps: society must change gradually. *Natura nihil agit frustra* – Nature does nothing in vain: society grants to each his appointed task. Gradualism and functionalism in the new theodicy replaced the static teleology of the old. And if the old theodicy had spared industrial

Britain Tennyson's 'red fool-fury of the Seine', then in a day when the Paris sky again glowed red, as the communards wreaked revenge, the theodicy of a New Reformation could promise nothing less. 'We have been to the brink of the volcano', wrote Stephen of his forebears, 'and we did not like the glimpses we caught of the seething masses of inflammatory matter at the bottom. The effect was fairly to startle us back into any old creed which led to less disastrous results.' Just 'any old creed', however, did not suffice, for in order 'that a creed may be permanent it must satisfy the intellect'. Among the generation of dissident intellectuals, the new creed of scientific naturalism filled the bill. W.R. Grove, whose doctrines of the correlation and the continuity of physical forces buttressed the naturalistic creed, spoke their mind when he reminded the British Association that revolutionary ideas and *a priori* reasoning 'are far more unsound and give us far less ground for improvement of the race than the study of the gradual progressive changes arising from changed circumstances, changed wants, changed habits. Our language, our social institutions, our laws, the constitution of which we are proud, are the growth of time, the product of slow adaptations, resulting from continuous struggles. Happily in this country practical experience has taught us to improve rather than to remodel; we follow the law of nature and avoid cataclysms.'[67]

But in asserting that a counter-revolutionary creed must 'satisfy the intellect' if it is to be 'permanent', Stephen also recognised that the first impulse towards its acceptance 'comes from the passions'. 'Therefore,' he said, 'a revival of belief may be due much more to a change in social conditions than to any process of logical conviction.' Stephen wrote better than he knew. The 'revival of belief' in which he participated, whatever permanence it derived from the 'intellect' and 'logical conviction', owed its existence fundamentally, I submit, to a 'change in social conditions' in Victorian Britain. Scientific naturalism was the creed of a movement, as Clifford put it, that had 'grown out of the strong impulse given to the moral sense by political freedom'. The theodicy of the dissident intellectuals was related organically to the social crisis of their times.[68]

NOTES

1. *The Post-Darwinian Controversies: A Study of the Protestant Struggle to Come to Terms with Darwin in Great Britain and America, 1870–1900* (Cambridge, 1979) 12–16, 346–52; 'Creation and the Problem of Charles Darwin', *British Journal for the History of Science*, 14 (1981) 189–200; '1859 and All That: Remaking the Story of Evolution-and-Religion', in *Charles Darwin, 1809–1882: A Centennial Commemorative*, ed. Roger G. Chapman and Cleveland T. Duval (Wellington, NZ, 1982) 167–94; 'Geologists and Interpreters of Genesis in the Nineteenth Century', in *God and Nature: A History of the Encounter between Christianity and Science*, ed. David C. Lindberg and Ronald L. Numbers (Berkeley, Calif., 1986).

2. The case for this view is developed by Frank M. Turner, 'The Victorian Conflict between Science and Religion: A Professional Dimension', *Isis*, 69 (1978) 356–76.

3. Maurice Mandelbaum, *History, Man, and Reason: A Study in Nineteenth-Century Thought* (Baltimore, Md, 1971) 30.

4. See Robert M. Young, 'The Historiographic and Ideological Contexts of the Nineteenth-Century Debate on Man's Place in Nature', in *Changing Perspectives in the History of Science: Essays in Honour of Joseph Needham*, ed. Mikuláš Teich and Robert Young (London, 1973) 344–438, and 'The Naturalization of Value Systems in the Human Sciences', in *Problems in the Biological and Human Sciences*, by Michael Bartholomew, *et al.* (Milton Keynes, Bucks., 1981) 63–110; and Sheridan Gilley and Ann Loades, 'Thomas Henry Huxley: The War between Science and Religion', *Journal of Religion*, 61 (1981) 289.

5. J.A. Froude, *The Nemesis of Faith* (London, 1849) 95; Thomas H. Huxley, 'Prologue' (1892) *Collected Essays*, 5 vols (London, 1893–4) 5: 54–5.

6. Robert Chambers, *Vestiges of the Natural History of Creation* (1844; Leicester, 1969) 385.

7. [J.R. Seeley,] *Natural Religion* (1882) 3rd edn. (London, 1891) 61–2; Leslie Stephen, 'An Agnostic's Apology' (1876), *An Agnostic's Apology, and Other Essays* (1893) 2nd edn (London, 1903) 21, 39.

8. [David Brewster,] 'Railway Accidents', *North British Review*, 34 (1861) 400.

9. [W.S. Lilly,] 'Railway Accidents', *Quarterly Review*, 145 (1878) 165, 170.

10. For typical statements of the older theodicy, see Warren Burton, *Cheering Views of Man and Providence Drawn from a Consideration of the Origin, Uses, and Remedies of Evil* (Boston, Mass., 1832), and James McCosh, *The Method of the Divine Government, Physical and Moral* (Edinburgh, 1850). For the old and the new at work side-by-side, cf. [James Hinton,] *The Mystery of Pain: A Book for the Sorrowing* (London, 1866), with I. Burney Yeo, 'Why Is Pain a Mystery?', *Contemporary Review*, 35 (1879) 630–47; and see also J.S. Blackie, 'The Utilization of Evil', *Good Words*, 20 (1879) 770–5; George A. Gordon, *Immortality and the New Theodicy* (Boston, 1897); and the two series of Gifford

Lectures by Alexander Balmain Bruce, *The Providential Order of the World* (London, 1897) and *The Moral Order of the World* (London, 1899). On views in the Church of England, see Jennifer Hart's synthetic study of over 200 sermons and pamphlets published from about 1830 to 1880, 'Religion and Social Control in the Mid-Nineteenth Century', in *Social Control in Nineteenth Century Britain*, ed. A.P. Donajgrodzki (London, 1977) 108–37. There is considerable indirect evidence of Anglican and nonconformist attitudes in Eileen Yeo, 'Christianity in Chartist Struggle, 1838–1842', *Past and Present*, no. 91 (1981) 109–39. For Scotland, see John F. McCaffrey, 'Thomas Chalmers and Social Change', *Scottish Historical Review*, 60 (1981) 32–60. Among American interpretations of evil that were read and reviewed on the opposite side of the Atlantic, the transitional views of Ralph Waldo Emerson had a wide impact. See Peter A. Obuchowski, 'Emerson, Evolution, and the Problem of Evil', *Harvard Theological Review*, 72 (1979) 150–6. Charles D. Cashdollar concludes in 'The Social Implications of the Doctrine of Divine Providence: A Nineteenth-Century Debate in American Theology', *Harvard Theological Review*, 71 (1978) 265–84: 'The providential theory worked as a sort of practical theodicy for the conservatives. Essentially, they saw the socio-economic order as God-ordained, a perfectly composed "preceptive" moral order operating to the benefit of man. Social evils were disciplinary or punitive actions which served the ultimate good' (274). For the natural history context, cf. Frank N. Egerton, 'Changing Concepts of the Balance of Nature', *Quarterly Review of Biology*, 48 (1973) 322–50, with parallel discussions in A.L. Loades, 'Analogy, and the Indictment of the Deity: Some Interrelated Themes', *Studia Theologica*, 33 (1979) 25–43.

11.   See D.L. LeMahieu, 'Malthus and the Theology of Scarcity', *Journal of the History of Ideas*, 40 (1979) 467–74; Edwin N. Santurri, 'Theodicy and Social Policy in Malthus' Thought', *Journal of the History of Ideas*, 43 (1982) 315–30; Maxine Berg, *The Machinery Question and the Making of Political Economy, 1815–1848* (Cambridge, 1980); David de Giustino, *Conquest of Mind: Phrenology and Victorian Social Thought* (London, 1975); and Roger Cooter, *The Cultural Meaning of Popular Science: Phrenology and the Organization of Consent in Nineteenth Century Britain* (Cambridge, 1984).

12.   John Blakely, *The Theology of Inventions; or, Manifestations of Deity in the Works of Art* (New York, 1856) 94–5.

13.   John F.W. Herschel, 'About Volcanos and Earthquakes', *Familiar Lectures on Scientific Subjects* (London, 1867) 2–3.

14.   Lilly, 'Railway Accidents', 173, 180.

15.   Robert Gray, 'Bourgeois Hegemony in Victorian Britain', in *The Communist University of London: Papers on Class, Hegemony, and Party*, ed. Jon Bloomfield (London, 1977) 78.

16.   Jeffrey Cox, *The English Churches in a Secular Society: Lambeth, 1870–1930* (New York, 1983) 112.

17.   J. Baldwin Brown, *First Principles of Ecclesiastical Truth: Essays on the*

Church and Society (London, 1871) 219, 221, 222–4, 225, 234, 243, 250.

18. ibid., 257, 272, 273, 276, 278, 279.
19. ibid., 283.
20. ibid., 279, 286–7, 289, 293, 294.
21. ibid., 321, 324, 325.
22. ibid., 349, 350, 353, 354, 355, 364.
23. Here I distinguish between the 'intelligentsia' as genteel men and women of letters and the 'intellectuals', whose emergence at mid-century within the intelligentsia as relatively alienated commentators on national life marked 'the splintering of earlier Victorian cultural cohesion' (T.W. Heyck, *The Transformation of Intellectual Life in Victorian England* [London, 1982] 15 and *passim*).
24. Richard Kennington, 'Descartes and Mastery of Nature', in *Organism, Medicine, and Metaphysics: Essays in Honor of Hans Jonas on His 75th Birthday, May 10, 1978*, ed. Stuart F. Spicker (Dordrecht, Holland, 1978) 221–2.
25. Ernest Becker makes a similar point in *The Structure of Evil: An Essay on the Unification of the Science of Man* (New York, 1968), where he refers to the new 'secular' theodicy of the Enlightenment and after as an 'anthropodicy' (18). See the overview in Leroy E. Loemaker, 'Theodicy', in *Dictionary of the History of Ideas: Studies of Selected Pivotal Ideas*, ed. Philip P. Wiener, 5 vols (New York, 1973–4) 4: 378–84.
26. Brown, *First Principles*, 250, 293.
27. William Kingdon Clifford, *Lectures and Essays*, ed. Leslie Stephen and Frederick Pollock, 2 vols (London, 1879) 1: 71–2.
28. Olive Brose, 'F.D. Maurice and the Victorian Crisis of Belief', *Victorian Studies*, 3 (1959–60) 228.
29. Frederick Denison Maurice, *Theological Essays* (1853) 4th edn (London, 1881) 410.
30. Geoffrey Rowell, *Hell and the Victorians: A Study of Nineteenth-Century Theological Controversies Concerning Eternal Punishment and the Future Life* (Oxford, 1974) 123.
31. Frank M. Turner and Jeffrey von Arx, 'Victorian Ethics of Belief: A Reconsideration', in *The Secular Mind: Transformations of Faith in Modern Europe; Essays Presented to Franklin L. Baumer, Randolph W. Townsend Professor of History, Yale University*, ed. W. Warren Wagar (New York, 1982) 94–5. See also James C. Livingston, *The Ethics of Belief: An Essay on the Victorian Religious Conscience* (Tallahassee, Fla, 1974).
32. Brose, 'F.D. Maurice', 230; Maurice, *Theological Essays*, 237.
33. Froude, *Nemesis of Faith*, 86; Francis William Newman, *Phases of Faith; or, Passages from the History of My Creed* (1850) new edn (London, 1865) 135.
34. Stephen, quoted in Christopher Harvie, *The Lights of Liberalism: University Liberals and the Challenge of Democracy, 1860–86* (London, 1976) 38.
35. Frederic Harrison, 'My Memories – 1837–1890', *Memories and Thoughts: Men – Books – Cities – Art* (London, 1906) 9.

36. Leslie Stephen, 'An Apology for Plainspeaking', *Essays in Freethinking and Plainspeaking* (1873) new edn (London, 1907) 375.

37. Clifford, 'The Influence upon Morality of a Decline in Religious Belief' (1877) *Lectures and Essays*, 2: 250.

38. Gordon S. Haight, *George Eliot and John Chapman, with Chapman's Diaries*, 2nd edn (Hamden, Conn., 1969) 20, 32, 33, 42.

39. M. Evans, 1852, in Haight, *George Eliot and John Chapman*, 60; Eliot, 1852, quoted in Heyck, *Transformation of Intellectual Life*, 17. For the parallel movements among liberal Anglicans and nonconformists, see Ieuan Ellis, *Seven against Christ: A Study of 'Essays and Reviews'* (Leiden, 1980) ch. 1, and Dennis G. Wigmore-Beddoes, *Yesterday's Radicals: A Study of the Affinity between Unitarianism and Broad Church Anglicanism in the Nineteenth Century* (Cambridge, 1971).

40. Frederic Harrison, 'Apologia pro Fide Mea', *The Creed of a Layman: Apologia pro Fide Mea* (London, 1907) 23, 28; see 95–157 for his review, 'Septem contra Fidem', originally published as 'Neo-Christianity'.

41. Herbert Spencer, 'A System of Philosophy', *An Autobiography*, 2 vols (London, 1904) 2: 484.

42. Harvie, *Lights of Liberalism*, chs 2, 7.

43. R.H. Hutton to J. Lubbock, 1 July 1869, in Horace G. Hutchinson, *Life of Sir John Lubbock, Lord Avebury*, 2 vols (London, 1914) 1: 101. A number of members had joined in support of *The Reader*, a 'Review of Literature, Science, and the Arts', which attempted to represent a kind of high-level consensus among the intelligentsia from 1863 until its demise in 1867. '*The Reader*', writes David A. Roos, 'offers abundant evidence that Huxley and other admittedly "unorthodox" men of science were in fact still struggling to maintain a broad, public intellectual context that would replace the faltering natural theology of earlier generations and transcend any divisive "professional" points of view' ('The Aims and Intentions of "Nature"', in *Victorian Science and Victorian Values: Literary Perspectives*, ed. James Paradis and Thomas Postlewait, *Annals of the New York Academy of Sciences*, 360 [1981] 164). See Robert M. Young, 'Natural Theology, Victorian Periodicals, and the Fragmentation of a Common Context', in *Darwin to Einstein: Historical Studies on Science and Belief*, ed. Colin Chant and John Fauvel (London, 1980) 69–107.

44. Harvie, *Lights of Liberalism*, chs 5, 6.

45. T.H. Huxley, quoted in Bernard Lightman, 'Pope Huxley and the Church Agnostic: The Religion of Science', *Historical Papers* (1983) 158; Stephen, 'Religion as a Fine Art' (1872) *Essays*, 81.

46. Newman, *Phases of Faith*, 175.

47. Froude, *Nemesis of Faith*, 42; Herbert Spencer, *The Study of Sociology* (1873) 14th edn (London, 1889) 306, 350.

·48. John Stuart Mill, 'Nature', (*c.* 1850–8), *Nature, The Utility of Religion, and Theism* (1874) 4th edn (London, 1875) 26; Stephen, 'Darwinism and Divinity' (1873) *Essays*, 123; Stephen, 'The Scepticism of Believers' (1877) *Agnostic's Apology*, 82.

49. John Tyndall, 'Scientific Use of the Imagination' (1870) *Fragments of*

Science: A Series of Detached Essays, Addresses, and Reviews (1879) 6th edn, 2 vols (New York, 1899) 2: 133; Harrison, 'The Basis of Morals', *The Philosophy of Common Sense* (London, 1907) 147; Clifford, 'Cosmic Emotion' (1877) *Lectures and Essays*, 2: 274.

50. Stephen, 'Religion as a Fine Art', *Essays*, 82; Clifford (1870), quoted in Frederick Pollock, 'Introduction', in Clifford, *Lectures and Essays*, 37; Stephen, 'Apology for Plainspeaking', *Essays*, 388; Tyndall, 'Apology for the Belfast Address' (1874) *Fragments of Science*, 2: 220; Tyndall, 'The Sabbath' (1880) *New Fragments* (1892) 3rd edn (New York, 1900) 45.

51. Spencer, *Study of Sociology*, 327.

52. Huxley to C. Kingsley, 23 September 1860, in Leonard Huxley, *Life and Letters of Thomas Henry Huxley*, 2 vols (London, 1900) 1: 221; Huxley, 'Administrative Nihilism' (1871) *Collected Essays*, 1: 284; John Lubbock, *The Use of Life* (London, 1894) 223.

53. Ruth Barton, 'Evolution: The Whitworth Gun in Huxley's War for the Liberation of Science from Theology', in *The Wider Domain of Evolutionary Thought*, ed. David Oldroyd and Ian Langham (Dordrecht, Holland, 1983) 286, n. 122; de Giustino, *Conquest of Mind*, 128–9.

54. [James Anthony Froude,] 'The Book of Job', *Westminster Review*, NS 4 (October 1853) 444.

55. [Francis Newman,] 'The Reformation Arrested', *Westminster Review*, NS 23 (April 1863) 392, 393; Colenso, quoted in A.O.J. Cockshut, *Anglican Attitudes: A Study of Victorian Religious Controversies* (London, 1959) 100.

56. Newman, 'Reformation Arrested', 393. The 'phoenix' metaphor appears in Froude, 'Book of Job', 421.

57. F.D. Maurice, *The Conflict of Good and Evil in Our Day: Twelve Letters to a Missionary* (London, 1865) 171; A.P. Stanley to J.C. Shairp, 1865, in Rowland E. Prothero, *The Life and Correspondence of Arthur Penrhyn Stanley, D.D., Late Dean of Westminster*, 2 vols (London, 1893) 2: 239 (cf. 238); A.P. Stanley, 'The Theology of the Nineteenth Century', *Fraser's Magazine*, 71 (February 1865) 252–68.

58. Thomas Henry Huxley, 'Species and Their Origin' (1860), in *The Scientific Memoirs of Thomas Henry Huxley*, ed. Michael Foster and E. Ray Lankester, 4 vols (London, 1898–1902) 2: 393; Huxley, 'Universities Actual and Ideal' (1874) *Collected Essays*, 3: 191–2; Huxley to his wife, H.H. Huxley, 8 August 1873, in L. Huxley, *Life and Letters of T.H. Huxley*, 1: 397; Huxley, 'Prologue', *Collected Essays*, 5: 40.

59. Carlyle, quoted in Tyndall, 'Matter and Force' (1867) *Fragments of Science*, 2: 74.

60. Huxley, 'Agnosticism' (1881) *Collected Essays*, 5: 245, cf. 310 and S. Laing, *Modern Science and Modern Thought* (London, 1895) 282–3, 286–7. Cf. Huxley's *confessio fidei* in 'An Apologetic Irenicon', *Fortnightly Review*, NS 52 (1 November 1892) 557–71.

61. John Tulloch, 'Thomas Carlyle as a Religious Teacher', *Movements of Religious Thought in Britain during the Nineteenth Century: Being the Fifth Series of St. Giles' Lectures* (London, 1885) 196–7; Richard Holt

Hutton, 'Creeds and Worship' (1870) *Aspects of Religious and Scientific Thought* (London, 1899) 5; Froude, *Nemesis of Faith*, 33; William Kirkus, 'Morality and Creeds', *Theological Review*, 4 (1867) 541.

62. Stephen, 'Apology for Plainspeaking', *Essays*, 406; Spencer, *Autobiography*, 2: 468; Stephen, 'Agnostic's Apology', *Agnostic's Apology*, 10; Stephen, 'Scepticism of Believers', *Agnostic's Apology*, 51. See Kingsbury Badger, 'Christianity and Victorian Religious Confessions', *Modern Language Quarterly*, 25 (1964) 86–101.

63. George Henry Lewes, *Problems of Life and Mind*, 4 vols (1874–9) vols 1–2, First Series: *The Foundations of a Creed* (London, 1874–5) 1:2; John Morley, *On Compromise* (1874) 2nd edn rev. (London, 1877) 125; Harrison, 'Septem contra Fidem' (1860) *Creed of a Layman*, 151.

64. Auguste Comte, *A General View of Positivism* (1865) trans. J.H. Bridges, 2nd edn (London, 1880) 67.

65. ibid., 268, 280; Francis Galton, *English Men of Science: Their Nature and Nurture* (London, 1874) 260.

66. Froude, 'Book of Job', 448; Herbert Spencer, 'The Social Organism', *Westminster Review*, NS 17 (January 1860) 90–121.

67. Stephen, 'Are We Christians?' (1873) *Essays*, 145, 147; W.R. Grove, 'Address of William Robert Grove, Esq., President of the British Association for the Advancement of Science, Nottingham, 1866', *On the Correlation of Physical Forces . . . Followed by A Discourse on Continuity* (1843) 5th edn (London, 1867) 346.

68. Stephen, 'Are We Christians?' *Essays*, 147; Clifford, 'Influence upon Morality', *Lectures and Essays*, 2: 250.

6 W.R. Greg: A Manchester Creed

Richard J. Helmstadter

As if to remind his readers that his was not a voice crying in the wilderness, W.R. Greg prefaced *The Creed of Christendom*, which Chapman published in 1851, with a few lines on faith and doubt written by famous contemporaries. He included Coleridge's comment that 'even with regard to Christianity itself, like certain plants, I creep towards the light, even though it draw me away from the more nourishing warmth'. And from *In Memoriam* he took the optimistic assertion, 'There lives more faith in honest doubt, Believe me, than in half the creeds'. We no longer need reminding now, that in mid-nineteenth-century England, at least among men and women of letters, many were perplexed with doubts about the fundamental truths of Christianity, and many fell away from Christian orthodoxy. The themes of childhood faith abandoned and saints once dear, now lost, were commonplace among the literary élite at that time. Within this group there seems to have been a widespread crisis of faith, a crisis that was, for some, highly personal, deeply felt, and marked by anguish. W.R. Greg was not among that number.

Man of letters though he was, Greg's outlook on the world was that of a provincial manufacturer, a cotton spinner whose social and intellectual vision was conditioned by the life of Manchester business circles at the time of the Anti Corn Law League.[1] It is, in a sense, misleading to refer to a crisis of faith in connection with Greg if that term is taken to mean a critical phase in personal spirituality. Greg experienced no dramatic conversion to unbelief. He suffered no pangs of anxious uncertainty. Like his contemporaries in the Anti Corn Law League, he inclined much more towards dogmatism than towards doubt. He rejected Christianity as he rejected aristocratic tradition, the corn laws, and the unreformed constitution. He embraced political economy, utilitarian morality, and the liberal idea of progress. Greg's qualifications for inclusion in a study of faith in crisis are found in his interweaving of fundamental religious, political and cultural ideas and assumptions. His attitudes were shaped at a time when the traditional structures of English society and politics were under powerful attack from new powers that were emerging through industrialisation and the growth of democracy.

Greg himself was keenly aware, especially in the two decades following the Reform Act of 1832, that he lived at a time of grand political crisis. For him, as for many nonconformists, that political crisis had profound religious implications. A new, energetic, rational and industrial England confronted a still powerful aristocracy whose hold on governing institutions and governing beliefs seemed to be weakening. The Church of England, emblem of tradition in so many ways, seemed vulnerable to the tides that were sweeping away the crumbling institutions of the past. Raised as a Unitarian, on the radical, rationalist wing of nonconformity, Greg included Christian orthodoxy along with the Church in his vision of the benighted past. At the beginning of his writing career, Greg was an enthusiastic soldier in the army of political progress. His major contribution to the warfare of modernity with tradition was his attack on conventional faith, a faith he associated with an effete and outworn aristocracy. *The Creed of Christendom*, his first book, provided him the occasion to articulate in religious terms that general orientation towards material progress and scientific rationalism that is associated with the emergence of industrial society. He saw the crisis of his age as essentially political. His views of every aspect of life were coloured by his political commitment. For him, the attack on Christianity was a political act.

In spite of his clear and unmistakable rejection of much that he himself considered central to Christianity, Greg found that Christian tradition retained a hold on him. While he attacked the general thrust of Christ's moral teaching, he professed admiration for Christ's moral being. While he argued that all which lay beyond the realm of reason belonged to the world of superstition, he continued to find comfort in prayer and solace in the hope for life after death. Ironically, Greg's emotional attachment to a minimal remnant of conventional religiosity helped keep him in touch with the mainstream of mid-Victorian culture and made it possible for him to be a popular journalist. The world of letters gave him the platform from which he preached his version of the Manchester creed.

In *The Creed of Christendom* Greg applied the methods of German historical criticism to both the Old Testament and the New, and he wrote plainly enough to make the book accessible to a broad audience. This work sold steadily throughout the nineteenth century, reaching seventeen editions before the first world war. John Morley accounted Greg's *Creed* an important part of that dissolvent literature which attacked the traditional status of biblical authority, and he commented on the impact it had among Oxford undergraduates at the time he was up at Lincoln College.[2] *The Creed of Christendom*, Greg's only book that was not a collection of essays, is now almost entirely forgotten. It is left out of most accounts of the rise of biblical criticism in England, and it has been entirely ignored by those who seek to unravel the nature of mid-Victorian scepticism.

To some extent the current obscurity of Greg's book results from the character of the work itself. Greg announced no original critical or historical discoveries in *The Creed of Christendom*. As far as scholarship goes, the book was derived from the Germans. Nor did Greg attempt any original interpretive theories in *The Creed*, or any thoughtful discussion of the place of the Bible in the Christian tradition. Greg's work is deceptively simple; it rests, apparently, on the surface of its subject. It has not proved an attractive source for those who would study Victorian religiosity and its critics. Greg, no doubt, deserves more footnotes in the study of biblical criticism in Victorian England. In so far as that study is concerned with the advance of scholarship, however, or with the way that scholarship was received by the most intellectually sophisticated men and women of the time, he deserves no more than footnotes. For the popular reception of biblical criticism, and for the growth of popular scepticism generally, he deserves a great deal more, not so much for his influence as for the complex of attitudes that he reflects.

Greg reflects the Manchester man's crisis of faith at the time when liberal hopes ran high, when the constitution had just been reformed, free trade just achieved, and the era of triumphant reason and industry seemed at hand. The men and women whose views he helped to articulate, were of his own social class and his own time in history. He made no effort to appeal beyond those boundaries, and in this limita- tion lies a great deal of his interest for historians. It is an interesting feature of Greg's career that his writings were always received with respect. He wrote a great deal, mostly essays for the great and near-great periodicals, many of which were reviewed when collected and published in books. His contemporaries found much to criticise in his particular views of social, political, economic, and theological issues. But no reviewer approached his work in a spirit of hostility. Greg's lucidity, his transparent sincerity, his honest good will, and his appearance of plain commonsense were qualities that his reviewers noticed and appreciated. Along with his limited imagination, these qualities helped make him seem a spokes- man for his time. A.V. Dicey, who had kind words in *The Nation* for Greg's 'outspokenness and common sense', sug- gests that Greg's work 'gives us information as to the beliefs of a whole host of persons. It is almost certain that the same feelings which consciously influence a thinker of ability, unconsciously and indirectly weigh with persons who have never, even to themselves, put their thoughts into the form of a definite creed. We cannot doubt for a moment that [Mr Greg's views] are the views of thousands whose sentiments are not fairly represented by the dogmas of confident orthodoxy or by the dogmas of equally confident heterodoxy.'[3]

Along with Greg's passion and gift for clarity went a natural bent towards coherence. His many articles dealt with a wide variety of subjects, with a range of political, social, religious, and literary questions of the day. It is, of course, a sign of Greg's limitations as well as a sign of strong- mindedness, that his various views on many different issues form a coherent mosaic in which the parts clearly interrelate. Not only did he approach each of his subjects in the same spirit of calm rationality; he saw, as well, that each of his subjects constituted but a part of a larger cultural whole. He had a strong sense of the unity of his culture, and he believed that every aspect of that culture was subject to the same principles of analysis and criticism. 'He applies to religious problems', wrote Dicey, 'exactly the same qualities which he brings to the solution of social enigmas.'[4]

W.R. Greg is a useful subject for a case study in how ideas about a number of major public issues of the mid-nineteenth century were related to and affected ideas about religion. This is not to suggest that Greg was a typical Victorian, still less that he constitutes a microcosm of Victorian opinion. But his ideas, and the ways his ideas interrelate with each other, must be accorded some representative value. Unless his ideas called forth echoes from his readers, largely, one suspects, well-to-do middle-class readers, Greg could not have gone on writing for the periodical press. From 1851 until his death thirty years later, Greg never lacked takers for his prodigious output of essays. The first three volumes of *The Wellesley Index of Victorian Periodicals* identify 158 essays by Greg, scattered among ten different reviews: the *Edinburgh*, the *Quarterly*, the *Westminster*, the *Fortnightly*, *Fraser's*, the *National*, the *Cornhill*, *Nineteenth Century*, the *Contemporary*, and the *North British*. This is only a portion of his output. Incomplete as it is, this range of periodicals lends force to John Morley's comment: 'Mr. Greg is not one of the thinkers we can place in any school, still less in any party.'[5] Eight separate collections of his essays were published during his lifetime or just after, most of them by Trübner, and some of these sold very well indeed. Twenty editions of *Enigmas of Life*, which first appeared in 1873, are identified in the *National Union Catalog*. This publishing record demonstrates a willing readership.

Greg did not take up writing seriously until he had reached his mid-thirties, and he did not become primarily a writer until, in 1851, at the age of 42, he moved to London. He quickly became, in London, a man of letters, and he took on many of the attributes of that characteristically Victorian genus. He moved in a circle of literary friends, developed a taste for good wine and a talent for pleasant conversation. Shortly after his wife died in 1873 he married a daughter of Janes Wilson, thus becoming Walter's Bagehot's brother-in-law. In London he became, wrote John Morley, who was for a time his neighbour in Wimbledon, 'the good type of the man of the world. . . . He was urbane, essentially modest, and readily interested in ideas and subjects other than his own."[6] He led a comfortable, club-oriented life, acquainted with men of power as with the literary élite. His friend George Cornewall Lewis assured him a steady income by appointing him a commissioner of customs in 1856; from 1864 to 1877 he was head of the stationery office. He was among those whose literary reputations made them welcome guests of Lady Amberley. Towards the end of his life he was one of the founding members of the Metaphysical Society. Man of letters though he was, fond as he became of the urbane style of life he cultivated in London, Greg's point of view, throughout his literary life, remained solidly rooted in Manchester.

Greg was born in Manchester in 1809, the last of thirteen children of Samuel Greg. His father had made a fortune as a cotton spinner, and the Gregs lived a life of restrained luxury in Quarry Bank, their home near Manchester. Quarry Bank was a Unitarian household, and the young William Rathbone was made aware of the virtues of rationality from his early years. His mother was a descendant of Philip Henry, one of the ejected two thousand, and Matthew Henry of the *Commentaries*; this helped reinforce Greg's sense of nonconformity and his suspicion of the aristocratic Church of England. Quarry Bank, filled with books, and aggressively liberal, with a picture of George Washington over the dining-room fireplace, left its imprint on Greg for life.

W.R. Greg followed his two older brothers, Robert Hyde and Samuel, to school in Bristol, where he studied under Lant Carpenter, as did so many Unitarian boys of talent in the 1820s. From Bristol he went to the University of Edinburgh, again a family tradition, studying with both Sir William Hamilton and his rival, John Fraser. At that time, 1827–8, Hamilton was engaged in an attack upon phrenology and mesmerism, and Greg's interest in those subjects date from this time. It is likely, also, that Greg's later agnosticism derives, at least in part, from the influence of Sir William Hamilton. In both *The Creed of Christendom* and *Enigmas of Life* there are echoes of Hamilton's distinction between conditioned and unconditioned knowledge, between the knowledge of this finite world, derived through reason and logic, and knowledge of the infinite derived through intuition.

In 1828 Greg returned to his father's house to work in his father's factory. From the beginning, Greg was deeply dissatisfied with his life as a cotton spinner. He missed the intellectual stimulation of Edinburgh and he resented the time away from reading that his work demanded. His life as a manufacturer, he told a sister in 1833, was 'a dog's life. I never open a book, but shun them as if they were poison, rise at half-past five o'clock, go to bed at ten, and toil like a galley slave all day, willy nilly. Man labours for the meat that perisheth, and the food which satisfyeth not.'[7] Greg never did settle happily into the manufacturer's life. From the autumn of 1831 he spent a year wandering on the continent and in Greece and Turkey. When he returned he began business on his own account in Bury, with £40 000 from his father. He married a Manchester woman in 1835 and, in 1842, for the sake of her health, he moved his household to Ambleside. From there he tried to manage his business on a part-time basis, spending more than half his time in the Lake District. In 1847 his favourite brother, Samuel, lost his health in the midst of a major dispute with his employees, and W.R. Greg took on Samuel's firm in addition to his own. Inevitably, management from afar proved unsuccessful; in 1850 Greg lost both firms and almost all his capital.

For a few years after his return from Europe and the east in 1832, Greg played a minor role in Lancashire politics, but he had no taste for the rougher side of public affairs. 'I am sick of public life,' he wrote in 1832, just after a riotous nomination meeting in Manchester, 'I mean sicker than ever.'[8] He longed for 'scientific studies, and calm, quiet and refreshing society'. In 1837 he stood in the Liberal interest for Lancaster, was soundly beaten, and that ended his active association with politics. Except, that is, for his participation in the campaign to repeal the corn laws. The campaign against the corn laws made an enormous impression on Greg. His work with the Anti Corn Law League was the highlight, in a sense the only real success, of his Manchester days. Throughout his life in London after 1851 he frequently referred to the League and its victory. It is evident that his experience with the League played an important part in shaping his views of English politics. The League, moreover, provided him with a practical model for the mechanics of social progress, a model within which he himself could play a congenial role.

Greg was a passionate, whole-hearted supporter of the Anti Corn Law League, a true believer in its historic mission. In the light of his own lack of ambition in business and in politics, his deep commitment to the cause of the League is a little surprising; one senses here that Greg was moved by emotional pressure to identify with the business class, the class in which his father and his older brother, Robert Hyde Greg, had been so successful. He himself, of course, grounded his support of the League on scientific principles, on what he considered the solid rock of political economy. The basic principles of economics, as expounded by David Ricardo and Nassau Senior were, to Greg, scientific discoveries whose validity was beyond doubt. Secure in his conviction that the League espoused a cause blessed by science, Greg took even more time from his business and raised money, spoke to public meetings, and wrote in the interest of corn law repeal. His most important contribution was an essay, *On Agriculture and the Corn Laws*, which won a prize from the League in 1842. In that essay Greg developed the argument for the economic interconnectedness of English society. Each sector of the economy affects every other. There can be no long-term agricultural prosperity without commercial prosperity, 'the elevation of one class of the community cannot be permanently procured by the depression of the rest'. Assuming that the case against the corn laws as they affected trade and manufacturing had already been made, he concentrated on the benefits that farmers and labourers would gain from repeal. This essay was polemical, of course, and it helped Cobden in his efforts to soften the impression that the League was the instrument of a single class. For Greg, however, the essay was also an opportunity to espouse economic truths in which he had come to believe deeply. He held fast to those truths for the rest of his life, and they lay beneath almost everything he wrote.

In the year that Greg published his prize essay on the corn laws he moved his family to the Lake District, and there he turned his attention in a sustained way to religious matters. From 1845 until 1848 he worked on *The Creed of Christendom*, 'a contribution', he called it, 'to the progress of religious science'.[9] For three years the finished manuscript lay on his desk while he wrestled with his failing business. He published it in 1851; it launched his career as a man of letters.

There is some evidence that Greg, in the course of writing *The Creed*, experienced the pain and anguish that is generally associated with a personal crisis of faith. He writes movingly in the Preface to the first edition of *The Creed* about the 'divided allegiance' of 'the searcher whose affections are strong, whose associations are quick, whose hold upon the Past is clinging and tenacious'. Such a one 'loves the Church where he worshipped in his happy childhood; where his friends and family worship still; where his grey-haired parents await the resurrection of the just: but where *he* can worship and await no more. He loves the simple old creed, which was the creed of his earlier and brighter days; which is the creed of his wife and children still, but which inquiry has compelled him to abandon. . . . To such a man the pursuit of Truth is a daily martyrdom.'[10] This suggestion of pain and reluctance struck, no doubt, sympathetic chords in many of his readers, and it helped establish the reverential posture that he tried to maintain throughout the book. But there is no further evidence in *The Creed*, or in any of his other writing, that Greg was deeply troubled by his encounter with biblical scholarship. The tone of *The Creed of Christendom* is the same bright, confident, cheerful tone that he gives to all his writing. He writes of the Bible with the calm assurance that marks his writing for the Anti Corn Law League.

Greg wrote *The Creed of Christendom*, a sustained essay in biblical criticism, because, he notes in the Preface, he wished to share the results of his reading and thinking with others who were pursuing the same inquiries. He also wrote in an effort to combat the popular notion of scriptural authority, a notion that had social and economic as well as religious and intellectual implications. 'I was compelled to see', he writes, 'that there is scarcely a low and dishonouring conception of God current among men, scarcely a narrow and malignant passion of the human heart, scarcely a moral obliquity, scarcely a political error or misdeed, which Biblical texts are

not, and may not be without any violence to their obvious
signification, adduced to countenance and justify.' His
strongest qualification for undertaking a critical study of the
Bible, he thought, was his commonsense, 'the ordinary
education of an English gentleman, and a logical faculty
exercised in other walks'. It was essential, he believed, for
such work to be undertaken by laymen, for clergymen of all
denominations were 'restrained and shackled at once by their
previous confessions of faith, and by the consequences to
them of possible conclusions'.[11] Here begins an attack on the
professional bias of the clergy that Greg pursued for many
years. Their professionalism itself, Greg believed, tied the
clergy to the past both intellectually and politically and made
them poor guides for the future.

Characteristically, Greg approaches the Bible, and the
Christian religion generally, from a decidedly élitist point of
view. Because men are finite creatures, he asserts, following
Sir William Hamilton, they cannot attain a completely pure
and accurate view of religion. Educated men, men of science,
can approach truth much more closely than can children or
the great majority with their undisciplined minds. Indeed,
the majority, like children, can only understand religion
when it is presented in coarser images. Popular religion,
then, was by its very nature likely to be vulgarised and
suffused with error. Popular religion, he said, was his target.
'The rapid spread and general reception of any religion may
unquestionably be accepted as proof that it contains some
vital truth (the usual view); it may be regarded also as equally
certain proof that it contains a large admixture of error, – of
error, that is, cognizable and detectable by the higher human
minds of the age.'[12] Greg's mission in *The Creed* was to detect
that body of error in the Bible so that the best educated men
and women of his generation and beyond might concentrate
on the truth that remained.

Greg wrote his book in Ambleside, at a time when he was
making regular business trips to Manchester and Bury. He
had access to no great library, but he was certainly not
working in provincial isolation. Manchester New College had
recently moved back to Manchester from York, and John
Kenrick, a biblical scholar of note, was professor of history
there. Kenrick had spent time in Germany, and he served as

an important guide to Greg. Also on the staff at Manchester New College was J.J. Tayler, a very successful Unitarian minister in Manchester, a man whom James Martineau called 'the English Schleiermacher'. Tayler, like Kenrick, had spent time in Germany and sometimes conducted services in German. Greg knew no German and, indeed, appears to have consulted no foreign language sources while preparing his book. He relied on the best recent English and American works, and on a few German works in translation. This linguistic limitation circumscribes the value of Greg's work as a contribution to scholarship, but as an essay in popularisation *The Creed* is a considerable success. With relatively few available sources, Greg was able to grasp the methods and current controversies of the German critics, and he reported the results of his reading with a vigour, force, and political point of his own.

For the Old Testament the only German critic Greg used to any extent was Wilhelm Martin Leberecht De Wette, and De Wette's only work available in translation was *A Critical and Historical Introduction to the Canonical Scriptures of the Old Testament*, translated by the American Unitarian, Theodore Parker, and published in Boston in 1843. This work dominates Greg's treatment of the Old Testament. He also drew on John Kenrick's *Essay on Primaeval History* (1846), and F.W. Newman's *A History of the Hebrew Monarchy*, which appeared in 1847, when Greg had almost completed his discussion of the Old Testament.

Greg deals relatively quickly with the Old Testament. He announces that the German critics have proved beyond controversy that the Old Testament does not contain a literally true history, with the Pentateuch written by Moses, with genuine prophecies in the prophetical books, with the law written under the immediate dictation of Jehovah. 'That this is the popular belief in which we are all brought up, and on the assumption of which the ordinary language of Divines and the whole tone of current literature proceeds, no one will entertain a doubt.'[13] This popular belief is wrong. Scientific criticism, meaning close linguistic analysis and a critical and logical examination of the text, demonstrates that the Pentateuch was given its present form about 800 years after the death of Moses. The Pentateuch ought to be viewed as a collection of national traditions. Greg accepts Kenrick's view that the accounts of creation in Genesis represent early speculative attempts to explain phenomena that cannot fail to interest men. He dismisses the elaborate attempts of Whewell and Buckland to harmonise Genesis and geology, and he argues plainly that 'the cosmogony of Moses was the conception of an unlearned man and of a rude age'.[14] The proposition that the Bible was intended as a revelation of moral and religious truth, not physical science, seemed to Greg an ecclesiastical evasion. 'The bible professes to give information on all these points alike.... All the statements are made in the same affirmative style, and on the same authority.'[15] The biblical accounts of creation cannot be read as divine revelation, and neither can the prophets or, indeed, any part of the Bible. That prophecy is prediction is the general assumption upon which the prophets are inter-preted. Greg concludes that there is not sufficient evidence to prove that even one case of Old Testament prophecy was fulfilled. 'There is no case in which we can say with certainty that the narrative has not been tampered with to suit the prediction, or the prediction modified to correspond with the event.'[16]

Much the longer portion of *The Creed* deals with the New Testament, where Greg finds, particularly in the gospels, issues more interesting, more immediately relevant to his time, and more difficult to penetrate than those he had examined in the Old Testament. His principal German source for New Testament criticism was Johan Leonhard Hug, whose *Introduction to the Writings of the New Testament* was translated by D.G. Wait in 1827 and then, much more effectively, in 1836 by Moses Stuart, the father of biblical criticism in America. Friedrich Schleiermacher's *Critical Essay on the Gospel of St Luke* was translated and published with a critical introduction by Connop Thirlwall in 1825, and Greg makes much use of both Schleiermacher and Thirlwall. Surprisingly, David Friedrich Strauss is not a major source, even though George Eliot's translation of *The Life of Jesus* appeared in 1846, well before Greg finished writing. Perhaps this is because Strauss did not serve Greg's purpose well; Greg wanted to separate truth from error, while Strauss developed a theory of the myth of Jesus in which literal truth was inextricably mixed with reflections of the aspirations and needs of the society in which Christ lived. In addition to the Germans, important sources for Greg's New Testament studies included John Kenrick's articles in the *Prospective Review*, Charles Hennell's *Inquiry Concerning the Origin of Christianity* (1838), and Anders Norton's three volumes on *Historical Evidences for the Genuineness of the Gospels* (1837 and 1844).

Greg's purpose in turning critical attention to the gospels was, he writes, to provide a means 'of extracting Religion from Orthodoxy – of rescuing Christianity from Calvinism'.[17] There is some sectarian colour to his effort to establish Christ's exclusive humanity and to his arguments against the Resurrection. But Greg's work went far beyond the defence of Unitarianism. He tried to create, for men of commonsense, a way in which they could accommodate their Christianity to their practical experience and to their knowledge of physical and social laws. In this effort he was, of course, much less protective of orthodoxy than were the authors of the *Bridgewater Treatises*, works for which he had little respect.[18] While professing a strongly stated commitment to the moral grandeur and spiritual beauty of Christianity, Greg proceeded to attack, without reservation, the status of the Bible as a repository of revealed truth. 'There is no text in the evangelists', he maintains, 'the divine (or Christian) origin of which is sufficiently unquestionable to enable it to serve as the foundation of doctrines repugnant to natural feeling or to common sense.'[19] Through his emphasis on commonsense and practical knowledge, moreover, Greg produced a case against Christianity which was ultimately more destructive than he had intended.

To what extent are the gospel narratives authentic and accurate accounts of historical events? This is the question that Greg, paying little attention to Acts or the Epistles, asked of the New Testament. 'This inquiry', he wrote, 'we consider as of paramount interest to every other question of criticism; for on the conclusion to which it leads us depends the whole – not of Christianity, which, as we view it, is unassailable, but – of *textual* or *dogmatic Christianity*; i.e. the Christianity of nine tenths of nominal Christendom.'[20] Following his German guides, particularly Schleiermacher, Greg rehearses at length the various critical theories about the origin of the four gospels. Naturally he dismisses the doctrine of plenary inspiration, and he discusses at some length the ways in which Coleridge and Thomas Arnold, 'one the most subtle thinker, the other the most honest theologian' had begun to modify the idea that the Bible contains God's word as revealed through his chosen scribes.[21] The gospels are historical documents. 'In a word, we are to examine them and regard them, not as Mohametans regard the Koran, but as Niebuhr regarded Livy, and as Arnold regarded Thucydides – documents out of which the good, the true, the sound, is to be educed.'[22] Greg reports general agreement among scholars that the first three gospels, the synoptic gospels as we know them, date from late in the first century. None of them was written by an eyewitness to the events they record. Convinced by Schleiermacher's work on Luke, Greg rejects the theory associated with Eichhorn which posits an original gospel, written in Aramaic, whence Matthew, Mark, and Luke derive. He accepts Schleiermacher's view that the synoptic gospels were each compiled from a variety of sources, written and verbal, which are now lost. The fourth gospel is a problem. Greg accepts the possibility that it might have been written by an eyewitness, but he strongly inclines to the view that it was not. Its credibility as evidence for Christ's life is weakened in Greg's eyes by its sophisticated tone, its philosophic unity, and by its Grecian character, alien to Christ and his disciples. He is confident that 'nearly all the discourses of Jesus in the fourth gospel are mainly the composition of the evangelist'.[23]

Greg, therefore, concentrates his search for the historical Jesus on the first three gospels, books in which morality is, for the most part, elevated over dogma. Here he does more than follow the Germans; he adopts some of their methods of literary and historical criticism and employs them himself. He subjects the King James text of the gospels to a very close reading, looking for inconsistencies and improbabilities in the narratives; and he tries to establish the immediate intention of the compilers, from textual inference and from his historical knowledge. Given that the gospels were assembled forty years or more after Christ's death, from a miscellany of texts and oral traditions, Greg assumes that the narratives contain much that is distorted and much that is false. Inconsistencies and improbabilities are easy for him to find. Why are there two feedings of the multitude in Matthew, and only one in Luke and Mark? Why two demoniacs in Matthew? Sensible men prefer the accounts of one in Luke and Mark. In all three gospels, Christ predicts his own death and his resurrection, and more than once in each gospel. Can commonsense accept these prophecies, given the gospel record of the shock of the disciples at Christ's death and their amazement at his resurrection? 'The conclusion, therefore, is inevitable – that the predictions were ascribed to Jesus after the event, not really uttered by him.'[24]

The account of the birth of Christ in Matthew is, Greg argues, a product of the polemical intention of the author, who is intent on demonstrating how Christ fulfilled the Old Testament prophecies. Luke's treatment of the Virgin Birth is suspect not only because the event is physically unlikely, but also because, as Strauss demonstrated in *The Life of Jesus*, the account follows closely the established conventions of Hebrew poetry.[25] When the gospel is read as poetry it cannot also be read as a record of the plain truth. Polemical intention, again, explains why Christ is reported in Matthew as saying: 'that thou art Peter, and upon this rock I will build my church.' This verse conferring the power of the keys upon Peter is understood within the context of the need to establish central spiritual authority for the church in the late first century. 'The whole passage, with its context, betokens an ecclesiastical, not a Christian spirit.'[26] And besides, observes the practical Greg, no sensible man like Christ would have given such power to a man so unfit, so impetuous and unstable as Peter.

Having established through these and numerous other cases that the gospels are not uniformly reliable as historical records, Greg turns specifically to the teachings of Christ. Are Christ's words, as reported by the evangelists, really what he said? Here Greg parts company with Coleridge, who had argued in *Confessions of an Inquiring Spirit* that the directly quoted language of Christ must be excepted from the general rule that the Bible should be subjected to the same critical examination as any other book. Greg finds many errors in the accounts of what Christ is reported as saying.

Christ himself refers to two miraculous feedings of the multitude in Matthew. He refers in the same gospel to John the Baptist as long dead when he was in fact still alive. And he comments on the death of Zacharias, son of Barachias, who did not die until thirty-five years after the crucifixion. More important than these minor errors are the sustained passages in which Christ speaks of his second coming as if that event were not far off. The destruction of Jerusalem and the end of the world are closely linked: 'Verily I say unto you, This generation shall not pass away, till all these things be fulfilled.' Now that nearly 1800 years have passed since the destruction of the Holy City, there are for Greg only two possible conclusions. Either Jesus was entirely in error and did not possess the prophetic spirit, or the evangelist has presented announcements that Christ never uttered.[27] These are some of the cases Greg uses to press the point that even in the matter of Christ's own words, the biblical account cannot be considered reliable.

The New Testament, for Greg, contains much that is false as well as much that cannot be verified. The 'most questionable doctrines of modern orthodoxy', Greg thought, were all founded on texts that were false, in the sense that they did not represent Christ's authentic teaching. He offers three illustrations. The doctrine that belief is essential and the one thing essential to salvation is based on a spurious portion of Mark.[28] The idea of Christ's divinity is based upon texts written from ecclesiastical motives.[29] And in the revised third edition, published in 1873, he adds, since it was by then so much disputed, the doctrine of eternal punishment, based on one textual reference in Matthew and contradicted by the spirt of Christ.[30]

What, then, remains of truth and value in the gospels? Do they constitute a report of Christ's teachings that is sufficiently reliable to be useful? Greg's answer, phrased in definite and positive language, is an evasion, an evasion that was to become commonplace among educated Victorians later in the century. Even this evasion, moreover, in which Greg seems to rest confidently in *The Creed of Christendom*, was undermined by Greg the political economist and anti corn law leaguer. After his critical examination of the gospels, Greg concludes that the Bible does contain 'a fair and faithful *outline* of Christ's character and teaching'.[31] We cannot verify with certainty the authenticity of any specific utterance of Christ, but we can judge between what is in harmony with our general impression of his spirit and what is not. 'Most reflecting minds rise from a perusal of the gospel history with a clear, broad, vivid conception of the character and mission of Christ, notwithstanding the many passages at which they have stumbled, and which they have felt – perhaps with needless alarm and self-reproach – to be incongruous and unharmonizing with the great whole.' This style of judgment, up to a point, conveniently permitted Greg to accept what seemed sensible and to reject with a clear conscience what caused him to stumble. 'A true revelation, addressed to all mankind, and destined for all ages . . . must carry with it its own permanent and unfading credentials.'[32] The moral beauty of Jesus has that convincing character; his moral teaching constitutes the core of biblical truth.

Greg does not devote much energy to Christ's moral beauty. While he repeatedly asserts that *The Creed of Christendom* is a search after truth, in fact the book is concerned, almost entirely, with error. He maintains consistently the view that the character of Jesus is vastly more important than the doctrines associated with the church. But he does no more than merely suggest the outline of that character, and the outline is very general. Christ is pure, forgiving, spiritual and sincere – little more. *The Creed of Christendom* is not a life of Christ, and it contains no serious or extended discussion of the personality of Jesus. Greg, it is clear, was much more at ease with doctrines and principles than he was with character. Almost in spite of himself, he is driven to reducing the meaning of Christ's personality into a list of moral principles. With the enthusiastic comment that Christ's life contains 'more truth, purer truth, higher truth, stronger truth, than has ever yet been given to man', Greg introduces his list of Christian principles, each of which he considered both authentic and true.[33] The list, with a comment on each truth, comprises only two pages. Jesus teaches: (1) the worthlessness of ceremonial observances and the need for essential righteousness; (2) the obligation of purity of heart as security for the purity of life; (3) the wisdom of unfeigned good will to all men; (4) the obligation to forgive injuries; (5) the necessity of self-sacrifice in the course of duty; (6) the obligation of humility; (7) the obligation to be genuinely sincere, being not seeming; (8) the fact of God's fatherhood of mankind. This list of Christian virtues is not unsubstantial, but in the context of his long book Greg downgrades the importance of these principles by devoting so little space to them. None of these precepts receives more than a line or two of explication.

Greg is very much more interested in whether or not one is justified in hoping for a future life. The question of a future life, a life after death, is, for him, the great enigma, as it must have been for many Victorians. There is a chapter on the prospect of life beyond the grave in *The Creed*, and Greg developed further his position on this question in *Enigmas of Life* (1873), the most popular of all his books. A future life, he held, was a matter of faith, hope, and earnest desire, not a question of revelation. Even if the resurrection was a fact, which he does not accept, it would not demonstrate a future life for the rest of mankind. It is certainly true, Greg observes, that Christ taught the existence of another life. 'He gave to the doctrine, for the first time, an authoritative sanction; he announced it as a direct revelation from the Deity.'[34] But this authentic teaching of Jesus might not be accurate. He may merely reflect ideas then current among the Pharisees and the Essenes. Human reason does not support the future life. 'Logic never originated it, logic can never establish it. All that can properly be called reasoning, i.e., inference deduced from observation, points the other way. Appearances all testify to the reality and permanence of death.'[35] Yet Greg continues to hope the larger hope. 'The truth we believe to be, that a future existence is, and must be, a matter of *information* or *intuition*, not of *inference*.'[36] The faculty which intuits the future life is not the mind, but a spiritual sense, the soul. The soul is not subject to the ordinary rules of evidence; it is 'anterior to reasoning, independent of reasoning, unprovable by reasoning'. The intuition of the soul is for Greg a matter of undoubting faith. 'The only occasions on which a shade of doubt has passed over my conviction of a future existence, have been when I rashly endeavoured to make out a case, to give reasons for the faith that is in me, to assign ostensible and logical grounds for my belief.'[37] In *Enigmas of Life* Greg restated this case and added a physical description of heaven, 'a home', a place he envisioned as much like the Lake District at its very best during the summer, 'gentle streams, and shady groves, and woodland glades, and sunny valleys, and eternal mountains, and the far off murmur of a peaceful ocean'.[38] Little wonder that the reviewer for *Blackwood's Magazine* (February 1873) knew a woman 'who fell acrying as she closed the book, and burst forth into a broken prayer (all his arguments notwithstanding) that a man so near the kingdom of heaven might have the Christ in whom she trusted revealed to him yet'. Her reaction might have been more restrained had she given *The Creed of Christendom* a close reading.

Towards the end of *The Creed*, following the two pages in which approved Christian principles are listed, she would have found thirty pages on erroneous principles in the authentic teaching of Jesus; twenty more pages on authentic Christian errors appeared in the introduction to the third edition, which Greg published in 1873. These false principles, moreover, were at the core of genuine Christianity. They served to undermine the value of the beauty Greg saw in the general outline of Christ's personality. This attack on the central teachings of Christ constituted a general attack on Christianity, although, clinging to the rhetoric of moral grandeur, Greg repeatedly denied that such was the case. *The Creed of Christendom* constituted an elaborate argument that Christianity was either irrelevant or antagonistic to the mainstream of modern life. That Greg himself refused to admit the boldness of his case adds an interesting dimension to his work. His fundamental criticism of the place of Christ in western civilisation did not emerge from his foray into biblical criticism. It flowed, rather, from a view of the world that he had developed as a Manchester man, a cotton spinner, a leaguer, a devotee of political economy, and a nonconformist. Politics more than scholarship provided the context for *The Creed of Christendom*.

Those fundamental errors in Christianity, which Greg associated both with Christ and with the mainstream of subsequent Christian teaching, constituted a clear pattern. They were antagonistic to the conception of natural law in general, and they ran against the thrust of particular natural laws. Those errors were actually espoused by Jesus, and they harmonise with our general picture of his character and his message. But reasonable men must reject them because the progress of knowledge has established their falsity. These particular errors and, by implication, Christianity in general reflect a discredited view of the world.

Greg identifies and discusses at length three major Christian fallacies. The first is the common Christian conception of the forgiveness of sin upon repentance and conversion.[39] This means that God saves the repentant sinner from the consequence of his sins. Greg refuses to accept that this is possible. 'A sin without its punishment is as impossible, as complete a contradiction in terms, as a cause without an effect.' Every action has a result, and the relation between action and result is a matter of natural law. 'The punishment of sin *consists* in the consequences of sin.'[40] The punishment is the natural and inevitable result of the offence. Forgiveness of sin would 'violate the eternal and harmonious order of the universe.'[41] The idea that the consequences of sin might be avoided is also mischievous from a practical, utilitarian point of view. 'It has encouraged millions, *feeling that a safety was in store for them in ultimate resort*, to persevere in their career of folly or crime, to ignore or despise those natural laws which God has laid down to be the guides and beacons of our conduct.'[42] Concluding his discussion of sin, Greg urges his readers to study those fixed laws upon which their well-being depends, the physical laws, the moral laws, the intellectual laws, the social and economic laws.

The idea of the efficacy of prayer, at least prayer of petition, is the second Christian fallacy. From time to time in the nineteenth century the problem of prayer was debated in the popular press, and Greg, with his journalist's instinct, wrote an essay on the question for *Enigmas of Life*. In both the essay and *The Creed* he advanced the argument that asking God to intervene in our lives is asking God to upset the natural order. This God will not do; he prefers order to chaos. Greg reaffirms his 'conviction that all things in life are arranged by *law*'.[43] While he does not think that prayer is effective – does a toothache, he asks, last less long with those who pray? – Greg is content that Christian practice continue, though not the Christian theory. He did not see prayer as positively harmful in practical life.

Far different is the case of Greg's third Christian fallacy, the ascetic and depreciating view of life that he locates in the gospels, the epistles, the traditions of the Christian churches, and in preachers of his own day. This most pernicious fallacy poses a practical danger because it runs against the most effective progressive forces in modern civilisation, and because it makes hypocrites of those who seem to accept it. With startling audacity and surprising simplicity, Greg attacks the Christian emphasis on spirituality, and the Christian tendency to downgrade the material side of life. 'Lay not up for yourselves treasures upon earth, where moth and rust do corrupt, and where thieves break through and steal.' Or, 'What shall it profit a man if he should gain the whole world and lose his soul?' These exhortations, and their incorporation into the teaching of organised Christianity, roused Greg's passion. It seemed to him a profound error 'to cry down this world, with its profound beauty, its thrilling interests, its glorious works, its noble and holy affections' and to urge men to fix their minds and hearts on a spiritual world that is to come.[44] Existence, for Greg, was a two-stage affair. First, life in this material world, a stage that was good and essentially important in its own right. Next, a different stage of being in which spirituality will predominate. The two stages must not be confounded. Men should love this world and commit themselves to its material problems until they enter the spiritual realm. There will be time a plenty for spirituality then. Premature concentration on the qualities of the next world leads men to undervalue the good things of this world. Spirituality stands opposed to economic and social progress. 'I question', wrote Greg, 'whether the whole system of professing Christians is not based on a mistake, whether it be not an error to strive after *spirituality*.'[45] So convinced was Greg that it was man's nature to love prosperity, this life, and the fruits of economic progress, that he, with uncharacteristic intemperance, claimed that those who professed dedication to the spiritual element in Christianity were hypocrites. The preacher who Sunday after Sunday urges his flock to fix their eyes on heaven goes home to his claret, his dinner, his children, and his professional ambition. How many prosperous mid-Victorian men of business shared this view?

In 1873, in the long introduction to the revised edition of *The Creed of Christendom*, Greg returns to the dangers that lie within Christian moral precepts. Relating Christ's preference for the spiritual side of life to his mistaken belief that the end of this world was at hand, Greg argues against five specific aspects of Christian other-worldliness. Christ commanded non-resistance and submission to violence, whether directed against persons or property. Greg holds this as clearly unrealistic, against all common sense. 'The whole of our criminal law and our police arrangements are based upon a systematic repudiation of the precept in question.'[46] In the international sphere, especially, the doctrine of non-resistance is obviously absurd. 'Any people that habitually and notoriously submitted to violence would simply be overrun, enslaved, or trampled out.'[47]

Alms-giving is another dangerous precept. Greg, who had been a strenuous supporter of the new poor law, was entirely at one with the spirit of the Charity Organisation Society in its pursuit of scientific philanthropy. 'No conclusion has been more distinctly or definitely proved than that nearly all charity, popularly so called – more especially all indiscriminate alms giving – is simply and singularly noxious.'[48] Jesus 'never reflected on the danger of creating a whole tribe of begging imposters.' Experience and social science have generated conclusions that supersede Christ's outdated philanthropy.

In the Sermon on the Mount, Jesus preached improvidence: 'Take no thought for your life, what you shall eat. . . .' This is clearly not a healthy principle of behaviour. Especially the working classes need to be encouraged to store up something against the times when their earnings are interrupted. If business men did not take thought for the morrow they would have nothing to invest and economic progress would cease. 'Providence, if not the very first duty of social man, ranks very high among his duties.'[49]

Denunciation of wealth as a peril and temptation to the soul is another Christian error. The prevailing tone and teaching of the gospels cannot be denied: wealth should be shunned, not sought, for it distinctly stands in the way of salvation. Greg disapproves of ostentation and excessive luxury, with its fatal torpor and apathy, but he fiercely defends wealth. The accumulation of capital is a necessary part of the progress of civilisation, a fact not disputed now, but a fact that was as yet unrecognised in the simpler days when Christ lived.[50]

Lastly, Greg maintains that the general tone of Christ's exhortations tends towards support for communism. That every man should work according to his capacities, and should receive according to his wants might be a noble idea. Even John Stuart Mill saw something in it to approve. But every man of affairs recognised that communism would not work. 'Private property alone calls forth adequate exertion, alone controls indefinite multiplication of the population, alone counteracts inveterate laziness, alone raises nations out of squalor and barbarism, alone lifts man above the condition of the beasts that perish.'[51] Such was Greg's creed.

Greg's view of Christianity was closely related to his attitude towards women. Along with many Victorians, Greg associated the hard, progressive, analytical, and worldly side of life with men. Women he associated with what was soft, tender, unscientific, conservative, and compassionate. He makes these associations clear in the literary and social criticism he wrote after moving to London in 1851. In 'The False Morality of the Lady Novelists', Greg offers the opinion that many women and some young men take their ideas of correct behaviour from novels.[52] But many novels are written by women who have no proper basis for judging conduct because they have, necessarily, a limited experience and knowledge of the world.[53] Their vision is sentimental; and they, along with the church, tend towards a false hierarchy of sin. Weak flesh is castigated severely; weak understanding is forgiven. Mrs Gaskell, in *Mary Barton*, treats John Barton with feminine compassion, forgiving his improvidence, forgiving his association with the misguided Chartists, entirely misunderstanding the true situation of the working classes. Gaskell, moreover, in a scene of emotional and religious reconciliation, rescues Barton from the consequences of the murder he commits. False morality indeed! Greg approved the soundness of Harriet Martineau's *Political Economy Tales*, of course, but even Harriet Martineau, he suggests, lived within the conventional limitations of her femininity. She abounded in 'views' that she mistakenly called 'principles'; her opinions were instantaneous insights, not deliberate or gradual deductions; her conscience dominated her intellect.[54] Greg's strong inclination was towards science and rationality, towards worldliness and practical experience, and towards material progress. In conventional Victorian parlance, he favoured masculine qualities and manly spheres of action. The language of Christianity, in Greg's opinion, the language as it appears in *The Creed of Christendom*, is feminine. Indeed the image of Christ, in *The Creed*, is feminine, loving, unphilosophic, meek, and forgiving.

Greg associates the conventional feminine qualities with blacks as well as women. In the course of a long review of 'Dr. Arnold's Lectures on Modern History', Greg remarks that it is possible that the time might not be far off when western civilisation shall have run its course.[55] Scientific and economic progress are bringing us towards the point at which further advance is unlikely. There is still work for several generations, but what then? Possibly, Greg speculates, an antithesis to European culture will then come out of Africa. The European character has been energetic, revengeful, and proud; it has been a pagan character. 'The spirit of Christianity is at variance with the whole tone and elements of the European character.'[56] African blacks, on the other hand, are less aggressive, less energetic, more contemplative, less independent, more forgiving. The African character is essentially well adapted to the 'mild and passive excellencies which the gentle spirit of Christianity delights to honour'. It may well come to pass that a Christianised Africa will set its impress on the next age of man, an age that will be very different from nineteenth-century Europe. 'There is a place, and an hour, in the divine plan, for all modifications of human character. Intellectual energy and Christian perfection are the fruits of different trees.'[57] This fanciful Hegelian vision, explicitly racial and with strong sexual overtones, is powerful evidence for the psychological profundity of Greg's rejection of Christianity.

Although the extent of that rejection is evident to a careful reader, Greg never made it explicit, perhaps not even to himself. He claimed in *The Creed of Christendom*, and he continued to maintain, that his goal was to rescue true Christianity from that orthodox dogma that rested on spurious or misinterpreted texts. Even in the introduction to the third edition of *The Creed of Christendom*, in which he details the antagonism between political economy and the gospels, Greg continues to dwell on the moral perfection of Christ. Consequently he did not alienate readers who might have been shocked and repulsed by a more explicit attack on the foundations of their religion. In this matter of brotherhood with his readers, Greg's strongly stated, unquestionably sincere belief in a future life undoubtedly played a significant role. His solid conviction in the existence of life beyond death, and his emotionally charged attempt at a description of heaven, must have helped make his writing acceptable in those many respectable households where families hoped to be reunited beyond the grave. With so many bridges to conventional responsibility, and holding so many conventional liberal opinions himself, Greg had no difficulty finding publishers for his essays when he entered upon literary life in London.

As a man of letters Greg wrote several important articles on religious matters after the appearance of *The Creed of Christendom*. James Martineau judged the new introduction to the third edition of *The Creed* the most able of all Greg's essays.[58] He dealt again with the efficacy of prayer as well as with heaven in *Enigmas of Life*. And he made in 1863 a most interesting contribution to the debate on the Colenso case.[59] After 1851, however, Greg turned his attention mainly to politics, economics, and social problems. His writing on these subjects is, in the main, based on the same bedrock of attitudes and assumptions that lay under *The Creed of Christendom*. This is not to suggest, of course, that readers who accepted his political views accepted his religious views as well, for such was certainly not the case. Walter Bagehot observes in *The English Constitution* that most men, especially men of business, live in an intellectual haze; they are not fond of implications or abstractions; they like abstract principles diluted and dissolved into real life. Greg's political articles could be read without reference to his other writing, as practical discussions of practical problems. The links among his various opinions are there nonetheless. His outlook on the world was sufficiently consistent, and sufficiently clear, that the links connecting Greg's religious writing with his work on politics and literature are clearly there for those who look for them. It has been suggested above that the matrix within which *The Creed of Christendom* was conceived was essentially political. The following discussion of Greg as a political and literary critic is intended to demonstrate how closely his role as a spokesman for Manchester liberalism relates to his place in the history of Victorian faith in crisis.

In politics Greg was chiefly concerned with the extension of the franchise and the implications of democracy. Along with Bagehot and Mill and other mid-Victorian liberal men of letters, Greg distrusted democracy. An élitist in politics as well as theology, he always held suspect the views of the popular mind. That education helped men to exercise their vote sensibly was a mid-Victorian commonplace that Greg did not doubt. Nevertheless, in the period before the second reform act, he did not agree that franchise qualifications ought to be lowered as increasing numbers of the working classes were educated. He opposed franchise extension on the ground of class interest, and he explained his position at length in two major articles in the *Edinburgh Review* in 1852.[60] All his subsequent political writing consisted of variations on themes established in these two articles. These two essays define his political creed.

For Greg the Reform Act of 1832 was a great turning point in modern English history. Before 1832 power was too highly concentrated in the hands of the aristocracy. The aristocracy controlled parliament and governed according to decisions taken within the two legislative chambers. After the great reform act, power passed from exclusive aristocratic control, and power passed, as well, from parliament to public opinion. 'Parliament now responds more than it initiates. Public opinion is formed out of doors; and is only revised, ratified and embodied within'.[61] Before 1832 political power lay with the professional politicians who consulted the laity outside parliament only when it seemed in their interest to do so. Now every man has become a politician, and every man studies less the qualifications of his member of parliament and more the merits of specific political issues. The most important pieces of legislation originate outside parliament. Able and well-informed individuals, 'sometimes men of business, sometimes philanthropists, sometimes theoretical economists', take up particular social or economic questions, and bring their solutions to parliament while educating the community. This method of governing through response to pressure from without was, Greg thought, working very well. The clinching evidence of the successful operation of the current arrangements was 'the wise and wholesome moral of the anti-corn law agitation', an instance of public opinion governing through 'the simple might of truth and justice, sobriety and union'.[62] Indeed, the history of the Anti Corn Law League provided Greg with a model of politics that became his ideal. It seemed to him that the victory of the League was 'perhaps even greater than that of parliamentary reform, and against a phalanx of foes even more formidable to begin with'.[63]

The age of public opinion gave a new importance to businessmen, to men who were not distinguished by 'the comprehensiveness of their views, or the delicacy of their tact', but by their energy and 'tenacity of purpose which was rebutted by no obstacles'.[64] These men needed scientists and writers to guide them, and therefore, in the new age political economists and men of letters have a noble role as the shapers of effective political opinion. Together, the captains of industry and men of learning would work to further the progress of the entire community. Greg was evidently so certain that political economy was a science through which natural laws were discovered that he never questioned his assumption that businessmen and their philosophic guides operated for the political and economic good of the whole society. He did not raise the spectre of a selfish middle class concerned primarily with its own well-being.

The working classes were another matter. If they received the franchise they would dominate politics by their numbers, and working-class views of their own interests would always be different from the interests of the nation as a whole.[65] Whether or not the working classes were educated did not signify; they would always act in the spirit of exclusive class concern. This was demonstrated by the new model unions; their leaders were educated, but they acted against the interests of their employers none the less. Besides, it was self-evidently wrong 'that those who labour with their hands should have supremacy over those who labour with the brain'.[66]

Consequently, throughout the fifties, Greg offered a number of suggestions for parliamentary reform that he hoped might forestall a general extension of the right to vote. After all, he argued, efficiency, technical expertise, was now what government required; the times were not what they were before 1832. 'All the great battles have been fought. All the great victories have been won. All the more stupendous works have been achieved. All the more formidable difficulties have been surmounted.'[67]

Greg responded manfully to the second reform act. The new regime can be regarded with hope, as well as fear, if the upper and middle classes recognise that different means of rule are now necessary.[68] The governing classes must exert themselves to shape and lead a larger public opinion. The people must be instructed in political economy. Leaders will have to develop new techniques for reaching the voters. He was confident that 'rank, wealth, character, and education, are sure to win with us if they fairly and courageously enter the arena'.[69] These promising comments notwithstanding, Greg's political views did not change much after 1867. He did not accept democracy. He did not generate specific ideas about how to lead the more democratic public or how to influence its opinions. Unable to acclimatise to the new regime, he remained faithful to the philosophy of politics he had developed in the *Edinburgh Review* in 1852. At the time of his death in 1881, Greg was still, A.V. Dicey noted in *The Nation* (18 September 1884), a man of 1852.

Even in the fifties Greg's ideas about parliamentary reform seemed, to those better informed than he, too rigid, too doctrinaire, too remote from the practical realities of government. John Stuart Mill approved the general thrust of the *Edinburgh Review* articles of 1852, particularly the opposition to the ballot, but he feared that Greg's unyielding opposition to democratic change was not realistic. George Cornewall Lewis, Greg's friend and patron, recognised that his client was so much an outsider that he did not understand the nature of cabinet government.[70] Nor did Lewis think that

Greg's evaluations of leading politicians were well founded. Greg's political writing did not proceed so much from close observation of ongoing political life as it did from a set of positions taken up during his Manchester days. A.V. Dicey might well have characterised him as a man of 1846.

In his essays on economic questions, Greg took a line that was firm and clear. He consistently favoured employers over employees, he attacked socialism, and he optimistically argued the possibility of continuing economic growth, continuing progress in prosperity for the entire community. Economic theory was not Greg's metier. He wrote almost nothing on theory, and there is no evidence that he read much in this area. Apart from Malthus, whom he read in order to refute, the only economists he refers to by name are Nassau Senior and John Stuart Mill. On economic matters Greg wrote as a layman and he wrote for laymen. He believed that the most important principles of economnics had been discovered, that they had the status of natural laws, and that his role as a writer was to show how these laws applied to practical situations. While he wrote nothing systematic or comprehensive on economic principles, it is clear that, for him, the fundamental economic law was that which established the relation of supply and demand. Economic well-being was promoted when supply and demand were left free for natural adjustment in the market place. This implied freedom of commercial competition and freedom of contract between employers and their workpeople.

Reviewing Charles Kingsley's *Alton Locke*, Greg dismissed Christian socialism and the Christian socialist scheme for producers' cooperatives.[71] No doubt he found readers who were receptive to his claim that the greatest recent achievement of civilisation was the emergence of modern industry in which scientific discoveries were applied to methods of production. 'Natural philosophers and engineers have been the real poets and wonder workers of our day.'[72] A socialist society could not have fostered such progress. Kingsley, he thought, was moved altogether too much by emotion and misguided Christian compassion. This is a theme Greg developed further in a major article on 'Kingsley and Carlyle'.[73] Of Kingsley he writes: 'competition – which political economy recognizes as the law of trade – he sees, truly enough, to be the source of much selfishness and jealousies, and occasionally of bitter animosities and heart burnings; and hence he tries to sweep the whole system away with the strong wind of religious faith.'[74] The human suffering that moves Kingsley is for Greg a matter of 'social anomalies' that will in time be rectified as progress continues. To cry out in pain, as Kingsley does, and to preach Christian socialism, is to give way to irrational religiosity. Competition is a law of nature. Socialism will work only if human nature is miraculously transformed into the image of Christ.[75]

Writing in the *Westminster Review* at mid-century, Greg maintained that of all the 'disorders and anomalies of society', the industrial problem is the central issue of the time.[76] What obligations have masters to their workers? What principles ought to define the now troubled relation of those two groups? A 'silent social revolution' has, in England, moved that relation beyond the servile bond of feudal times. In the age of liberty, the only proper principle of association between an employer and his employees is the principle of free contract. Free contract reflects the free market-place in which the laws of supply and demand should operate. Wages and conditions of work should be determined, at any given time, by the demand for labour and its supply. 'Neither the most boundless benevolence, nor the most consummate ability, can fight against the clear moral and material laws of the universe.'[77] Through this clearly stated application of a commonplace economic precept, Greg demonstrated the irrelevance of Christianity to an area of human relations that he considered of central importance.

Trade unions were anathema to Greg, who had nothing at all to say in their favour. He took the Sheffield outrages as the occasion upon which to argue that the essential logic of trade unions implied personal violence.[78] Trade unions had as their goals limiting the amount of work done by individual tradesmen, and limiting the number who entered the trade. Both goals, particularly the first, implied coercion, and both involved interference with the free market-place. Prices were driven up and foreign competitiors were given an advantage. Here again is the businessman's point of view. 'Trade unions are a miscalculation and a gigantic blunder.'[79]

Greg reserved for the clergy an even stronger antipathy than that he accorded the trade unionists. The reviewer of *Enigmas of Life* in *Blackwood's Magazine* (February 1873) remarked that Greg seemed 'cruelly and unjustly, and sometimes we think ignorantly, contemptuous of all religious teachers of every class, creed and country'. This is a fair comment. Greg's style is usually calm, reasonable, polite. He was always forthright and direct, and it is not surprising that he was once seriously threatened with physical violence by some trade unionists.[80] There was, however, little apparent emotion in Greg's case against the unions; he wrote against them in the same confident tone that he used when reporting the conclusions of Schleiermacher about the origin of the gospels. His language changed, however, when he commented on the clergy; he condemned them, as a body, in language surprisingly extreme. He wrote of the repellant power of sermons, and he commiserated with those who listened every week to 'a string of astounding propositions . . . from a shallow and narrow preacher whose intellect it is often impossible to respect'.[81] The clergyman is of an intellectual calibre that cannot compare favourably with that of the geologist or the naturalist. When the clergyman is asked a question about the religious implications of modern science, 'either he talks nonsense, or he talks irrelevancies, or he denounces the question, or he shirks it'.[82] This harsh judgment, not often expressed in polite circles in Victorian England, is unusually severe even for the outspoken Greg. It indicates, as a change in tone often does, that Greg harboured a peculiarly sharp animus towards the clergy. The clergy were associated with the superstitious and aristocratic past. For him, the clergy were an especially important enemy, a group whose traditional social role was out of place in the modern world.

Greg was, indeed, suspicious of all the professions. Professionalism, he thought, implied traditionalism. Professionals tended to be conservative, to place emphasis on consistency with the past, to be bound by outdated conventions. This was the case with parliamentary politics before 1832, when men, many of them aristocrats, entered politics as 'a profession, . . . as others enter the navy or the Church'.[83] The clerical

profession had yet to experience their great reform act. The
clergy remained, as did their churches, a dangerous anomaly
left from the old regime.

Reform of the clergy would take place, in Greg's view, only
through pressure from outside the profession. During the
early stages of the Colenso case, Greg took sharp issue with
the position Matthew Arnold assumed in 'The Bishop and
the Philosopher', *Macmillan's Magazine* (1863). Arnold had
argued that Colenso's attack on the historicity of the Pentateuch served no valid purpose and ought to be condemned.
Colenso, according to Arnold, did not advance the cause of
truth or inform the instructed; scholars were already aware
of the difficulties in the Pentateuch. Neither did Colenso
edify the uninstructed; the foundation of their morality will
be weakened by hearing a bishop question the authority of
the Bible. On the contrary, Greg protested, Colenso's work
both instructs and edifies.[84] Who are the instructed who have
nothing to learn from Colenso, he asks. Certainly not the
clergy. Of the 30 000 ministers of religion in England, at least
25 000 have not the slightest knowledge of biblical criticism.
Their sermons display such ignorance that 'the thoughtful
are unspeakably disgusted'.[85] Those clergymen who fully
understand the advances in biblical science, men like Bishop
Tait and Bishop Thirlwall, act to suppress Colenso because
they fear he will unsettle the faith of the laity. They do not
recognise that such suppression, that insistence upon professional oaths and traditional creeds, isolates the clergy from
the intellectual mainstream and makes religion seem
irrelevant to the laity. To save religion from its ministers,
Greg wrote, the reformer must appeal to the clergy through
the laity. He must seek to reform theology as politics has
been reformed. 'He must convince the public – not the
ministers; and when the public is enlightened and persuaded
and grows noisy, then the officials follow tardily, reluctantly,
and grumblingly in its wake. Ecclesiastical tenacity in adher-
ing to old ideas, established formulas, obsolete errors, and
exploded routine, is at least a match for bureaucratic
immovability.'[86] This reforming work was Greg's religious
mission. It was towards this end that he published *The Creed
of Christendom*. His model for action was the political pressure
group.

Throughout his life Greg claimed that his attack on orthodoxy would preserve the truth of Christianity, just as he had once maintained that the attack on the corn laws would benefit agriculture. He prided himself on being a reformer, not a revolutionary. His moderation, his common sense, his reasonableness all helped him to share his ideas with his readers. Like many patriotic Victorians, he disdained French political life with its extreme confrontations and volatile shifts of government. 'France is the land of experiment', he wrote, 'as England is the land of compromise.'[87] His entire view of life, moreover, was essentially political. 'The peculiarities of the English mind', he thought, harmonise with 'the spirit of the British constitution. . . . Whatever exists, and has long existed, may plead more than mere prescription in its favour.'[88] With an eye on tradition, and susceptible himself to the power of convention, Greg wrote about Christianity, and Christ in particular, in terms reverentially respectful. Nevertheless, he made it clear that he believed economic growth to be the driving force in the progress of civilisation, and that life in this world was regulated by laws that science had begun to discover. Whenever Christianity and material progress seemed opposed, Greg associated himself with progress. At base, he thought that Christianity worked counter to progress, and that its conservative influence must fade away. 'It would be rash', he once wrote, 'to say that, on a balance of considerations, the Church and the clergy of all denominations have in the course of ages done more harm than good to the Christian world; but probably it would be rasher still to assert the contrary.'[89] He did not often write thusly. More typical is the style of the introduction to the revised edition of *The Creed of Christendom*. There he asks, 'can a Christian life be lived out in modern days?'[90] Most clearly, Greg's answer is implicitly no. Christianity is spiritual and other-worldly. He shows in detail that the core of Christ's teaching is inapplicable to life in a dynamic, industrialised society, and he leaves his readers no room to misinterpret his position. His explicit answer, however, is yes, one can certainly lead a Christian life in Victorian England, provided one rejects dogmatic orthodoxy. Christ's beautiful and loving character is an example for all the ages. This explicit answer runs contrary to the basic thrust of Greg's religious writing. It is an answer in the spirit of the British constitution, the half-conscious compromise of a moderate liberal and a successful man of letters who is sensitive to his audience. It masks the crisis of faith that it serves to encourage.

NOTES

1. The most extensive work on the Greg family is by Mary B. Rose. Her book, *The Gregs of Quarry Bank Mill* (Cambridge, Cambridge University Press, 1986), concentrates on the business affairs of the family, as does her unpublished PhD thesis, 'The Gregs of Styal: the Emergence and Development of a Family Business' (Manchester, 1977). W.R. Greg's cultural context is discussed by John Seed, 'Unitarianism, Political Economy and the Antinomies of Liberal Culture in Manchester, 1830–1850', *Social History*, 7 (1982) pp. 1–25; and by Simon Dentith, 'Political Economy, Fiction, and the Language of Practical Ideology in Nineteenth-Century England', *Social History*, 8 (1983) pp. 183–99. No substantial collection of the papers of W.R. Greg has been uncovered.
2. John Morley, 'W.R. Greg – A Sketch', *Macmillan's Magazine*, 48 (June 1833) p. 120. Morley's 'sketch' of Greg is the best informed account of his life and character. The family papers to which Morley had access have since disappeared.
3. A.V. Dicey, 'Enigmas of Life', *The Nation*, 5 June 1873, 386.
4. ibid.
5. Morley, 123.
6. ibid., 109.
7. Quoted by Morley, 118.
8. ibid., 117.
9. W.R. Greg, *The Creed of Christendom*, 5th edn (London, 1878) 65. All references will be to this edition. The first edition was published in 1851; it was revised once, in 1873, and the revisions were clearly indicated by square brackets in that and subsequent editions.
10. *The Creed*, 71–2.
11. ibid., 64.
12. ibid., 71.
13. ibid., 106.
14. ibid., 119.
15. ibid., 124.
16. ibid., 131.
17. ibid., 223.
18. ibid., 121–4 on Buckland and Whewell, 264–5 and 272 on Babbage.
19. ibid., 233.
20. ibid., 169.
21. ibid., 97.

22. ibid., 95.
23. ibid., 220.
24. ibid., 195.
25. ibid., 202.
26. ibid., 188.
27. ibid., 197.
28. ibid., 225.
29. ibid., 228.
30. ibid., 231.
31. ibid., 223.
32. ibid., 224.
33. ibid., 318.
34. ibid., 352.
35. ibid., 359–60.
36. ibid., 373.
37. ibid., 374.
38. W.R. Greg, 'Elsewhere', *Enigmas of Life* (London, 1872) 269.
39. *The Creed*, 335 ff.
40. ibid., 336.
41. ibid., 337.
42. ibid., 340.
43. ibid., 328.
44. ibid., 344.
45. ibid., 347.
46. ibid., 39–40.
47. ibid., 42.
48. ibid., 44.
49. ibid., 47.
50. ibid., 52.
51. ibid., 54.
52. W.R. Greg, 'The False Morality of the Lady Novelists', in *Literary and Social Judgements*, 4th edn, 2 vols (London, 1877) 1: 106.
53. ibid., 1: 108.
54. W.R. Greg, 'Harriet Martineau', in *Miscellaneous Essays* (London, 1882) 180.
55. W.R. Greg, 'Dr. Arnold's Lectures on Modern History', in *Essays on Political and Social Science*, 2 vols (London, 1853) 1: 6.
56. ibid., 1: 12.
57. ibid.
58. James Martineau, 'The Creed of Christendom', *Nineteenth Century*, 13 (February 1883) 199–216.
59. W.R. Greg, 'Truth versus Edification', in *Literary and Social Judgements*, 2: 91–116.
60. W.R. Greg, 'The Expected Reform Bill', and 'Representative Reform', in *Social Science*, 2: 422–517, 518–94.
61. Greg, 'The Expected Reform Bill', 467.
62. W.R. Greg, 'Constitutional and Autocratic Statesmanship', in *Political Problems of Our Age and Country* (London, 1870) 4.
63. Greg, 'The Expected Reform Bill', 430.

64. ibid.
65. Greg, 'Representative Reform', 532–3.
66. ibid., 2: 533.
67. Greg, 'The Expected Reform Bill', 463.
68. W.R. Greg, 'The New Regime and How to Meet It', in *Political Problems*, 311.
69. ibid., 314.
70. *The Letters of Sir George Cornewall Lewis*, ed. Gilbert Frankland Lewis (London, 1870) 302 ff.
71. W.R. Greg, 'English Socialism', in *Social Science*, 1: 458–88.
72. ibid., 1: 458.
73. W.R. Greg, 'Kingsley and Carlyle', in *Literary and Social Judgements*, 1: 156 ff.
74. ibid., 1: 166.
75. Greg, 'English Socialism', 488.
76. W.R. Greg, 'The Relation between Employers and Employed', in *Social Science*, 1: 252–302.
77. ibid., 1: 290.
78. W.R. Greg, 'The Intrinsic Vice of Trade Unions', in *Political Problems*, 110–20.
79. ibid., 128.
80. Dicey, 372.
81. W.R. Greg, 'Why Skilled Workmen Don't Go to Church', in *Literary and Social Judgements*, 2: 256.
82. ibid., 2: 257.
83. Greg, 'The Expected Reform Bill', 429.
84. Greg, 'Truth versus Edification', in *Literary and Social Judgements*, *passim*.
85. ibid., 2: 100.
86. ibid., 2: 101.
87. W.R. Greg, 'France since 1848', *North British Review*, 15 (May 1851) 1.
88. Greg, 'The Expected Reform Bill', 449.
89. W.R. Greg, 'Realisable Ideals', in *Enigmas of Life*, 19.
90. *The Creed*, 37.

Part IV
The Faith of Scientific Naturalism

7 Scientific Discourse as an Alternative to Faith
George Levine

The enemy of knowledge, as Huxley saw it, was faith: 'The man of science has learned to believe in justification, not by faith, but by verification.'[1] Huxley's language shapes itself paradoxically, as the negative form of the language of religion; that is, in its often witty and bitter rejection of religion as a method of knowing, it retains the religious structure and the sanction of feeling that goes with it. The fondest 'convictions of barbarous and semi-barbarous people' are the convictions Huxley associates with religion: 'that authority is the soundest basis of belief; that merit attaches to a readiness to believe; that the doubting disposition is a bad one, and scepticism a sin.' Huxley assumes 'the exact reverse ... to be true'. The 'semi-barbarous' sounds like the John Henry Newman of the *Apologia pro vita sua*, published two years before. But 'the improver of natural knowledge', Huxley affirms, 'absolutely refuses to acknowledge authority, as such. For him, scepticism is the highest of duties; blind faith the one unpardonable sin.'[2] The reversal is 'exact', the refusal 'absolute', and faith, in the deliberate paradox, becomes an 'unpardonable sin'. Huxley's language depends upon the mode it is rejecting.

Such reversals provide the form of that 'naturalising' of religion of which James Moore talks in this volume. Huxley is constructing a naturalistic 'theodicy', as Moore calls it, in which the justification is established by virtue of naturalism's powers, first, to explain – to make the world even more intelligible than previous ('metaphysical') theodicies had done – and, second, to *change* the world for the better in material ways. The true God is nature, the true worship, science.

Moore's argument implies paradox: the secular is the religious. Huxley indulges that paradox. In praise of scepticism, doubt, intellectual openness, Huxley, notoriously, sounds like a dogmatist. He aspires, like any good believer, towards the absolute. He believes that 'as our race approaches maturity' it will discover 'that there is but one kind of knowledge and but one method of acquiring it'.[3] Such faith is as difficult as Newman's, and takes the breath away in its superb and unreasoning confidence.

But Huxley was making his argument in a philosophical and critical climate that makes the paradoxical form more intelligible. While the substance of his philosophical position is now easy to dismiss, he wrote not as a philosopher but as a self-conscious propagandist for a science that was still struggling to make a place for itself in the culture, and that could only be practised adequately if it were protected against established intellectual authority. It had to be defined, Huxley believed, apart from the religious context in which, as it were, it had incubated during the first half of the century. Such definition constituted not only a crisis of faith; the turn from religion, as Jeffrey von Arx shows in his study of Leslie Stephen's 'crisis', entailed a crisis of vocation. The non-Oxbridgean Huxley and the naturalists were not only arguing for 'truth', but for the respectability of science as a vocation. In this light, the struggles of the naturalists can seem merely self-serving. Frank Turner and Adrian Desmond have demonstrated how thoroughly this aspiration for professional status helped define even the smallest details of Huxley's scientific arguments.[4]

Many recent historians would agree that even the most abstruse intellectual struggles reflect ideological and socio-economic structures, if usually in much mediated ways. And it is no denial of the importance of Huxley's literal arguments to say that his concern for professional status accounts for much of his rhetorical excess. Like Matthew Arnold, whose respectability has not been in question, he defended a vocation while he was also a critic of culture, ranging often beyond his ostensible subject, modern science, to illuminate non-scientific subjects with its brilliant light. So Arnold ranged beyond literature to subject all of his society to the light of criticism, or culture.

Without defending Huxley's dogmatic ideas in defence of the anti-dogmatic, I want to reconsider the rhetoric, the writer, and much of the nineteenth-century movement of

which Huxley's is a characteristic expression. Without mini-
mising the baleful consequences of some of the naturalists'
positions, we can see that their responses to 'the crisis of faith'
– their energetic exacerbating of it – constituted a fruitful,
historically understandable alternative to the Victorian sages'
mode of secularising religion. As an imaginative construction
aimed at redefining vocation, and getting out from under
repressive and failing intellectual and social organisations,
the naturalists' vision retains a strong claim to respect.

I am not suggesting a proselyte's unqualified admiration of
the naturalists' positions, but a sceptic's reconsideration of
them. Aware as we are of their dogmatic tendencies, we need
to recall how central to their method and faith was their
opposition to authority and dogma. Not great original thinkers, they nevertheless helped create a cultural context in
which challenge to authority, demystification, and intellectual scepticism became continuing and healthy tendencies.
And that opposition took science and philosophy and culture
itself into positions that would ultimately undermine their
own.

This argument runs directly counter to Moore's, although
I find him very persuasive. He is obviously right, for example, that the naturalists were totally unable to entertain the
bare prospect of a tremendous calamity in human affairs
resulting from attempts to master nature. Nevertheless,
Huxley came round in *Evolution and Ethics* to the view that
human mastery of nature is necessarily limited, that nature
will have its way ultimately, and with catastrophic consequences. Moore is certainly right, in his masterly book on
Protestant responses to Darwinism, that the metaphor of
warfare between science and religion, so common in Huxley's writing, among others, distorts the complex history of
those responses.[5] Religion was not by any means uniformly
antagonistic to Darwin (or Huxley), and many of those who
were first ready to receive Darwin's theory were themselves
religious. To make my argument yet more difficult, there is
Frank Turner's discussion of the movement he has called
Victorian 'scientific naturalism'. Turner's strong analysis and
critique of it (and his study of various more or less eccentric
scientific or quasi-scientific reactions) belongs in the strong
tradition of anti-positivist polemic that has marked much of

the philosophy, literature, and cultural history of the last half century. Mincing no words, Turner takes the writing of the great publicists of science, in England – Huxley, Tyndall, Clifford, Spencer, Galton – as demonstrating 'the existential, intellectual, and moral bankruptcy of scientific naturalism'.[6]

For someone who has read Huxley and Tyndall and Clifford with admiration, this assertion, too, takes the breath away. How can those graceful writers, so passionate, morally engaged, and imaginatively resourceful, be seen in such a way? Tyndall argues that Huxley, Clifford, Helmholtz, and Du Bois Reymond show remarkable command of a great 'breadth of literary culture. Where among modern writers can you find their superiors in clearness and vigour of literary style?' he asks, and I have no answer.[7]

The validity of the critiques of the reductionist, positivist-like views of the naturalists by Moore and Turner, or by contemporaries like Sidgwick, Arthur Balfour, and William James, are not in question; nor are latter attacks on positivism by strong philosophers like Adorno and Marcuse, Gadamer and Habermas. But I want to call attention to a curious aspect of the discussion. While science retains in the culture at large much of the mystique of authority that Huxley tried to build for it a century ago, there are few serious thinkers and almost no humanists who talk positively about positivism, which is now something like a four-letter word, except longer; and thus the aggressive scientism of the popularisers, who were often also serious scientists, takes its place in intellectual and social history as self-deluded, self-righteous, self-interested. The reductionism (despite some echoes from modern socio-biology), and the apparently blind optimism about the possibilities of scientific and technological advancement, are no longer seen as exclusively 'scientific' arguments, but political and ideological as well.

Thus, while the critics of positivism and scientism tend to argue as from an embattled position, seeing positivist science as the voice of the dominant culture, they are acting out, again in negative, the strategies of Huxley and Co., who similarly saw themselves (at least at the start of their crusades) as arguing from embattled positions, in a culture where traditional authority was sanctioned by political and social institutions. Indeed, Turner reminds us that the push for science in post-Darwinian years significantly failed: 'scientists confronted frustration on all sides.'[8] We, however, tend to see the naturalists as belonging to the dominant new capitalist culture, confirming a version of Darwinism that sanctioned individual enterprise, reducing morality to the physically calculable, disbarring non-material causes, turning psychology into physiology, increasing alienation by insisting on the absolute separation of subject and object, and reading into the laws of evolution and the conservation of energy a justification of unequal distribution of wealth and of social as well as biological superiority. Valid enough in its way, this reading is unequal to the sense of repression felt by the naturalists, and blames scientific thought for the sins of the economic system that adopted it.

Similarly, the critics of positivism write as embattled, but surely, at least within the academy, belong to the dominant intellectual tradition. Popular culture itself is obviously divided, feeling the authority of science but distrusting it: witness the staples of one of its most successful genres, science fiction. With tedious predicability, the merely intellectual scientist villainously keeps alive, simply for the sake of knowledge, hideous and hungry mutants. The popular majority is not positivist, and tends to regard scientific intellect as a threat. Our tendency to believe in the culture's commitment to positivistic values and science needs to be qualified. In the name of spiritual truth we are still likely to kill – as in the fire-bombing of family planning clinics, for example, or in the suggestion that our enemies are 'godless'.

One of the most significant of the anti-positivist arguments rebounds upon the anti-positivists: that is, that all intellectual positions are ultimately also ideological. While, in recent years, anti-positivist positions have often been associated with leftist ideologies, there is no inevitable connection. The instabilities now endorsed by relativists and hermeneutic thinkers can play as easily into right-wing as into left-wing positions. The commitment to positive knowledge has often supported rigidly Marxist arguments. But almost universally, anti-positivist positions are associated with the arts or humanities or religion, and imply strong support for high culture. While science has accumulated money and power, status within the humanist disciplines has tended, from the time of the great debate between Huxley and Arnold, to require support for the kind of general position outlined by Turner. Humanists until recently, at least, have been agreed that science is a narrow and dehumanising experience, that it does not describe experience in all of its felt richness, that it ignores the complexities introduced by feeling, that it can at best be taken as a narrow supplement, for practical purposes, to the knowledge that derives from the life of the spirit. So Turner describes the defection of Victorian scientists from the strict positivist standards of knowledge toward knowledge of the world of spirit. In their own ways they were affirming the Arnoldian view that all of us require the satisfactions of 'conduct' and of 'beauty', satisfactions that cannot be supplied by scientific knowledge. And the Arnoldian humanist position remains in the majority. Positivism is simply not respectable these days.

While science was often a handmaiden to technology, we should notice Huxley's Carlylean insistence that he would not have remained a student of natural knowledge had he thought that knowledge was only a 'comfort-grinding machine'.[9] High-minded as he saw himself, however, he was also interested in the kinds of social improvements science might bring about; and that concern connects him with the idea of mechanism, a 'buzz word' with Arnold, Carlyle, and others for the unspiritual, the morally banal, the merely pragmatic. The association with the idea of mechanism not only set science against the highly valued 'organicism' of romantic tradition, but against the Platonic idea of contemplation. It was moving from the world of the gentleman to a lower class: the mechanical does more than contemplate, and the 'mechanic' belongs at the bottom of the social structure, a human who was, socially speaking, a mere machine.

As members of the academy, we are likely to look with melancholy at the strength of positivist thinking near the end of the century. The difficulties science was having in getting the kind of support it most wanted did not prevent a strong and rapid reaction against it. And scientists, until right up to the time of Sputnik, probably had a right to feel as beleaguered as the humanists. The reaction was against both technology and science, their frightening reductivism and mechanisation of the human. We can call to mind writers like

Butler and Shaw, among many others, mounting witty and ironic attacks. As early as the 1880s Arthur Balfour, whose two books, *A Defence of Philosophic Doubt* and *The Foundations of Belief*, constituted a very powerful – and representative – assault on the scientific idea of truth, complained about the intellectual dominance of the scientific naturalists:

> Speculation seems sadly in want of destructive criticism at the present time. Whenever any faith is held strongly and universally, there is a constant and overpowering tendency to convert Philosophy, which should be its judge, into its servant. It was so formerly, when theology ruled supreme; it is so now that Science has usurped its place: and I assert with some confidence that the bias given to thought in the days of the schoolmen through the overwhelming in-fluence of the first of these creeds was not a whit more pernicious to the cause of impartial speculation than the bias which it receives at the moment through the influence of the second.[10]

Ironically, Balfour can use precisely the sort of rhetorical move – identifying science with 'faith', finding it governed not by pursuit of truth, but by bias – that the scientists themselves used against their enemies. Huxley's inversion of the language of faith comes back to haunt him here (he died in the midst of writing his refutation of Balfour's *Foundations of Belief*). Given the extravagant claims of the naturalists, Balfour had every right to challenge science as though it had become a faith. Yet, as I have been suggesting, the natural-ists' pugnacity was not unreasonable in a society that was only slowly and reluctantly allowing them serious professional status, that had traditionally resisted the 'mechanical', even in its later secular phases – as so many of the Victorian prophets make clear; and the reaction, once set in, has been unre-lenting.

In the halls of military power it may be possible, but where scientists, philosophers, critics engage the questions serious-ly, we cannot now think of science as a purely rational activity. After the analyses of Kuhn, Lakatos, Feyerabend, Robert Young, Stephen Jay Gould, we cannot accept unqual-ified the Popperian (and Huxleyan) view that falsifiability is the determining test of true science. Philosophy and literary criticism are currently busy reading science as unprivileged discourse, containing within it remnants of the mythical, being in fact a kind of fiction.[11] And the major move in modern philosophy of science is to recognise the multiplicity of scientific methods, the impossibility of the sort of disinterest Huxley wanted to claim for it, the possibility that science does not progress, and the influence of social, political, historical, personal forces. Who now would agree that there is but one kind of knowledge, dare to identify it, and, yet more perilously, to identify it with empiricism?

It may be that we prefer the solutions of Balfour, or of Arnold, Ruskin, Samuel Butler, Henry Sidgwick, to the intellectual, moral, and social problems to which Huxley, Tyndall, and Clifford were responding in their more popular writings; I am not so sure I do. While Balfour's intelligent criticism establishes a radical scepticism which finally readmits the old faith because *all* belief is based on 'non-rational' cases,[12] this move hardly resolves the issues. More secular responses get not much further. Ruskin's moral passion and glorious prose have little to do with the large epistemological questions the naturalist position raised; and his movingly paternal proposals for social reorganisation seem wildly out of touch with the world he was addressing.[13] I can be moved by the vision but am not sure that it would have been better than disastrous in enactment. I would want to say the same of Huxley who may, indeed, have been less pugnacious, bulldog though he was, than either Ruskin or Arnold.

Thus, recognising the ideological implications of ostensibly disinterested scientific work is only part of the story; what are the ideological implications of its alternatives? The pursuit of disinterest, and the (now, to us) misguided ideal of objectivity and natural observation, was not merely 'scientific'. Arnold's 'disinterest' is a version of John Herschel's, or Huxley's; Carlyle's *Selbsttödung* was a requirement of scientific study; George Eliot's 'duty' entailed precisely that refusal to allow interest to interfere with judgment and moral act that we find Huxley urging in essay after essay.[14] The alliance of science with a powerful and morally crude social authority came only when science, having failed to establish its authority on its own terms, allied itself to the nation's military and imperial ambitions.[15] It was not absurd of scientific writers to think of themselves as in the minority, to go out with intellectual six-guns blazing against all forms of authority, imagining the possibility of revolutionising the moral and social structures of the country.

I want then to affirm that however vulnerable the scientific naturalists were to the kinds of criticism Moore and Turner level at them, they were involved in one of the great imaginative responses to the difficulties of modern culture – as rich and imaginative as, say, Arnold's. And I want to argue that the positions they adopted, however arrogant the formulation might sometimes be, however implicated in political and self-interested actions for the advancement of new professional power, developed the intellectual strategies for the very critiques we use against them. It is surely worth considering how, in the light of the transparent failure of traditional religion and philosophy or even the sages to improve the condition of the ordinary person very much, science could be seen as a genuinely liberating possibility. The battle was part of a class war, and science certainly served the interests of the capitalists. But its methods pointed towards the developments of a meritocracy, and implied a far more democratic social order, so that what it affirmed it could also, eventually, negate.

I want, in what follows, to look at the substance, rather than the ideological implications of some of the naturalists' basic arguments. I shall be setting up polarities, which need to be qualified very heavily, between traditional assumptions and those to which the naturalists tended – at least by virtue of their arguments about science and scientific method. (Tyndall, for example, was so Carlylean outside his scientific work that his moral and social positions seem to belong rather to the sage-like secularisation of experience – which often becomes another form of mystification – than the naturalists' kind.) These polarities can, crudely, be described in this way:

— faith in *a priori* knowledge as opposed to 'faith' in experience as the source of all knowledge.
— valuing the spiritual and the timeless as opposed to change and the material (which incorporates the spiritual).

— commitment to the past as model as opposed to the past as origin.

— imagination of a nature hierarchically and purposively organised for the benefit of humankind as opposed to a nature democratically organised, without divine purpose; meaning here is humanly imposed, and nature's 'usefulness' entails human manipulation of it.

— confidence in the possibility of objectivity as opposed to a heightened sensitivity to the difficulties of objectivity and of the safeguards required to avoid the distortions of human consciousness, the limitations of human perspective.

— faith in the humanly satisfying meaning of nature (based on a prior faith in the divine organisation of nature) as opposed to belief that 'objective' investigation may lead to dangerous discovery; on this latter model 'Truth' becomes both an intellectual and a moral virtue, and entails rigorous self-discipline and courage to confront a world inimical to human consciousness. Truth inheres in any study in which scientific method is preserved, and thus serves to protect against any subject matter which might seem, on traditional grounds, immoral.

— faith in language as accurately 'representing' reality and (consider Carlyle and Ruskin's etymologies) somehow bearing truth within itself (i.e., Adamic language) and a sense of language as an arbitrary tool, not representing reality but useful in allowing manipulation and understanding of it.

By virtue of its positions, Victorian scientific naturalism was implicated in its own displacement, and the requirement that all knowledge be tested, which often turned into dogmatic denials of alternative models of knowledge or into a philosophically evasive agnosticism, became part of that continuing critique of authority that is now subverting all foundationalist thought – including, of course, positivism.

So, 'scientific method' begins with the refusal of a lie, continues in dogged determination to learn the truth, allows, in the discovery of truth, rational change. Its method is saintly suppression of all interest. Scientific knowledge is beyond prejudice, and claims the authority lost by traditional religion. It is based not in inherited assumptions, but in experience itself, in the confirmation given by a community committed to the same values and procedures, and it looks not backward to a source, but forward, to a development.

Such was the official position of the naturalists. But it is important to recognise some of the difficulties implicit in it. If we look for philosophical consistency we find instead a mass of contradictions. Since, however, the primary object of the naturalists was to clear space for free scientific practice (just as Arnold's was to clear space for poetry) they sought to avoid full philosophical elaborations of their position – with the possible exception of Clifford, who died too young to write more than tentative essays on philosophic problems. Particularly, as Turner points out, the naturalists refused confrontation with ontological questions.

The naturalists' essential move was against any form of the *a priori*, for, as they saw it, the *a priori* made further discussion impossible; it could be affirmed but not verified, and thus it undercut the whole enterprise of science. But of course, as they also understood, their science could not verify its own initiating assumptions, and hence the Spencerian preoccupation with the unknowable and Huxley's coinage of 'agnosticism'. Huxley would unabashedly affirm, for example, that 'physical science starts from certain postulates', and that, by definition, these are not 'demonstrable'. One of the postulates is 'the objective existence of the material world'. We are in metaphysics here, but Huxley does not want to play, and he settles for the view that use of these postulates is justifiable because 'expectations logically based upon them are verified, or, at any rate, not contradicted, whenever they can be tested by experience'. This is not good philosophy, but Huxley knows he is not writing it. Perhaps less excusable is his assumption that 'rational order ... pervades the universe'.[16] This he does not even affirm as an undemonstrable postulate. Science, for Huxley, is the attempt to discover this order! But, not having discovered it, how can he know it is there?

Perhaps the most difficult contradiction was the one that led to reductionism in the naturalists' treatment of matters traditionally regarded as spiritual. Huxley dismissed the charge of 'materialism' since, as he said, 'I am utterly incapable of conceiving the existence of matter if there is no mind in which to picture that existence'. But he could not understand, nor could any of his colleagues, what connection there might be between the physical and the immaterial, particularly consciousness (although Clifford struggled toward a half-formed conception of 'mind-stuff' as a way around the difficulty). This became one of the great issues of late nineteenth-century thought, another version of Cartesian dualism, of the mind–body problem. Huxley and Tyndall settled for the view that one could not have consciousness without parallel physical phenomena. As Tyndall was to put it in his notorious 'Belfast Address': 'We can trace the development of a nervous system, and correlate with it the parallel phenomena of sensation and thought. We see with undoubting certainty that they go hand in hand. But we try to soar in a vacuum the moment we seek to comprehend the connection between them. . . . Man the *object* is separated by an impassable gulf from man the *subject*.'[17]

This impassable gulf did not stop the naturalists from attempting to extend the scientific mythos from inorganic, to organic, and finally to human phenomena. Taking up the injunction of Comte and Mill, they saw no discontinuity, of the sage-like sort, between material and spiritual. If they did not know what the connection was, they believed there was one, and that belief played a critical role in the whole development of psychology and social science. The rhetorical inversions of Huxley's prose are not merely satirical. They reflect his commitment to find an alternative to the religion whose values he accepted and whose power is still manifest in his language.

The rational order of the universe, which religion had sustained, but which seemed to stop short at the human, was now to be extended to human organisation; the naturalists sought to develop the social sciences on the model of the physical, to seek in human behaviour and organisation 'laws' that would explain and predict – as Herschel, whose astronomy was the model for all science, could predict the movements of the planets. Darwin's extension of 'law' to the biological seemed to Darwinians like Huxley to mean the extension of the kinds of laws discoverable in Newtonian physics. The differences entailed by a study whose definition required historical, phylogenetic explanation and whose subjects were always *unique* organisms, was not apparent to Huxley.[18] Recognising the fundamental intellectual contradiction that supported this move, we need not regard it as intellectual bankruptcy (in the context of religious arguments, which insisted that humans were somehow exempt from the orderly structure of the rest of the inorganic and organic world, it was invaluable). An unfortunate consequence of the rhetorical shift was that the authority formerly inhering in religious tradition shifted to a science which could naturalise the prejudices of the culture and reinstate them in theories of racial and sexual superiority. While the scientists were in no way superior to their culture, and their subversion of tradition often merely reinstated it in other forms – which can help account for its ultimate successes – yet that sanctioning of subversion made it an essential part of post-Darwinian thought, allowing for further subversions of new naturalising mystifications.

As cultural critics, Huxley, Tyndall, and Clifford offered refreshing alternatives to the kind of humanist arguments we find in Matthew Arnold. For most of us, the ideal of Victorian culture has been shaped by Arnold, and by the other great critics of society we have come to call 'sages'. But against that notion of culture, it is worth looking at a more naturalistic one. The struggle to perceive a rational order of the universe is here most clearly ideological; the failure to recognise the interested elements in ostensibly disinterested study is most clearly damaging. Yet the work of E.B. Tylor, in its attempt to translate religious experience into rationally explicable phenomena, offers an interesting example of the kinds of correctives the more existentially alert sages often needed, and of ways in which a radically imperfect scientific method opened new possibilities of value and social organisation.

Reading *Primitive Culture* now is a curious experience. If one had wanted to predict how a 'social scientist' would apply the methods of science, Tylor's first chapter would have fulfilled almost all expectations. It is uniformitarian and evolutionary, and it attempts to apply the methods of natural philosophy to the study of mankind. Thus, Tylor sets to work assuming the 'unity of nature, the fixity of its laws', and 'the definitive sequence of cause and effect through which every fact depends on what has gone before it'.[19] Indeed, although with less belligerence, Tylor sounds rather like Tyndall: 'To many educated minds there seems something presumptuous and repulsive in the view that the history of mankind is part and parcel of the history of nature, that our thoughts, wills, and actions accord with laws as definite as those which govern the motion of waves, the combination of acids and bases, and the growth of plants and animals.'[20] Taking too literally the scientific ideal of 'law', 'regularity', and measurement, Tylor assumes too readily his own capacity for detachment. Needing a 'scale', he invents one, as though it were self-evidently *in* nature; to nobody's surprise, he places Western European civilisation at the top, as the standard of measurement. Yet in so doing, he only makes formal the assumptions of all his contemporaries (which is why the scale seemed so self-evident). Nevertheless, having the idea of a 'scale' actually loosens the grip of religious and ethnic complacency at the very moment that it seems to be getting scientific sanction.

Tylor's overview of anthropology implies two theories of culture, which distinguish the naturalists and the sages. These were formulated, Tylor argues, in the eighteenth century: the 'degenerationist' theory, formulated by Joseph de Maistre, who argued against the 'perverse' modern idea that civilisation has grown from savagery; and the 'progressionist' theory, formulated by Gibbon. Where de Maistre argues that civilisation degenerated from a higher stage of culture, Gibbon argues that mankind developed from savage beginnings, from an 'abject condition, perhaps the primitive and universal state of man', to a condition from which 'it is able to command the animals, to fertilise the earth, to traverse the ocean, and to measure the heavens'.[21]

For Tylor, as for Darwin, the scientific ideal of 'regularity', and the cultural ideal of 'progress' are threatened by the recognition that retrogression is possible, and extinction common. Yet Tylor, more unambiguously than Darwin, allies himself with the mythos of progression. He even formulates it, as he puts it, 'in mythic fashion': 'We may fancy ourselves looking on Civilization, as in personal figure she traverses the world; we see her lingering or resting by the way, and often deviating into paths that bring her toiling back to where she had passed by long ago; but, direct or devious, her path lies forward, and if now and then she tries a few backward steps, her walk soon falls into a helpless stumbling. It is not according to her nature, her feet were not made to plant uncertain steps behind her, for both in her forward view and in her onward gait she is of truly human type.'[22] The view is familiar: we need only recall George Eliot's 'melioristic' invocation, less than a year after the publication of *Primitive Culture*, of 'the growing good of the world'.

Tylor's formulation might be taken as an elaboration of what she probably meant by this unsatisfying phrase. In George Eliot, the disparity between the bleak local narratives and the quasi-religious faith in ultimate goodness becomes evident. Tylor's 'scientific' justification has its elements of faith, too:

> In striking a balance between the effects of forward and backward movement in civilization, it must be borne in mind how powerfully the diffusion of culture acts in preserving the results of progress from the attacks of degeneration. A progressive movement in culture spreads, and becomes independent of the fate of its originators [read here Dorothea Brooke's 'incalculably diffusive acts' and Jubal's invention of music]. What is produced in some limited district is diffused over a wider and wider area, where the process of effectual 'stamping out' becomes more and more difficult. Thus it is even possible for the habits and inventions of races long extinct to remain as the common property of surviving nations; and the destructive actions which make such havoc with the civilizations of particular districts fail to destroy the civilization of the world.[23]

But the evidence, as Tylor himself often admits, might be read in other ways. Underlying the view is an evolutionary model: 'the institutions which can best hold their own in the world gradually supersede the less fit ones';[24] and this idea of development gives Tylor both the assurance of meaningful-ness so essential after the displacement of religious explanation, and the method he needs to make sense of the phenomena of culture.

Gradual if locally irregular progress allows for a scale and for a position from which to judge the past, while at the same time it makes a kind of cliodicy, justifying the ways of history to man, making the secularisation of experience tolerable. As for Huxley and Darwin, Tylor can only understand the present by seeing it historically. One of Darwin's most striking moves was to find the evidence he needed not in the formal functioning of organisms, but in their vestigial and functionless parts. He was delighted by 'mammae in men', for example. Such 'vestiges' could only be explained historically, as evidence for an earlier stage of the organism, in which the 'vestiges' had been functional. Similarly, Tylor focuses on what he calls 'survivals', cultural phenomena with no obvious contemporary function. Their apparent meaninglessness argues a past in which they had performed useful functions. This strategy depends, as Darwin himself was to admit, on a Paleyan assumption 'that every detail of structure, excepting rudiments, was of some special, though unrecognised, service'.[25] But even if irrational data could eventually be framed within a rational theory, the world that theory explained was clearly not the one imagined by natural theologians, not designed and intentional down to the last hair of the head.

This shift of perspective from the tradition of natural theology, which restricted earlier modes of explanation and, for example, made it extremely difficult to arrive at a theory of evolution, was only one element in the naturalists' alternatives to the humanist idea of culture. Another is suggested by George Stocking, Jr, in an important essay on Tylor and Arnold. Tylor's title, *Primitive Culture*, Stocking suggests, would constitute an oxymoron in Arnold's language. The concept that 'primitive' peoples might even *have* a culture begins, though it does not for Tylor fully mean, the idea of cultural relativity – an idea that the Victorian sages, on the whole, sorely lacked. A scale of civilisation, after all, implies many different *kinds* of civilisation, even if there is a flat judgment built into the scale. Even the view that primitive animism is an early form of science makes the primitive and the civilised dangerously kin. Thus, the ethnocentric Tylor offers an argument that, according to Stocking, 'contained at least the germ of cultural plurality': 'one way (although perhaps not the most direct) to the idea of different cultures was through the concept of stages of culture. Perhaps more importantly, cultural evolutionism implied a kind of func-tionalism in the realm of morals and values which, if it was not the same as modern anthropological relativism, was a major step toward it.'[26] Gillian Beer argues that Tylor's project was 'the recognition of the "real culture" and the imaginative energy of peoples throughout the world and throughout history'.[27] Such a self-consciously comparativist position, based on what Tylor took to be the evidence of the total continuity between primitive beings and 'higher' ones, could find no place in Arnold's qualitatively organised scheme of things. Culture is something higher than and different from mere civilisation; and poor Wragg has no culture.

In the short run, at least, the naturalists inevitably won out against religious dogmatism; but their most difficult combat came against those, like the writers Turner discusses, with scientific interests of their own, and those, like the sages, who were secular and oriented toward the arts and literature. Most of the great Victorian sages, however anti-clerical they became, tended to assume more or less precisely some impersonal power of conscience, spirit, intelligence. Finding the source of value in imagined pasts, secular and divine, the sages viewed the new with fear and scepticism, and therefore paradoxically worked out strategies that would allow them to cling to the institutions and authority they so marvellously criticised. (At the same time, their criticism of contemporary culture – particularly Carlyle's – had a strong influence on the decision of several of the naturalists to enter scientific work.)

The naturalists' attack on traditional religion had much to do with the Fall, the quintessential degeneration myth. And Huxley, at the very end of his life, directly attacked that myth, on both moral and intellectual grounds. How rational can a world be, he asks: what sort of God could have created man 'in his own image' and then have allowed him to fall 'away from goodness' on the 'most trifling temptation'? Yet more cruelly, he goes on to say, in a diction self-consciously

borrowed from the New Testament, as a consequence of that
fall 'the whole creation travaileth and groaneth in the bonds
of sin and misery; now, as ever since Adam and Eve were
expelled from Eden, all but a mere fraction of the human
race have lived sorrowfully and sinfully, and at death have
passed to endless torment.'[28] Degeneration, of course, need
not be from a literal paradise; but it was characteristic of the
Victorians to value some pure, authoritative, and immediately apprehended experience; or the Fall might have been
from an ideal community, or from language in touch with its
experiential sources, or from classical order and balance.
Arnold finds an ideal possibility for culture in the Greeks, of
whom, Richard Jenkyns argues, he has 'an inadequate
notion'.[29] The Greeks were his myth of culture – balance,
order, sanity, health – as mediaeval Gothic architecture
became Ruskin's, with its 'savage-ness' and spiritual freedom.
The ideas seem radically different, but the resort to a
'factual' past as model and authority reflects the same sort of
resistance to the new, the same attempt to relocate an older
spiritual authority. The corollary of degeneration, the 'golden age', lies tacitly in the background of much of their
cultural criticism.

But the Golden Age, as Gillian Beer has shown, was
disbarred by Darwinian theory. Darwin locates our ancestor
in that 'hairy quadruped, furnished with a tail and pointed
ears, probably arboreal in its habits',[30] so unappealing, as
Matthew Arnold put it – half-smiling, we hope – to the sense
in us for conduct, the sense in us for beauty. And beyond
that unidyllic source lies the true organic origin in unicellular
hermaphroditic organisms. On the evolutionary account
origins trail no clouds of glory. As Beer puts it, where the
biblical paradise should have been we have only an 'empire
of molluscs'.

The foundation of truth, once wrested from God, had to
be located in some impersonal source. But the 'impersonal',
outside of God, is without value; and the great quest of
nineteenth-century secular culture was for an impersonal
authority that could include the normal human preoccupation with 'value'. The Cartesian dilemma, as Richard Bernstein calls it, is central to the Victorian debate. Descartes,
Bernstein says, 'leads us with an apparent and ineluctable

necessity to a grand and seductive Either/Or. *Either* there is some support for our being, a fixed foundation for our knowledge, *or* we cannot escape the forces of darkness that envelop us with madness, with intellectual and moral chaos.'[31] According to Descartes, the human mind, though limited, has the equipment to know the truth; error results from misuse. The ideal of 'self-purification', so dear to the hearts of Victorian thinkers and artists, is part of the Cartesian method. And the quest for some ultimate authority for knowledge through purging of all inherited traditions and the turn to Experience is similarly Cartesian. Descartes wipes out the golden age of knowledge because what we know cannot come to us through 'authority'. We retreat to the internal 'cogito' and construct from there.

But once the secular move is made, and the reliance on Descartes's divine source is dismissed, we are left with a fundamental dualism. Like their most obvious antagonists, Huxley and the naturalists shared the terror of 'darkness', 'madness', and 'moral chaos' that would come if we could find no foundation for our knowledge. Like them, they believed that the source was entangled with value: the rational order of the universe is, without question, a good in Huxley's world; and when he asks himself whether he would rather be free, in the theological sense, to choose evil, or be constrained, in the deterministic naturalists' sense, to do what is necessary, he prefers the 'necessary' – as long as he can rely on the necessary being a good. Huxley believes, with a conviction beyond ideology, that the religious view of the world is 'bad': it implies an irrational disorder and leads to that worst of sins, ignorance. Better, in the Cartesian dilemma, objectivity and determinism than subjectivity and chaos. Value can be excluded from the surface of the objectivist's thinking because it is deeply bound in the idea of objectivity itself. In the struggle between the naturalists and traditional religion, the question was not about whether objectivity was possible, but whether it was possible without God.

Despite the quest for value-free judgments, the scientists, as the examples of Huxley and Tylor should have demonstrated, were constantly engaged with problems of value; ideas matter. Further complications arise, however, because the naturalists knew, in spite of their Baconian protestations, that ideas do not come on the empiricist formula. The scientists' preoccupation with 'imagination', as in Tyndall's famous lecture, or G.H. Lewes's massive attempt to reconcile science and metaphysics in *Problems of Life and Mind,* is a symptom of widespread recognition that the Baconian method had little to do with the actual procedures of science, and that 'science' was not as rational as its apologists often argued. Here again the scientific mythos is not so clearly opposed to the mythos of the sages. We find in Huxley sentiments we might have expected from Ruskin or Arnold, and in all of the scientists a view for which they are often not forgiven, that science is integral with culture and enriches life, not merely materially and quantitatively, but with a sense of history and art and the complexity of social relations.

Of course, the myths diverge. In rejecting the past as model, the naturalists inevitably questioned standards of morality and taste as well. While they constantly waged war against those who argued that rejection of conventional religion was licence for immortality, and lived with a puritanical austerity that might have been the envy of the strictest evangelicals, their inversion of religious rhetoric and secularisation of meaning subverted traditional supports for morality. When Darwin traced the aesthetic sense back to sexual selection, and conscience to the usefulness of social sympathy in natural selection, he wrested those authoritative categories from the absolute. Ironically, while finding their source in natural phenomena, he initiated a tradition the sages could not contemplate, of denaturalising morality and taste. That is, Art and Morality are not in 'nature' but are human developments from anaesthetic and amoral phenomena; human effort has transformed these and tried to give them the same status in nature as physical phenomena.

In modern parlance, the scientists' project was demystification. If they often remystified (as we can see Tylor doing) by giving nature a *moral* authority, they did not make remystification the kind of high cause we can see in Carlyle, or in Arnold's wonderful impressionistic catch-phrases like 'Reason and the will of God', or 'Sweetness and Light', or, more telling still, 'to see the object as in itself it really is'. The methods announced by the naturalists would have forced them to criticise many of their own positions had they been fully aware of the contradictions.

Some of the richness of the naturalists' position can be inferred from Huxley's part in the great debate with Arnold on Literature and Education. Most of us assume that Arnold was the winner. The upholder of culture, concerned with the full human experience, should indeed triumph over the philistine proponent of an exclusively scientific education. Insisting on the 'need of humane letters', Arnold connects that word, 'humane', with 'the paramount desire in men that good should be for ever present to them', and he goes on to argue that humane letters will build the necessary bridge between 'the new conceptions' provided by science and 'our instinct for beauty, our instinct for conduct'.[32] The unGothic Arnold invokes the Middle Ages against modern science as he tries to explain the function of humane letters. In those days, Arnold says, 'knowledge was made to engage ... emotions ... powerfully'. We may deny the religious substance of the medieval vision, but we must sustain the form. Poetry replaces the religion that science has displaced, and Arnold finds his values by looking backward: 'The medieval universities came into being, because the supposed knowledge, delivered by Scripture and the Church, so deeply engaged men's hearts, by so simply, easily, and powerfully relating itself to their desire for conduct, their desire for Beauty.'[33]

When Huxley looked backward it was to find indications of developments to come, and in essay after essay, reviewing the history of science in European culture, he sees the Middle Ages' preoccupation with the supernatural as an obstacle to knowledge. So much had been lost through the Dark Ages that the new scientific men of the Renaissance, 'though standing on the shoulders of the old philosophers, were a long time before they saw as much as their forerunners [the ancient Greeks] had done'.[34] The naturalists did not participate in the mediaevalism that turned so many Victorian eyes to the distant past. Huxley's vision, in good post-Darwinian fashion, is developmental, his interest in history is an interest in origins, not models.

Arnold's 'understanding of science', a recent critic has noted, was 'extraordinarily naive': 'he constantly stresses the importance of knowing the results of scientific study, but he seems curiously insensitive to the claims of science as a mode of intellectual culture and thus as an important element in a liberal curriculum.'[35] He thinks of the natural sciences as mechanisms for gathering facts, some of which develop into new 'concepts'. But he does not imagine scientific imagination, or that scientific fact might have moral and emotional significance. Neither he nor the other sages could share John Stuart Mill's touching view that 'The intensest feeling of the beauty of a cloud lighted by the setting sun, is no hindrance to my knowing that the cloud is vapour of water, subject to all the laws of vapours in a state of suspension.'[36]

For Huxley, whatever Arnold might have thought of scientific discourse, knowledge and feeling were not disjunct, and truth was not morally neutral. The attempt to achieve dispassion is necessary precisely because so much is at stake; we must be brave enough, so the rhetoric of all the naturalists goes, to discover what we think we do not want to know. Despite their perhaps disingenuous bravado, Huxley's arguments were anything but obvious. We may want to take a deep breath at some of his aggressively scientistic passages now, but despite the apparent excess, they rightly make the scientist no mere recorder of the way things are but a visionary, a more convincing sage for his time than the sage himself: 'the improvement of natural knowledge whatever direction it has taken, and however low the aims of those who may have commenced it – has not only conferred practical benefits on men, but in so doing has effected a revolution in their conceptions of the universe and for themselves, and has profoundly altered their modes of thinking and their views of right and wrong. I say that natural knowledge, seeking to satisfy wants, has found the ideas which can alone still spiritual cravings.'[37] It is precisely for such views as this that humanist historians have condemned the naturalists. Their sin was high valuation of reason and intelligence, the assumption that knowledge is always vitally connected to human values; their utopianism was a result of the historically excusable view that the most potent kind of knowledge western civilisation had produced could extend helpfully to all areas of human experience, and of the assumption that such knowledge was the condition for human improvement.

In his debate with Arnold, Huxley was not asking for a

purely scientific education. He was responding to a critical failure in English curricula. When he wrote, as Lyon Playfair pointed out in his Presidential Address to the British Association in 1885, there was 'a lamentable deficiency of science education' almost everywhere in England. In the endowed schools, for example, 'while twelve to sixteen hours per week are devoted to classics, two to three hours are considered ample for science. . . . The old traditions of education stick as firmly to schools as a limpet does to a rock; though I do the limpet injustice, for it does make excursions to pastures new.'[38]

'Science and Culture' was as daring in its way as Ruskin's 'Traffic'. In Birmingham, the den of the practical men of practical England, at the opening of a science college, Huxley dared to attack merely 'practical' views. With a rhetoric more devious if less thrilling than Ruskin's, he weaves an argument around Josiah Mason's condition that there be 'no mere literary instruction and education' at the new college, and ends with an apologia for languages and the humanities. Arnold's objectives are sound; what is wrong is his view that they can only be attained through exclusively literary education. Huxley in fact smuggles Arnold into the Josiah Mason curriculum.

Huxley insists on the importance of 'a wider culture than that yielded by science alone'.[39] The object of scientific education, and of science itself, according to Huxley, is neither prosperity nor education, but, as Ruskin would have been proud to argue, 'the enhancement of life'. 'If the increasing perfection of manufacturing processes is to be accompanied by an increasing debasement of those who carry them on, I do not see the good of industry and prosperity. . . The prosperity of industry depends', Huxley tells the founders of the science college, 'not merely upon the improvement of manufacturing processes, not even upon the ennobling of the individual character, but upon a third condition as well, namely a clear understanding of the conditions of social life, on the part of both the capitalist and the operative.'[40] Nothing could be more sage-like, except perhaps the implicit trust in the ordinary student.

If there was to have been a triumph, it probably should have been Huxley's: his essay, rhetorically, is the model of balance that Arnold's is often taken to be, as he argues for remediation of an intolerable condition in education, demonstrates a rich sense of what humanistic study was and should be, and implies a new model, not built on mediaeval retrospects, of what it might mean to connect knowledge and feeling. While Arnold revealed what should have been a disqualifying ignorance of science, Huxley risks extending culture out into the world of social and political action.

Of course Huxley and Arnold were friends, and the public encounter, while serious enough, reflects the playfulness of both great writers in their pugnacity. The solemnity with which both are read these days misses the flexibility of spirit that made them effective cultural critics but bad philosophers. Their dogmatism in support of flexibility suggests inconsistency; their willingness to play in public suggests ultimate consistency. Substantively, they agreed far more than they disagreed. Both sought to humanise and broaden the understanding of the society which they mutually regarded as narrow and 'philistine'. As Huxley wanted to insure that modern languages and literature were part of the 'science' curriculum (for 'practical' reasons, of course), so Arnold would allow study of Euclid and Newton and Darwin. Elsewhere, Arnold agreed that science should be part of everyone's curriculum; Huxley is said to have agreed that the Bible should be taught to all students.

Taking into account this fundamental agreement, however, we need to return to the divergence. We may think of Arnold as a spokesman for rounded culture, for a rich contextual sense of art and human experience, but in his formulaic insistence on beauty and conduct, with its appeal to the Hellenic or Hebraic past, and with his intense distrust of the complacency of the modern, he remained closed to the widening of the humanist position implicit in Huxley's argument. Arnold looks back, and tends to freeze the past into an ideal; it becomes a point of comparison. Huxley sees the past developmentally, not as a model but as part of the condition that accounts for where we are now. The most profound divergence between the two friends comes, I believe, just here: with all its failures, the constantly transforming present, Huxley would argue, is where value resides.

At this point, I want to consider more generally, though briefly, some aspects of the naturalists' thought (many of them suggested in the work of Huxley and Tylor discussed earlier) that led them to believe they were able to provide a better alternative to the religious vision or the visions of the more secular sages. The basis of the naturalists' arguments, we can now see, was 'faith', or a cluster of not entirely compatible 'faiths', and to sustain these they had to look not for philosophical consistency or comprehensiveness, but for pragmatic confirmation. They built their church on assumptions that remained 'assumptions', and their spiritual consolation was in the pride with which they were willing to make the sacrifice of traditional consolation for the sake of making their society better. A form of spiritual pride, perhaps. But pragmatic effects aside, they were remarkably effective intellectually in opening everything to question, in suggesting the arbitrariness of conventions that had always been taken as inescapably real.

They tended to accept the uniformitarian dogma that knowledge is possible because the world has always worked uniformly, according to laws now in operation, and that ostensibly massive changes and extraordinary phenomena can be accounted for by minute incremental effects of minute causes. *Natura non agit per saltum* was Darwin's watchword, and Lyell's. Knowledge, they believed, can only be achieved when the data of experience are organised into laws.

Although law did come to replace religion as the guarantor of order in the universe and society, a testimony to God's ordering intelligence, the central naturalist move was to demystify it. At their most rigorous, the naturalists regarded laws as having no teleological implication. Laws existed in nature as the human formulation of regularity of sequence;[41] and such sequence operates by means of uninterrupted cause and effect (cause and effect themselves were often drained of metaphysical implications and understood only as phenomena in constant conjunction). Finally, while Herschel himself understood that 'naming' was merely an arbitrary convenience to avoid getting lost in particularities, later science, particularly after Darwin, was leaning imperfectly away from the essentialist view that classification, and its language, represent some reality in nature, and was tending to conceive all things as in flux.

The question of what determines the truthfulness of a 'discovery' in such conditions was the major one of scientific method. Discoveries stick, the naturalists argued, because of their power to connect other 'partial generalisations', to explain more than they were intended to explain, and to be subjected to 'exact verification' (or, in Popper's later formulation, to be 'falsifiable'). Scientific truth implied a community of understanding. The truth, finally, lay beyond words, which were to be severed from Platonic essentialism and regarded as convenieces of discussion and ordering, subject only to the rules of language, while truth depended finally on experience. The establishment of this myth of objectivity and positivity, even against the insights implicit in the overt rejection of essentialism and Adamic language, is what gave to science that tinge of orthodoxy Balfour assails. Objectivity belonged to a religious intellectual frame. The Cartesian dilemma becomes most intense at the point at which a divine source of authority 'disappears'. And thus the strategy of the naturalists in adopting the structure of religious language without its substance.

Barring language and spirit as 'real', the naturalists took the material world as the only real subject of knowledge. Thus, in the demystifying but reductive move that most fully alienated the religious and the humanists, Huxley and Tyndall discussed human life as they discussed physical phenomena; science, as Tyndall put it, attempts 'to explain the unknown in terms of the known'. He takes as example the excited actions of a merchant who leaps from his chair after reading a letter and makes complicated moves to avert financial disaster. This complex mass of action, emotional, intellectual, and mechanical, is evoked by the 'impact upon the retina of the infinitesimal waves of light coming from a few pencil marks on a bit of paper.... What caused the merchant to spring out of his chair? The contraction of his muscles. What made his muscles contract? An impulse of the nerves, which lifted the proper latch, and liberated the muscular power. Whence this impulse? From the centre of the nervous system. But how did it originate there? This is the critical question, to which someone will reply that it had its origin in the human soul.'[42]

If anything justifies Turner's severe judgment, it is writing like this. Needing to bring behaviour within the order of reality recognised by physical science, Tyndall argues that his explanation is better than the conventional religious one, which in insisting on a willing and free self implies that there is a 'self within the self which acts through the body as through a skillfully constructed instrument'.[43] Finally, Tyndall admits, he cannot answer the question, 'Whence this impulse?' He cannot discover the connection 'between molecular motions and states of consciousness'.[44]

There are, then, spiritual possibilities, both for Tyndall and for the 'agnostic' Huxley, but only if they are not invoked as explanations for material phenomena. As W.H. Mallock's version of Tyndall says, 'Let us beware, then, of not considering religion noble; but let us beware still more of considering it true.'[45] Exposing the metaphysics implicit in our conventional way of talking about 'self', and demystifying the language of 'spirit', were part of the programme to make the material respectable in a world whose values were at least professedly 'spiritual'. Unfortunately, Tyndall's materialist reading of human behaviour sounds silly (while it seems to expose in its choice of example something of his ideological concerns). It is clear enough now that the attempt to assimilate biology to physics was a mistake. As Ernst Mayr argues, 'The explanatory equipment of the physical sciences is insufficient to explain complex living systems.'[46] But underlying the reductionist moves of the naturalists was the metaphysical assumption, acceptable to humanist and scientist alike, that the world is unified and coherent: there is 'but one science about the one real world'.[47] Kuhn's theory of scientific revolutions has put this nineteenth-century view in doubt; and Mayr and Stephen Jay Gould have argued persuasively against the view that biology is reducible to physics. The absurd example of Tyndall's robotic merchant suggests that the naturalists understood that there was a problem. Their strategy was not to yield belief in unity but to confess that they did not understand *how* it worked. At stake was the possibility of science in a culture that preferred *a priori* authority, and took the idea of the unity of nature as unproblematic.

Arnold, we remember, urged the importance of 'disinterest' too, and he found his model in Burke. He might have looked to the scientists who even when smugly dogmatic about the atomic-Newtonian model of matter, insisted that they could be wrong. After all, Huxley's institutionalised science rejected Huxley's model of the world. As Stephen Toulmin and June Goodfield put it, 'the men responsible' for the dogma of classical physics 'wished to establish neither a political nor an ideological tyranny and when the time came they refused to shut their eyes to the necessity for fundamental change'. Late-nineteenth-century positivism was not, says John Passmore, 'an attack on philosophy by arrogant and self-satisfied scientists'. Rather, it prepared the way for revolutions in science, 'associated with the name of Einstein'.[49] There vested interest was not in particular theories, but in the cultural conditions that allow for free discussion of them. We can recognise the political and social implications of this, yet find also that the energy for free enquiry valuably enhanced the possibility of our questioning the disinterest even of that move.

Our rejection of the naturalists' apparently naive faith in objectivity in general – the 'objective existence of the material' which Huxley affirmed – and in their own objectivity in particular, should not distract us from the moves by which they put the whole idea of objectivity in doubt. Since their enterprise entailed constant testing of the validity of their knowledge, the scientists had to ask themselves what they were knowing and how they were knowing it. Preoccupation with method follows from radical scepticism. The struggle to achieve the objectivity many of us now believe was another form of mystification implied distrust of the *a priori* as institutionalised superstition, wariness of perception itself as distorted, subject to angles of perspective and limitations of point of view, and disbelief in Adamic language. Science, that is to say, threw everything in doubt, at the same time as it was arguing strenuously that at last a positive method had been found to clear things up.

Consider how the naturalists handled change, a traditional motif of poetry. Not only did they see that change was continuing and ineluctable, but they had been convinced by Darwin that change was a condition for life itself. The ideal stability and stasis of Platonic and Aristotelian philosophy becomes, for the naturalists, a disastrous myth. It would be misguided to minimise some of the unhappy consequences of the new focus on change as it was translated by many naturalists and by much of the culture into the idea of progress. Spencer, Clifford, Tylor, Galton, among others, opened the way for social Darwinism as a real force in social programs. But the distinction between change and progress is critical. While Darwin was adapted to the progressive idea, and much of his writing justifies that adaptation, his theory itself argues not for progress, but for change. While the naturalists too tended to believe in 'progress', they did not in fact assume that all change is in the direction of the better. As Huxley put it in *Evolution and Ethics*, the word '"Fittest" has a connotation of "best"; and about "best" there hangs a moral flavour. In cosmic nature, however, what is fittest depends upon the conditions.'[50] The only certain 'progress' is adaptation to current environmental conditions. 'I believe', says Darwin, 'in no law of necessary development.'[51] 'Natural Selection', he says in his *Autobiography*, 'is not perfect in its action, but tends only to render each species as successful as possible in the battle for life with other species, in wonderfully complex and changing circumstances.'[52]

The emphases on change, instability, and demystifying produced a discourse more complex than any of its arguments or than the dogmatic form it often took. The mixture of messages infiltrated the culture. Yet the naturalists' discourse offered the culture a possibility that it still, on the whole, refuses – to live with the tentative, to risk not knowing, to recognise that action must precede certitude, and, most difficult of all, to understand that there can never be absolute proof.

While holding the line against science and technology, capitalism and democracy, the sages joined religious critics in refusing to be bound by the epistemological limits insisted on by the naturalists. Regarding preoccupation with the material nature of the universe as a kind of moral disease, they rejected an attitude that would risk anarchy in its displacement through reason and experience of an intuitively grasped, historical locus of authority. While scientists were saying that the world was under the reign of law and progressively developing from rude beginnings to higher levels of civilisation, the sages were detecting in the withdrawal of authority from the *a priori*, and therefore from clerisy and inherited power, and in the extension of authority to experience and to 'observation and experiment', the democratisation of nature and the threat of an ultimate disorder.

But with all the ideological and cultural limitations of the naturalists they were at least as committed to a total vision of knowledge and culture as were the sages. As Donald R. Benson has said, 'It is more than a passing irony that' the scientific theorists, like Tyndall and W.B. Carpenter, Jevons and Karl Pearson, 'should have treated science as an essentially human and even humane activity while the humanists . . . resignedly accepted the reductive popular conception of it.'[53] When, for example, Huxley was asked to write the opening article for the important scientific journal, *Nature*, in 1869, he turned to Arnold's own culture hero, Goethe, and offered a translation of some of his aphorisms on nature. Those aphorisms are full of paradoxes – a sense of nature's mysterious refusal to resolve itself into rational human structures. The work is Whitmanesque, yet, as Huxley says, 'with a bitter truth in it'. Still, Goethe's vision is progressive. Having described a nature that both gives and takes away, creates life through ingenious modes of death, isolates and unites, completes, but never finishes, he talks of science, in a letter also translated by Huxley, as moving progressively from the 'comparative' to the superlative.[54] Huxley is, of course, pleased with that view, but it is important for our sense of what the scientific methods of the late century was, that he sets it in the context of the moving, gnomic, lyrical utterances of the great romantic poet-scientist.

The humane, intellectual, and moral elements of the writing of the great naturalist-publicists are there in the freshness, clarity, cockiness, and energy of their prose. That the reaction to them was so strong testifies to the power and originality of their vision, not to its consistency or its philosophic depths. In her brief study of the 'scientific movement', as she calls it, Tess Cosslett may take too literally the naturalists' claims for disinterested moral engagement. But she is right that Huxley, Tyndall, and Clifford 'insist passionately that science matters unto men, . . . demonstrate the importance of Imagination in scientific thought, and . . . present their view of the universe with a Carlylean Awe and Mystery'.[55] What she does not adequately insist on are the points I want to conclude with here, by looking briefly at the most notorious and adventurous of them – Clifford. I would want to emphasise their role as cultural critics, operating feistily and exuberantly in a context where their excesses were almost parodic responses to traditions of faith and authority. They were intellectual risk-takers, and the excitement of their work is, at this late date, far more in the disruptions than the solutions.

Clifford, for example, was surely a 'provincial' in Arnold's scheme of things. His object is to disrupt, and to demystify nature and indeed science itself by depriving idealist or religious positions of their hiding-places in the mysteries of science, or in the limits of empiricist epistemology. And thus his writing is full of abrupt reversals. (The naturalists' inversions of commonsense readings of experience seem to anticipate, at least run parallel to, the Wildean pleasures of paradox that become so prominent in *fin de siècle* literature.) As a mathematician who helped bring non-Euclidean geometry from the continent to England, he was impressed by the evidence that Euclid's axioms themselves, far from being universal or *a priori*, were here and now bound. For Clifford, all statements, including those that had been taken to be axioms, are ultimately empirical, contingent on physical conditions: 'No maxim can be valid at all times and places for all rational beings', he wrote. 'A maxim valid for us can only be valid for such portions of the human race as are practically identical with ourselves.'[56] Such a vital recognition of western provincialism is extraordinary refreshing among Victorian writers.

'Universal statements', he argues, are merely exercises in definition: 'the moment we use language at all, we may make statements which are apparently universal, by which we really only assign the meaning of words.'[57] His sensitivity to the way language works, especially to substantiate abstractions, led him to question almost everything the culture – and science itself – authorised. He cannot allow the idea of law, which, as I have suggested, science had used to replace the banished God, to mean more than perceived regularity of sequence. He argues, 'Now it is quite true, that the word *law* in the expression "law of nature", and the expressions "law of morals", "law of the land", has two totally different meanings, which no educated person will confound; and I am not aware that any one has rested the claim of science to judge moral questions on what is no better than a stale and unprofitable pun.'[58] While Clifford has what might be regarded as too confident a sense of 'fact', he has an equally strong sense of the disguises language affords – in science and out – for prejudices.

Language harbours for Clifford, as for Derrida, a metaphysic of presence, of which we need constantly to be reminded. 'Language is part of the apparatus of thought', but its reference when it aspires to universality is always to itself. The metaphors latent in 'law' are only one of many traps for the idealist consciousness.

One does find dogmatism in Clifford, but primarily in resistance to dogma, where inherited authority threatens to close discussion. 'It is wrong,' says Clifford, 'always, everywhere, and for anyone, to believe anything upon insufficient evidence.'[59] He releases into his world, through discussions of perception, a giddying stream of relativity: he reduces the self to a cable of feeling. Beginning his lecture 'On Some of the Conditions of Mental Development' he asks his audience, 'what it is that you have done most often during this day'. The answer is stunning: 'I think you can hardly avoid being drawn to this conclusion: that you have all done nothing else from morning to night but *change your mind*.[60] Consciousness exists only in change. Nothing in Clifford's world is stable or univocal and thus nothing can be *defined* as we normally expect. Character itself is the accumulation of changes, changing in the act of identification.

Although Clifford's Tyndallian insistence that all things human are subject to physical laws is deterministic, his conception of change outreaches that definition. For, as he says, 'the character which will *roughly* represent the law of a man's action for some considerable time will not accurately represent that law for two seconds together. No action can take place in accordance with character without modifying the character itself.'[61] Again, to have consciousness 'is to have fifty thousand feelings at once, and to know them all in different degrees'.[62] Elsewhere, he argues that every sensation includes, 'besides the actual message, something that we imagine and add to the message . . . ; not the whole of sensation is immediate experience . . . but this experience is supplemented by something else which is not in it.'[63] To explore the implications of these various arguments would take us far into aesthetic theory, into developments in art and thought in the late century. What I want to emphasise is the way these arguments reshape common perceptions. Addressed to audiences who were, by all reports, enthralled, Clifford's lectures are designed to destabilise, to turn the world on its head, so that new possibilities, alternatives to traditional notions of faith and order, might come in. Clifford was the Oscar Wilde of the naturalists.

In the reaction to scientific dominance at the turn of the century, we lost some of Clifford's kind of daring originality, that commitment to change normally missing from nostalgic Victorian constructions of bulwarks against anarchy. Though often wonderfully flexible, and aware that culture's pursuit of perception is always a becoming, never a finality, Arnold persistently opposes any sort of crudeness, excess, provincialism. Culture becomes 'a principle of authority' to counteract the threat to anarchy. Alarmed at the threat, he refuses Clifford's kind of risk and fantasises a state that would be the embodiment of right reason, a state that would exercise the authority necessary to discriminate true culture, and thus suppress anarchy.

A characteristic sage-like passage will serve as a final contrast to the scientist's view of things:

Great changes there must be, for a revolution cannot accomplish itself without great changes; yet order there must be, for without order a revolution cannot accomplish itself by due course of law. So whatever brings risk of tumult and disorder, multitudinous processions in the streets of our crowded towns, multitudinous meetings in their public places and parks, – demonstrations perfectly unnecessary in the present course of our affairs, – our best self, or right reason, plainly enjoins us to set our faces against. It enjoins us to encourage and uphold the occupants of the executive power, whoever they may be, in firmly prohibiting them. But it does this clearly and resolutely, and is thus a real principle of authority.[64]

To be fair, one must concede that this is not so far from the naturalists' position as I am suggesting by the juxtaposition with Clifford. But Arnold is embodying here that terror of disorder that might justify any reaction to it; it is the culture's response to the sort of risks the naturalists were willing to take intellectually. And it closes itself to the new. If we cannot have the ideal, we still must support the state, whatever it may be; order and decorum are more important than change.

One of Clifford's essays talks about two qualities of mind, 'crystallisation' and 'plasticity'. The former is the condition of death: 'to become crystallized, fixed in opinion and mode of thought, is to lose the great characteristic of life, by which it is distinguished from inanimate nature: the power of adapting itself to circumstances.'[65] For Clifford, crystallisation is, in fact, 'propriety'. It is reliance on past forms and inherited authority, and it denies the risks and the vitality of movement into an unknown future. He talks of 'the immense importance to a nation of checking the growth of conventionalities'. We shall see, in Jeffrey von Arx's chapter, how even so potent a spokesman for agnosticism as Leslie Stephen sought a scientific theory that would 'impose order on the chaos of events'. Of course Clifford, who near the end of his life was warmly befriended by Stephen, shared many of the materialist and agnostic principles that led Stephen to his crisis, and he, too, sought ordering principles; but he plunged recklessly into disorder, risked paradox more pugnaciously than Huxley or Stephen would, 'consciously holding [every theory] as an experiment, and being perfectly ready to give it up when found wanting'.[66] Stephen, von Arx shows, withdrew from politics in the quest for stability and order. And in these respects Clifford was probably unique, pushing to their dangerous limits some of the destabilising implications of science's anti-authoritarian strategies. What Stephen would have been uncomfortable with, what Arnold, leaning back toward the stabilities of an earlier age, could not have endured, can perhaps be summed up in the last sentence of Clifford's essay, printed in fact in Arnoldian italics: *It is not right to be proper.*

NOTES

1. T.H. Huxley, 'On the Advisableness of Improving Natural Knowledge' (1866) *Methods and Results* (London, 1893) 41.
2. ibid., 40.
3. ibid., 41.
4. Adrian Desmond, *Archetypes and Ancestors: Palaeontology in Victorian England, 1850–1875* (Chicago, 1984); Frank M. Turner, 'Public Science in Britain, 1880–1919', *Isis*, 71 (1980) 589–608; Frank M. Turner, 'The Victorian Conflict between Science and Religion: A Professional Dimension', *Isis*, 69 (1978) 356–76.
5. James R. Moore, *The Post-Darwinian Controversies: A Study of the Protestant Struggle to Come to Terms with Darwin in Great Britain and America, 1870–1900* (Cambridge, 1979).
6. Frank M. Turner, *Between Science and Religion: The Reaction to Scientific Naturalism in Late Victorian England* (New Haven, Conn., 1974) 36.
7. John Tyndall, 'The Belfast Address', *Fragments of Science*, 2 vols (New York, 1899) 2: 199. Since this chapter was written, Peter Allan Dale has published what is certainly the most extensive and important study of nineteenth-century positivism in relation to literature and to the development of modernist and post-modernist theory. Much of what he says confirms in detail and in fine-grained argument the general tenor of my argument in this chapter; much might be taken to supersede my argument. Dale's is perhaps the first book by a literary critic to allow to positivism the complexity and richness that it surely embodied. His book is not at all a 'defense' of positivism, but it keenly describes the vagaries of its development and of its influence on the thinkers and writers of the period. He demonstrates that positivist thought was constantly forced to return to the recognition that 'imaginary projection' is inevitably a condition of scientific knowledge. The truly imaginary being, he concludes, is 'a serious positivist thinker who was unaware of the necessary intervention of the mind's intentional structure between himself or herself and the world as in itself it really is.' (Peter Allan Dale, *In Pursuit of a Scientific Culture* (Madison, Wisonsin, 1989) 280–1.)
8. Turner, 'Public Science', 592.
9. Huxley, 'Improving Natural Knowledge', 30.
10. Arthur Balfour, *A Defence of Philosophic Doubt: Being an Essay on the Foundations of Belief* (London, 1879) 293–4.
11. For two diverse but powerful approaches to the mythological

elements in science, see Gillian Beer, *Darwin's Plots* (London, 1983), and Michel Serre, *Hermes: Literature, Science, Philosophy*, ed. Josué V. Harari and David F. Bell (Baltimore, 1982) esp. xxix: 'The domains of myth, science, and literature oscillate frantically back and forth with one another, so the idea of ever distinguishing between them becomes more and more chimerical.'

12. Balfour, *Defence*, 366.
13. Cf., however, the soon-to-be-published study by Jeffrey Spear, who argues that Ruskin's economic theory and practice were, in fact, alert responses to contemporary conditions.
14. See my 'George Eliot's Hypothesis of Reality', *Nineteenth Century Fiction*, 35 (1980) 1–28.
15. Turner, 'Public Science'.
16. T.H. Huxley, 'The Progress of Science' (1887) *Methods and Results*, 60–1.
17. Tyndall, 'The Belfast Address', 2: 195.
18. On this point, see David Hull, *Darwin and His Critics: The Reception of Darwin's Theory of Evolution by the Scientific Community* (Chicago, 1973) 64–74; and Ernst Mayr, *The Growth of Biological Thought* (Cambridge, Mass., 1981) 36–67.
19. Edward B. Tylor, *Primitive Culture*, 2 vols (London, 1920) 1: 2.
20. ibid.
21. ibid., 33.
22. ibid., 69.
23. ibid., 39.
24. ibid., 69.
25. Charles Darwin, *The Descent of Man and Selection in Relation to Sex* (1871; Princeton, NJ, 1981) 1: 153.
26. George W. Stocking, Jr, *Race, Culture, and Evolution* (Chicago, 1982) 87–8.
27. Beer, *Darwin's Plots*, 118.
28. First published in Houston Peterson, *Huxley: Prophet of Science* (London, 1932) 326.
29. Richard Jenkyns, *The Victorians and Ancient Greece* (Cambridge, Mass., 1980) 266.
30. Darwin, *Descent of Man*, 2: 389.
31. Richard J. Bernstein, *Beyond Objectivism and Relativism* (Philadelphia, 1983) 18.
32. Matthew Arnold, *Philistinism in England and America*, ed. R.R. Super (Ann Arbor, Mich., 1974) 66.
33. ibid.
34. Huxley, 'Progress of Science', 44.
35. Robert A. Donovan, 'Mill, Arnold, and Scientific Humanism', in *Victorian Science and Victorian Values: Literary Perspectives*, ed. James Paradis and Thomas Postlewait (New York, 1981) 189.
36. John Stuart Mill, *Autobiography* (1873) ed. Jack Stillinger (Boston, Mass., 1969) 92.
37. Huxley, 'Improving Natural Knowledge', 31.
38. Lyon Playfair, 'Science and Technology as Sources of Natural Power'

(1886), in *Victorian Science*, ed. George Basalla, William Coleman, and H. Kargon (Garden City, NY, 1970) 69.

39. T.H. Huxley, 'Science and Culture' (1880) *Science and Education* (London, 1894) 156.
40. ibid.
41. See the famous clarification by Darwin in later editions of the *Origins of Species*, ch. iv, and his almost exact duplication of it in the 'Introduction' to *The Variation of Animals and Plants under Domestication* (1866) 2 vols (New York, 1900) 1: 7. For Darwin, laws are merely 'the sequence of events as ascertained by us'.
42. John Tyndall, 'Science and Man' (1877) *Fragments of Science*, 2: 353.
43. ibid., 354–5.
44. ibid., 355.
45. W.H. Mallock, *The New Republic* (1877) ed. J. Max Patrick (Gainesville, Fla, 1950) 42.
46. Mayr, *Growth of Biological Thought*, 52.
47. Ian Hacking (ed.), *Scientific Revolutions* (Oxford, 1981) 2.
48. Stephen Toulmin and June Goodfield, *The Architecture of Matter* (New York, 1962) 240.
49. John Passmore, *A Hundred Years of Philosophy* (Harmondsworth, 1967) 324.
50. T.H. Huxley, *Evolution and Ethics* (London, 1911) 80.
51. Charles Darwin, *The Origin of Species* (1859) ed. J.W. Burrow (Harmondsworth, 1968) 348.
52. Charles Darwin, *The Autobiography of Charles Darwin* (New York, 1958) 90.
53. Donald R. Benson, 'Facts and Contrasts: Victorian Humanists and Scientific Theorists on Scientific Knowledge', in *Victorian Science and Victorian Values*, 315.
54. T.H. Huxley, 'Nature: Aphorisms by Goethe', *Nature*, 1, no. 1 (4 November 1869) 9–11.
55. Tess Cosslett, *The 'Scientific Movement' and Victorian Literature* (Sussex, 1982) 2.
56. W.K. Clifford, *Lectures and Essays*, 2 vols (London, 1910) 2: 279.
57. ibid., 1: 390.
58. ibid., 2: 125.
59. ibid., 2: 175.
60. ibid., 1: 79.
61. ibid., 1: 84–5.
62. ibid., 2: 20.
63. ibid., 2: 308–9.
64. Matthew Arnold, *Culture and Anarchy* (1869) ed. Ian Gregor (Indianapolis, 1971) 79.
65. Clifford, *Lectures*, 1: 116.
66. ibid., 1: 15.

8 The Victorian Crisis of Faith as Crisis of Vocation
Jeffrey von Arx

Much of the understanding we have of the Victorian crisis of faith is shaped by the literature of conversion and reverse conversion: autobiographical accounts like Newman's *Apologia*, barely concealed autobiography like Froude's *Nemesis of Faith*, or novels of conversion like Mrs Humphry Ward's *Robert Elsmere*. These personal or personalised accounts focus on the crisis of faith as an issue of conscience and intellectual integrity: the protagonist must ask whether it is ethical to assent to religious doctrines that one has ceased to believe. The answer, of course, in good conscience can only be no, and yet the decision to abandon the creed in which one was raised is always a process of agonised soul-searching and deeply-felt personal loss.

It would be unfair to call these and similar accounts of the Victorian crisis of faith self-serving. Quite understandably they were intended to convince an audience that would be hostile to heterodox religious choice of the moral and intellectual integrity of those who suffered much and sacrificed much for the sake of conscience and of truth.

Yet recalling his own loss of faith while he was a fellow and the chaplain at Trinity Hall, Cambridge, in the early 1860s, Leslie Stephen described the event as 'not discovering that my creed was false, but that I had never really believed it. I had unconsciously imbibed the current phraseology; but the formulae belonged to the superficial thought, instead of fundamental convictions.'[1]

On the one hand, Stephen's laconic and restrained recollection suggests that the Victorian crisis of faith was not always a dramatic and agonised struggle with religious doubt. His account of ceasing to assent to what he did not believe indicates that loss of the spiritual consolation of

Christianity – a consolation Stephen seems never to have felt – caused no great emotional or intellectual dislocation in his life.

On the other hand, there is evidence that something connected with the decision not to believe was deeply painful to Stephen. F.W. Maitland records the reminiscences of 'one who was intimate with [Stephen] from about 1859 onwards and whose memory may be confidently trusted' (the informant is the judge, Sir Robert Romer):

> There is one subject connected with Stephen's life at this time, which perhaps I ought not to pass over, for it was the most important in every aspect; and yet I will only refer to it briefly, for even now I do not like to dwell upon the mental torture which he went through. When I first went up [to Trinity Hall, Cambridge], Stephen was a clergyman and took his part in the clerical services in the chapel. I was a grieved witness to the misery endured by my friend during the time when doubt as to the truth of revealed religion according to the orthodox view gradually increased until he made up his mind that his views were incompatible with his continuing to be a clergyman of the Church of England. The pain he suffered was very acute, as was sure to be the case when a highly sensitive and loving nature like his had to pass through such a crisis of life, and was made doubly so because he knew what grief his determination would cause to some of his family who were nearest and dearest to him.[2]

Professor Bernard Lightman of York University has discovered a letter in the Maitland Papers from Sedley Taylor, another of Stephen's contemporaries at Cambridge, written to Maitland while the latter was preparing his biography of Stephen. Taylor records that Henry Fawcett (Stephen's closest friend at the time) told him that while Stephen was undergoing his crisis of vocation 'he was with Stephen late one night and that when he quitted him, Stephen's state of mind was such that Fawcett entertained serious fears he might cut his throat during the night'.[3]

Stephen scholars tend to discount this story because Fawcett is its ultimate source. According to Lord Annan, Fawcett habitually exaggerated, and John Bicknell argues that Faw-

cett would scarcely have left Stephen that night had he
entertained serious fears that he might kill himself.[4] Still,
Taylor's report and the more reliable testimony of Romer
indicate that Stephen did suffer at this time. How is one to
reconcile these contemporary reports of Stephen's anguish
with his own later testimony that loss of faith caused no great
crisis of intellectual conscience in his life?

This conflicting evidence makes clear the need to establish
just what was critical about Stephen's crisis of faith. To do
this, we may begin by considering Stephen's motives for
entering a clerical career, which he did when he was
ordained deacon in 1855 and priest in 1859. Stephen himself
reports that he took this step 'rather – perhaps I should say
very – carelessly. . . . My real motive was that I was anxious to
relieve my father of the burden of supporting me.'[5] There is
testimony from Stephen's sister Caroline that Leslie experienced subtle pressure from their father to realise the elder
Stephen's desire that one of his sons should enter the
ministry. Caroline believed that her brother had no vocation
to the clerical life and urged these doubts on Leslie right up
to the eve of his ordination – but to no avail.[6]

This evidence suggests that it was not the experience of
doubting truths of faith that had once been important to him
that Stephen found so existentially wrenching. Rather, his
agony of mind came from the discovery that he had mistaken
his vocation in deciding to be ordained, and must draw back
from a commitment he had made, as it must now have
seemed, irresponsibly.[7]

From the perspective of what had been the traditional
conception of the relationship between clerical status and the
role of a tutorial fellow at university, Stephen had been
neither unusual nor irresponsible in taking orders without
much thought. Because of the Anglican character of the
universities, it was part of the college statutes that almost all
fellowships involving contact with undergraduates were clerical. And it had been for decades, indeed for centuries, an
accepted road of advancement for bright but impecunious
young men like Stephen that they should accept clerical
university fellowships as a first step toward a career in the
Church.

That Stephen should come to feel his decision to accept

ordination was a mistake and cause for regret and bitter personal reproach illustrates an important change that affected both clerical and academic life in the 1860s. That change was nothing less than a revolution in the conception entertained by men in Stephen's position of what were the commitments they had undertaken as clergymen and as dons.

In recent years there have been a number of studies devoted to the transformation in the self-understanding of dons in the ancient universities. In his *Revolution of the Dons*, Sheldon Rothblatt has traced the change at Cambridge and explained it as a general movement at mid-century to define professional status in terms of culture, gentility, and an ideal of service over against what was perceived as the acquisitive, competitive, and self-interested character of a career in business. Academics, and especially college dons, played an important role in working out this definition, and in so doing, came to a new understanding of their own profession.[8] A.J. Engel, in his study of the transition of Oxford academics from clergymen to dons, has made even more explicit the shift in career expectations that occurred in the third quarter of the nineteenth century. No longer did resident fellows consider their time at the university an interlude between the completion of undergraduate studies and a career in the Church. The new emphasis on the responsibility of teaching at a reformed Oxford led dons to desire for their profession not only a status comparable in social position to traditional learned professions, but also a security and remuneration commensurate with that status.[9]

Leslie Stephen in many ways personified this new tendency toward viewing academic life as an independent and permanent profession. He was much involved as a don in the reform of curriculum and the improvement of teaching. This involvement grew out of Stephen's conviction that English intellectual life was inferior to that on the continent, especially in Germany, and contributed to a narrowness of mind in leaders in church and state.[10] His conviction as to the inadequacy of English higher education led him, as we shall see, to seek ways of revising the system of cramming and competitive examinations that held sway in Cambridge, and to propose reforms that would have involved a greater and longer-term commitment to research and teaching on the part of instructors at the universities.

Stephen's reforming zeal was not just a function of social criticism and high educational policy. A very large part of his desire to see curriculum and instruction reformed was the result of his experience as a tutor dealing with pass men, the majority of Cambridge undergraduates who, lacking the ability or the desire to read for honours, took a pass on their examinations. These pass men spent their time either in stultifying rote memorisation of set texts, or, what was more likely, in such amusements as fertile undergraduate imagination could devise and Cambridge and its environs provide. Stephen's commitment to these victims of academic neglect was not limited to concern for their instruction. The Reverend Leslie Stephen was a new breed among Cambridge tutors in the frequency and informality of his contacts with undergraduates. He invited undergraduates regularly to his rooms, and was a pioneer and great enthusiast for college athletics, especially rowing. Twice during his tenure at Trinity Hall he coached the college boat head of the river.

Stephen undoubtedly saw athletics and his other activities with undergraduates as a way of occupying the idle time of the pass men. But it is clear from the appealing portrait Noël Annan paints of Stephen's tenure at Trinity Hall that Stephen enjoyed these contacts, and experienced his roles as tutor, coach, and friend of students as a deeply satisfying way of life.[11] In the course of his years at Cambridge, Stephen was one of those who had redefined the position of a don as a profession in its own right, and not a mere stepping stone to a country rectory. Nor is there any doubt that Stephen would have continued in this life had he been able to do so in good conscience.

But Stephen was not only a college tutor. He was also a clergyman of the Church of England, and it is in this latter capacity that a new understanding of the clerical profession coupled with his own doubts precipitated a crisis that led him to abandon the academic life he had chosen and come to love.

Just how his status as a clergyman fitted in Stephen's own mind with his engagement in university reform and undergraduate life is far from clear. We know that he took his regular turn in conducting religious services in the college chapel. But Stephen's own testimony cited above and the evidence of others suggests that having accepted ordination under the old understanding of what it was to be a clerical don, Stephen now gave the religious implications of his status little thought in comparison to his activities as a college tutor. In trying to explain her own conviction that her brother had been ordained without a vocation to the ministry in the accepted Evangelical sense of the word, Stephen's sister Caroline wrote to Maitland, 'Perhaps it would give the wrong impression to say that at the time of his ordination his whole soul was in the boats! but I believe it to be very much the truth.'[12]

To understand how it was that Stephen's clerical status mediated his crisis of faith, one must realise that academics were far from being the only group engaged in redefining career status in the fifties and sixties. The clergy, too, were in the midst of a movement toward greater professionalisation, and, as Anthony Russell has indicated in his study of the clerical profession in the mid-nineteenth century, that transformation affected every aspect of clerical duties and therefore the very heart of how a Victorian clergyman understood his role and his relationship to society.[13]

The effect of professionalisation on dons considered as academics has been carefully studied both at the general level, in works like Rothblatt's and Engel's, and at the level of the individual, in a work like Noël Annan's biography of Stephen.[14] But no one, so far as I know, has yet considered the impact of professionalisation of the clergy on the lives of dons who were also deacons and priests of the Church of England. What were the implications of the professionalisation of the clergy for someone like Stephen, whose decision to take holy orders was a function of an older understanding of the identity of a clerical don?

In the *Mausoleum Book*, the memoir he wrote for his children in 1895, Stephen again recalls his state of mind as a young don at Cambridge: 'I was a liberal after the fashion of those days; a follower of J.S. Mill like my friend Fawcett, a reader of Mill's *Logic*, as well as of his "Political Economy". I read a little philosophy, Kant, Hamilton, etc., and was supposed at Cambridge, where the standard was very low, to

know something about it. I read Comte, too, and then
became convinced among other things, that Noah's flood was
a fiction (or rather convinced that I never really believed in
it) and that it was very wrong of me to read the story as if it
were sacred truth. So I had to give up my position at Trinity
Hall.'[15]

We shall return to this passage later as an account of how
Stephen understood his own loss of faith, but in the mean-
time it will serve to illustrate the peculiar logic affecting
clerical profession in the mid-1860s. In a characteristically
understated fashion, Stephen indicates that the immediate
consequence of his first doubts about the literal historical
truth of the biblical accounts (presumably Noah's flood
stands as symbol for other *incredibilia*) was the resignation of
his position as chaplain to undergraduates. One might
contrast the moral sensitivity manifested in such a decision
with what was surely the easier attitude toward clerical
subscription that had characterised Oxford and Cambridge
in the eighteenth century and well into the nineteenth. One
can scarcely imagine a Georgian clergyman-don who entertained similar doubts abandoning his responsibilities and
jeopardising his prospects.[16]

It must always be remembered, however, that the background and context for a decision like Stephen's that he
could no longer in good conscience conduct the college
services was a period of ecclesiastical and devotional revival.
The emergence of the vocational crisis as a dimension of the
ethics of belief was one by-product of the religious renewal
within the Church of England. The leaven of Evangelicalism
still touched the lives of young men coming of age in the
1840s and 1850s. The Tractarian influence continued to
work its way after the departures of Newman, Manning, and
others to Rome. Moreover, the Broad Church party was
stressing both a learned ministry and a heightened sense of
social responsibility on the part of the Establishment. All of
these developments meant that those people who were
religious tended to regard both doctrine and devotion more
seriously than in the first quarter of the century and that the
ministry itself had come to be considered a more distinctly
religious vocation. The problem of defining the ethics of
belief was almost always related to the problem of vocation.

And at the centre of the crisis over the ethics of belief were young men about to enter the Anglican priesthood or recently ordained. The sense of the ministry as a religious vocation rather than one of social status was one result of the religious revival that had marked the Church of England in the first half of the century.

The revival of the first half of the century stirred a new understanding of the Church of England as a corporate religious body and its priesthood as a devotional vocation actively supporting defined doctrine. The ethics of belief could become problematical only for clergymen or potential clergymen who had learned to take seriously and earnestly the life of the Church and its theological foundations. Such was the state of mind of a significant number of vocal clergymen by the third quarter of the century. The Oxford movement had initially called forth a new religiosity and devotion on the part of the Anglican ministry. The theological extremes to which for better or worse some of its leaders had carried their convictions elicited a reaction that sought to delineate more strictly and dogmatically the parameters of Anglican doctrine. As a result of this new awareness of doctrine, devotion, and religious duty, those people who grew up either in Tractarian or, like Stephen, in Evangelical homes during the 1840s and 1850s always viewed the Church of England primarily as a religious institution and its ministry as a body of men called to devotional service and theological loyalty. For such people, who became the articulate spokesmen of the 1860s, the ethics of belief became problematical. It was for this reason that to the end of his life Henry Sidgwick, himself an unbeliever, argued that the Anglican clergy must genuinely believe the doctrines of the Articles and the Creed. Unlike Matthew Arnold, the heir of the latitudinarian tradition, Sidgwick and others like him even in their unbelief could not regard the Church merely as an institution of national culture.

This new sense of the Church and especially the clergy as a distinct corporate body had the effect of exacerbating and hardening differences between churchmen and doubters within the Church. As clergymen came increasingly to understand themselves in terms of membership in an exclusive caste clearly defined by devotion, doctrine, and ministry, for a person even to begin to doubt was to place himself beyond that charmed circle and even over against it. It is this dynamic affecting doubt within a clericalised church that explains the action of Leslie Stephen in the present instance. Immediately he began to entertain doubts about the Flood, he could no longer in good conscience conduct the college services that fell to him. This decision in its turn precipitated a request from college authorities that he resign the position of tutor to undergraduates, which he held by virtue of being a fellow in orders. In 1864 Stephen left Cambridge for London to embark on a career in journalism, never to return again in an academic capacity.

It is not possible to reconstruct, from any contemporary account, the genesis of Stephen's loss of faith. The best sources there are for this event are to be found in two later reminiscences. In his autobiographical 'Early Impressions', published in the *National Review* in 1903, Stephen stated that it was Mill's *System of Logic*, avidly studied by reading men at Cambridge in the fifties and sixties, that led him to agnosticism.[17] In another place, the passage from the *Mausoleum Book* already quoted, he indicated that it was Comte that undermined his belief in the literal truth of biblical stories like Noah's Flood.

It is somewhat surprising, considering the quantity and sophistication of objections Stephen would later raise against Christianity, that disbelief in the historicity of Noah's Flood should mark the beginning of his agnosticism. Of course, specific problems in sacred history were the focus of more than one crisis of faith – in the case of Henry Sidgwick, for example, it was the virgin birth – and, as we have suggested, the Flood served as a symbol of what Stephen felt was incredible in much of the biblical account. Even so, these recollections point to the limited extent of Stephen's initial questioning. This is not to say that Stephen's doubts were insignificant, or his understanding of Christianity so superficial that it could be knocked down by the first wind of higher criticism. He was, he says in the *Mausoleum Book*, 'in a vague kind of way, a believer in Maurice, or in what were called "Broad Church" doctrines'.[18] But Maurice's effort to represent Christianity in a form acceptable to modern thought ceased to satisfy the Reverend Leslie Stephen as he read more deeply in Mill and Comte. Because of Stephen's own reticence about this period of his life, it is necessary to speculate about why this should be so. The simplest explanation lies in the very combination of Mill and Comte. As the more rigorous epistemological standards of Mill's *System of Logic* convinced Stephen that Christian belief was problematic, Comte's account of the three stages of history and of the mythological character of the first theological stage provided an explanation of how such erroneous belief arose. Mill's empiricism, therefore, and the developmentalism learned from Comte acted in a pincer movement that first denied and then explained away Christian belief. It was an intellectual technique that would be characteristic of Stephen's controversial style in years to come.[19]

Whatever Stephen's reasons at the time for questioning the faith in which he had been raised, it is essential to recognise that his doubts were not worked out on a purely intellectual plane, nor was the resolution of those doubts in the decision to abandon Christian belief and practice a matter only for his own conscience. Stephen's decision to resign his tutorship and abandon the ministry occurred at a time when he and a group of Cambridge friends were active in the cause of university reform. Stephen's involvement in university reform had begun with the Commission set up by the Act of 1856 to investigate the conditions of the universities. When the Commission finally began its work at Trinity Hall in 1859, among the reforms that Stephen supported – unsuccessfully, as it turned out – were the abolition of clerical restrictions on teaching fellowships, and an abrogation of a provision that required fellowships to be vacated upon 'open secession from the Church of England'.[20] Of course at this time it was not for his own sake that Stephen sought these changes. For himself, he was content to function within the old structures, since he accepted ordination to the priesthood in that same year, 1859. It was not, therefore, for personal or religious reasons, but for scholarly and educational ones that Leslie Stephen had joined a group of reformers in his college, disciples of Mill and led by his friend and mentor, Henry Fawcett. A liberal-minded clergyman could associate himself with such a group because they had no direct intention of doing away with the role of the Church in the university. Their purpose in advocating measures of declericalisation was merely to remove obstacles to the efficient functioning of the competitive examination system that already existed.[21]

Stephen approved and supported the reforms proposed by Fawcett and his friends through the 1850s.[22] But in the early sixties – at the same time, in other words, that he was beginning to experience religious doubts – he began to be dissatisfied with the narrowly utilitarian character of Fawcett's reform programme. Fawcett held that the mental discipline acquired by intense competition for places in the rigidly defined classical and mathematical triposes was itself a sufficient justification for university education. So while Fawcett supported efforts to make the rewards of that competition as attractive and accessible as they could be, he opposed measures to broaden the curriculum, or to strengthen university instruction and research at the expense of college revenues devoted to fellowships.[23] Stephen, while he admitted the virtue of the mental discipline that a competitive system provided, thought that other studies besides mathematics and classics were important for the formation of those who might some day govern the nation. As he recognised the need for a better quality of instruction in more areas, Stephen moved closer to another school of university reformers, who had a much broader ideal of university education, and a more radical programme of reform. Led by J.R. Seeley at Cambridge and Mark Pattison at Oxford, and with the support of Matthew Arnold, this group advocated a major reorganisation of the university to support an independent professorate, and to endow advanced research out of the revenues of the colleges.

There are several reasons that together account for the change of Stephen's opinions about university reform. Fawcett was certainly Stephen's closest friend at Cambridge from his undergraduate days until he left the university in 1864.[24] It was Fawcett who introduced Stephen to Mill,[25] and if Stephen entered the lists over university reform under the banner of Philosophical Radicalism, it may have been because this was the army of reformers who first recruited him.[26] But as the young Stephen broadened his own intellectual outlook and questioned his beliefs during his years as a college tutor, he became increasingly dissatisfied with Fawcett's constricted idea of university education. The ambitious course of philosophical reading that Stephen undertook in 1859 and 1860, which he says contributed to his loss of faith, can be seen as the link between growing religious doubts, and the conviction that education must provide a broader intellectual culture for future leaders. By 1861, with this newly acquired philosophical background, Stephen began to examine in the newly established Moral Science Tripos, an innovation that Fawcett did not approve.[27]

Of course, both the limited reforms advocated by Fawcett and the much broader programme of Seeley were opposed by those who wished to preserve and strengthen the exclusively Anglican character of the universities. W.R. Ward in his study of Victorian Oxford describes the very successful rearguard action carried out by E.B. Pusey and other high churchmen in the fifties and sixties to limit drastically the effects of the Reform Commission at the older university.[28] Stephen had recognised clerical opposition as the main obstacle to reform while still a clergyman himself, and he and Fawcett had failed to convince their colleagues at Trinity Hall to remove clerical restrictions from all fellowships. But now, just as he began to realise the needs of the age required a far more radical change than Fawcett's programme for free trade in fellowships, Stephen found himself excluded from any chance of participating in the reform. This exclusion had been effected by the same clerical establishment that had successfully resisted every effort to change the Anglican character of the university, save the admission of Dissenters to degrees. Not only the instruction and the educational programme, therefore, but the doctrinal and ecclesiastical assumptions that underlay the structure of English university life became questionable for Stephen after he had lost his own belief in Christianity. The debate over university reform assumed for him the added dimension of a struggle between a small group of enlightened thinkers trying to shape the nation's youth for life in the world of modern scientific thought, and the still powerful defenders of a creed he had rejected, who had been able to manipulate reform to preserve Anglican exclusivism in all its essentials.

The resistance of the universities to reform thus became a

symbol of the entrenched power of the Church, which Stephen gradually came to see as pervading English social life. In short, while it is accurate to view Stephen's loss of faith as an instance of transformation of opinions of a young Victorian intellectual, far more significant was the transformation that conversion worked at the level of vocation: i.e. in Stephen's perception of and participation in the dominant institutions of Victorian cultural life, especially the university and the Church. Where once he had been a willing participant in the ecclesiastical establishment that controlled British higher education, he now saw that establishment as the principal obstacle to the successful reform of the university and to adequate preparation of Britain's future rulers for the task of governing in an age of changing ideas and values.

Stephen finally left Cambridge in 1864 at the age of 32, a ten-year veteran of active participation in university politics, with an enthusiasm for reform that had been shaped by his experience at Cambridge. When he settled in London in 1865, after the interlude of an American tour to observe and report on the Civil War, the first problem he faced was a consequence of the vocational crisis: the necessity of choosing a new career. This problem was especially acute, not merely because of his age and the understandable fear that his years as a don had unfitted him for any other work, but because his status as a clergyman barred him, both by law and by custom, from the other professions.[29]

There is some indication that, except for this obstacle, Stephen would have pursued his political and reform interests in a parliamentary career.[30] This, too, was legally impossible, however, and the limitation thus placed on his choice by a calling he no longer felt provided further grievance against the position of the clergy in English public life.

Even while he was still at Cambridge, Stephen had been involved not only in university reform politics but also in radical politics more generally. Stephen's votes as an undergraduate in the Cambridge Union, his support of the North in the American Civil War, his involvement in the Jamaica Committee and in the parliamentary campaigns of 1863 and 1864 of his radical friend Henry Fawcett all indicate that university reform was only part of a larger concern about leadership and direction in an age of transition. It is not surprising that Stephen tended to see national political issues from the perspective of university reform: as a struggle between an older entrenched élite and a competing élite of talent, ability, and new ideas. What is surprising is the way in which the vocational dynamics of Stephen's crisis of faith structured his perception of the destructive role of the clergy in national politics in the reform era. The dogmatic, exclusive, aggressive character that the Anglican clergy had assumed as a result of the religious revival by mid-century had driven Stephen from the Church and prevented his contribution to the university. That same resurgent clericalism now threatened to block progressive reform and to deprive men like Stephen of the political leadership they believed they deserved in the wider arena of national politics.

One can trace the growth of Stephen's concern over the role of religion and the clergy in politics in his reaction to the events of Gladstone's first ministry, a period for which we are fortunate enough to have Stephen's regular contributions as English correspondent for the American magazine the *Nation*. Stephen had begun his participation in national politics as a supporter of radical causes, especially franchise reform, and as a follower of Gladstone.[31] The way in which the Reform Act was passed, however, was disturbing to Stephen, who thought it demonstrated a lack of ability among Liberals and a lack of integrity among Conservatives.[32] With the passage of the Act itself and with the installation of the Liberal reform ministry that followed it, Stephen expected 'a thorough over-hauling', not only of church and education, but of Poor Law, Irish Land Law, army and legal system.[33] The first hint of his disappointment with the new ministry occurred over the vast amount of time and parliamentary effort required to pass the Irish Church Act. Parliament's preoccupation with the bill had prevented consideration in that session of other much needed legislation in education and poor law reform. 'Some', Stephen reported in the *Nation*, 'were disgusted with the parliamentary system of government' and convinced that 'Parliament should use its power and knowledge to conduct business, instead of frittering away time on party struggle.'[34]

Complaints about the inefficiency of Parliament recurred

in Stephen's contributions to the *Nation*, causing him to lament, 'when shall we get to the end of knocking down old restrictions and begin some process of reconstruction?'[35] As early as February 1871 he noted dissatisfaction with Gladstone's leadership: with his indecision, his wish to conciliate all parties, the impulsiveness that was manifested in the controversies over the Education Bill of 1870.[36] But one theme came to predominate in Stephen's analysis of the failure of Gladstone's ministry as it wore on, and it is the key to his own disillusionment with politics. Sectarian strife, 'The Religious Difficulty', as Stephen called it in an 1870 essay of that name in *Fraser's Magazine*, was the chief reason for the failure of the ministry to produce the constructive legislation for which he had hoped.[37] Controversy over the Education Bill – the struggle for control of national education between the Church of England on the one hand and Dissenters and secularists on the other – had occupied Parliament for most of a session, and resulted in a compromise so unsatisfactory that Dissenters threatened to destroy both the new system by their non-compliance and the Liberal party by their defection.[38] The furore over education, however, was only one instance of how the religious context in which British politics were conducted could complicate, delay, and even frustrate desperately needed reforms; for Stephen believed that the religious issue permeated almost every aspect of British political life from the Irish question to poor law reform. Intervention in politics by religious groups was inevitable, however, as long as the power of the state church remained a political factor: 'outsiders have to fight it with political weapons, and to preserve a "watchful jealousy" because their opponents have a political power to back them. The evil cannot be thoroughly eradicated unless the state becomes absolutely impartial in regard to all religions, or unless we are converted to one religion.'[39]

It was precisely the susceptibility of the state to corruption by religious politics that Stephen saw as the most ominous sign of the disordered condition of public affairs late in Gladstone's ministry. The inability of the Church of England to provide any longer a source of national unity meant that one had to look to government itself for that unity. Real leaders in public office, by constructive acts of legislation, could point the way out of intellectual confusion and anarchy, and toward a new organic age. In an essay composed late in 1872, Stephen wrote of the need for the state to exemplify 'moral authority based on reason' – to organise and direct public opinion, rather than merely to reflect it.[40] He proposed Bismarck as an example of a leader who had been able to unite his people, and compared his firm treatment of religious parties in Germany with the 'timidity, shuffling, and underhand flirtations of that which calls itself our Liberal party'.[41] British party politics, on the other hand, were characterised 'by infinite speech-making, by dexterous balancing of parties, and by angling for the votes of Irish members, by carefully watching every shifting mood of a many-headed monster, introducing measures to catch a few cheers, and allowing all serious legislation to fall into an ever-increasing muddle and entanglement because it could not be made into party capital'.[42] This chaos of party politics was both symptom and consequence of religious disunity and sectarian strife among the British people. It was clear indication, Stephen wrote, of a national lack of faith. What England needed was the kind of secular faith in the nation and in the nation's leadership that enabled a great leader like Bismarck to 'feel that he can wield the whole force of the nation, and had a fair chance of being permitted to carry out a bold and definite line of policy'.[43]

Stephen's unfavourable comparison of Gladstone's England with Bismarck's Germany implies an association of fundamental importance in the development of his thought: that is, the implication of parliamentary party politics – the politics of emerging mass democracy – in what thinkers like Stephen viewed as the miasma of religious controversy and deception. There is a basic continuity between Stephen's experience of personal failure in his effort to reform the university – and the crisis of vocation mediated by that failure – and his perception of national politics threatened by clerical resurgence. Just as he had hoped that reform of the university would prepare England's leaders for life in the modern world, so he expected to see the new post-reform ministry lead the nation out of sectarian bickering and in a new, positive, constructive direction. He had hoped the Liberal administration would give the lie to the revived claims of the Anglican Church to national leadership. What he found, instead, through the course of Gladstone's ministry, was a conflation of national and religious politics, a willingness among political elders to submit to clerical pressures and emulate their counterparts in the Church by using popular sentiment and exploiting popular causes to gain partisan advantage. In Stephen's case, the transfer or, better yet, the expansion of resentment of religious politics to encompass parliamentary politics corresponded to a perception that the corrupting influence of religious controversy threatened to permeate national politics as well with self-interested expediency.

It is not clear whether Stephen really thought this corruption of national politics might lead to some new kind of clerical domination. In an essay of 1873 he warned of the danger posed by newly emancipated masses without developed political convictions, and of the possibility that priests and demagogues might unite the people into a party that threatened freedom and property.[44] Here the Irish example is not mentioned but is certainly implied. What is clear, in this essay and elsewhere, is that Stephen feared and abhorred the new politics of manipulation and exploitation or, to use neutral terms, of pressure groups and party management. These were an extension of the techniques religious leaders used to maintain their own power, and had the same effect of blocking national unity based on an emergent cultural synthesis and depriving men like Stephen of the leadership in national affairs they deserved.

Stephen's growing disillusionment with the politics of parliamentary democracy led to an important turning point in his own life. From the late sixties through the early seventies, Stephen had been actively involved, through his contributions to the periodical press, in the political controversies of the day; he had even considered standing for Parliament at this time. But in 1873, as Gladstone's ministry wore on to its inglorious end, Stephen gave up writing political leaders for the *Nation*, explaining to Charles Eliot Norton that he had grown 'rather too indifferent to our wearisome politics to be a good correspondent'.[45] And, in the next few years, his political contributions to English journals became more and more infrequent as he devoted himself to less topical writings, first to the *History of English Thought in the Eighteenth Century* and then to his *Science of Ethics*. These works, coming as they do hard upon Stephen's disappointment with the politics of the post-reform era, represent a return to some of the intellectual preoccupations of the period of his conversion. They illustrate that the rationale for this conversion, especially as it was conditioned by Stephen's own unsuccessful participation in reform at Cambridge, continued to function in response to similarly unsatisfactory political situations.

For politics, in Stephen's experience, whether the politics of religious parties within the universities or of parliamentary parties, had come to be characterised by confusion, by amibiguity and even by wilful deception. In contrast to the negativity of the events that surrounded him, at the time of his conversion Stephen had found in the philosophy of history – especially in Auguste Comte's Law of the Three Stages, and his alternation of critical and organic ages – ordering ideas that could account for this confusion, while pointing beyond it to an intellectual and cultural synthesis. In fact, there were events, like the agitation for disestablishment, that convinced Stephen that the country was on the verge of great changes. But if the age refused to turn – if, in other words, the country still found itself in the midst of chaos and conflict long after Stephen had hoped to see social order and intellectual consensus restored – this required special explanation. The explanation that Stephen offered was given in terms of the theory that had led him to expect change in the first place: the theory of progressive historical development that he had learned from Comte. He would explain, by means of history written from a developmental point of view, not only the course of progress, but also the causes that had prevented the emergence of the new synthetic age. Then, since its effectiveness as a solvent for Christian belief had convinced Stephen that the developmental theory was itself the first fruit of the new scientific age, he would use that theory to specify the shape of the new age in the form of a social ethic.

This turning away from a willingness to participate in politics as a process of emergent resolution of social conflicts to the search for a developmental theory that would impose order on the chaos of events represents a crucial change in stance for Stephen and for other thinkers who followed him in this shift. Fear of religious resurgence and disillusionment with the political process provided the impetus for a recourse to a theory of progress, and played a large role in shaping the future that theory envisioned.

But once before at Cambridge Stephen had removed himself from a political conflict and explained the necessity in terms of a theory of development. It was his loss of faith that precipitated this removal, but precisely what was significant about Leslie Stephen's crisis of faith had been its vocational dimension: the fact that the peculiar dynamic of loss of faith in an age of clerical resurgence required his withdrawal from the struggle for university reform. In turn, the experience of vocational crisis was paradigmatic for Stephen's later participation in a wider arena of political reform. It structured his perception of his own role, of the enemy he faced, and even of the way events would and should unfold. To understand the Victorian crisis of faith as a crisis of vocation is therefore to hold the interpretative key to a whole pattern of thought and behaviour, at least in the case of one representative Victorian thinker.

NOTES

1. Leslie Stephen, 'Some Early Impressions', *National Review*, 42 (1903) 214.
2. F.W. Maitland, *The Life and Letters of Leslie Stephen* (London, 1906) 146.
3. Letter from Sedley Taylor to F.W. Maitland, quoted by John W. Bicknell in a paper, 'Mr. Ramsay Was Young Once', delivered at the Modern Language Association meeting of December 1982, with acknowledgement to Professor Lightman (C.U.L. Add. 7007.296).
4. Letter of Lord Annan to the author, 1 October 1983; Bicknell, 'Mr. Ramsay Was Young Once'.
5. Leslie Stephen, *Mausoleum Book*, MS, 3, British Library, Add. MSS 57920; published in *Sir Leslie Stephen's Mausoleum Book*, ed. Alan Bell (Oxford, 1977) 3.
6. Caroline Stephen to F.W. Maitland, 8 January 1905 (Maitland Papers, Cambridge University Library Add. 7008.305).
7. Such is Lord Annan's conviction: 'I now believe that LS suffered agonies of remorse that he had thoughtlessly accepted ordination & of embarrassment that his mother and family would be deeply

shocked' (Lord Annan to the author, 1 October 1983).
8.   Sheldon Rothblatt, *The Revolution of the Dons* (London, 1968).
9.   A.J. Engel, *From Clergyman to Don* (Oxford, 1983).
10. 'A Don' [Leslie Stephen], 'University Organisation', *Fraser's Magazine*, 77 (1868) 144.
11. Noël Annan, *Leslie Stephen* (New York, 1984) 29–34.
12. Caroline Stephen to F.W. Maitland, 8 January 1905.
13. Anthony Russell, *The Clerical Profession* (London, 1980).
14. Annan, *Leslie Stephen*.
15. Stephen, *Mausoleum Book*, MS, 4; published ed., 6.
16. For an excellent description of how clergymen/dons could live with doubt and even with outright disbelief in certain religious formulas under the old dispensation see Stephen's own portrait of the 'average Cambridge don of my day': 'a sensible and honest man who wished to be both rational and Christian. He was rational enough to see that the old orthodox position was untenable. He did not believe in hell or in "verbal inspiration" or the "real presence". He thought that the controversies on such matters were silly and antiquated and spoke of them with indifference, if not with contempt. But he also thought that religious belief of some kind was necessary or valuable, and considered himself to be a genuine believer. He assumed that somehow the old beliefs could be "rationalized" or "spiritualized". He could accept them in some sense or other but did not ask too closely in what sense. Still less did he go into the ultimate questions of philosophy. He shut his eyes to the great difficulties and took the answer for granted' (Maitland, 150–1). Stephen's inability to do the same is what needs to be explained in terms of a new understanding of the commitments one undertook with ordination.
17. Stephen, 'Some Early Impressions', 217.
18. *Mausoleum Book*, MS, 3; published edn, 5.
19. Support for this interpretation of Stephen's loss of faith can be derived from his 1874 article on Maurice ('Mr. Maurice's Theology', *Fortnightly Review*, 21 [1874] 595–617). Stephen's main criticisms of Maurice are: (1) that he confuses reason and feeling, and what satisfies the criteria of truth with what satisfies his feelings (604–6); and (2) that he lacks historical sense, and cannot distinguish between Christianity as an historical creed with a definite content, and that element of it which satisfies his own emotions (608).
20. For Stephen's own view of these controversies see his *Life of Henry Fawcett* (London, 1885) esp. 110–11.
21. ibid., 105.
22. See ibid., 102 ff., for details of Stephen's participation in the reform of Trinity Hall in this period.
23. ibid., 90, 114.
24. Maitland, 48.
25. Stephen, 'Some Early Impressions', 216–17.
26. In 'Some Early Impressions', Stephen recalls that while he was active with Fawcett in the cause of freeing fellowships from restrictions, 'some people were beginning to talk about "endowment of re-

search"'. He goes on to mention Mark Pattison's book on 'academical reorganisation' and in another place (his essay 'University Organisation') J.R. Seeley's essay 'Liberal Education in the Universities' as being characteristic products of this group. But Pattison's book did not appear until 1868, and Seeley's essay was published in 1867 in *Essays on a Liberal Education*, ed. F.W. Farrar (London, 1867).

27. Stephen, *Life of Fawcett*, 90–1, 115.
28. W.R. Ward, *Victorian Oxford* (London, 1965).
29. The Clerical Disabilities Act, opening to former clergymen professions that had been closed to them, was not passed until 1870.
30. Maitland, 106, 173.
31. *Nation*, 28 February 1867, 172.
32. *Nation*, 23 May 1867, 418; 20 June 1867, 500; 15 August 1867, 135.
33. *Nation*, 12 September 1867, 214.
34. *Nation*, 8 April 1869, 273.
35. *Nation*, 26 August 1869, 169.
36. *Nation*, 8 February 1871, 87.
37. Leslie Stephen, 'The Religious Difficulty', *Fraser's Magazine*, NS 1 (1870) 623–34.
38. *Nation*, 16 November 1871, 319.
39. Leslie Stephen, 'Matthew Arnold and the Church of England', *Fraser's Magazine*, NS 2 (1870) 426.
40. Leslie Stephen, 'Social Macadamisation', *Fraser's Magazine*, NS 6 (1872) 168.
41. ibid., 162.
42. ibid., 161.
43. ibid., 162.
44. Leslie Stephen, 'Are We Christians?' *Essays on Freethinking and Plainspeaking* (New York, 1877) 152.
45. Leslie Stephen to Charles Eliot Norton, 18 August 1873 (Norton Papers, Houghton Library, Harvard University MS AM 1088, No. 6887).

9 *Robert Elsmere* and the Agnostic Crises of Faith
Bernard Lightman

An outspoken critic of excessive emotionalism, whether its origin be religious or otherwise, Leslie Stephen nevertheless experienced during his crisis of faith the pain and anguish to which countless Victorians attest in their novels, poetry, memoirs, and letters.* Speaking through the protagonist of *The Nemesis of Faith* (1849), J.A. Froude told his readers that those who treat doubters like himself so coldly would be far more sympathetic could they see 'the tears streaming down his cheeks' when he recalled the peacefulness of his lost childhood faith.[1] A.H. Clough, whose poetic ability seemed to be devoted to the elegant depiction of the agony of decision in a time of crisis, asked in 1851 if man's purpose were 'to spend uncounted years of pain/Again, again and yet again/In working out, in heart and brain/The problem of our being here'.[2] Perhaps most vivid of all is Mrs Humphry Ward's description in *Robert Elsmere* (1888) of the trials of an earnest Anglican minister in the process of losing his faith in conventional Christianity. Coming to terms with the idea of a purely human Christ 'broke his heart', and the ensuing three months, 'marked by anguished mental struggle', were 'the bitterest months of Elsmere's life'.[3]

Situations wherein excessive emotion and intellectual despair are displayed can possess an almost irresistible attraction for historians. Just as Freud found that to study the elusive unconscious it was necessary to take it unawares in dreams and (Freudian) slips of the mind, the historian must take advantage of all opportunities to examine the interior spiritual life of individuals and classes, normally hidden from view. We are shamelessly interested in the agonising crises of faith of numerous Victorians because they present one of

* The author would like to express his gratitude to Henry Alley, James Moore, John Bicknell, Ruth Barton, and Richard Helmstadter for helpful suggestions in regard to revising this chapter.

those occasions when the tensions within an intellectual framework are laid bare to our scrutiny. The Victorian crisis of faith was an emotional and intellectual upheaval brought on by the questioning of a set of assumptions and values (not always restricted to the religious realm) which the doubter previously had shared with his or her social circle.

Although many of the Victorians who passed through a crisis of faith agree that it was a painful time in their lives, the kinds of doubts and questions with which they grappled were not always the same. The term 'Victorian crisis of faith' is a label which covers a rather broad range of experience. The majority of those who questioned the values and norms of the old order, centred on the ideals of an agrarian, aristocratic, and conservative Christian society, found solace in the construction of a new intellectual synthesis acceptable to the modern, industrial, scientific, and urban mind. Although considered by its proponents as competing with the old cluster of beliefs, the new *Weltanschauung* still retained within itself much of its rival, not least of all in the area of religious and Christian ideas.

In order to begin an outline of some of the types of crises of faith experienced by Victorians, and to illustrate how these crises embody both change and continuity characteristic of the development of Victorian thought, it is only appropriate to start with a discussion of Mrs Humphry Ward's *Robert Elsmere*. Scholars concur that *Robert Elsmere* contains a significant portrait of the Victorian crisis of faith. In an extensive examination of all the major novels of faith and doubt, Wolff contends that *Robert Elsmere* is 'the great classic novel of Victorian doubt'. Schieder treats Ward's book as an example of the basic pattern which the conversion theme followed in Victorian fiction. Finally, referring directly to the representative nature of Robert's crisis of faith, Jones states that 'it seems plain enough today that the ideas that shake young Robert Elsmere are those which agitated Matthew Arnold, T.H. Huxley, Mark Pattison...'.[4] Many Victorians agreed that *Robert Elsmere* was an important sign of the times. Even the book's critics admitted that it was so. Gladstone wrote in his review that 'the book is eminently an offspring of the time', while the *Quarterly Review* conceded that 'a success of this kind [in terms of sales] is proof that a book has touched some general and deep sources of public feelings, and has given vivid expression to thoughts or interests which are widely spread'.[5]

Book sales were immense. Even though the three-decker novel was published late in the eighties, Peterson refers to it as the 'best-seller of the decade' with good reason. A first edition of 500 copies, which appeared on 24 February 1888, was sold out by the end of March, and two more editions were called for within the next month. By March 1889 it was said that somewhere between 30 000 to 40 000 copies had been sold in England.[6] *Robert Elsmere* also enjoyed a huge readership in the United States, where over 200 000 copies had been published by 1889. The book's popularity was so great that the Maine Balsam Fir company elected to give one copy away free to each purchaser of a single cake of their soap, advertising that their customers would receive both 'cleanliness and godliness'.[7] Canadians also were taken with the novel. Writing from Toronto late in 1888, Goldwin Smith told Mrs Ward, 'you may be amused by seeing what a stir you are making even in this sequestered nook of the theological world, and by learning that the antidote to you is Ben-Hur'.[8]

No doubt sales of the book were boosted by the controversy it engendered. The book's theological position was attacked by outraged conservative Christians in sermons, letters to the papers, and in the leading journals. The book did receive some notable reviews of praise from Walter Pater and Henry James, but far more noticeable was the criticism of men such as Gladstone, Henry Wace, and Randall Davidson.[9] The colossal circulation of *Robert Elsmere*, combined with the hoopla surrounding its reception, has led one scholar to see in the appearance of Ward's book 'one of the publishing events of the century'.[10]

At the centre of the storm of controversy surrounding *Robert Elsmere* was the book's author, Mary Augusta Ward (1851–1920). Born an Arnold, she was the granddaughter of Thomas, the great master of Rugby immortalised in *Tom Brown's Schooldays*, and the niece of the illustrious poet and essayist Matthew. Thomas Arnold the younger, her father, however, did not follow in the liberal footsteps of his famous brother or father. He converted to Catholicism in 1856 and thereupon was forced to give up his post as inspector of schools in the public service of Tasmania and return to England with his family. Then began a trying period of separation. Mary attended boarding school and lived with her mother, while Thomas worked under J.H. Newman both at the Catholic University, Dublin, and later the Oratory School at Birmingham. Mary's mother, a staunch anti-Catholic, refused to reside with a papist and was determined to bring up her daughter as an Anglican. A family reunion was made possible when Thomas turned against Rome in 1865 and went to Oxford to take on pupils.

Oxford delighted Mary. Being an Arnold, she was treated like royalty by the university liberals. Although not formally a student, the teenager was welcomed into the halls of Balliol and Lincoln, was invited for dinners by Benjamin Jowett and Mark Pattison, was advised by T.H. Green, and enjoyed working in the Bodleian. Living and conversing with the intellectual élite of the nation turned her interests towards writing and research. She published articles throughout the 1870s in *Macmillan's Magazine*, the *Saturday Review*, and the *Fortnightly Review*. It was also at Oxford that she met Thomas Humphry Ward, a young Fellow and tutor of Brasenose College. They were married by Dean Stanley in 1872. When the Wards left Oxford for London in 1881 Mary was considered one of the most promising scholars of her generation. The only memory that marred her otherwise happy remembrance of Oxford was her father's reconversion to Catholicism in 1876 and his subsequent departure to the Catholic University in Ireland.

In London, where Mr Ward became a member of *The Times'* staff and Mary wrote for a variety of journals and papers, she began work on *Robert Elsmere* in 1885, and after three years of gruelling writing and rewriting it was complete. With the success of *Robert Elsmere* her career as a novelist was guaranteed. Although she dealt with a variety of issues in her twenty-five novels, the theme of the conflict between modern thought and Christianity often surfaced. Besides *Robert Elsmere*, the subject of religious doubt was dealt with directly in *The History of David Grieve* (1892), *Helbeck of Bannisdale* (1898), *Eleanor* (1900), and *The Case of Richard Meynell* (1911).

A number of intriguing aspects of Mary Ward's life, outside her work as a novelist, should attract the interest of

Victorian scholars. There is, of course, her role as representative of the third-generation Arnold who continues the liberal transformation of her family's tradition. There is the enticing story of her turbulent relationship with her father, whose own crises of faith drove him to seek out the advice and friendship of her grandfather's greatest enemy, J.H. Newman. Also of note is her connection with so many of the leading intellectuals of the day. In addition to her liberal friends at Oxford, she was acquainted with Walter Pater, Henry James, W.E. Gladstone, Frederic Harrison, T.H. Huxley, and John Morley, and met Swinburne, Eliot, Taine, and Renan. Many Victorianists will find a list of Mrs Ward's practical accomplishments impressive. Although she was a prolific writer, she still found the time to work among the poor of London, founding settlement houses, organising children's recreational centres, and setting up an educational programme for crippled children.

But perhaps most compelling of all is the fascinating blend of contradictory attitudes and ideas she represented. She was an enthusiastic supporter of the movement for the higher education of women and by virtue of her success as an outspoken novelist and organiser seemed to symbolise the aggressive 'new woman' of the modern age. Yet she professed a very traditional notion of the role of women in society, founded the Women's National Anti-Suffrage League (1908), and quoted with approval John Morley's response to those who supported the enfranchisement of women, 'For Heaven's sake, don't let us be the first to make ourselves ridiculous in the eyes of Europe!'[11] She had a reputation for theological unorthodoxy, accepted all the findings of German biblical criticism, and for many years did not think it possible for the Anglican Church to reform itself from within. But she valued institutionalised religion, yearned for a national church as a good Arnoldian should, continued to attend church, and displayed in her novels tremendous sympathy for characters who remained committed Anglicans. Finally, her political temperament called both for progressive change and a distrust of liberalism. The two worlds that uneasily existed side by side in late Victorian society and that she continually depicted in her novels were embedded in her own consciousness.

Robert Elsmere begins by painting a rosy picture of the old and new worlds co-existing in peace in Victorian society and within the mind of the young hero of the novel. Although we first see Robert as an ardent supporter of liberalism and neo-Hegelianism at Oxford, it is clear that he places the fruits of his philosophical idealism in the service of orthodox Christianity. The step of taking orders presents no difficulties in his mind. After teaching brilliantly for three years, Robert's ill-health forces him to take up the family living as rector of Murewell. There he woos and marries Catherine, attracted by her evangelical zeal and selfless devotion to the poor of his parish.

If Robert's idealism presents no serious difficulties to his relationship to the strictly orthodox Catherine (described in the novel as 'the Thirty-nine Articles in the flesh'), neither does his growing 'passion for science'.[12] He organises a Natural History Club for his parishioners, keeps a copy of Darwin's *The Formation of Vegetable Mould through the Action of Worms* on his study table, and marvels at the complexity of *The Origin of Species*. 'It is a revelation', Robert exclaims, but he is reminded by his old Oxford tutor, Langham, that 'it is a revelation ... that has not always been held to square with other revelations'.[13] Robert defends Darwin, claiming that the initial panic concerning evolutionary theory was due to the misconception that it was hostile to Christianity: 'But the panic is passing. The smoke is clearing away, and we see that the battle-field is falling into new lines. But the old truth remains the same. Where and when and how you will, but somewhen and somehow, God created the heavens and the earth.'[14] Robert sees no threat to his faith from natural science or Darwinian theory.[15]

The harmonious relationship between liberal and orthodox Christianity within the older order, symbolised by the joyful marriage of Robert and Catherine, is soon disturbed by the appearance of the sinister squire of Murewell, Mr Wendover, who embodies the negative force of historical criticism. Squire Wendover is a brilliant scholar, an expert in the subject of Christian origins, and at work on a history of testimony. As Robert attempts, with success, to awaken in Wendover a concern for the plight of the poor who live on his land, he inadvertently exposes himself to the squire's scepticism.

Wendover becomes obsessed with the thought of converting the young rector to his radical faith. In conversation he
constantly presses Robert on the issue of the nature and
value of testimony at different times in history. Did the man
of the third century understand, or report, or interpret, facts
in the same way as the man of the sixteenth or nineteenth
century? If not, what is the deduction to be drawn? By
focusing on this crucial question, the squire drives Robert
toward the position that humanity's power of apprehending
and recording has grown and developed through the ages.
In order to understand the origins of the testimony of any
time, the squire argues, the historian must look at the
intellectual preconceptions of that period.

Ironically, it is Robert's recent research on the origins of
modern France that renders his mind fertile ground for the
seeds of doubt planted by Wendover. He is determined to
follow his intellect wherever it may lead, even if his feelings
are trampled in the process. He feverishly studies the validity
of Christian testimony, only to come to the horrible realisation that the uncritical acceptance of the reality of miracles in
the time of Christ must lead the historian to conclude that
the testimony of that period must be considered pre-
scientific, half-trained, and incompetent. The climax of this
wrenching experience is Robert's confession that he can no
longer believe in 'the Man-God, the Word from Eternity',
nor can he profess faith in the Incarnation, in the Resurrection, in the Atonement, or in miracles.[16] This crisis of faith
severely strains both the harmonious union of reverence for
the intellect and feeling for doctrine within liberal Christianity, and the blissful marriage between Robert and Catherine.

Because of the sceptical conclusions brought about by his
crisis of faith, Robert believes it only proper to give up his
living and his orders. But before he takes this final step, he
returns to Oxford to seek advice from Grey, his old neo-
Hegelian teacher. After hearing the story of Elsmere's dark
night of the soul, Grey remarks that 'the process in you has
been the typical process of the present day', and that it 'has
all been a question of literary and historical evidence'.[17] Grey
agrees with Elsmere that it would not be honourable to
remain within the Church.

As Grey does not attempt to convince Eslmere to reconsider leaving the Church, the whole issue of the role of Oxford in Robert's difficulties is raised. Robert's training as a scholar and historian at Oxford are admitted by the narrator to have played a role in his questioning of orthodoxy, his tutor Langham is a sceptic (with distinct affinities to Mark Pattison), and Grey, definitely modelled on T.H. Green, is one who has broken with popular Christianity. In 1888 the *Quarterly Review* charged that the atmosphere of infidelity which surrounded men like Robert at Oxford was one important reason for his crisis of faith. Warning English parents that many Oxford colleges exposed their immature sons to crafty sceptics who deliberately undermined their faith, the *Quarterly Review* declared that 'Oxford is the place to which good German philosophies go when they die'.[18]

However, the place of Oxford in Robert's crisis of faith is not merely destructive, for it is his intellect, his philosophical idealism, his historical sense, first developed as an undergraduate, and his friendship with Grey, which enable him to find a way out of the impasse created by his doubts. 'The parting with the Christian mythology', Grey tells Robert, 'is the rending asunder of bones and marrow. It means parting with half the confidence, half the joy, of life!' But Grey comforts Robert with the thought that this agonising crisis of faith is the education of God. 'Do not imagine', Grey solemnly asserts, 'it will put you farther from Him! He is in criticism, in science, in doubt, so long as the doubt is a pure and honest doubt as yours is. He is in all life, in all thought.'[19] Unlike the squire, whose very title suggests the old order wherein biblical criticism can only play a negative role, Grey helps Robert to envision a positive place for criticism in the search for religious truth.

Grey's words cure Robert's spiritual sickness and the remainder of the book centres on his efforts to heal the rupture between Catherine and himself and to construct a new faith from the ashes of the old. Elsmere is painfully aware of how his doubts will hurt his orthodox wife. Even after he has resolved his crisis his relationship with her is strained. He is alive to the feeling of liberation his new faith has brought him while his wife continues to hope for his return to the fold. There seems to be an unbridgeable gulf between Robert's neo-Christianity and Catherine's orthodoxy. But Mrs Ward reunites Robert and Catherine by the end of the novel. Catherine begins to understand that Robert's faith, though different from hers, still has value. Mrs Ward conceives of a new marriage between freethought and orthodox Christianity.

As husband and wife reach a new understanding, Robert works to build a new relationship with God. Robert still believes in God, convinced as he is that the theistic explanation of life can never be disproved. Unlike Christianity, whose grounds are literary and historical, and therefore always open to question, theism is in a much stronger position, being philosophical in nature.[20] Like Grey, Robert locates God in the human conscience, moral life, and history of man. Robert also retains a belief in Christ the teacher, martyr, and ethical exemplar. Both notions are incorporated into the New Brotherhood of Christ, a religion Robert develops for those of the working class who are alienated from Christianity and yet who thirst for spiritual friendship. Even the tragic death of its founder at the close of the novel does not prevent the New Brotherhood from growing and flourishing, demonstrating the spiritual energy and enthusiasm possessed by the new church.

Robert's crisis of faith is portrayed by Mrs Ward as being relatively brief in duration, intense in its quality, and intellectual in its origins. His crisis lasts less than four years, the whole novel taking place between May 1882, when Robert visits Long Whindale, and March 1886, when he dies.[21] In the three months during which the crisis reaches its peak, Robert is shown to be suffering deeply. By focusing on a neo-Hegelian Oxford graduate who loses his faith while engaged in biblical research in a secluded library somewhere in isolated rural England, Ward portrayed the Victorian crisis of faith as a process that originated from purely intellectual considerations. The larger political and social world seems to be relatively unimportant for Robert's deliberations. Although one of the main themes in *Robert Elsmere* concerns the effect of an individual's crisis of faith on his personal and family relationships, especially Robert's wife Catherine in this case, Ward does not really extend her point to include society as a whole. There is no sense in the novel that Robert's radical beliefs alienated him from his social class. Neither does Mrs Ward deal with changes in social conditions, such as those accompanying the process of urbanisation, industrialisation, the parallel shifts in population patterns, and their impact on religious institutions and ideas. She concentrates on the intellectual, not the social, dimension of the Victorian crisis of faith.

Convinced that Robert's painful intellectual odyssey was a paradigm of the experiences of other doubters, Mrs Ward claimed that her novel was representative of the period – that to some extent 'the generation in which it appeared had spoken through it'.[22] Notwithstanding the claims made by Mrs Ward, her contemporaries, and some scholars, *Robert Elsmere* can be considered as being representative only of the experience of a particular group of Victorian intellectuals, and typical of a specific period in Victorian history. Robert's crisis of faith reflects a state of mind common to those who, like Mary Ward herself, were influenced by the Oxford environment in the seventies and eighties.

If we compare the experiences of Mrs Ward with those of a number of eminent agnostics, it will become clear that Robert represents only one strain of the doubt developed in her generation. T.H. Huxley (1825–95), biologist, zoologist, and professor at the Royal School of Mines, coined the term agnosticism in 1869. To him the true agnostic believed that the very nature of the human mind ruled out the possibility of dogmatic certainty on theological and transcendental matters. Other unbelievers adopted a similar position, including Leslie Stephen (1832–1904), philosopher, critic, essayist, and biographer, John Tyndall (1820–93), professor of natural philosophy at the Royal Institution, W.K. Clifford (1845–79), professor of applied mathematics at University College, and Herbert Spencer (1820–1903), the great 'synthetic philosopher'. The agnosticism of these men represented an important component of their commitment to the cause of scientific naturalism, a movement that limited human knowledge to the realm of natural phenomena and centred new interpretations of man, nature, and society on concepts derived from the theories, methods, and categories of empirical science. Mrs Ward was neither a fully fledged scientific naturalist nor was she an agnostic. Though she defended German biblical criticism on the grounds that it was science, and though she sympathised with some aspects of the agnostic attack on Christian theology, her chief concern was not the popularisation of a scientific world view.

Despite her differences with the agnostics, Mrs Ward nevertheless became friends with a number of them. She and the Huxleys were always on terms 'of the closest intimacy and affection'. Her eldest sister's marriage to Huxley's eldest son, Leonard, in 1885, brought them into frequent contact. When Huxley died in 1895 Mrs Ward remarked that 'there was never a man more beloved – more deeply mourned'. Although acquainted for a number of years, Stephen and Mrs Ward became close friends after the death of Stephen's second wife in 1895. Long heart-to-heart talks throughout the late nineties had established a warm, sympathetic rapport between them. When Mrs Ward published *Helbeck of Bannisdale* in 1898, she had a special copy of the book bound for Stephen without the final chapter, 'that the book might not, by its tragic close, depress one who had known so much sorrow'.[23]

Behind the novel *Robert Elsmere* lies the story of Mary's own personal crisis which began when, still a teenager and fresh from boarding school, she arrived at Oxford in the late sixties. In her own words, she had not progressed beyond an 'Evangelical phase'.[24] On Sunday she would dine with the Pattisons. Dressed in her dark woollen frock and sometimes offended by the speculative freedom of talk at the table, she stood out from the other young persons invited to supper. But slowly she was drawn into the Oxford atmosphere of religious controversy that surrounded her. The worldly scepticism of Pattison, Balliol's defence of unfettered history and criticism, the penetration of Darwin into all realms of thought, and the latest works of Renan, Strauss, and her uncle Matthew, began to exert an influence upon her. Mrs Ward openly conceded the important role her life at Oxford played in the creation of *Robert Elsmere*. Although the novel was begun in 1885, Mrs Ward found herself 'once more in the heart of that Oxford life' when she tried to 'trace back some of the causes which led to its composition'.[25] Stephen and Clifford, who both lost their faith during the sixties while at Cambridge, no doubt also experienced the unsettling effect of encountering powerful new influences in a university environment. But Huxley, Tyndall, and Spencer all came from outside the English university system, and many of the features of Ward's, Stephen's, and Clifford's crises, endemic to Oxbridge, are missing from their experience.

By 1871 Mrs Ward was repelled by the arrogance of the orthodox party at Oxford, attracted by liberal Anglicanism, and dreamed of a substitute for conventional Christianity that would still be Christian.[26] Two years later she wrote to her father that belief should be kept simple, rather than encumbered with supernatural legend and what her uncle called *Aberglaube* (extra belief): 'Of dogmatic Christianity I can make nothing. Nothing is clear except the personal character of Christ and that view of Him as the founder and lawgiver of a new society which struck me years ago in *Ecce Homo*. And the more I read and think over the New Testament the more impossible it seems to me to accept what is ordinarily called the scheme of Christianity.'[27] Although Mary Ward had travelled a long way on the road to liberalism by the early seventies, the crisis did not come until the late seventies, the outcome of her decision to act on Pattison's advice to 'get to the bottom of something . . . choose a subject, and know *everything* about it'.[28] She selected early Spanish history as a subject worthy of study, and began to work in the Bodleian some time in 1868. A few years later she had already built a reputation as a knowledgeable scholar in the field. She maintained an interest in early Spain throughout the seventies, and received an invitation in 1878 from Henry Wace, later Dean of Canterbury and one of the most vociferous critics of *Robert Elsmere*, to write the lives of the early Spanish saints and ecclesiastics for his *Dictionary of Christian Biography*.

Two years of research on the *Dictionary*, concentrating as it did exclusively on religious history and drawing upon German criticism for aid, crystallised in her mind the problematic question of testimony. To her friend Mandell Creighton she wrote in 1888:

> what convinced *me* [of the difficulties raised by historical considerations] finally and irrevocably was two years of close and constant occupation with the materials of history

in those centuries which lie near to the birth of Christianity and were the critical centuries of its development. I then saw that to adopt the witness of those centuries to matters of fact, without translating it at every step, into the historical language of our own day – a language which the long education of time has brought closer to the realities of things – would be to end by knowing nothing actually and truly, about their life.[29]

Like Robert, Mrs Ward's crisis of faith, wherein her vague liberalism was transformed into disbelief, was relatively short in duration. This was also the case with Stephen and Clifford. Stephen's crisis of faith was as spectacular as Robert Elsmere's, in that both began as Anglican ministers who in a short period of time found themselves beyond the pale of the Church. Clifford entered Trinity College, Cambridge, in 1863, won second wrangler honours in the tripos of 1867, and one year later was elected to a fellowship. During the late sixties, when he was still at Cambridge, Clifford experienced a profound religious crisis. Before he took his degree and for some time after he was a high churchman. His close friend Frederick Pollock reported, 'when or how Clifford first came to a clear perception that his position of quasi-scientific Catholicism was untenable I do not exactly know; but I know that the discovery cost him an intellectual and moral struggle'.[30]

Spencer, Huxley, and Tyndall, however, experienced no sudden or swift crisis of faith. They seem to have drifted slowly into unbelief. Spencer discarded the creed of his Wesleyan Methodist parents during the late thirties and forties. In his *Autobiography* he explained that 'the current creed became more and more alien to the set of convictions formed in me, and slowly dropped away unawares'.[31] Born and raised by an evangelical family, Huxley nevertheless supported the disestablishment of the Church of England and no longer accepted evangelical theology by 1840 when he was fifteen.[32] But, like Spencer, Huxley did not have the benefit of college tutors or a university environment to help him think through the issues or speed up the process. While on the Rattlesnake voyage during the late forties he grappled with the chaotic state of his religious emotions. 'Morals and religion are one wild whirl to me,' Huxley wrote in May of 1847, 'of them the less said the better.' In January of 1849 he added beside the same entry, 'Is it better with me now? A little.'[33] However, when he returned to England in 1850 he had worked out the basis of his agnostic creed with the help of J.S. Mill's *Logic* and Sir William Hamilton's philosophy of the conditioned.[34]

Tyndall was also looking for a replacement for traditional Christianity during the forties and fifties. It is not clear when he first began to have doubts about his Irish family's Protestantism with its strong Quaker connections. But by 1847 he had given up many of the main Christian doctrines. 'I cannot for an instant imagine', Tyndall wrote, 'that a good and merciful God would ever make our eternal salvation depend on such slender links as a conformity with what some are pleased to call the essentials of religion. I was long fettered by these things, but now thank God they are placed upon the same shelf with the swaddling clothes which bound up my infancy.' But, during this time and throughout the fifties, Tyndall yearned for a sense of direction that could only be supplied by a definite creed.[35]

A comparison of the role played by biblical criticism in the crises of Ward and the agnostics uncovers further differences in their experiences. Mrs Ward believed that Europe owed to the Germans 'the *rise of history*, in the modern sense', which had 'shaken the traditional fabric of Christian orthodoxy as nothing earlier had been able to shake it'.[36] Looking back in her memoirs on the work she undertook for Wace, Mrs Ward declared that it 'led directly to the writing of *Robert Elsmere*'.[37] The intellectual and emotional contortions to which Robert is driven by his study of the origins of modern France are modelled on Mrs Ward's experiences while she investigated the early Spanish Church. 'The astonishment awakened in Elsmere', Mrs Ward wrote, 'as his task develops by those strange processes of mind current in the historians of certain periods, processes which are often more significant and illuminating than the facts which the historians are trying to relate, was in truth my own astonishment.'[38] *Robert Elsmere* was actually a thinly veiled account of Mrs Ward's own religious crisis and inner struggle, so much so that writing this private confession was an extremely painful process for her. Even two years after publishing the book she confessed to a friend that 'I have never quite recovered from the strain of *Robert Elsmere*'.[39]

Although biblical criticism may have plunged Mrs Ward and other Victorians into a crisis of faith, the original agnostics were not as profoundly affected. There is little evidence that Huxley, like Tyndall and Spencer, lost his faith from reading German higher criticism. Huxley held Mrs Ward's *Robert Elsmere* in high regard. He jokingly wrote to her in 1888 that she deserved no credit for the 'charming style' of the novel since her literary talents were 'in the blood'. While professing a great deal of sympathy for the squire, he praised the picture of Catherine as 'the gem of the book'. Although Huxley believed that Mrs Ward had painted an admirable 'picture of one of the deeper aspects of our troubled time', he made no mention of a feeling of personal identification with Robert or his experiences.[40] A reading of the German critics was not involved in Huxley's struggle to free himself from the slavery of the 'Pentateuchal Cosmogeny' in his youth. Huxley did devote a considerable amount of time to undermining bibliolatry, particularly towards the end of his life, when he engaged Gladstone in heated controversy. He believed that bibliolatry was at the root of the struggle between dogmatism and the free spirit of scientific investigation. It may well be that Huxley's work in bringing the results of biblical criticism to the attention of the Victorian public converted many to agnosticism. But he himself was not led to his new creed by this route.

Of all the agnostics, Stephen was most influenced by biblical criticism. In his *Some Early Impressions* Stephen pointed to Buckle, Darwin, Spencer, *Essays and Reviews*, and Colenso as the powerful dissolvents of religious belief in Victorian society during the early sixties.[41] Stephen himself was familiar with biblical criticism. His 'Are We Christians?' (1873) is full of allusions to the German higher criticism, especially the work of Strauss. But more important throughout Stephen's writings is the theme of the unpleasant implications of evolutionary theory for dogmatic Christianity. Whereas Mrs Ward's crisis of faith took place in the seventies, when the furore over Darwin had died down, Stephen was in the throes of his crisis at the height of the controversy over evolution in the early sixties.

Stephen realised that his loss of faith would constitute a

major turning point in his life, for it altered his whole relationship to the social scene. He could no longer play the moderately liberal, muscular Christian don at Cambridge, nor could he hypocritically stay within the system by desperately clinging to a Broad Church compromise. After his loss of faith in the late sixties while at Cambridge, Clifford, too, felt duty bound to declare war on the Church and the conservative society to which he had formerly belonged. Throughout the seventies Clifford published a series of essays famous for their outspoken religious radicalism and in 1878 helped found the short-lived Congress of Liberal Thinkers. For both Clifford and Stephen, the upshot of their crises meant that they would have to pit themselves against the establishment from a position outside the Church and in alliance with other unbelievers and radical liberals. They would be called upon to break the hold of the Anglican Church over Victorian institutions and ideas. This crucial social dimension to their crises has no parallel in Ward's portrait of Robert's spiritual odyssey.

Coming from outside both the Oxbridge system and well-to-do middle-class society, Huxley, Spencer, and Tyndall were confronted by the social dimensions of their doubt early on. All three were of humble, lower-middle-class origins and had no famous fathers or grandfathers as had Mrs Ward and Stephen to pave the way for their rise to fame. Instead of studying at Oxbridge, Huxley and Tyndall received their schooling by attending to the lessons of the hungry forties. Huxley's experiences as a medical assistant in London's poverty-stricken East End and Tyndall's work as a surveyor, which exposed him to riots in Preston by starving weavers and the topsy-turvy world of the railway mania, rendered them receptive to Thomas Carlyle's indignant attacks on complacent Victorian society. The youthful Huxley and Tyndall became inspired with a passion for social reform, which they now linked to a disdain for conventional Christianity. During the early fifties, when both Huxley and Tyndall were searching for a place in the scientific world, controlled largely by the Church, they had to suffer through years of frustration as men of lesser talent and ability were preferred to them for posts. Although ultimately successful in finding themselves jobs, their initial failures only streng-

thened their resolve to work towards breaking the strangle-
hold of the Anglican Church on the universities as well as on
the larger social scene.

The very different experiences of Mrs Ward and the
agnostics when they wrestled with religious doubt hint at the
complexity underlying the deceptive simple term 'crisis of
faith'. The crisis could take place in the volatile atmosphere
of the major universities of the land, or upon the decks of a
sea-going vessel; it could disrupt the individual's life, or leave
it relatively untouched; it could last over ten years, or rush to
its conclusion in a matter of months; it could originate in
doubts over the infallibility of the Bible, or in problems
raised by philosophical speculation or evolutionary theory,
or even in dissatisfaction with the Church's power in English
society. Each individual's crisis differed in regard to its
origins, intensity, and chronology. It would be more accurate
to speak of crises of faith to indicate a recognition of the
individual quality of each crisis. Since Mrs Ward's personal
experience at Oxford during the seventies were the prime
source for her portrait of the Victorian crisis of faith, Robert
could never be the representative doubter.

One of the few factors that all these crises of faith shared
was the pain and agony felt by those who dared to question
commonly-held beliefs and values. But the pressing of brave
souls in a variety of different directions in response to a sense
of crisis does not point to a profound rupture in the
intellectual framework. When the crises of faith had run
their course, and many painful questions had been resolved,
the initial feeling of loss was replaced by a new-found
perception of gain. Many intellectuals retraced some of their
steps and constructed a new faith that retained important
elements of the old one they had given up.

The majority of agnostics, like Mrs Ward, found a place
for theism and religion in their new creeds, although they
had lost faith in orthodox Christianity.[42] For Mrs Ward the
great fact in the world and in the history of man was
'progress'. The teachings of T.H. Green had revealed to her
the presence of a great Power in history, and 'in the life of
conscience, in the play of physical and moral law' she saw 'the
ordained means by which sin is gradually scourged and
weakened both in the individual and in the human society'.[43]

Huxley did not share Mrs Ward's love for neo-Hegelianism. But when she scolded him in 1892 for berating Caird and Green he replied that he sympathised with their theism though he was not well acquainted with their works. 'And if you please, Ma'am,' Huxley protested, 'I wish to add that I think I am *not* without sympathy for Christian feeling – or rather for what you mean by it. Beneath the cooled logical upper strata of my microcosm there is a fused mass of prophetism and mysticism, and the Lord knows what might happen to me, in case a moral earthquake cracked the superincumbent deposit, and permitted an eruption of the demonic element below.' Clifford and Spencer were also quick to defend the religious nature of their agnosticism against unbelievers. Pointing to the 'dual' theological and ethical aspect of evolutionary theory, Spencer maintained that his synthetic Philosophy did not necessitate a divorce from 'inherited conceptions concerning religion and morality, but merely a purification and exaltation of them'. Clifford referred to his sense of religious feeling as 'cosmic emotion', by which he meant a sense of awe in regard to the order manifested throughout the universe.[44]

A genuine commitment to their new faith gave the agnostics and Mrs Ward confidence that the present unsettlement of orthodox Christianity could only strengthen religion in the long run. 'The world would survive even if Anglicanism were a thing of the past', Stephen declared, 'and would probably find itself much better off than clergymen expect. Whatever happens, the religious instincts of mankind will survive and will find some mode of expression.' Likewise Tyndall talked confidently of the survival of religion. Since religion was 'ingrained in the nature of man' it would be reconstituted, as it had been many times in the past.[45] The growing sense of crisis was, for Mrs Ward, a positive sign. It represented one more step of progress in man's long history. 'What was taking place in Robert during this period of his young intellectual development', Mrs Ward affirmed, 'was the reproduction in miniature of what takes place on a large scale in any of the critical moments of human history. It was the slow and gradual substitution of one set of perceptions for another.'[46] The guiding hand of God himself lay behind the intellectual and religious crisis, for, as Robert Elsmere discovered, the death of the old order and the growth of criticism and science were the fruits of the 'process of Divine education'.[47]

To underline the essentially religious quality of the present crisis, branded by orthodox Christians as heretical and anti-religious in nature, Mrs Ward and the agnostics often compared the nineteenth century to periods of turmoil and unsettlement immediately preceding a time of growth in religious history. For Stephen, the decline of Christianity in the nineteenth century, and the corresponding vacuum that now existed, created a situation resembling the age prior to the birth of Christ. He could not predict which sect of his time was analogous to the ancient Christians, but he was confident that the new religions that would emerge would be superior to modern Christianity.[48]

Mrs Ward viewed the nineteenth-century religious crisis as similar in kind to other moments in human history when God revealed to man the antiquated quality of his ideas and beliefs. But she also saw in the modern condition a particular resemblance to the sixteenth century. In an article published in the *Nineteenth Century* for 1889, intended as a response to the critical reviews of *Robert Elsmere* by Wace and Gladstone, Mrs Ward referred to the present unsettled situation as the 'New Reformation'. The idea of a 'New Reformation' is developed in a dialogue between two fictional characters, Ronalds, a conservative Anglican minister, and his old Oxford friend of two years before, Merriman, who delayed taking orders in favour of studying historical criticism in Germany. Merriman speaks directly for Mrs Ward when he perceives a vast religious movement at work throughout Europe. '"All round us",' Merriman declares, '"I feel the New Reformation preparing, struggling into utterance and being! It is the product, the compromise of two forces, the scientific and the religious."'[49]

Mrs Ward looked toward the birth of a new religion once the 'New Reformation' had run its course. This new religion would 'demand a trust in God, independent of all "schemes of revealed religion"', and would require a faith called upon to meet suffering, the mystery of life, and the agony of death, 'without any cut and dried formulae of explanation'.[50] Mrs Ward did not advocate a complete break from the

Christian tradition, rather, for her, 'the problem is how to replace Christianity of one type by Christianity of another'.[51] The simple faith of Elsmere's New Brotherhood, essentially a reconstructed and revitalised form of Christianity, represented the ideal Mrs Ward envisioned for the future.

Huxley read Mrs Ward's article on 'The New Reformation' with avid interest. At the time he too was engaged in controversy with Wace in the pages of the *Nineteenth Century*. Large sections of Huxley's 'Agnosticism: A Rejoinder' (1889) were devoted to a merciless dissection of Wace's orthodoxy. Expressing his delight with Mrs Ward's article to Knowles on 20 February 1889, Huxley added, 'If it should be possible for me to give a little shove to the "New Reformation", I shall think the fag end of my life well spent.'[52] Actually Huxley had already been pushing for a 'New Reformation' for over thirty years. In 1859 he had observed in a private letter that 'we are on the eve of a new Reformation and if I have a wish to live thirty years, it is that I may see the God of Science on the necks of her enemies'.[53] A year later Huxley presented his idea of the 'New Reformation' to the public in his 'On Species and Race, and Their Origin': 'The general mind is seething strangely,' Huxley announced, 'and to those who watch the signs of the times, it seems plain that this nineteenth century will see revolutions of thought and practice as great as those which the sixteenth witnessed. Through what trials and sore contests the civilized world will have to pass in the course of this new reformation, who can tell?'[54]

Like Mrs Ward, Huxley used the term 'New Reformation' to imply more than a reference to the revolutionary changes sweeping through the religious world. The 'New Reformation' was both a continuation and the climax of the movement of thought that produced the Reformation centuries ago.[55] As such it was essentially religious in nature. Just as Luther had opposed free thought to traditional authority in order to undermine the strength of the decaying Catholic Church, Huxley believed that the new spirit of intellectual freedom instilled into the modern mind by science would reform the obsolete orthodoxy of the day and make room for a purer, more ethical, and less dogmatic religion.

It is unclear whether Mrs Ward simply borrowed the term

'New Reformation' from Huxley. A number of Victorians were intrigued by the parallel between the upheaval preceding Luther's era and that of the nineteenth century.[56] Mrs Ward may even have heard her uncle Matthew mention the coming of a 'New Reformation'. In 1873 Arnold wrote to Huxley, 'I think, however, we shall see in our time a change in religion as great as that which happened at the Reformation, and, like that, a decided advance on the whole'.[57] Whatever the case, Mrs Ward's anticipation of a 'New Reformation' brought her and Huxley together as allies against Wace. When they met socially soon after the publication of Huxley's attack on Wace in 'Agnosticism', Mrs Ward recalls that they could not resist 'dancing a little on our opponents'.[58]

Although the agnostics and Mrs Ward all retained a place in their souls for a type of religion with affinities to Christianity, and even though Mrs Ward sympathised with one of the cardinal agnostic principles – the idea of the unknowability of God – she did not count herself among the agnostics.[59] Where she affirmed her faith in a neo-Hegelian God behind human conscience, the agnostics tended to believe in the unknowable neo-Kantian God behind nature. Furthermore, Huxley and Stephen never believed that it was possible to reform Christianity, and especially the Anglican Church, from within. Mrs Ward initially held to the same position. Robert Elsmere could not espouse his views on the Bible and remain an Anglican. However, Mrs Ward later came to believe that the Church could be saved through internal reform. In 1899 she protested that it was wrong to exclude liberal Christians as well as ritualists from the English Church. She felt that she had been 'driven out' from the Church forms 'natural and dear' to her heart.[60] By 1911, in her novel *The Case of Richard Meynell*, she was defending the right of modernists to be a part of the Church of England and to stay within the Church to fight from within to have their views recognised as fully legitimate. 'These great national structures that we call churches', Mrs Ward stated in her memoirs, 'are too precious for iconoclast handling, if any other method is possible. The strong assertion of individual liberty within them, as opposed to the attempt to break them down from without; that seems to me now the hopeful course.'[61] Since Mrs Ward's interest was centred on the transformation of the Church, she was highly critical of those who would not join in the task of rebuilding Christianity. 'Let me only say that to me . . . ,' Mrs Ward declared, 'the distrust and weariness of Christianity, which is common among some of the best men and women of the present day, is the most wasteful, the most uncalled-for surrender of its own wealth that modern life can make.'[62] None of the agnostics exhibited Mrs Ward's reverence for the Church as an institution to be dealt with delicately and carefully.

For the agnostics, the Church not only was incapable of reforming itself, it also was the chief obstacle to effecting the reform of English society. The Anglican Church, the agnostics believed, had a vested interest in preserving the status quo and protecting its privileged position in society as well as its control over the English educational system. Mrs Ward, who desired reform as well, did not view the Church's impact on social and political change so negatively. Her years at Oxford had brought her into close contact with a brand of liberal Anglicanism at Balliol that concerned itself with social reform and bettering the daily life of the masses. Jowett, whom she reverently referred to as 'the master', and Green filled the minds of their students with the issues of temperance, housing, workers' wages, electoral reform, and the condition-of-the-people question. In *Robert Elsmere* Mrs Ward does not blame the Anglican establishment for the plight of the poor. Robert's work in his parish before his crisis stands as an example of the contribution made by the Anglican clergy to alleviate the suffering of the poor in opposition to the selfishness of wealthy landowners like the squire.

In the end there was a social dimension to Mrs Ward's portrait of the crisis of faith in *Robert Elsmere*, although she, like other Oxford intellectuals, treated the origins of the crisis in purely intellectual terms. When Mrs Ward moved to London in 1881, just after her crisis in the late seventies, she was confronted by a series of events that contributed to her decision to begin work on *Robert Elsmere* in 1885. Shortly after her arrival Mrs Ward began to watch the tense situation in Ireland closely, largely because her uncle, William Forster, was stationed in Dublin as Chief Secretary. Convinced that he was in personal danger, Mrs Ward was relieved when he resigned on 2 May 1882. She was horrified when only four days later Forster's successor, Lord Frederick Cavendish, was assassinated by Irish terrorists. 'On myself, fresh from the quiet Oxford life,' Mrs Ward recalled, 'the Irish spectacle, seen from such a point of view, produced an overwhelming impression.'[63]

The violence and social disorder in Ireland combined with a new awareness of the potential for strife in England to drive her into the Tory camp, and her political conservatism increased with age. Among the events that led her and others to recognise the wretched condition of the labouring poor in London was the publication of *The Bitter Cry of Outcast London* (1883), one of the earliest of many religious pamphlets focusing attention on the London slums. While Mrs Ward was writing *Robert Elsmere* in 1886 there were street demonstrations by unemployed workers. Throughout the late eighties London was continually rocked by labour unrest. Annie Besant's matchgirls' strike occurred in 1888, followed by the great Dock Strike a year later. Many liberals responded to the 'social problem' by reformulating traditional liberalism in order to fuse individualism with socialism.[64] The revival of Christian socialism during this period, a development not unrelated to the birth of a new liberalism, was manifested in the establishment of settlement houses in urban slums and the founding of the Christian Socialist Society in 1886. Even ivory-towered Oxford reacted to the social problems of the day with the founding of the Christian Social Union in 1889.[65] The CSU was guided by Gore, Scott Holland, and Westcott, all contributors to the modernist *Lux Mundi* and all influenced by the idealism of T.H. Green.

Mrs Ward, like the members of the CSU, saw an intimate connection between religion and social reform. In *Robert Elsmere* her concern for social questions is expressed in Robert's fear that 'a war of classes' would take place 'unsoftened by the ideal hopes, the ideal law of faith'. Mrs Ward wanted to modernise Christianity so that it could provide the new faith needed to humanise the 'period of social struggle which undeniably lies before us'.[66] Like the Christian socialists, Mrs Ward believed, and wanted to convince her readers, that lasting and constructive social change could only be effected through religious means such as Robert's settlement work and the founding of a new Christian sect.[67] Mrs Ward's social, as well as her literary, work can be seen as an attempt to retain in the lives of the masses a form of Christianity. To Gladstone she wrote in 1888 that 'for the masses, in the future, it seems to me that charitable and social organization will be all-important. If the simpler Christian ideas can clothe themselves in such organization – and I believe they can and are even now beginning to do it – their effect on the democracy may be incalculable.'[68] Mrs Ward aimed at directing the present crisis of faith into a positive, neo-Christian path, towards the new religion she predicted for the coming age. 'It is about the new forms of faith', Mrs Ward affirmed, 'and the new grounds of combined action that I really care intensely. I want to challenge those who live in doubt and indecision from year's end to year's end, to think out the matter, and . . . to count up what remains to them, and to join frankly for purposes of life and conduct those who are their spiritual fellows.'[69] Mrs Ward's *Robert Elsmere*, which she openly admitted was 'religious propaganda', was meant to resolve, not deepen, the crisis of faith, and to illustrate an alternative to orthodox rigidity that would work towards social reform.[70]

In the end, the agnostics found their authority in science, while Mrs Ward held out hope that a catholic, national church, along the lines suggested by her grandfather, would be established by Elsmeres of the future who would elect to remain within the Church and modernise it. She was attracted to the sense of community offered by religious institutions, and was not sure that secular institutions could foster strong human relationships. In choosing to place authority within a Christian institution, Mrs Ward found common ground with some of her enemies. Most striking was her ability to maintain a close relationship with Gladstone despite his critical review of *Robert Elsmere*. Gladstone had in fact taken the extraordinary step of arranging two friendly interviews with Mrs Ward prior to writing his review as, according to her, 'he had never read any book on the hostile side written in such a spirit of "generous appreciation" of the Christian side'.[71] Their 'tearless battle', as Gladstone called it, never disrupted their friendship.[72]

Mrs Ward's position as a link between the agnostics and Gladstone resembles her attempt to arrange a new marriage between freethought and orthodox Christianity in *Robert Elsmere*. Both stand as a reminder that the intellectual historian cannot interpret the movement from the old order to the new order as a sharp break with the past. The term 'crisis of faith' can be somewhat misleading if it connotes solely a radical break with previous forms of thought. Undoubtedly, for many, Revelation could no longer be a source of truth, and orthodox Christian dogma was unacceptable. The crisis experienced by many Victorians as they gave up old beliefs generated great pain, agony, and suffering. However, emotional turmoil is not proof positive of the existence of a war between two irreconcilable and totally opposed world views. Ultimately, the similarities in how each crisis was resolved is more impressive than the diversity in the origins of crisis. Although Mrs Ward's portrayal of the crisis of faith as originating in purely intellectual factors reflects the unsuitability of characterising Robert as the typical doubter, Robert's endorsement of a form of neo-Christianity at the end of the book is representative of the agnostics' attempt to retain a place for religion in their thought. The pain experienced by those who underwent the process should not lead us to lose sight of the fundamental continuity running throughout the spectrum of faith in Victorian England.

NOTES

1. J.A. Froude, *The Nemesis of Faith* (1849) 2nd edn (London, 1849) 107.
2. Arthur Hugh Clough, 'To Spend Uncounted Years of Pain', in *Victorian Poetry and Poetics*, eds Walter E. Houghton and G. Robert Stange (Boston, Mass., 1968) 365.
3. Mrs Humphry Ward, *Robert Elsmere* (1888) 3 vols, Westmoreland Edition (Boston and New York, 1911) 2: 49. (Hereafter cited as RE.)
4. Robert Lee Wolff, *Gains and Losses* (New York and London, 1977) 454; R.M. Schieder, 'Loss and Gain? The Theme of Conversion in Late Victorian Fiction', *Victorian Studies*, 9 (1965) 36; Enid Huws Jones, *Mrs. Humphry Ward* (London, 1973) 83. See also Margaret Maison, *The Victorian Vision* (New York, 1961), 255, 268; David Wee, *The Forms of Apostasy: The Rejection of Orthodox Christianity in the British Novel, 1880–1900* (Ann Arbor, Mich., 1984) 80. Peterson is far more

careful in his assessment of the significance of *Robert Elsmere*. Although he sees Robert as bearing 'the heavy symbolic burden of being the representative modern doubter', he is not willing to view Robert's crisis of faith as a paradigm for the entire Victorian period. Carlyle's *Sartor Resartus* he regards as the more important spiritual autobiography of the early Victorian age, as therein is found an experience recognised by many readers as an expression of their own spiritual doubts and longings. For the same reason Tennyson's *In Memoriam* and Newman's *Apologia* are emblematic of the mid-Victorian age, and *Robert Elsmere* claims a similar position for the late Victorian period (William S. Peterson, *Victorian Heretic* [Leicester, 1976] 132, 14).

5.   W.E. Gladstone, '"Robert Elsmere" and the Battle of Belief', *Nineteenth Century*, 23 (1888) 767; [Henry Wace,] 'Robert Elsmere and Christianity', *Quarterly Review*, 167 (October 1888) 273.

6.   Peterson, *Victorian Heretic*, 160; Basil Willey, 'How "Robert Elsmere" Struck Some Contemporaries', *Essays and Studies*, 10 (1957) 56; Peterson, *Victorian Heretic*, 159, 221–2. In 1909 Mrs Ward estimated that nearly one million copies of *Robert Elsmere* had circulated in English-speaking countries.

7.   Janet Penrose Trevelyan, *The Life of Mrs. Humphry Ward* (New York, 1923) 75.

8.   Mrs Humphry Ward, *A Writer's Recollections*, 2 vols (New York and London, 1918) 2: 93.

9.   For a full list of reviews of *Robert Elsmere* see Peterson, *Victorian Heretic*, 248–50.

10.   Schieder, 'Loss and Gain?', 34. Considering Ward's popularity with the Victorian reading public and her tendency to act as the mouthpiece of the spirit of the age, she has been relatively neglected by scholars until recently (see Esther Marian Greenwell Smith, *Mrs. Humphry Ward* [Boston, Mass., 1980] 142). One explanation for the decline in influence after her death stems from the very topicality of her work. By centring on a burning question of the day she assured her books immediate success, but in the process fated them to eventual obscurity. The fortunes of Mrs Ward's reputation resemble those of Herbert Spencer, whose importance has also recently been recognised on the grounds that his influence was pervasive though he now makes dull reading.

11.   Trevelyan, 229.

12.   RE, 1: 293, 489.

13.   ibid., 1: 307.

14.   ibid.

15.   Quoting approvingly from a letter on *Robert Elsmere* she had received from an Owens College professor, Mrs Ward wrote to Gladstone in 1889, 'it is not the scientific (in the loose modern sense of the word), . . . but it is the education of the historic sense which is disintegrating faith' (Trevelyan, 63). Peterson points out that Mrs Ward had initially planned to deal with the scientific issue but later came to believe that the main Darwinian battle had been over before 1870 (Peterson, *Victorian Heretic*, 148).

16. RE, 2: 84.
17. ibid., 2: 105.
18. Wace, 275.
19. RE, 2: 109.
20. ibid., 2: 204.
21. Peterson, *Victorian Heretic*, 132.
22. RE, 1: xiv.
23. Ward, *Writer's Recollections*, 1: 138, 2: 175, 84.
24. ibid., 1: 138.
25. RE, 1: xvi.
26. Trevelyan, 32–3.
27. ibid., 33.
28. Ward, *Writer's Recollections*, 1: 141. Ironically, what was for Pattison his own method of coping with religious crisis, faith in learning and the critical intellect, touched off Mrs Ward's crisis of faith (see Duncan Nimmo, 'Learning against Religion, Learning as Religion: Mark Pattison and the "Victorian Crisis of Faith"', in *Religion and Humanism*, ed. Keith Robbins [Oxford, 1981] 311–24).
29. Mrs Humphry Ward to Mandell Creighton, 13 March 1888 (Pusey House Library, as cited in Williams S. Peterson, 'Mrs. Humphry Ward on "Robert Elsmere": Six New Letters', *Bulletin of the New York Public Library*, 74 [November 1970] 591).
30. Frederick Pollock, 'Biographical', in William Kingdon Clifford, *Lectures and Essays*, 2 vols, ed. Leslie Stephen and Frederick Pollock (London, 1879) 1: 32.
31. Herbert Spencer, *An Autobiography*, 2 vols (New York, 1904) 1: 173.
32. Leonard Huxley, *Life and Letters of T.H. Huxley* (1900) 3 vols (London, 1913) 1: 10; Bruce Gordon Murphy, *Thomas Huxley and His New Reformation* (Ann Arbor, Mich., 1977) 17.
33. *T.H. Huxley's Diary of the Voyage of the H.M.S. Rattlesnake*, ed. Julian Huxley (Garden City, NY, 1936) 278.
34. T.H. Huxley, 'Mr. Balfour's Attack on Agnosticism II', in *Huxley: Prophet of Science*, ed. Houston Peterson (London, New York, and Toronto, 1932) 315.
35. Tyndall Papers (Royal Institution of Great Britain, London), journals of John Tyndall, 220, 216; correspondence with Thomas Archer Hirst, 15 (R.I. MSS T., 31/B4, 12), 112 (R.I. MSS T., 31/B8, 38); Arthur Stewart Eve and C.H. Creasey, *Life and Work of John Tyndall* (London, 1945) 70.
36. Mrs Humphry Ward, *New Forms of Christian Education* (New York, 1898).
37. Ward, *Writer's Recollections*, 1: 202.
38. RE, 1: xix. The Westmoreland edition was published over a decade after the novel first appeared. But Mrs Ward did not fabricate this story in later life, for soon after *Robert Elsmere* was published in 1888 she wrote to the Broad Churchman Reverend Hugh Haweis that the 'historical experience' of Elsmere 'is my own' (see Mrs Humphry Ward to H.R. Haweis, 8 May 1888, Harvard College Library, as cited in Peterson, 'Mrs. Humphry Ward on "Robert Elsmere"', 596).
39. Mrs Humphry Ward to Frances Power Cobbe, 15 August 1890

(Huntington Library, as cited in Peterson, *Victorian Heretic*, 121).

40.   L. Huxley, *Life and Letters of T.H. Huxley*, 3: 64.
41.   Leslie Stephen, *Some Early Impressions* (1924; London, 1952) 54.
42.   The essays by James Moore and George Levine have already addressed facets of this issue. See also Bernard Lightman, *The Origins of Agnosticism: Victorian Unbelief and the Limits of Knowledge* (Baltimore, 1987). Here I shall concentrate on those points that pertain specifically to a comparison of the thought of Mrs Ward and the agnostics.
43.   Mrs Ward to Gladstone, 15 April 1888 (British Museum, Add. MS 44503, fol. 170–5, as cited in William S. Peterson, 'Gladstone's Review of *Robert Elsmere*: Some Unpublished Correspondence', *Review of English Studies*, 21 [1970] 456).
44.   Ward, *Writer's Recollections*, 2: 174; *The Letters of John Fiske*, ed. Ethel F. Fiske (New York, 1940) 479; Clifford, *Lectures and Essays*, 2: 253–85.
45.   Leslie Stephen, *Essays on Freethinking and Plainspeaking* (London, 1873) 7; John Tyndall, *New Fragments* (New York, 1896) 29.
46.   Peterson, *Victorian Heretic*, 146.
47.   RE, 2: 206.
48.   Leslie Stephen, *An Agnostic's Apology and Other Essays* (London, 1893) 302, 353–5.
49.   Mary A. Ward, 'The New Reformation: A Dialogue', *Nineteenth Century*, 25 (1889) 479.
50.   Mrs Humphry Ward, 'Sin and Unbelief', *North American Review*, 148 1889) 177.
51.   ibid., 178.
52.   Huxley, *Life and Letters of T.H. Huxley*, 3: 107. In his 'Agnosticism: A Rejoinder' (1889), a sequel to his 'Agnosticism', Huxley thanked Mrs Ward for saving him time by responding so powerfully to many of Wace's points (see Thomas H. Huxley, *Science and Christian Tradition* [London, 1909] 263).
53.   Huxley to Dyster, 30 January 1859 (London, Imperial College of Science and Technology, Huxley Papers, 15: 107).
54.   T.H. Huxley, *The Scientific Memoirs of Thomas Henry Huxley*, ed. Sir Michael Foster and E. Ray Lankester, 5 vols (London, 1898–1903) 2: 393.
55.   L. Huxley, *Life and Letters of T.H. Huxley*, 2: 111; T.H. Huxley, *Science and Education*, 1893; New York and London, 1914) 191–2.
56.   P.O.G. White, 'Three Victorians and the New Reformation', *Theology*, 69 (August 1966) 352–8.
57.   Matthew Arnold to Huxley, 13 February 1873 (London, Imperial College of Science and Technology, Huxley Papers, 10: 155).
58.   Ward, *Writer's Recollections*, 2: 121.
59.   RE, 2: 556.
60.   Mary A. Ward, 'The New Reformation: II. A Conscience Clause for the Laity', *Nineteenth Century*, 46 (1899) 668.
61.   Ward, *Writer's Recollections*, 2: 74.
62.   Ward, *New Forms of Christian Education*, 22.

63. Ward, *Writer's Recollections*, 1: 235.
64. Michael Freeden, *The New Liberalism: An Ideology of Social Reform* (Oxford, 1978) 257.
65. Peter d'A. Jones, *The Christian Socialist Revival, 1877–1914: Religion, Class, and Social Conscience in Late-Victorian England* (Princeton, 1968) 177.
66. RE, 2: 205.
67. ibid., 2: 463.
68. Trevelyan, 61.
69. ibid., 68.
70. Ward, *Writer's Recollections*, 2: 66.
71. ibid., 2: 78.
72. Gladstone to Mrs Ward, 14 May 1888 (Pusey House, as cited in Peterson, 'Gladstone's Review of *Robert Elsmere*', 461).

Part V
The Faith Abroad: Two
Case Studies from
the Empire

10 On Redefining 'Crisis': The Victorian Crisis of Faith in the Punjab, 1880–1930

Jeffrey Cox

Almost all academic thinking about religion in the modern world has been governed, in one way or another, by the assumption that we are in the midst of a transition from a world in which religion was universally important to a world in which religion will be universally marginal. Scholars who would vigorously deny holding any theory of the nature of religion in the modern world fall back upon this assumption unwittingly. As the sociological theory of secularisation, the same assumption dominates the social history of religion, and scholars who set out to escape from the theory find themselves entrapped within its tentacles before they can get away.[1]

I have argued elsewhere that we need a new set of hypotheses to guide our thinking about religion in the modern world, and I have also attempted to apply some of those hypotheses in a new explanation of the declining importance of the British churches in the late nineteenth century. Briefly stated, I suggested that all theories of secularisation, even the most sophisticated, are linear models of decline that should be replaced with a model of religion in the modern world that leaves the question of growth and decline open. I also suggested that the declining importance of the Protestant churches in Britain during the last century has been at least as much a consequence of specific British historical developments as a consequence of global technological, intellectual, and social trends.[2]

But not explicit in either of those efforts was a further hypothesis about the relationship between the Victorian crisis of faith as an intellectual and moral crisis, and the

Victorian crisis of faith as an institutional crisis of confidence that led to a near disastrous decline in support for Britain's Protestant churches. In the old-fashioned view, the intellectual crisis caused the institutional crisis. The more recent view attributes both crises to the hidden hand of secularisation. In both hypotheses, British religion in all its forms has been a casualty of the 'transition to modernity'. My own hypothesis is that the two crises were largely if not entirely independent in origin, but mutually reinforcing in their effects.

That 'modern' religion differs from 'pre-modern' is true enough, and the distinction is a serviceable one if thought of in the right way. But we should think of this transition as one that *allows* religion to become unimportant rather than one that *forces* it to become unimportant. A religion buttressed by state power and an all-encompassing religious cosmology differs fundamentally from a religion that has to compete in a market-place of institutions and ideas. A secular society is one in which religion may or may not be important depending on historical circumstances.

The single most important condition influencing the status of 'modern' religion is the role of the state. Is religion to be promoted by the state, as it was almost everywhere, with widely varying degrees of success, up until the eighteenth century? Is religion to be suppressed or discouraged, or barely tolerated? Or is the state to function as a formally neutral arbiter in a competing market-place of religious and irreligious ideas and institutions?

If religion is allowed to compete, the questions of success or failure, growth or decline, crisis or confidence, become questions for specific historical investigation rather than abstract sociological prediction. The contrast between Britain and America is instructive. In the late nineteenth century both Britain and America allowed some rough approximation of a free competitive market in religious ideas and institutions, and both countries saw a partial falling away from Christianity among their literary and intellectual classes at this time.

Yet the plain fact is that, one hundred years later, Christianity is more *plausible* in the United States than in Great Britain,[3] not because one nation is more scientific, more technological, more intellectual, or in possession of a larger percentage of intellectuals or scientists, not because intellectual life is more thoroughly rational or technocratic or scientific in one country than in the other, but because American churches of all kinds managed to recruit people into religious institutions much more effectively than their counterparts in Britain. The reasons for this are understandable in the light of the historical circumstances that in the early days of the Republic forced the American churches to scramble for members merely in order to survive, and that created a passion for recruitment characteristic of American churches ever since.

This contrast between Britain and America has led to a great deal of nonsense about the allegedly unique hypocrisy, shallowness, and materialism of American religion,[4] and also to a bemused style of reporting about religion in periodicals such as the *New York Times*, a style that prominently features the key phrase 'still important despite' or a synonymous one, and in which the polar opposition between 'secular' and 'religious' generates hopeless confusion.[5]

The apparent paradox of religion thriving in a secular society confronts us just as forcefully when we consider those portions of Africa, Asia, and Latin America where religion is allowed to compete. There is an astonishingly large body of scholarship, much of it mixed with advocacy of the missionary cause and therefore likely to be ignored by secular scholars, on the spectacular worldwide expansion of Christianity in the nineteenth and twentieth centuries.[6] Thanks to the labours of an Anglican evangelical missionary in Kenya, for instance, we now know that there are at least 20 000 distinct Christian denominations in the world, most of them small but growing rapidly, many of them a consequence of the Victorian missionary movement.[7] Barring a worldwide triumph of totalitarianism, or nuclear obliteration, this growth probably ensures that religion will continue to be important for several centuries to come.

Study of the missionary movement not only provides opportunities to examine the future of Christianity, but promises to shed light on the nature of faith in the sending countries as well. One of the most interesting of the Victorian missionary enterprises was the sustained effort to Christianise the Indian Province of the Punjab, which only fell into British hands in the first half of the nineteenth century and where missionary effort was almost entirely in the hands of British and American Protestants, competing and cooperating with each other directly in the nearest thing a historian will ever get to a controlled, laboratory environment. There were no Christians of any kind in the Punjab until the nineteenth century. The problems that British and American missionaries faced there were the problems that British and American Protestants faced at home writ large. In a competitive situation it was not possible to ignore entirely fundamental questions of strategy and mission. What is the church? What is it for? What is the essence of Christian faith? How do you explain it to someone who must be persuaded to believe it?

The British and American effort to Christianize the Punjab began in the 1830s and reached its peak between 1880 and 1930. The most important British missionary society at work in the Punjab was the Anglican evangelical Church Missionary Society (CMS). By the middle of the nineteenth century the CMS was the largest and most prestigious of the many British missionary societies at work throughout the world; in the late nineteenth century it was the largest single missionary society of any country at work in India.

But the CMS was slow in beginning its work in the Punjab, and the beginnings of its work were accompanied by a bitter dispute about the proper role of the state in Christianising the province. A number of prominent civil and military colonial officials of the famous 'Punjab School' of administration wanted the government of India to intervene directly with a programme of state-sponsored promotion of Christianity.[8] The battle lines were drawn in the 1850s, primarily over the question of the Bible in the schools, with John Lawrence, Chief Commissioner of the Punjab, and Herbert Edwardes, Commissioner of Peshawar, fighting and losing a long struggle to overturn the established policy of secular education.[9] Before losing, however, they caused the government of India a great deal of trouble, especially by going on speaking tours in England denouncing, with inflammatory illustrations, the wicked consequences of the government's secular neutrality, and driving the frustrated

Viceroy, Lord Canning, to fantasies of having Edwardes's head shaved.[10]

The loss of this fight meant that the primary task of Christianising the Punjab would belong to missionaries, not administrators. It was a source of considerable embarrassment to the Punjab School that the British churches, especially the established churches, were so slow to respond to the new opportunities for spreading the gospel after the final British conquest of the entire Punjab in the 1840s, and that British administrators were forced to patronise the ambitious missionaries of the Presbyterian Church in the USA, who had been active since the 1830s in the areas of the southern Punjab under direct British rule. But the CMS, always a cautious bureaucracy, worried about over-extension, and their formal involvement did not begin until 1852, when the first two missionaries arrived from England.[11]

These clergymen, Robert Clark and T.H. Fitzpatrick, symbolised the particular strategy the CMS planned to follow, a strategy of concentrating on the educated élite. Both were university men, since the CMS believed that it was particularly important to put their most highly educated recruits into those parts of the world characterised by centuries of learning on the part of sophisticated rivals to Christianity. Within ten years there were eleven ordained CMS men in the Punjab, some of them with their wives, who invariably did missionary work too. The number remained stagnant in the 1860s, when the CMS was having financial problems at home, but began to grow in the 1870s. By 1881 there were thirty-three European agents, with an additional fourteen ladies of the Church of England Zenana Missionary Society, which sponsored single women. In the early nineties, after CMS statisticians, in a burst of feminist enthusiasm began counting married women as missionaries, the Punjab missions of the CMS and CEZMS numbered 170. A peak of 180 workers was reached about 1911; after some wartime decline there were still 150 Anglican evangelicals at work in the early 1920s, substantially more than in the 1880s.[12]

What did these people do? Missionaries have at one time or another tried almost everything, and performed an extraordinary variety of historical roles. Within the Anglican evangelical missionary effort there were multiple gaps between theory and practice that tell us a great deal about the character of Victorian faith. A number of other missionary societies began work in the 1850s, including the United Presbyterians (a second American Presbyterian group), the Church of Scotland, and the Anglican United Society for the Propagation of the Gospel, but the Punjab School placed the primary responsibility for Christianising the Punjab on the CMS. Having awarded the contract, as it were, to Anglican evangelicals, the Punjab School were willing to leave the precise details of missionary strategy to the missionaries themselves. Even extremists like Herbert Edwardes recognised important limits to the use of state power to propagate Protestant Christianity, and agreed that Punjabis had ultimately to be *persuaded* to become Christians. Spreading Christianity was a task for professional clergymen and other kinds of missionaries, and it was up to them to come up with the precise details about how it was to be done. Laymen should raise money, lend moral support, encourage high standards of missionary effort, and use their considerable social influence on behalf of the church; clergymen should provide the precise programme and bear the primary responsibility for carrying it out.

The CMS had an official set of theories about what missionaries should do, theories developed by the presiding genius of the CMS at home, Henry Venn, who dominated the society throughout the mid-Victorian period until his death in 1872. Missionary strategists today regard Venn as something of a prophet of the allegedly enlightened missionary strategies of the post-colonial, post-imperial age, and it is easy to see why, for he was keenly aware of the ephemeral nature of British rule and even of the western presence in what we now call the Third World. Venn understood better than most Victorians that religion in the nineteenth century was operating under a new set of rules, and that social influence was no substitute for individual persuasion. If missionaries were merely colonialists who happened to perform religious tasks, then the effects of missionary work would not be permanent, for they would not outlast the colony.

Venn believed that *all* missionary effort should be directed toward the goal of creating an indigenous 'native', that is, non-western, non-English church. The missionary goal was, in his phrase, 'the euthanasia of the mission', an event that would leave behind a native church that was – again his phrases, and very important ones for the CMS – a native church that was 'self-supporting, self-governing, and self-extending'.[13] CMS missionaries in the Punjab necessarily took this famous 'three-self' formula very seriously. A majority of them believed that the development of a self-supporting, self-governing, and self-extending Punjabi church was what they *should* be doing, and until the 1880s even believed that it was what they *were* doing.

Missionary historians often assume that mid-century CMS missionaries attempted to follow Venn's advice, which was later abandoned in the 1880s and 1890s when a new generation of missionaries infected the mission field either with new and more virulent forms of racism and imperialism, or with the theological perfectionism promoted in Anglican evangelical circles at the yearly Keswick Conventions.[14] But given the kind of people who were entrusted with the missionary task in the Punjab, and given the kind of people who became Christians in the Punjab, it is not at all clear that Venn's policy could have been put into effect by anyone. The three-self formula turned out to be a poor guide to everyday practice.

A missionary arriving, usually alone or with his wife, in Amritsar, or Multan, or Peshawar, had to decide what to do. He could build a church and preach in it, but no one would be there to listen. He could go and preach in the bazaar, and almost always gather a crowd that was usually polite although on some occasions violent. But bazaar preaching was soon discovered to be an ineffective means of gathering together a native church, and cold weather itinerating tours of rural villages produced similarly barren results. A missionary could, however, become an important local figure almost at once by opening a school, and from the 1850s through the 1880s education was the primary activity of CMS missionaries.

The demand for education was primarily related to the desire to obtain government jobs, but it went beyond that and extended out into rural villages, whose leaders often begged missionaries to open schools and offered to share in the costs. Missionaries opened village schools – including schools for girls – and 'Anglo-Vernacular' high schools for boys and girls, mainly non-Christian. They opened up boys' and girls' boarding schools for Christians, with separate institutions for each social class. The boys' Christian Boarding School in Batala advertised itself as 'the Rugby of the Punjab'; its girls' counterpart was the Alexandra School in Amritsar, the site also of a 'middle class girls school' for Indian Christians with insufficient social standing for the Alexandra School. The teachers at the girls' orphanage and school at the Christian village of Clarkabad dealt with the lower end of the social scale; despite strenuous efforts to make sure that these girls were trained to be the wives of Christian ploughmen and nothing more, this school continued to graduate school teachers with social ambitions above their station.

This educational strategy was not merely a question of responding to demand. Missionaries created other Christian institutions when they could, and they did it because the building of Christian institutions was central to the conception of Christianity that CMS clergymen brought with them from England. In 1864 the Reverend T.P. Hughes arrived in Peshawar and spent the next twenty years more or less in charge of the CMS mission there. By the early 1880s Peshawar had the usual CMS high school, occupying a former palace. Not one of the 473 students was a Christian. A number of the non-Christian teaching staff had graduated from the school, which offered no religious teaching at all except to the upper forms.[15]

In addition to tending his school, Hughes spent a great deal of time and money on entertainment. The CMS sponsored a guest house (*hujra*) operated according to missionary notions of the traditional hospitality of Afghan chiefs. Hughes reserved it, according to the chaplain of the Bishop of Calcutta, for 'native visitors to the city who may desire to converse with or hear, or at least have the reflected honor, of becoming guests of so great a *moulvi* as the Christian missionary'.[16] Mr Hughes was evidently willing to discuss any subject, even religion, with his visitors, one of whom in 1881 was 'a very aged and very learned Wahhabi *moulvi* who owed to Mr. Hughes his reinstatement to a position from which he had been driven by the Akhund of Swat'.[17]

Hughes believed in what sociologists call 'stratified diffusion': influence the upper classes and lesser creatures will follow. The Peshawar mission sponsored a hostel for the sons of distinguished Afghan chiefs who wished to attend the CMS high school, where children were routinely identified in public procession according to their social rank. Unenthusiastic about bazzar preaching, Hughes instead chose to open a Christian *Anjuman*, a kind of literary society with reading rooms in the bazaar, where English lectures were given on improving subjects, including religion.

When Robert Clark, the Secretary of the CMS Punjab and Sindh Mission, visited Peshawar in 1883 he wrote enthusiastically of Hughes's strategy now 'bearing fruit'. Where was the fruit? Large numbers of Christian converts? A self-supporting, self-governing, self-sustaining native church? No. The fruits were the 473 scholars in the school, many of *good* family, who would one day have influence. He cited as a particular fruit one of the school's first pupils in the 1850s 'who, although not a Christian, had evidently received many benefits to his own spirit and mind from his *contact* with Christianity, and is still in charge of the Persian and Urdu department'.[18]

The goal was neither converts nor an indigenous Indian church; it was *influence*. When the Bishop of Calcutta visited Peshawar, Hughes proudly took him around to visit Afghan villages, where they were greeted with great pomp and exchanged gifts while admiring and making notes on 'the handsome and stalwart physique and courteous gentlemanly manners of the upper classes of the Pathans'.[19] Although Hughes was something of an extreme case, virtually all the CMS missionaries believed that Christianity could best be propagated by establishing Christian institutions. Christian values would radiate from these institutions and leaven and enlighten society as a whole. Christian institutions would create an environment where Christianity would be intelligible, and if only Christianity could be made intelligible then conversions would follow in due time. A rational mind, freed from error, would be likely to see the persuasive power of truth.

Furthermore, Christianity was not some hole-and-corner,

back-street religion, like English Dissent. It would not further the cause of Christianity to have a group of outcastes worshipping in a mud hut. Hindus and Muslims of the influential classes would reject a Christianity that appeared to them in that form. No, Christianity was a great world religion that had to challenge Hinduism and Islam with institutions of a grandeur equal to theirs. The Sikhs were regarded as followers of a local religion that would disappear during the course of the demolition of Hinduism and Islam, or Mohammedanism, as Christians called it. It was true that Muslims had to be informed of the textual superiority of the Bible to the Koran, and public polemics between the two religions concerned, almost obsessively, the comparative reliability of the texts. Both Hindus and Muslims also had to be reminded that the immorality and idolatry of their religions, which extended even back to basic texts,[20] were repugnant to universally held natural principles of reason and ethics. But the fundamental form of competition was in the construction of improving social institutions. It was there that the superiority of Christianity as the greatest of world religions was to be manifested.

The crowning glory of Hughes's tenure in Peshawar came with the construction of a native church for the eighty or so native Christians who huddled around the CMS institutions. Hughes wished to erect a building 'in harmony with the tastes and feelings of the people – a purely oriental structure',[21] and personally raised £2000 for the church building and vested ownership in the CMS. The prospect of Peshawar's Christians building their own church was never seriously considered. How could they afford it? Poor Christians in England were not expected to build their own churches. When the church was opened in 1884 the CMS claimed it as the most beautiful church in India, an adaptation of mosque architecture, with painted windows given by Mrs Herbert Edwardes in memory of her husband, a baptistry adapted for baptism by immersion, Persian biblical texts on the walls, a chancel floor set with patterned Peshawar pottery, wood carvings of native Peshawar patterns, and one transept set aside for women in purdah.[22]

This was Hughes's concept of an indigenous church, the translation of Christian cultural forms into Asian cultural forms. Every generation of missionaries has been criticised by the succeeding generation of missionaries, and by outside critics, for importing western culture, but to interpret Hughes's strategy along those lines is to miss the point. Almost every western missionary has been concerned to fashion a form of Christianity that will be palatable to his potential converts. Almost all Christian missionaries, despite their best efforts, import western culture to a greater or a lesser degree, although perceptions of what is and is not western and non-western change. The important thing about Hughes's strategy is that it was an *institutional* strategy. He did not appear to worry excessively about failing to produce converts, who numbered about eighty in the 1880s when the Christian community was actually shrinking. He recognised that opportunities to win converts were strictly limited in a city like Peshawar, and that in the absence of converts 'influence' is almost as important.

There is a great deal of evidence, in both word and deed, to indicate that CMS missionaries regarded 'influence' as just as good as converts. The educational missionary in Kashmir admitted in 1890 that 'I do not see, humanly speaking, any greatly increased prospect of any considerable accession to the church by baptism of either Mahommedans or Hindus. But there is an impression being made literally upon thousands, a feeling after God – dimly – a widespread knowledge of spiritual truths, and above all a widespread belief in Jesus Christ. This must eventually come to a head.'[23]

Omit the reference to non-Christian religions, and this might have been written by a slum parson in Leeds or Bethnal Green, pondering the significance of empty pews and working-class 'heathenism' while raising middle-class money for a network of Anglican educational and philanthropic institutions designed to perform the same task of diffusing Christianity. The competitive strategy that Anglicans adopted in the nineteenth century was an institutional strategy that evolved naturally from their professional self-image. They rejected charismatic revivalism, intense door-to-door canvassing, media appeals through pamphlets or newspapers, and a concentrated effort to demonstrate the intellectual superiority of Christianity to its alternatives, including secularism, although they did attempt the latter as a kind of by-product of their institutional work. They also rejected, unconsciously and unintentionally, the views of Henry Venn, a fact that did not escape the attention of the CMS Committee (the 'Parent Committee') and CMS bureaucrats in London. In the 1880s CMS officials wrote increasingly urgent and forceful letters to Robert Clark, the Punjab Secretary, asking, in effect, 'Where are the fruits?' Where are the converts? Where is the self-supporting, self-governing, self-extending native church? When can we expect to see the euthanasia of the mission?

Clark was used to this kind of letter, and when he received one he filed it in the wastepaper basket and wrote his usual and often lengthy reply: 'The seeds of truth have long been sown.... They will in due time germinate and take root.'[24] The actual progress of the Gospel in the Punjab is up to God, but we are doing his work and there are signs of revival all around; 'We are being used as God's instruments for totally disintegrating false religion and we are persuaded that the issue is not far off.'[25] The CMS could, of course, hasten this great work by sending more men and more money.

But in the course of the 1880s CMS officials found this line of argument increasingly unsatisfactory. Perhaps your strategy is wrong, they gently suggested. Perhaps you should spend less time and effort supervising non-Christians who teach non-Christians. Furthermore, perhaps the native church is not growing, i.e., not self-extending, because you are not allowing Indian Christians to be self-governing. The CMS Parent Committee began to demand results: more converts, more native pastors, more native Christians in positions of authority.

In obedience to Venn's prescriptions, and amid much fanfare, the CMS had established in 1878 a Punjab Native Church Council, with theoretical authority over the pastorate of the native congregations.[26] But in spite of the sincere good intentions of everyone involved, the CMS Native Church Council never worked. Some missionaries, including Hughes, refused from the first to recognise or participate in the Native Church Council on the grounds that it was an embryonic ecclesiastical body that should emanate from the diocese rather than from a purely voluntary, private society like the CMS. The Church of England in the Punjab, like the

Church of England in England, suffered from an almost unbelievable degree of internal administrative chaos and confusion about authority, and for all his foresight Henry Venn had never successfully solved the problem of how a voluntary society could start an episcopal church.

Even more debilitating than this insoluble theological dilemma was the actual condition of the CMS congregations whose pastors, along with leading Christian laymen, had been organised into the Native Church Council (NCC). The designers of the NCC assumed that Christian parishes were the central missionary institutions in the Punjab and everywhere else in the world, but in the Punjab and many other places the Christian congregations were small, poor institutions on the periphery of much larger educational and medical institutions that employed many members of the congregation. Whatever authority Indian pastors might exercise in parochial affairs, they were necessarily dependent upon the missionaries within the large CMS institutional structure. The theoretical independence they were offered with the NCC only disclosed their real powerlessness and dependency in their relationship with the missionaries, a situation that was the inevitable consequence of an institutional strategy based upon no formal missionary theory. Within five years of its creation, everyone associated with the NCC agreed that it was a failure with no responsibility, no funds, and no real authority. Robert Clark supplied a variety of contradictory explanations for this failure, but the Parent Committee had a simpler explanation, and their letters in the 1880s showed an increasing tendency to blame the missionaries for excessive paternalism.

This was the Victorian crisis of faith in the Punjab in the 1880s. An institutional strategy generated an institutional crisis of confidence. The CMS existed to win converts and foster an indigenous native church, but after a generation of work in the strategically sensitive Punjab, with their prestige as a missionary society on the line, there were few converts and no native church.

The first problem, lack of growth, was solved in the late 1880s, to the enormous relief of everyone, by the appearance of substantial numbers of converts, the majority of whom initially were gathered into the CMS as a consequence of a decision made in Philadelphia, the headquarters of the missionary society of the United Presbyterian Church. There were two distinct American Presbyterian denominations at work in the Punjab. Missionaries of the Presbyterian Church in the USA had pursued since their pioneer days in the province a strategy similar in many ways to that of the CMS, with an emphasis on education and influence, and with similar results.[27] The United Presbyterians had been labouring in the Punjab since the 1850s and were having some difficulty explaining their lack of success to contributors at home. 'But what are our encouragements,' one UP missionary wrote in 1877 to home supporters, acknowledging that 'it is the question in which all contributors are deeply interested. If we look only at the number of additions to the church, our encouragements in the Gurdaspur District are nothing at all, since we have baptized none during the year. And yet we do not remember of ever feeling as much encouraged as at this time. Why this is so we may not be able to make very clear to others.'[28]

One of their missionaries, the Reverend Samuel Martin, decided after some hesitation to exploit a situation that UP missionaries had for some time been aware of, i.e., that it was possible to convert large numbers of village 'outcastes' who discovered, or hoped, that they could shed some of their caste disabilities by becoming Christians. Martin went on rural tours in which he appeared to go into a kind of frantic spiritual high while baptising literally thousands of people a year. Net United Presbyterian growth in the Punjab in the 1880s was roughly 10 000.[29]

In the late eighties this growth began to spill over into the CMS as village Chuhras (the 'sweeper' community affected by this 'mass movement') began to present themselves to baffled Anglican missionaries, asking for baptism. This wholly unanticipated development directly contradicted the Anglican expectation that conversions would begin at the top of society and work their way down. Furthermore, CMS missionaries drew a sharp (and largely non-sensical) distinction between 'secular' and 'religious' motives in matters of religion, and the 'secular' motives of the Chuhras were more than usually clear. They wished to use the village well. They wished to be buried facing upwards rather than downwards.

They wished to have the help of the missionaries in confrontations with the landowners to whom they were traditionally bound to do agricultural and household labour. But finally two CMS missionaries who actually worked in villages decided after much prayer that God must be behind these conversions despite the brazen opportunism of Chuhra leaders, and the Punjab Mission established a Central Punjab Village Mission Board to deal with the special problems of Chuhra Anglicans.[30] The creation of this board allowed the overwhelming majority of missionaries simultaneously to claim credit for the growing number of Christians and to avoid thinking about unsavoury problems such as whether Christian Chuhras should be prohibited from continuing to eat their traditional fare of carrion.

After a period of no net growth at all in the largely urban, middle-class Punjabi CMS community of roughly 1500 in the early 1880s, the CMS suddenly added 233 new members in 1886, 555 in 1887, and 517 in 1888, many of them in villages.[31] But the important breakthrough came in 1890, as the CMS repulsed 'Presbyterian aggression'. The Protestant missionary societies in the Punjab had divided up the province into exclusive territories in order to avoid direct competition with each other, and to prevent wily native catechists and schoolmasters from playing one missionary society off against another for higher pay or better conditions of work. But Martin refused to recognise such distinctions. Claiming to be led by the Holy Spirit, he marched right into CMS territory in the southern Sialkot district, baptising right and left and leaving behind congregations and schools in the care of locally recruited catechists.

The CMS missionary at Narowal, who found himself in direct competition with the United Presbyterians, was unusually flexible and productive for an Anglican missionary. The Reverend Rowland Bateman came from the minor northern gentry, he had a university degree, and he had a passion for souls and a willingness to do what was necessary to win them. He more or less abandoned his wife and went to live like an Indian in the obscurity of the village of Narowal. His tactic was to influence young unmarried men by playing cricket with them, befriending them, exercising a kind of charismatic influence over them, and encouraging them forcefully to convert. Conversion often involved what amounted to kidnapping them from their parents and family, and in some cases taking them away to England. He exercised a paternal sway over a group of highly intelligent young Indian Christians who would often accompany him as he donned Indian dress, mounted his camel, and went off on village itinerant tours.[32]

Bateman did not fit the image of an English clergyman, most of whom would not consider riding around on a camel in obscure villages attempting to alienate young boys from their families. But he shared with his colleagues a belief in orderly methods of ecclesiastical discipline, a conviction that institution building was the most important missionary task even if it could not be expected to produce mass conversions automatically, and a conviction that the key to Christianising India lay in the creation of an educated, upper-class and professional Christian élite that would use its influence to Christianise the classes below. Consequently, he objected strenuously when an American marauder began converting thousands of outcastes in 'his' territory, and he objected even more bitterly when the United Presbyterians claimed that the Holy Spirit had instructed them to evangelise outcastes who had been neglected by the CMS.[33] Bateman's view was that the Holy Spirit instructed him to do many things, but never to violate a gentleman's agreement, and he vigorously denied the largely accurate accusation that the CMS had done very little work with the Chuhras.[34] These arguments persuaded the CMS Parent Committee to complain to the United Presbyterian governing body in Philadelphia.

In 1889 the United Presbyterian Mission persuaded Martin to hand over his converts to the CMS, which he did, lock, stock, and barrel, all 1500 of them, confident that the CMS was too incompetent and 'cold' to do anything with them and that the Holy Spirit would be vindicated before long. Bateman duly began to take his new outcaste following in hand, firing schoolmasters and catechists who could not repeat the Apostle's Creed, excommunicating and expelling ordinary believers who could not repeat the Lord's Prayer. But even these tactics could not prevent the CMS from growing in this district and another nearby, since village outcastes did not distinguish one Christian denomination from another, and the CMS, under pressure to produce converts, could hardly turn down entire communities demanding baptism.

The CMS began to grow, then, in the late eighties, and Clark used these growing numbers to justify all the other CMS activities, claiming the converts were the 'fruits' of their schools, their hostels, their guest houses, their divinity school. Never too particular about the precise details of local strategy, the CMS Parent Committee was satisfied that CMS methods were at last paying off, and one of the two issues in the crisis of the eighties was resolved. The Church in the Punjab was growing.

But what about a *native* church? Were these converts being organised into a self-supporting, self-governing, self-extending church? If not, why not? The Punjab Native Church Council had been established in 1878 for Indian pastors and prominent laymen, who were assumed to be the Indian equivalents of the kind of people who sustained and supported the Church of England at home. No one, not even on the Parent Committee in London, expected the missionaries instantly to organise illiterate Punjabi-speaking Chuhra converts into self-sustaining, self-extending, and self-governing communities, but the parent Committee did expect the missionaries to organise the Urdu-speaking middle-class and professional converts into such a community. Why, they wondered, was the NCC a failure?

What were the Indian Christians on the NCC interested in? In the creation of a self-governing, self-sustaining, and self-extending Indian church? In principle, yes, like everyone else in the CMS. In practice, well, not exactly. For one thing, they had some difficulty in adopting the practice of cleanly distinguishing between religion on the one hand and society on the other, a distinction that is one of the axioms of western thought about religion. Like other religious communities in the Punjab, they were interested in defending the interests of, and gaining advantages for, their tiny middle-class and professional religious community.

How do you promote the interests of the Christian community in the Punjab? By asking for better terms and conditions of employment from your employer, the CMS; by agitating for an expansion of employment opportunities for Indians with the CMS; and, if you were not a CMS teacher or catechist but were instead a Christian lawyer or government official, by urging the CMS to improve and upgrade the social standing of the educational opportunities it supplied for the children of middle-class Indian Christians, especially at the two Christian boarding schools, the Baring School for Boys at Batala and the Alexandra School for Girls at Amritsar.[35] The NCC pressed in particular for formal equality between mission employees and missionaries, i.e., equal pay for equal educational qualifications. Mission employees should be treated like Indian civil servants, they argued, with a uniform scale of pay, rules governing dismissal, etc.[36]

Because of the institutional strategy pursued by CMS missionaries, a strategy that was a consequence of their own professional standards rather than CMS policy, many Indian Christians were badly needed as staff for the array of Christian institutions the missionaries had created. Only about one-third of the teachers at CMS post-primary schools were Christians, and the CMS in London constantly pressed the Punjab Mission to increase the percentage of Christian teachers, a task the mission found difficult in part because Christian teachers, in short supply, demanded more money and better conditions than non-Christians.[37] Most employees of these institutions were directly under the personal supervision of the missionary in charge, and requests for formal equality of status would be directed to him. It is difficult to imagine a request that would infuriate a Victorian clergyman more than a request for equality. CMS missionaries, like their brother clergymen everywhere in the world, were deeply committed to the spiritual value of *subordination*, and the principle of subordination was one they applied on a non-discriminatory, non-racist, non-imperialist basis at home as well as abroad.

In addition to believing in subordination to duly constituted authority, CMS missionaries adhered to a concept of *spirituality* that was a consequence of drawing a strict distinction between the religious and the secular, between religion and society, between secular motives and sacred motives. This sense of 'spirituality' was strengthened in the late nineteenth century by the spread of 'higher life' and 'perfectionist' doctrines and practices within Anglican evangelical circles, especially at the yearly Keswick Conventions.[38] But this theological emphasis only intensified a longstanding Anglican anxiety about the social standing and motives of the lower clergy. CMS recruits in England were treated with great suspicion, in part because the CMS from the very first had been highly sensitive to the charge that they were providing a back door into the clergy for people who would not otherwise have had a high enough social standing. Unable to recruit enough university graduates, the CMS established its own training schools and recruited missionaries from among the classes of people who probably would have entered the Nonconformist ministry if they had not been Anglicans, but would not have been able to attend a university and certify themselves as 'gentlemen'.[39]

Although they showed a certain flexible vigour in setting up their own training system and recruiting men who would not otherwise have found their way into the clergy, they remained almost neurotically anxious about the possibility of unfit persons using the CMS to ascend the social hierarchy. A clergyman whose motives were primarily worldly would not only subvert social discipline by using the CMS as a means of upward mobility, he would be 'unspiritual' and therefore unfit for his professional role. In order to maintain high standards, the CMS put its non-university recruits through a virtually totalitarian period of probation in which every detail of their conduct was supervised. No CMS missionary could marry without a detailed committee investigation of the fitness of the proposed bride. In the Punjab, senior CMS missionaries naturally attempted to apply the same standards of subordination and spirituality to young missionaries, lay English schoolmasters, single female CEZMS missionaries (who vigorously defended their own professional autonomy), and lay male medical missionaries (who refused to tolerate such clerical impudence).

In the light of all this it is not surprising to find that the efforts of the Native Church Council and other Indian Christians to secure regular conditions of employment embittered relations between missionaries and Indian Christians, and led to accusations of a 'lack of spirituality' among Indian Christians. The CMS Missionary Conference in the Punjab even went so far as to establish a special committee on 'The Shortcomings of the native Church', which reported to

London in 1884.[40] Clark and other missionaries encountered some difficulty in resisting the logic of the civil service analogy, although Clark could not resist pointing out that 'many of our native friends have been brought up by Americans, who are *Republican* in principle'.[41] But to the formal principle of liberal equality they counterposed the Christian principles of humility, poverty, obedience, and sacrifice. They also argued that subsistence (the formal principle of missionary pay) for an Indian meant a lower standard of living than subsistence for an Englishman, an argument Indian Christians quite rightly criticised as hypocritical and patronising.[42]

Indian Christians of course thought it most unfair to find themselves first encouraged to be independent, and then accused of insubordination when they followed that advice, and equally discouraging to find that utilising an organisation that was set up in order to allow them to express the interests of their community led at once to accusations of base motives and a lack of spirituality. Dissatisfaction with employment prospects led to a series of acrimonious resignations over what one CMS Indian pastor described as the CMS's 'despotic principle of administration'.[43]

These incidents were very painful to missionaries who thought, with some justice, that they had submitted to their share of subordination in the course of becoming missionaries, and their dismay was not allayed by the Parent Committee, which by no means automatically took the side of the missionaries in this dispute. CMS bureaucrats were suspicious of missionary paternalism, which contradicted their own Vennite principles, and in their bland bureaucratic way nagged the missionaries to do more to put native pastors in positions of responsibility and authority.[44] Proposals to shift a larger share of the burden of pastoral care from Indian pastors to missionaries were rejected by the Parent Committee as 'retrograde'.[45] As employers they were naturally suspicious of their missionary employees, who were paid large salaries but were often beyond their practical control. As bureaucrats they were naturally attracted to arguments in favour of regular rules and procedures, which is what the Indian Christians were asking for.

What finally brought the Parent Committee around to the

missionary view that Indian Christians were unspiritual careerists was the difficulty the committee had in persuading the Native Church Council to do more for self-support and self-extension, difficulties that appeared to confirm missionary complaints about a lack of spirituality among Indian Christians.[46]

Given the enormous task facing the CMS, i.e., the evangelisation of the entire world, and given the difficulty they had raising enough money for that task, they regarded a self-propagating, evangelistic native church as the world's only hope. In Venn's view of the missionary task, self-support and self-extension went hand in hand with self-government, and while the Native Church Council might accept that burden in principle, in practice they were never ready to assume it. The Punjabi church was, in the view of Indian Christians, too small for self-support, too weak for self-extension, ready only for self-government. What the NCC wanted now was more money from the CMS for their work, an expansion of the CMS sector of the economy. Instead the Parent Committee in the 1880s attempted to force self-support upon the Native Church Council by annual reduction of 1/40th in their grant.[47] Unlike many British schemes for colonial self-government, the CMS scheme had an actual timetable; with a 1/40th annual reduction the Indian Church would be self-supporting in forty years, and the euthanasia of the mission accomplished.

But the Native Church Council took the view that this was an insult to native Christians, demonstrated a lack of confidence in their work, and would damage the work of the church in India, which was 'not yet strong enough to allow any reduction',[48] and needed to be built up to a respectable level before self-support was introduced.[49] It was particularly cruel, they argued, to respond to requests for better terms of employment for Indian employees by cutting back on funds used for salaries, which was how most NCC funds were spent. In this dispute with the Parent Committee the Native Church Council could count on the support of the missionaries in the field, especially the secretary Robert Clark, who had become persuaded that neither self-support nor self-government were possible or appropriate yet, and who agreed with the Native Church Council that the CMS should allocate more rather than less money to the Punjab.[50]

This controversy had the unintended consequence, however, of getting the missionaries off the hook, for in their frustration at their failure to persuade the Indians to do more for self-support, the Parent Committee began to resort to an explanation that the missionaries often used: the Indian Christians were not yet ready for self-government. Indian unwillingness to do more for self-support appeared to be evidence for this argument. By 1890 the Parent Committee had come to agree with the missionaries, although for different reasons, that there was something wrong with the Indian Christians, that they were neither 'spiritual' enough nor 'responsible' enough to live up to the ideals of the great Henry Venn, that the day of an indigenous native church might have to be postponed, perhaps even beyond the forty-year limit they had hopefully set in the 1880s.[51]

CMS missionaries explained the failure of the native Church Council by persuading the Parent Committee that the shortcomings of the embryonic Indian church were the fault of the Indian Christians themselves. Although the Parent Committee's reasons for blaming Indians were not identical to those of the missionaries in the field, by the end of the 1880s both groups were persuaded that Indian Christians would have to improve before any progress could be made towards an indigenous Indian church.

This attitude was not, in my view, primarily a consequence of a new wave of racism and imperialism that swept over Britain in the eighties and nineties, nor was it the immediate consequence of the new emphasis upon theological perfectionism in evangelical circles, a movement that had large and immediate consequences in Nigeria. Nor was it *primarily* a consequence of the new dismissive attitude toward Indians that swept through Anglo-Indian society in the eighties and nineties.

All these things contributed to the new attitude, but even if Britain, and missionaries in India, and westerners in India had been seized with a new, broad-minded, tolerant liberal attitude toward Indians in the eighties and nineties, there would have been an inevitable conflict between the ideals of the CMS, the ideals of the professional clergymen hired to carry out CMS policy, and the ideals of the Indian Christians who were the ultimate point of all this activity.

The crisis of the 1880s was in essence a conflict between the values and aspirations of these three groups. Its resolution allowed the CMS missionaries in the Punjab to continue with their institutional strategy of church growth and church extension, for periodic waves of mass movements into the church allowed them all the legitimacy they needed for their highly inefficient policy of constructing schools and, after the 1880s and especially after the turn of the century, hospitals and dispensaries. The years from 1880 to 1920 were the heyday of Anglican mission work in the Punjab, as the number of CMS Indian Christians grew from 1378 to 32 218. By the end of the period the typical missionary was a nurse rather than a clergyman. By the 1920s however, the Victorian crisis of faith at home caught up with the church overseas, and falling numbers of missionary recruits and shrinking CMS budgets led to successive waves of retrenchment that were devastating for morale, even though there continued to be far more mission work in the early 1930s than there had been in the early 1880s.

The Victorian crisis of faith in the Punjab was not wholly unrelated to the Victorian crisis of faith in England, of course, and the striking thing about the Anglican clergy is the extent to which they followed the same strategy in Peshawar and Portsmouth. This strategy was a consequence of high-minded professionalism. In order to fulfil his social role, a clergyman should create prestigious social institutions and then preside over them paternalistically. The evangelical missionaries in the Punjab were far more likely to be interested in church growth than ordinary Anglican clergymen at home, yet even they were motivated primarily by their own professional self-image.

This professionalism interfered with their ability to recognise one crucial fact: the fate of any religious institution in a competitive, pluralistic society, where religion is not buttressed by state power or enveloped in a universally accepted religious cosmology, depends on its ability to recruit. The view of the modern world as one in which religion is inevitably shoved to the loony fringes of society has been falsified repeatedly. Churches and other religious institutions can do more than merely grow; they can be genuinely important in urban, secular, industrial societies, and indeed in virtually any kind of society. What distinguishes the modern world from the pre-modern world is the possibility that religion might be unimportant. The importance or unimportance of a particular set of religious ideas or religious institutions in a particular place at a particular time is a matter for historical investigation rather than sociological prediction.

Victorian clergymen in England and in the Punjab demonstrated among other things that it is possible for religious ideas and institutions to flourish accidentally. Church growth – growing numbers of church attenders, growing interest in religion – in Victorian England was an unintended by-product of the church's great campaign to cover England with parish churches, even in slums where no one attended church before or after a building with pews was provided. Victorian clergy expected recruitment to follow construction automatically; that is why they were so baffled at the empty pews they set up in slum parishes. But this vigorous religious campaign to influence, mould, and subordinate Victorian society attracted an enormous amount of support from upper, middle, and respectable working-class people who were worried about the condition of England and wanted to do something practical to see that society did not fall apart and that the poor were fed. The real Victorian crisis of faith in England occurred when people could no longer be persuaded that the church was important. An institutional strategy led to an institutional crisis. It was then, in the last two decades of the nineteenth century, that the Church of England began to decline in numbers and influence. This decline itself reinforced and was powerfully reinforced by the abstract intellectual notion that religion was declining automatically in the modern world, an idea that had been around since the Enlightenment and was greatly strengthened by a variety of important nineteenth-century intellectual changes.

The Victorians in the Punjab were no more interested in aggressive individual recruitment than their cousins at home, and they faced some of the same problems in the eighties and nineties: competition from secular institutions in education and medical care, biblical criticism, upper-class lay apathy among Anglo-Indians. But instead of declining in the eighties and nineties they stumbled upon a new, unintended social function that led to church growth and was their ideological salvation for a generation. The crisis of faith at home only caught up with them in the 1920s, but by then they had almost unwittingly created a small but significant Protestant minority in the Punjab, a community of landless rural labourers, the permanent legacy of their work.

NOTES

CMS = Archives of the Church Missionary Society, London.

1. See, e.g., Peter Burke, in *The New Cambridge Modern History*, 13, Companion Volume (London, 1979) 312; David Martin, 'Toward Eliminating the Concept of Secularization', in *Penguin Survey of the Social Sciences*, ed. Julius Gould (Harmondsworth, 1965); cf. his *A General Theory of Secularization* (New York, 1979).

2. Jeffrey Cox, *The English Churches in a Secular Society: Lambeth, 1870–1930* (New York, 1982), and his 'How to Think about Religion in the Modern World', paper presented to the Religion and Society History Workshop, London, July 1983.

3. On this see *The Gallup International Public Opinion Polls: Great Britain, 1937–1975*, 2 vols (New York, 1976); *Public Opinion, 1972–1977*, 2 vols (Wilmington, Del., 1978); or compare any other set of polls of British and American public opinion on assent to the traditional orthodox doctrines of the Christian faith such as the deity of Christ, Heaven, Hell, etc.

4. e.g., Bryan Wilson, *Religion in a Secular Society: A Sociological Comment* (London, 1966) ch. 6; Alasdair Macintyre, *Secularization and Moral Change* (London, 1967) 8.

5. e.g., John Herberts, 'Religion Enters a Political Revival', *New York Times*, 12 August 1984, Sec. 4, E7.

6. See E. Theodore Bachman, 'North American Doctoral Dissertations on Mission: 1945–1981', *International Bulletin of Missionary Research*, 7, no. 3 (July 1983) 98–134. He identifies 934 dissertations.

7. *World Christian Encyclopedia: A Comparative Survey of Churches and Religion in the Modern World, A.D. 1900–2000*, ed. David B. Barrett (London, 1982).

8. On the Punjab School and missions see Stanley Elwood Brush, 'Protestants in the Punjab: Religion and Social Change in an Indian Province in the Nineteenth Century' (PhD diss., University of California at Berkeley, 1964) 52–65; and his 'Protestants in Conflict: Policy and Early Practice in the British Punjab', *Al-Mushir*, 17, nos

4–6 (April, May, June 1975) 91–100; John C.B. Webster, *The Christian Community and Change in Nineteenth Century North India* (Delhi, 1976) 12 ff.; Eugene Stock, *The History of the Church Missionary Society: Its Environment, Its Men, and Its Work*, 4 vols (London, 1899 and 1916) 2: 193–213, 487–9, 560–78.

9. Stock, 214–61.
10. Brush, 'Protestants in the Punjab', 176.
11. For the chronology and statistics of this mission see Stock; Rev. Robert Clark, *The Punjab and Sindh Mission of the CMS, Giving an Account of Their Foundation and Progress for Thirty-three Years, from 1852–1884* (1885), 2nd edn (London, 1889); Rev. Robert Clark, *The Mission of the CMS and the CEZMS in the Punjab and Sindh*, ed. and rev. Robert Maconachie, late ICS (London, 1904).
12. These statistics are from the yearly *Proceedings* of the CMS.
13. For an introduction to the large literature on Venn, see the bibliography in Wilbert R. Shenk, *Henry Venn, Missionary Statesman* (London, 1983).
14. For a thorough discussion of the importance of this issue in Nigerian historiography, see Andrew Porter, 'Cambridge, Keswick, and Late Nineteenth Century Attitudes to Africa', *Journal of Imperial and Commonwealth History*, 5, no. 1 (October 1976) 5–34.
15. CMS G2/I4/PI/37/1882: *An Account of the Visit of the Lord Bishop of Calcutta to the Peshawar Mission, Contributed by His Chaplain the Rev. Brooke Deedes, M.A.* (printed 1881).
16. ibid., *moulvi*: a man learned in Islamic law; used as an honorific title.
17. ibid.
18. CMS G2/I4/O2/25/1883: 'Remarks of the Rev. R. Clark, Secretary of the Corresponding Committee, on a Visit to Peshawar, 9 Feb. 1883.'
19. *An Account.*
20. CMS G2/I4/O4/236/1887: Dr Martyn Clark, *The Principles and Teaching of the Arya Samaj, Lecture VI: The Vedic Doctrine of Sacrifice* (Lahore, 1887).
21. CMS G2/I4/PI/117/1882: T.P. Hughes to CMS Parent Committee, n.d.
22. *Lahore Civil and Military Gazette*, church supplement, 5 January 1884.
23. CMS G2/I4/O/415/1890: A. Neve to Mr Baring Gould, Kashmir, 17 September 1890; cf. similar comments in CMS G2/I4/PI/157/1882: Dr Neve to CMS Parent Committee, Kashmir, 10 August 1882; CMS G2/I4/O3/42/1886: W. St. Clair Tisdall to R. Clark, Amritsar, 22 January 1886.
24. 'Remarks of the Rev. R. Clark.'
25. CMS G2/I4/O4/180/1887: R. Clark, notes to the CMS, London, on 'Remonstrance against American Methodist Episcopal Mission Occupying Amritsar'.
26. See *A Native Church for the Natives of India, Giving an Account of the Formation of a Native Church Council for the Punjab Mission of the CMS and of the Proceedings of Their First Meeting in Amritsar, 31 March–2 April 1877* (Lahore, 1877).
27. See Webster.

28. Andrew Gordon, in *The Nineteenth Annual Report of the Board of Foreign Missions of the United Presbyterian Church of North America*, Presented to the General Assembly in May 1878, 53.

29. See Frederick and Margaret Stock, *People Movements in the Punjab, with Special Reference to the United Presbyterian Church* (Pasadena, Calif., 1975) ch. 5.

30. CMS G2/I4/O4/110/1888: *Rules of the Central Punjab Village Mission Board.*

31. CMS G2/I4/O/141/1890: R. Clark to W. Gray, Amritsar, 10 March 1890. Gray was the CMS Secretary in London with primary responsibility for India from 1874 to 1893.

32. See R. Maconachie, *Rowland Bateman, Nineteenth Century Apostle* (London, 1917).

33. CMS G2/I4/O/188/1889: 'Resolutions in Regard to Giving up to the CMS Certain Territory in Riah Tahsil, Adopted by the Sialkot Mission of the United Presbyterian Church of North America', 27 March 1889, Sialkot.

34. Marginal notes by R. Bateman, ibid.

35. CMS G2/I4/O3/152/1886: 'List of Girls at the Alexandria School', with parents' occupations.

36. See CMS G2/I4/O2/150/1884: R. Clark to W. Gray, summarising accurately their point of view.

37. On this see CMS G2/I4/O/81/1890: 'Examination of Mission Schools in the Diocese of Lahore by the Rev. T.R. Wade', MS, 1889.

38. See Porter, 'Cambridge', and his 'Evangelical Enthusiasm, Missionary Motivation, and West Africa in the Late Nineteenth Century: The Career of G.W. Brooke', *Journal of Imperial and Commonwealth History*, 6, no. 1 (October 1977) 23–46.

39. On this see C.P. Williams, '"Not Quite Gentlemen": An Examination of "Middling Class" Protestant Missionaries from Britain, c. 1850–1900', *Journal of Ecclesiastical History*, 31, no. 3 (July 1978) 301–15.

40. See CMS G2/I4/L2/1883–8: W. Gray to T.R. Wade, London, 22 May 1885, for the Parent Committee's chilly response to this report.

41. CMS G2/I4/O2/150/1884: R. Clark to W. Gray, Dalhousie, 17 May 1884.

42. See CMS G2/I4/O2/209/1884: Miss C.V. Bose, MA, to Miss Wauton, Calcutta, 30 July 1884.

43. CMS G2/I4/O4/146/1888: The Rev. Dina Nath to R. Clark, Ajnala, 3 March 1888.

44. CMS G2/I4/L2/1883–8: W. Gray to Robert Clark, London, 23 May 1884.

45. CMS G2/I4/L2/1883–8: W. Gray to T.R. Wade, London, 22 May 1885.

46. This is clear in a long letter from W. Gray to Robert Clark (CMS G2/I4/L2/1883–8), London, 23 February 1886.

47. CMS G2/I4/L2/1883–8: W. Gray to R. Clark, London, 15 February 1884, first suggesting such a reduction; and CMS G2/I4/L2/1883–8: W. Gray to R. Clark, London, 7 May 1886, instructing him to carry out the reductions.

48. CMS G2/I4/O3/212/1886: Minutes of the Executive Committee, Punjab Church Council, 14 June 1886.

49. CMS G2/I4/L2/1883–8: W. Gray to R. Clark, 21 October 1886, for his disappointed response.

50. See, for example, CMS G2/I4/PI/37/1882: R. Clark to W. Gray, 28 January 1882, and many subsequent letters.

51. See CMS G2/I4/O/536/1890: H.R. Wright (on tour) to W. Gray, Amritsar, 1 December 1890.

11 The Crisis of Faith and Social Christianity: The Ethical Pilgrimage of James Shaver Woodsworth
Mark D. Johnson

> Charlie, I am being driven on by some inevitable force to a kind of rationalistic
> unitarianism. I have struggled against the current – am struggling – but see no
> other end at present. I cannot believe against my will.
>
> (J.S. Woodsworth 1902)

Between the 1880s and the outbreak of the First World War
the Protestant churches in England and North America came
to share a pronounced and active concern for social problems. Until recently, 'Social Christianity', or the religion of
the Institutional Church, the Mission Hall, the Settlement
House, and the American Social Gospel movement, has
largely been explained by historians as an outgrowth of
Christian humanitarianism evoked in the Protestant churches by the pressing social needs of a modern age.* Whether
a direct Christian response to immediate urban and industrial problems,[1] or the expression of a reform spirit rooted in
the tradition of evangelical revivalism,[2] or as part of an
all-embracing religious mission to Christianise and Protes-
tantise the fledgling North American nations,[3] the prevailing
historical view of social Christianity has been one of church
extension, conditioned by the late-nineteenth-century concentration of urban and industrial life, and influenced by a
debate over the 'Social Question', which drew widespread
public attention in England and North America by the turn
of the century.

* I am grateful to the Social Sciences and Humanities Research Council of Canada
for financial support in completing the research for this chapter.

The tension between those who possessed the 'social passion' and their more orthodox evangelical fathers is acknowledged to have been doctrinal in part; but greater attention is paid to the frustration of the social prophets who believed that the reluctance of the churches to abandon an individualistic gospel for wider social responsibilities would ensure a future for the churches uncertain at best. Thus the rise of social Christianity is also understood as an attempt to save the churches by widening their doors to attract a greater number of unchurched adherents, thereby extending the moral influence of the churches in society;[4] or, in a more radical vein, to revitalise the churches spiritually in the drive to establish the Kingdom of God on earth. In the words of Josiah Strong, one of the cardinals of the American social gospel movement: 'If the church is willing to teach by her example that Christianity is divorced from philanthropy and reform and social service and the progress of civilisation, or that these are broader than Christianity, she must be content to occupy a little place and never dream of conquering the world.'[5]

One aspect of the rise of social Christianity that has received little attention is that escape, or the avoidance of doubt and theological difficulty, was also a motivating factor in the movement. This is not to suggest that those who promoted an ecclesiastical incursion into the realm of social service were all secret doubters, or that a declared faith in an enlarged gospel was a form of religious dissimulation. It is to suggest, however, that beneath a shared and articulated dissatisfaction with orthodoxy among those who embraced a socialised Christianity there lay deeper conflicts relating to belief that found a partial, and not entirely satisfactory, resolution in the enthusiasm for religious social service. On the level of historical generalisation one may explain social Christianity as 'called into being by the impact of modern industrial society and scientific thought upon ... Protestantism'.[6] But on the more complex level of individual experience one observes also intense theological difficulty, a wrestling with doubt, and a desperate search for a new basis of belief.

It is the purpose of this chapter to explore social Christianity as a retreat from faith in crisis in the early career of James

Shaver Woodsworth, who has been called 'the outstanding Canadian exponent of the social gospel'.[7] Woodsworth's entrance into the social work of Canadian Methodism and his eventual acceptance and promotion of the social gospel were directly related to his own struggle with unbelief. His experience is a reminder that the Victorian 'crisis of faith' was not by any means a uniquely English phenomenon.

Largely unknown outside his country of origin, James Shaver Woodsworth (1874–1942) was, and remains, a major Canadian historical figure. His name first rose to prominence as the author of *Strangers within Our Gates* (1909) and *My Neighbor* (1911), the first serious attempts to analyse the problems associated with immigration to Canada, written while Woodsworth was the Superintendent of the Methodist All People's Mission in Winnipeg. Typically these works have been described in the historiography of the Canadian social gospel movement as having 'helped to determine the *response* of the Protestant churches to one of the most important social problems confronting Canadians in the early twentieth century'.[8] As the founding secretary of the national Canadian Welfare League established in 1913, and as the first director of the Bureau of Social Research for the three prairie provinces of Manitoba, Saskatchewan, and Alberta during the War, Woodsworth became the pre-eminent Canadian expert in the field of social welfare and immigration. In 1917 he was fired from the Bureau for publicly opposing a national registration plan that he viewed as a prelude to conscription, and in 1918 he resigned from the Methodist ministry, the precipitating issue being his pacifist beliefs. In 1919 Woodsworth was catapulted into public notoriety by being imprisoned with other labour leaders during the course of Canada's greatest labour dispute, the Winnipeg General Strike. Although the charge of seditious libel was dropped before Woodsworth came to trial, his public martyrdom at the hands of the authorities only enhanced his well-established reputation in Winnipeg as a social reformer, and helped secure his election to Parliament in 1921 as a representative of the Independent Labour Party. As a widely respected, though at times troublesome member of Parliament for twenty-one years, Woodsworth exerted a significant influence over the passage of social legislation. He is best known, however, as the father and first leader of Canada's third political party, the Co-operative Commonwealth Federation (or the CCF, which became the New Democratic Party in 1961), a Canadian version of the British Labour Party founded in 1933 to seek a new order 'in which the principles regulating production, distribution and exchange will be the supply of human needs and not the making of profits'.[9] When he died in 1942 glowing tributes to Woodsworth's integrity, his selfless character, and his indomitable courage were delivered on both sides of the House and at commemoration services across the country. He was, according to one political observer, 'the most Christ-like man ever to sit in Parliament'.[10]

Woodsworth's prominence in the history of the Canadian political left has lent considerable importance to the progression of his career from traditional Methodism through the social gospel into socialism. The prevailing view, expounded in the two biographies examining Woodsworth's early development at greatest length, Kenneth McNaught's *A Prophet in Politics* (1959) and *J.S. Woodsworth: A Man to Remember* (1953), written by Woodsworth's daughter Grace MacInnis, contends that despite Woodsworth's religious background he was driven every step of the way by his 'social conscience' and his simple desire to serve humanity. According to this standard view, which diminishes the importance of religion and the churches in the history of Canadian socialism, Woodsworth's social conscience was awakened by the poverty he saw on the prairies as a young man, by the slum conditions he observed in Toronto while attending Victoria University in 1898–9, but most especially by his exposure to the East End of London, where he stayed for two weeks at the Mansfield College Settlement during a subsequent year of study at Oxford. 'Never again', writes his daughter, 'could he contemplate beauty and culture without being aware of the human wreckage that is everywhere in the back streets and hidden places. . . . Until he went to Mansfield House in East London he had no conception of the existence of submerged masses of people. Now he was to set himself resolutely to the task of preventing the spread of the blight in Canada. . . .' This awakening coincided with doctrinal difficulty, but, according to his daughter, Woodsworth was persuaded by 'qualified authorities' to remain in the ministry, and in 1907, despite a second attempt at resignation, he accepted the Superintendency of All People's Mission, which gave 'him the kind of work for which he had served so many years' apprenticeship'. In the words of McNaught, Woodsworth's 'mind undoubtedly flew back over his past experiences, his reading on social problems, his knowledge of Mansfield House and the London slums . . . and came to light irresistably on his prime urge to do immediately something to mitigate the emergent social problems of his own country. . . . And so Woodsworth accepted appointment as Superintendent. . . .' From that point on, the argument continues, his practical work among the immigrant population of Winnipeg 'led him to accept the ideas of the social gospel' and to 'consider the general question of socialism. . .'. A 'feeling of frustration while working within the denominational church framework had influenced him to move further and further from the centre of Manitoba Methodism. Increasingly his interests were becoming secular. . . .' The break finally came in 1918 over the issue of the church's support of the war effort. 'He had become convinced that he could no longer remain a minister of the Church and continue true to his ideals.'[11] With his back turned on the ministry, the militarism and conservatism of the church, he entered more directly upon the work of organising labour, and his political career began.

This secular description of Woodsworth as driven 'resolutely' by a social conscience 'stabbed awake during his Oxford days when he served soup in the welfare kitchens', first to church-sponsored social service, then outside the church in the interests of mankind 'without the screen of dogma between him and them,' is essentially the view that Woodsworth promoted of himself in later years, and has itself become orthodox doctrine.[12] But a close examination of the record reveals a young man who was far from resolute, who was late in blooming so far as matters of social conscience were concerned, and whose reasons for accepting the Superintendency of All People's Mission betray the significance of socialised Christianity as a temporary resolution of irresolvable religious conflict.

Woodsworth was raised in Brandon, Manitoba, where his

father, the Reverend James Woodsworth, DD, was appointed Superintendent of Methodist Missions in 1886. In reality his father's position meant that he was the man in charge of the west for the Methodist Church, which by the end of the nineteenth century, and except for the city of Winnipeg, was still a vast and sparsely inhabited frontier. James Woodsworth's 'parish', as Methodists delighted in describing it, extended westward from the head of Lake Superior to the Pacific Ocean, and north from the boundary with the United States to the Arctic Circle. 'Never again will any man in this whole world hold in his hand, and have under his supervision such an expanse.' During the first four years of his superintendency, James Woodsworth travelled 55 000 miles by horse and canoe, in temperatures sometimes reaching 50° F below zero, and against the mightiest enemy of the summer circuit rider – the mosquito. He was both a pioneer 'who blazed the trail for a better civilization west of the Great Lakes' and a 'pillar' of the society being born.[13]

The 'missions' James Woodsworth supervised were defined as Methodist circuits that were not self-supporting, and consequently dependent upon financial aid from the Missionary Society. The Society got its money from congregations in the east, and primarily from the wealthier churches in Ontario. Its national headquarters were located in Toronto. The responsibility of extending and consolidating the western circuits brought him necessarily into close association with the men who held the purse strings in Toronto and managed the political affairs of the church. It also took James Woodsworth frequently to England to seduce ministerial candidates, for the greatest demand on the western circuits was manpower. During the 1890s, by which time the evangelical enthusiasm of eastern Methodism had definitely waned, the church caught the enthusiasm for foreign missions, and graduates of the eastern theological colleges, from Victoria University in Toronto primarily, were attracted more to the glamour, the higher salaries, and the milder climate of China and Japan than they were to the harsh environment and ministerial penury of the prairies. By the turn of the century approximately 36 per cent of the western ministry had come from Great Britain, a large number of whom had been recruited personally by James Woodsworth and were known collectively as 'Woodsworth's Brigades'.[14]

James Woodsworth and his brother Richard, who also entered the ministry, were raised in Toronto at mid-century where their father had been a prominent architect and builder. Like most ministers of their generation who rose to positions of leadership in the Methodist Church, the Woodsworth brothers had been moulded by the great revivals of the 1850s and 1860s. 'I say revivals rather than evangelistic effort,' wrote Nathanael Burwash, Chancellor of Victoria University, in a tribute to the Woodsworths, 'for the revivals of those days led not only to decision and a practical religious life, but also to a clear knowledge of sins forgiven and to a spiritual baptism of power for a holier and higher life. . . . And the spirit of those days both these men helped to carry forward into our modern church.'[15] James Woodsworth carried it forward when he moved to the prairies, in part because of the special challenge facing the church there. Western Methodism had its wealthy and well-established congregations, like Grace Church in Winnipeg – the 'mother church' of the prairies where, as in many eastern congregations, an earlier emphasis on conversion had become church 'renewal' typified by the 'Special Meeting' and anxiety over why the children did not go forward. But the vast expanses of the outlying districts, which worked against the consolidation of communal church life, was being settled by European immigrants who had never heard of John Wesley. For this reason western Methodism, and the isolated circuits that James Woodsworth supervised, retained a stronger emphasis on the matter of individual conversion than in the east. It was not until the first decade of this century, when the flow of immigration became a tidal wave, and the strategy of individual conversion had proven a failure with 'foreigners', that western Methodists entered the field of social service as a way of bringing the strangers within their gates closer to the door of the church. This was the role of All People's Mission, and in accepting its superintendency in 1907 James Woodsworth's son was merely going about his father's business.

Such was the western Methodistical environment in which J.S. Woodsworth was raised. He was not another preacher's kid; he was the son of 'the ancient patriarch Abraham' in the wilderness, whose position in the national church was 'like that of a Bishop'.[16] His father's influence was the dominant one in his life, and in every stage of J.S. Woodsworth's religious development one must recognise the overwhelming presence of that paternal force. The family was close-knit, its moral standard exceedingly high, and the life of religious service its overriding orientation and expectation. This familial environment only reinforced the characteristics of Woodsworth's personality that were remarked upon throughout his entire life: his scrupulous honesty and a high sense of moral rectitude that bordered on perfectionism.[17]

In 1891, at the age of 17, Woodsworth entered Wesley College in Winnipeg. His undergraduate experience suggests a student of slightly more than average ability. Wesley had been established in 1888 to provide a higher standard of education for the children of the Methodist community in the west, and to provide a higher quality of minister for the churches. Woodsworth's ubiquitous father had been a founding member, served on the Board, and used the Theological Department, established in 1894, to upgrade the theological training of his brigades. During the early 1890s Wesley was not a centre of academic attainment. It opened three years previous to Woodsworth's arrival with a staff of two professors in addition to the Principal, the Reverend J.W. Sparling, and with a registration of seven students. 'The first lectures were given in two rooms at the back of Grace Church. One student alone took Chemistry and he performed his experiments in the Ladies Aid kitchen.'[18] Wesley grew quickly and by the turn of the century held its own in both academic prizes and student numbers compared with the other denominational colleges that made up the University of Manitoba; but Woodsworth's educational experience was obtained during the most precarious years of the College's existence. He graduated in 1896, the year that the college buildings were completed.

It took Woodsworth five years to complete Wesley's three-year BA, primarily because he spent a period of time teaching in rural schools. The first year of his programme was devoted to 'general subjects', while the final two years were reserved for specialisation in one of five departments. Woodsworth selected Mental and Moral Philosophy, the first outward indication of a lifelong concern with ethical problems rooted in an internal moral self-preoccupation. Moral Philosophy was taught by the Principal, J.W. Sparling, whose special talent was 'the noble work of administration', and who regarded 'the securing of the additional endowment of $250,000 as the crowning achievement of his life . . .'. Sparling was not a scholar. His religious position as stated in 1890 was that Christianity was 'a great system of facts – historical facts for which day and date can be given'.[19] His course was based on lectures in practical ethics, and surveyed the major schools of philosophical thought. The only other member of the Wesley faculty who could have influenced Woodsworth was the 'sane, serious, and serviceable' Professor Andrew Stewart, who taught English and History in the Arts stream, as well as Systematic Theology, Hebrew, and Old Testament Exegesis on the theological side; and who was so 'devoted to his work, there was no desire or time for published articles or treatises in theology . . .'. In 1899 Wesley 'honoured herself' by giving Stewart its first DD.[20]

On his graduation Woodsworth received a Bronze Medal (actually second prize) in Philosophy, and was voted 'Senior Stick' by his classmates in recognition of his all-round popularity. He took great pride in the Bronze – it was the only academic distinction he ever obtained – but it cannot be viewed as an indicator of special aptitude. As late as 1903 the programme in philosophy at Wesley was criticised as consisting 'in the memorization of notes dictated by professors', producing students 'crammed with ready-made estimates of the leading systems of philosophy and with cut and dried principles for daily application'.[21] In academic terms Woodsworth was at best a modest achiever. Although he envied the life of college professors, he did not possess an academic mind. Throughout his entire career Woodsworth displayed an inability to weigh matters on a philosophical level or to think in a detached or reflective way about them, and the understanding of symbolic meaning necessary to survive in the theological world of twentieth-century Protestantism created some difficulty for him. Woodsworth was, above all, a practical man who felt uncomfortable with intellectual considerations of moral problems. This led to an inner conviction that the determination of good and evil was ultimately a matter of stark simplicity. Woodsworth agonised over questions of right and wrong out of a personal need to *know* he was a good man, but when inevitably he found himself thrashing about in a realm of ambiguity he became all the more convinced that there had to be proximate answers to moral questions, as powerful as they were simple. Partly for these reasons his years at Wesley were the most pleasurable of all his student days. Ethics, as taught by J.W. Sparling at Wesley College, 'shut off from the University life of Eastern Canada and the United States',[22] gave him a sure philosophical footing in the narrow evangelical perception of the world he had inherited from his parents. He was ill equipped, both by ability and training, to meet the problems that soon faced him.

Evidence of this assessment is to be found in the diary Woodsworth kept while a probationer for the ministry after his graduation. While at Wesley in March of 1896, Woodsworth underwent a religious 'experience' that is best described as an act of personal consecration heightened by a spiritual awakening. 'I came into a fuller spiritual light', he described it a year later. 'On that Sunday evening I certainly had a new and deeper experience which I have felt ever since.'[23] He entered the circuits in south-western Manitoba, but his two years spent probationing were a period of difficulty for him. His problem, and the problem that fills the pages of his diary, was an inability to retain the level of spirituality he mercilessly expected of himself. 'I longed for personal purity . . . longed to be a saint, a sanctified man.'[24] Later, in 1907, when Woodsworth wished to resign the ministry, his sense of failure in the matter of perfect holiness became a denial that he had ever experienced conversion, but the very definition of conversion he used as a standard – Nathanael Burwash's discussion of the matter in *Wesley's Doctrinal Standards* (1891) – makes it clear that Woodsworth's earlier experience was certainly sufficient.[25] It was easier for Woodsworth in 1907 to deny his own conversion than to acknowledge his disbelief in an orthodox conception of the divinity of Christ. It was easier to admit personal failure than to challenge the beliefs of his parents. Woodsworth's earlier and real point of difficulty was the absolute and unattainable degree of holiness he expected of himself, and in this

insistent expectation one observes that strain of perfectionism that was so marked a feature of his character.

> Brandon people are all in a glow after their special services
> and when I came in contact with them it seems to have
> made me realize that my ardor is not as great as it ought to
> be. Mr. Gunty was talking of the Filling of the Holy Spirit. I
> prayed but I fear with very little faith. I could not help
> comparing my own condition with that of a few months
> ago. . . . That I did claim God's spirit in my life I cannot
> doubt. . . . That he has been and is now more fully in me I
> cannot but feel sure . . . although frequently my feelings
> would lead me to deny his presence. . . . Have I been
> faithful enough in prayers? I fear that here lies the trouble.
> That not long enough have I wrestled before God for
> power for the conversion of souls and held sweet commun-
> ion with him in my own soul. Here then I stand. May God
> help me *now*.[26]

He attributed a periodic 'ebbing' of spirituality to a private
'indifference' (a frequent theme of his social gospel sermons
later): 'the gradual indifference which is ever prone to creep
over me in regard to private devotions and . . . spending the
time of prayer in God's service. Oh how prone to wander
away. Is this very proneness not yet a remnant of the sinful
life . . . ?' Of course Woodsworth's internal struggle was common for young people raised in a closed evangelical world,
but like his father's powerful presence, Woodsworth's search
for purity and holiness dominated his entire life. He never
lost the feeling that his difficulty was a personal failing, but
later he began to believe there was something wrong with
Methodism too.

As a young probationer, Woodsworth not unnaturally
considered an outward sign of internal spiritual success to be
the conversion of others. His experience in this was mixed.
There were high points, as with the conversion of his
room-mate 'Forbes', kneeling on the floor of a boarding-
house: 'There and then he took the step and gave himself to
Christ, and there was joy among the angels. . . . Tonight I
rest satisfied that the Holy Spirit is abiding in me and gives
me peace. May God give me strength to fight the Devil when

he next tempts me to become indifferent.' 'Truly this pays
facing the inconveniences of circuit life and the mosquitoes.'
But there were low points when Woodsworth travelled for
miles in severe weather to find empty meeting houses, or
'that despite one's greatest efforts the people all sit apparently unmoved. . . . Oh that the Holy Ghost would work mightily
in the hearts of the people. Could we but have a revival of
spiritual Christianity in our midst.' At these times, and later,
Woodsworth considered foreign mission work as his future
vocation in the ministry, and one should recognise a pattern
of escape from internal difficulty in the recurrence of this
idea. But he felt a responsibility to the work of the Methodist
Church in the west to which his parents had devoted their
lives. 'When I think of the work abroad I am always thrown
back upon the great need at home.'[27]

Both of Woodsworth's biographers date the awakening of
his 'social conscience' to this early period. He harboured
'doubts . . . about the wisdom of approaching the problem of
decent social living only through the avenue of isolated
individuals'. This 'seed remained, to lie fallow until the slums
of London caused it to germinate and grow into one of the
overshadowing ideas of his life'.[28] But in examining the
diary, one is struck by the complete absence of evidence
relating to these concerns. MacNaught and MacInnis both
emphasise an encounter with 'Hughes', who Woodsworth
describes as belonging to 'the comparatively uneducated class
– narrow and bigoted and jealous of the upper classes'. He
sees 'a good deal of truth' in Hughes's complaint against the
wealthy, but he observes that Hughes fails to comprehend
the 'quality' of the work the rich do. And he ends the passage
with the blank and innocent assertion that 'in my own case I
am not envious of those wealthy business men I have met'.
There are a few passages describing scenes of poverty
Woodsworth encountered, but in every case his primary
concern is with the spiritual plight of those who suffered.
'But what was worse than the poor condition of the house
was the spiritual condition of the inmates.'[29] Far from
showing a man troubled by social inequities, the diary reveals
a young evangelical bound for the ministry, possessed with
an aggravated sense of his own spiritual poverty.

He furthered his training for the ministry by studying

theology in 1898–9 at Victoria University in Toronto. Victoria was federated with the University of Toronto, having moved from Coburg in 1892, and was the pre-eminent Methodist college in the country. The Chancellor and Dean of the Theological Faculty, who oversaw the move from Coburg against the forces of opposition, and whose authority permeated the life of Victoria, was the Reverend Nathanael Burwash, STD, LLD. A moderate liberal in theology whose study of *Wesley's Doctrinal Standards* (1881) was the unofficial bible of Canadian Methodism, Burwash was the outstanding proponent of a broadened liberal education, allowing for academic specialisation, that would bring the Methodist ministry in touch with advanced scholarship. Under federation Victoria retained its right to grant theological degrees, and Burwash staffed his theological faculty with the best he could get. His only error in this regard had been the appointment of the Reverend George Workman, fresh from five years at Leipzig, whose lack of public caution prompted a controversy over Biblical Criticism and his departure in 1892. 'The result was reached as a concession to popular feeling', explained Burwash. A similar controversy arose eighteen years later over the views of the Reverend George Jackson, a dynamic pulpit luminary from Scotland who was given a Chair of English Bible. Burwash defended both against conservative forces led by the Reverend Albert Carman, General Superintendent of the Methodist Church, who held that education 'may have some theory, some speculation, but education without some dogmatism is a contemptible rag. It would be . . . an unpardonable blunder, for a young man to be sent out from . . . a Methodist theological school with loose ideas or no ideas at all, of the Divine inspiration of the Holy Scriptures.'[30] The difficulty of Burwash's position was that he agreed with Carman, but believed equally that a ministry ignorant of advanced scholarship would jeopardise the future of the church. For these reasons he was a sympathetic adviser to young men in theological difficulty.

We know next to nothing about Woodsworth's year at Victoria except that he was severely troubled by the critical method and had difficulty integrating theology with the practical ethics he had absorbed at Wesley. McNaught informs us that 'he took pains to observe the growing slum conditions in Toronto and admired the work there of the Fred Victor Mission'.[31] There is no written evidence to confirm or contradict this in the Woodsworth collection, and the observation appears to be based on Woodsworth's mention of the Mission in *My Neighbor* (1911) long after he had entered the field of social service.

In order to fulfil the requirements of the BD, Woodsworth was forced to spend a considerable amount of time in the study of Hebrew, having picked up some Greek at Wesley. This brought him directly into contact with the 'quiet, diffident' professor John Fletcher McLaughlin, who held the Chair of Old Testament Exegesis and Literature after the outspoken and ill-fated Workman. McLaughlin had studied under S.R. Driver while attending Mansfield College, Oxford, in 1892 and 1897 and quietly held, without provocative public announcement, 'that the value and authority of the Old Testament . . . was not impaired or seriously endangered by the results of the historical and critical method of study'.[32] Despite McLaughlin's quiet confidence in the matter, Woodsworth's inherited framework of beliefs was severely shaken. He got over the initial shock soon enough, but his exposure to biblical criticism did contribute to the crisis he underwent two years later, which related more to an ethical search for personal purity. 'Take for instance the question of Bible criticism and Inspiration', he wrote to his mother one year later from Mansfield College in Oxford:

> Last year [at Victoria] I was turning intellectual summersaults at such a rate that the surroundings which had all seemed firm all seemed whirling and I hardly knew where I was. Well now I find things are becoming somewhat steady again. My summersaults may have changed my position somewhat; but after all things around me are *steady* even if my view point has altered a little.
>
> Of course I don't mean to say that all my problems are solved by any means and new ones have been raised.[33]

Woodsworth was soon ready to dispense with the Bible as having any role in establishing the authority of Christianity,[34] which was typical of the 'either/or' compartmentalisation of his thinking, and it may well have been a collective desire on the part of his father and the Victoria professoriate to 'steady' Woodsworth that led to his extended year of study at Mansfield College in Oxford.

Mansfield was established in 1886 as a Nonconformist outpost in Oxford to elevate the cultural level of the English Nonconformist ministry. It was a graduate, Congregational theological institution that had been moved to Oxford from Birmingham, and was not fully affiliated with the University. Its purpose was to provide a centre or 'rallying point' for Nonconformists of all branches who wished to pursue theological study as 'non-collegiate' students in Oxford. One of the major reasons for its establishment had been that the best and brightest Nonconformists 'going up' to Oxford after the liberalisation of the English universities had been 'going over' to the Church of England or to nothing. The College was a physical manifestation of R.W. Dale's 'New Evangelicalism', which sought the intrusion of Nonconformity into the cultural heart of the nation.[35] Under the strong leadership of its first Principal, the Reverend Andrew Martin Fairbairn, MA (Oxon by decree), DD (Edinburgh, Yale, Wales, Manchester), LLD (Aberdeen), DLitt (Oxon, Leeds), DTheol (Göttingen), who was by the 1880s the only real theologian of note in the Nonconformist community, young dissenters were to be grounded in their faith and tradition, and exposed under Fairbairn's sober and guiding hand to the world of higher learning.[36]

Tradition has it that Burwash advised Woodsworth to go. This is highly plausible, since Burwash knew Fairbairn, knew that the son of James Woodsworth was in difficulty, and knew James Woodsworth very well. His uncle Richard Woodsworth financed the trip (with interest), his father gave an envious blessing to it, and may have viewed his son's transferral to Mansfield as an investment for future traffic in the other direction. It is likely that McLaughlin, who found 'Principal Fairbairn's lectures very inspiring', also had a hand in the matter.[37]

Whatever the connection, Woodsworth arrived in Oxford on 24 October 1899 at the age of 25 and went straight to Fairbairn's office at Mansfield the next day. After hearing him out, Fairbairn advised that he not matriculate, nor even enroll as a non-collegiate student, but remain a 'private citizen' attending the lectures that interested him. Fairbairn granted him permission to attend his own lectures and wrote a note of introduction to Edward Caird for the same. Woodsworth was not offended by these arrangements; he viewed them innocently as a great 'favour'. It was, as Fairbairn pointed out to him, a less costly way to pursue his studies, leaving him free from any university regulations, with time to read for the special project he set for himself while attending lectures. To the lectures of Fairbairn and Caird, Woodsworth added those of Sanday and Driver during the Easter term, although he dropped Sanday's lectures because he 'did not like them'.[38]

The special project Woodsworth set for himself was a paper on 'Christian Ethics' by which he hoped to resolve the dichotomy in his mind between ethics or morality on the one hand, and what was for him the infinitely less pragmatic world of Christian theology on the other:

> During my arts course [at Wesley under Sparling] I was particularly interested in the subject of Ethics. It seemed to appeal directly to my inmost being. Unlike metaphysics it left one standing on the *firm ground of everyday experience*. . . . But when I entered upon the theological Course [at Victoria] I seemed to pass into a new world. Ethics had told me of man's dignity; Theology told me of his depravity. Ethics had spoken of works; Theology spoke of faith. Ethics claimed a *precise* truth; Theology a special revelation. Instead of Kant's calm and confident 'I ought therefore I can', I heard Paul exclaiming 'To me who would do good, evil is present . . .'. Here, then, I was trying in vain to hold two unreconciled and apparently irreconcileable systems. Each by itself appeared consistent; but reason demanded a higher unity and *practical* needs enforced the demand.[39]

In addition to this private academic endeavour, which reveals once again the segmented nature of his thinking, Woodsworth planned to expose himself to as much of English life as he could: 'To study life . . . to gain as many points of view as possible. . . . To get a fair idea of the principles of the religious and educational and social problems and work and try to understand the spirit which characterizes the whole system.'[40] It was to be his grand tour before ordination into the Methodist ministry.

Woodsworth's interest in understanding English life explains a great deal of his travel during his year at Oxford, but it is also true that his sightseeing was an avoidance of his academic project. During his first term he found it difficult to get down to work. 'Mother seems to think I am studying. Well this term is nearly gone and I have done practically nothing. Have not read more than an hour today and not taking any lectures – am taking a holiday.' He spent a considerable amount of time visiting the colleges, museums, and libraries of Oxford, touring the surrounding countryside, and describing his travels in lengthy letters to his family back home. 'The only trouble is I am doing no studying.' Part of his difficulty was that the Bodleian had no separate listing for the subject of Christian Ethics. 'So the only way was to read through hundreds of titles in the subject catalogue and examine scores of possible books.' Moreover, the lectures he heard from Caird and Fairbairn were not helping him: 'The Ethicists were busy thumbing the well-worn pages of Plato and Kant and the Theologians were too intent on Historical Theology and Biblical Criticism to trouble about such everyday affairs.'[41] But his greatest difficulty was an inability to grasp his subject.

He spent most of December and January 'on vacation' visiting London, Blyth near Rotherham where he had relatives, and Cambridge, returning to Oxford on 27 January. The first two weeks were to be spent at the Mansfield College Settlement in the East End where, as tradition has it, he was 'shocked at the dreadful slums, the wasted lives, the social neglect. . . . And he felt his own fresh country must not follow the same path . . .'[42]. But it is of utmost importance to understand that according to the record, Woodsworth was not shocked at all.

It is true that he viewed the slums of East London from the vantage point of the Mansfield College Settlement. It is true that he helped on one occasion to serve free lunches to school children, who 'pleaded for just a little more of the thicker soup near the bottom'; that he assisted one evening in the legal clinic; that he took an interest in the workings of the Settlement as a whole. But there is no indication that he was 'shocked' or that his emergent social conscience was 'stabbed' by what he saw. If anything he was disappointed: 'I have not seen anything of the slums as I imagined them.' Quite simply, the slums were another one of the 'sights' Woodsworth had planned for his itinerary. They were not described at length in his letters, nor with any degree of passion. 'You could buy nearly anything [from the hawkers]. The cries were bewildering and the cockney accents very amusing.' The truth about Woodsworth's stay at Mansfield House is that he spent most of this time visiting the sights in the Metropolis, taking day trips from the Settlement. 'Just let me mention a few places I have been this week: Natural History Museum, South Kensington Museum, National Gallery, Zoological Gardens, and Madame Tussaud's Wax Works – I get tired out trying to remember even a few things I have seen.' He also saw the British Museum, the Tower, toured places mentioned in Dickens's novels and, not to be forgotten, he visited the City Road Chapel and Wesley's house, which prompted the lengthiest description of anything he had seen in London. Instead of stabbing his social conscience, Mansfield House provided him with cheap accommodation. And the meals were very good: 'You can understand that I ought to grow fat when I am so well fed.'[43]

Before going north for Christmas, Woodsworth was unexpectedly invited to the north-east home of a minister by the name of Aldrich, who had married a Canadian woman. The conditions he saw there produced the only description of poverty that had any strength of feeling in his letters: 'It was really sickening to see the poverty and distress. . . . Of course a good share of the poverty is due to improvidence and drunkenness but that does not make it any the less real or pitiable. Then it seems that nothing permanent can be done. One can give a few coppers – alleviate the distress a little – that is all.'[44]

After attending a conference of the Student Volunteer Missionary Union on foreign missions (with free accommodation in St John's Wood), Woodsworth returned to the Aldrich home and visited some of the Mission Halls in the area with his host. But again this arrangement was one of convenience rather than keen interest in social conditions: 'I can't say that I am enjoying this week as much as others. . . .

You would be quite disgusted at the miserable little shops in this district. But my bed is clean and warm so I can put up with it for two or three days longer.... This week I have been into the city several days.... Next time I go to London I shall try to see a little more of the better parts.... I can quite easily understand how Dickens had such a rich field.'[45] Woodsworth's frequent reference to Dickens is an indication that his interest in poverty went as far as a tourist's desire to see the 'spots' that had kindled his imagination while reading the novels. 'Two months later he visited picturesque Chester which he described in great detail. But he also went to see the Black Country', writes MacInnis. Yet the following is from Woodsworth's actual description of the area: 'Well I wanted to get some idea of the Black Country. Many years ago I read Dickens' description – The Old Curiosity Shop. So I wanted to see it in all its horrors. Well you may be glad you don't live in such a place.... But do read Dickens ... he gives a good description. Why I saw the same old canal boats – the travelling shows and little Nell herself was about the only one I missed.... Oh how much more real things appear when one is right on the spot.'[46] After visiting Cambridge for a week, where he sought out 'Professor Sidgwick who [helpfully] told me that when he wrote his History of Ethics he had difficulty in gaining information on the subject',[47] Woodsworth returned to Oxford and his academic project. Such was James Shaver Woodsworth's exposure to the poverty of London. 'It is not *mere* sightseeing,' he wrote, justifying his vacation to his father, 'for one has constantly to try to understand and weigh methods and see things from new kinds of view.'[48]

Of greater importance to Woodsworth's development was his paper on Christian Ethics. In final form it was no more than an introductory statement and a 'tentative working outline' that defined the problem in the following terms: 'What is the relation of Religion to Ethics or more specifically Christianity to morality? Has Ethics the whole truth? Can religion exist independently? If Christianity is as universal as it claims to be, must it not combine in itself all morality – allow for its highest development – and be an essential factor in that development?' With an eye to Woodsworth's later career, McNaught suggests that these questions were social in nature: 'Along what lines should the reformation of society, distinct from, yet including, the regeneration of the individual soul, be conducted? In short, what was Christian ethics, and how was this scheme of behaviour to be applied to the modern world?'[49] But this obscures the nature of Woodsworth's dilemma. His moral self-preoccupation, rooted in an evangelical desire for personal purity, led him to ask an ethical question about Christianity, the simplistic logic of which was as follows: if Christianity is true, then it must represent the fullest embodiment of the good. It will foster man's highest moral development. If Christianity does not represent the fullest embodiment of the good and morality, then Christianity cannot be true. And if that is true, what is the basis of morality? Quite understandably these questions remained unanswered in his paper, and it is clear from his outline that he failed in establishing a complete and satisfactory integration of morality with Christianity in each of the categories he examined. It is here that Woodsworth's exposure to the wider world of English culture and history had a more telling influence on his development than his tour of the East End. What was dawning upon him, and marks the beginning of his crisis, was the realisation that morality and man's pursuit of goodness could exist and thrive apart from Christianity; that Christianity did not necessarily combine in itself all morality, nor was it necessarily 'an essential factor' in its development. Christianity was only one expression of man's moral striving within the vast and complex history of the human story. 'I think', he wrote in a sombre letter to his father, 'I am gaining an idea of a culture deeper than scholarship which many of us have utterly ignored.'[50]

That moral men live apart from Christ may not appear to be a particularly disturbing realisation for a young evangelical, but for Woodsworth it was. The difficulty was not that this realisation challenged a common Victorian evangelical assumption: that without Christianity there was no morality, and without morality there was chaos, etc. It was more personal than that. At the heart of Woodsworth's character was a desire to be pure, which meant on an intellectual level that he must find the ultimate seat of morality, the final test by which one could clearly determine the difference between good and evil and use it practically in attaining perfection.

He had assumed he would find all of this reaffirmed in Christianity, and preferably in its Methodistic form; but instead Woodsworth encountered a vast world of knowledge and achievement where there were no final answers, and where a final answer by its nature was suspect. 'One feels there are worlds all around, about which he is in dense ignorance. When I hear beautiful music – watch a painter or sculptor – see something of architecture . . . learn the hundreds of different subjects that men are reading or studying, I almost feel that it is useless to try to learn much because it can be such a small proportion of the world's knowledge. . . . And yet, sometimes an ignorant man practically sets up the claim that his ideas and standards should be the measure of the universe. . . .'[51]

At the risk of jumping too far ahead it is worth noting here that the source of Woodsworth's crisis of faith had little to do with Science, or Darwinism, or for that matter Biblical Criticism. Its source was essentially religious – a yearning for perfect oneness with God, or what his evangelical father called sanctification, what Woodsworth usually called moral purity or, when he wanted to be intellectual about it, what he called ethics. The moral relativism he feared most was what he called 'indifference'. The crisis itself was bound up in the realisation that he could not find what he wanted in orthodox Christianity, which in his case meant the Methodism of his father. Woodsworth spent his entire life in search of spiritual peace, and the logical ending point was pacifism rather than socialism, or the social gospel before that.

Woodsworth's letters to his parents do not reveal any serious reconsideration of orthodox doctrine during his year at Oxford, but they do reveal that toward the end of his stay he was anxious about entering the regular work of the ministry. He wrote to his father suggesting that the part of the church's work for which he was 'specially adapted' was that of a college teacher. 'In the West we need not so much erudite scholars who have the ability to devote themselves to original research or critical investigation, as men . . . who can grasp particular subjects and so present them as to enable others to do so.' What he meant was an appointment to Wesley College to teach Christian Ethics, enabling him to be a minister without preaching, and, in listing the advantage of such a post, he added that 'there would be opportunities for directly assisting in city mission work'. It is important to note the context of this first mention of mission work as an alternative to preaching in the work of the church. 'I don't know whether, as my father, and a member of the Board, you could do it ... but if you could talk this matter over quietly with one or two members of the Board ... it would at least give the Board a chance to consider my case. ... I want to find a place where I can be most useful.'[52]

Nothing came of this first of several attempts to remain in the ministry as a denominational college professor. In July, when he appeared at Victoria to receive his BD on the way back to Brandon, he presumptuously made the same proposal to Chancellor Burwash, who 'thought that my literary qualifications were probably sufficient to enter upon the work of teaching but strongly urged that I should spend a few years in pastoral work'. So he did. The following month he was ordained into the ministry, his proud parents in attendance. Woodsworth wrote in his notebook: 'Sincere in taking ordination vows. ... Dogmatic speculation less intense in the practical work of the ministry.'[53]

He was sent out to Carieval in Manitoba, then soon after to a small church at Keewatin in the wilds of Northern Ontario: 'the greatest town for lonely people.' His sermons were based on notes taken for the Christian Ethics paper, so there was time for further reading along these lines, and letters to his cousin Charles Sissons, who was studying at Victoria. By the fall of 1901 his thoughts were in a 'terrible tangle', and he began to feel he was violating his conscience by remaining in the ministry. 'There seems no opening in College for me; but perhaps I might be able to get into mission work.' In November 'there came a sudden revolution', and the unusual care taken in writing the following description in his diary, which he entitled 'My Apostasy', is indicative of the secret pride he took in his own unorthodoxy – his first real act of rebellion against his father.

> It was as if I had been travelling along an uneven mountain path. Lately the way had been smoother. I walked confidently notwithstanding the drifting mists. Suddenly the mists cleared and I found myself on the very edge of a precipice.

I looked down but could not see the bottom. There was no turning to right or left. I could not retrace my steps. Here was the end of it all. I thought of my parents – my dearest friends – their grief. I was leaving them.... Then it seemed as if the very rock on which I had stood began to slide with me. Cherished hopes and beliefs – *morality itself* – all were slipping. I had nothing to hold to.[54]

He had nothing, that is, but his own conscience and Jesus, whoever Jesus was. This was the substance of a letter he wrote at this time to Chancellor Burwash appealing for help: 'What is the ultimate authority in determining the truth and content of the Christian revelation?' Woodsworth dispensed with the Pope, the historical Church, and the Bible, 'whose historical accuracy cannot be maintained in the light of modern criticism', which left man with his own religious consciousness, 'whether called reason, conscience, intuition, or common sense'. What, according to this conscience, could be believed about the content of the Christian revelation? In Woodsworth's view, God revealed himself either 'miraculously' in the person of Jesus according to what theologians called the Incarnation, or 'Ethically according to spiritual laws'. His problem with the former was that it was simply irrational; it required 'a constant exercise of the "miraculous" from Jesus's conception by the Virgin to his bodily ascension' and belief in what he called 'inconceivable and irrational (super-rational!) conceptions such as the doctrine of the two natures in one person and the mystery of the Trinity'.

But the more rational ethical view 'cuts the Gordian Knot of theological subtleties, rejects the metaphysical doctrine of the Trinity', and accepts a spiritual revelation in Jesus. 'According to many exegetes, Jesus did not claim to be divine. In an ethical sense, he was the son of God – uniquely only because of his spiritual work.... Jesus has given us a revelation of God which bears upon it the impress of truth and is witnessed to by our spiritual needs and experience.'[55] Thus Woodsworth could now hold only as 'tentative' the doctrines of the Virgin Birth, the Incarnation, the Atonement, the Resurrection, and the Ascension, but he held on to the divinity of Christ in the poorly defined sense that Jesus revealed divinity in his life 'ethically'.

Woodsworth wrote to his cousin 'Charlie' Sissons that his first duty was to inform his parents that he must resign the ministry. 'It is bitter – so bitter – to bring grief to my home.' Without mercy he told them at Christmas, and recalled in 1930 that his father 'said to me steadily but with deep emotion, "I am afraid I cannot help you much in these newer problems, but of one thing I am certain; you must be true to your convictions."' The trip to Brandon 'brightened' his spirits, 'made me realize to be patient and to try to see things from a higher point of view'. He got a reply from Burwash, and commented: 'You can't know just how much the liberality and sympathy of friends has helped me . . .'. He visited Brandon again in January: 'In for a little father treatment.' But back in Keewatin the temporary foothold 'I thought – I hoped – I was gaining' after the Christmas break crumbled, and he resolved finally in April that unless 'new light comes between now and conference I propose to withdraw then. It will be a disappointment to the home. . . . Did you ever read Robert Elsmere by Mrs. Humphry Ward? I . . . have been reading it and taking a kind of bitter consolation from it. Robert Elsmere's experiences, till the time he left his living, have been mine during the past few months. But for one thing I am profoundly thankful . . . I have no wife.'[56]

What then happened immediately before and during Conference is of considerable importance in understanding Woodsworth's passage into social Christianity. There is little doubt that the matter was engineered by his father with the cooperation of his colleagues, and their purpose was to keep the son of James Woodsworth in the ministry. Woodsworth was given an escape from his crisis of faith in work that led along social lines, and his ambivalence allowed him to play the part assigned to him. It is important to note that Woodsworth uses the term 'escape' himself. He had reached a state of calm before Conference met, he wrote to his cousin:

> But sometimes I go over the ground wearily again and again – anxiously at times to see if there is no means of escape. For instance, the other day I received a 'Feeler' from Dr. Sparling [of Wesley College] re. accepting the position of junior pastor of Grace Church. . . . Now here is

a 'temptation' . . . the work would be largely in the S.S. – among the young people – and in practical work. It would give me an opportunity to teach and introduce me to city work with all its problems. Then it appeals to one's ambition somewhat. Grace Church has the largest membership of any Meth. Ch. in Canada. It would give me a recognized standing. Fair salary – congenial associations etc. . . . When it comes to the actual point of leaving, I would give anything if I could only stay. Again when I think of father's work in building up our Church – of the devoted lives of some of my friends, of the hopes that some have concerning me, and of the good wishes that have been expressed, its seems awfully hard to turn aside – to abandon that which still retains my sympathies.

But I cannot see any other course – . . . .

Then he was informed he was appointed Secretary to the Stationing Committee, over which his father presided, and which coordinated the rotation of ministers in the circuits.

This took me to conference several days earlier and gave me an opportunity for some long discussions with old friends. . . . One point that I had not considered very much was my duty to the church. The retiring President, in a confidential talk, pointed this out to me. He showed me that even the least radical men in the church would not be as exacting in their demands as I had been with myself – that even if I made public my difficulties they would urge further time in justice to myself and the church. . . . Then there were a few other men who think along these lines and I had a sense of fellowship with them. The strain of isolation was gone . . . and I felt that I must get out of the morbid state in which I have been living and *do* more – *do*, not to escape thought, but to stimulate thought. Right here comes Grace Church . . . work chiefly teaching and practical work among the young people. . . . Strange isn't it that six months of thought was set aside in two days – no not set aside . . .[57]

So he found himself at Grace Church, and the rapidity with which the appointment had been arranged produced a period of confusion: 'I hardly know just what I am supposed to be responsible for. . . .' He was promised he 'would not be required to preach. . . . They little know how thankful I am. . . . It may not develop preaching abilities – what do I care. I'm not ready to talk. . . . A very good salary. . . . Little or no anxiety and responsibility.' He got married (Mrs Woodsworth died in 1976), had the first of five children (now Mrs Grace MacInnis), and found his time consumed in the day-to-day running of the church. 'I almost despair of getting any reading done.' 'As to beliefs. Well they have largely sunk into the background at present. I have an idea that one day they will re-emerge from this bath of neglectful oblivion.'[58]

His principal duties were to supervise facets of Sunday School work, to organise clubs for church members, and to assist the pastor, the Reverend R.P. Bowles, in district visiting. This brought Woodsworth into the back streets of Winnipeg, where thousands of European immigrants had been left to find temporary shelter while awaiting settlement on the prairies. It was in the slums of Winnipeg, not London, where Woodsworth began to see an enlarged opportunity. 'Charlie, there is a great work ahead of us out here. . . . Our problem is to Canadianize and Christianize these people.'[59] Woodsworth came to share a western paranoia over the effects of immigration that was put succinctly by the Reverend S.D. Chown, who replaced conservative Carman as General Superintendent of the Methodist Church:

> The question of questions is, 'Which shall prevail; the ideals of Southern Europe or the noblest conceptions of Anglo-Saxondom?' Shall the hordes of southern Europe overrun our country as the Huns and Vandals did the Roman Empire? There is no disguising the fact that already in cities like Toronto and Winnipeg the foreign vote is reaching for control, if it has not already grasped it. The question that trembles in the balance is, 'How shall the foreigner govern us?' That they shall govern the west in a generation or two there is no doubt. The question, How? depends for its answer upon our assimilating power.[60]

It was not until Woodsworth's second attempt at resignation in 1907 and his subsequent appointment to All People's Mission that he became actively involved in promoting this 'assimilating power'. While at Grace Church he spoke of the needs of newly arrived immigrants as a field of Christian service, and he chided the congregation about the 'Sin of Indifference'. We know he was reading social gospel literature at this time, and there is some evidence that he caused 'uneasiness among the influential people of the congregation'.[61] But it appears that nothing practical came of these socially related concerns and that Woodsworth's work continued to revolve around the organised life of the church itself. In 1904 he added to his responsibilities some lecturing in ethics at Wesley College – 'enough to keep my hand in a bit . . .'. Wesley had plans to expand its faculty with an increase in student numbers, but it could no longer afford a staff without high academic qualifications and a record of publication, both of which Woodsworth lacked. 'Today', Woodsworth wrote to his cousin in July of 1904, 'I have started to prepare a paper on "The Stranger Within Our Gates".'[62]

He could not escape preaching entirely. Reverend Bowles, 'a splendid fellow', spent an increasing amount of time in Toronto, where he was appointed Professor of Homiletics at Victoria in 1905 (replacing Burwash as Chancellor in 1913), which meant that Woodsworth had to say something from the pulpit. But what was he to preach if he no longer held to orthodox doctrine? What was to be said in Grace Church if Jesus was only ethically divine? The answer lay in an outward search for salvation beyond the church with its orthodox theological formulas. Woodsworth's sermon notebook from the Grace Church period reveals a steady progression from a concern for personal piety and holiness to a concern for eradicating impurity in society, culminating in a sermon entitled 'The Wider Evangel'. There is no doubt that Woodsworth's discovery of Winnipeg's social problems and his reading of social gospel literature were influential factors in this reorientation, but also present was the avoidance of an internal moral struggle tied up in a Gordian knot of theological subtleties that was externalised into a search for piety in the redemption or perfection of society. In the matter of preaching, Woodsworth had no other direction but a social one in which to go. To contend with orthodox doctrine in the church was to contend with his own unbelief, but to enlarge the boundary of Christian concern to include social sin was to widen the scope of consecration and belief. The irony of Woodsworth's situation was that by orthodox church standards he was an apostate and therefore had to find a new basis of belief outside the church, or through the alteration of existing church doctrine. In the end he had to leave the church to retain his belief. For the moment Woodsworth's 'Wider Evangel', which was no more than the socialised 'New Evangelicalism' of late-nineteenth-century Protestantism, offered a renewed sense of purpose and a wider field of sacrifice in the act of *doing*, when orthodox formulations of belief proved to be tenable no longer. The 'Wider Evangel' led straight into the social gospel, as the following quotation from Woodsworth's sermon clearly demonstrates:

> The older type of religious life found expression in devotional exercises and partook largely of an emotional character.... It is not the contemplative life that appeals to us today. It is the strenuous life. As Christians we realise that the world must be conquered for Christ.... The old monastic idea of holiness was that of a life withdrawn from the world.... Thank God we are getting away from this exclusive spirit. We are gaining a nobler and truer doctrine of holiness.... Go ye into all the world – into the selfish impure sinful world ... to preach the good news of purity and unselfishness and holiness.... The church has never entirely overlooked the need of practical work for the welfare of men.... But we have begun to find out that our duty is more than this. We should not only feed the poor but should endeavour to change the conditions that lead to poverty.... In short our efforts ought to be preventative as well as remedial.... The work of the church is not merely to save men, it is to redeem – to transform society. Jesus said very little about saving souls. He spoke often about the establishment of the Kingdom.... The establishment of God's Kingdom means the purification and perfection of the home life ... the transformation of industrial and commercial organization ... the leavening of society with the Spirit of Jesus Christ.[63]

But the question remained: who was Jesus Christ? Was he divine or human? Curiously enough, although Woodsworth never abandoned a belief in God, it was his final realisation that Jesus was *only* a man – his ultimate break with evangelical orthodoxy – that led directly to the work of Christian social service as Superintendent of All People's Mission.

By the end of 1905 Woodsworth had decided to leave Grace Church. He had been forced into orthodox theological matters once again owing to the departure of Reverend Bowles, for the church's Bible Class had to be taught: 'This is about the first time that I have had courage to tackle some of the old church doctrines. . . .' He had suffered from colds and felt 'a bit run down'. He wrote to Dr Alexander Sutherland, the Superintendent of the Missionary Society, about work in China or Japan, but Sutherland was 'so uncommital' Woodsworth gave up the idea. The other route of escape, college teaching, also remained closed to him. He wrote to Chancellor Burwash: 'Do you know of any position in any of our Colleges for which I am fitted? . . . I cannot claim "Scholarship" and yet I am sure I could *teach*.' Burwash did not know or did not say, and Woodsworth decided that 'the best answer seems to be to take a year off'.[64]

He travelled to Switzerland, Italy, Egypt, and finally Palestine. He sought throughout the entire journey to clarify his beliefs, and the tone of his diary entries indicates depression. 'This is a big world – it grows bigger every day. . . . The old questionings again arise. Where to draw the line between history and legend – what are to be our criteria of truth? I must keep my mind open to the truth by following it whatever it costs.' The first truth to come home to him was a social one. Woodsworth's theological and ethical tribulations had already carried him in a social direction, or to a 'Wider Evangel', but it was not until Naples, where he watched men unloading coal on the docks, that he finally realised the 'system' was wrong.

> There is something wrong somewhere. The inequalities are too great. . . . There are incapables – and indolent and shiftless and criminal people – granted. But this does not account for the inequalities that exist. . . . Why should we have home and friends and opportunities and comforts while these people not even knowledge of what these mean? In the evening a walk along the Bay with some

American ladies. Yes there it is – the incongruity – the inconsistency of it all. Stand pitying these people. Then back to a good dinner – a pleasant stroll – and now a clean comfortable bed. Then tomorrow on to new pleasures! I don't know – but one thing I *do* know, that I shall be utterly unworthy of these privileges unless the knowledge and inspiration gained are used in the service of others. Yes let that stand written here in the book with the record of the experience – to my shame if I forget the call to service![65]

What is important about this passage is not that Woodsworth finally realised there were structural inequalities, but that he was still personally ambivalent in the matter of Christian social service.

While Woodsworth was travelling his father and his cousin, Charles Sissons, who was then teaching in Revelstoke, British Columbia, arranged for Woodsworth to take a temporary appointment in Revelstoke, where the church had undergone a ministerial 'scandal'. They sent a telegram to Jerusalem indicating that the job was his if he would only take it, and it is evident that Woodsworth mistook the offer to be a continuing appointment. But by this point he had decided once again that he must resign the ministry, for in Jerusalem he realised a second truth – that Christianity had more to do with legend than with factual history.

We have too much idealized and etherealized these Biblical scenes and stories! . . . I don't think that I could realize that these were really the places mentioned in the Bible. Not that the scene was disappointing – but that there seemed no connection between these places and those held sacred from our earliest childhood. The distances seemed short – that was one impression. Jerusalem such a small place and all the spots within a short radius. . . . All the sacred places built over by mosques churches monasteries and hospices. . . . My strongest impression then, I think, was the sense of the immorality of it all. . . . Then came a growing wonder that such a small barren hill could have meant so much in the history of the world. . . . The Jordan was much like the Assinaboia – only much smaller – more like the little Saskatchewan only muddier – only about 45 ft. across. . . . Strange that this could have been so idealized and spiritualized. . . . It all seems so ridiculous! . . . A mass of superstition. . . .[66]

This pointed to the third and final truth for Woodsworth – that after all Jesus had only been a man. What Jesus had said was inspiring and revealed divine truths, but he was not divinely inspired in the orthodox sense. Woodsworth had already come close to this position with the intellectual 'ethical revelation' about which he wrote to Burwash, but it was not until Jerusalem that Woodsworth *understood* that Jesus had been only a man – a man like himself.

This recognition of Jesus's humanity (or non-divinity) was the turning point in his career. It made Jesus's sacrifice all the more powerful and personal for him; it was an act that could be repeated in one's own life. In Jerusalem Woodsworth made the decision to sacrifice his own life in serving the material needs of men: 'One passage that has come to me strongly – "Pure religion . . . before the Father is this – to visit the Fatherless. . . ."' His Passion would be to resign the ministry in opposition to his parents' wishes, and to devote himself to the problems of the city. Realising Jesus's kingdom in the real world, with or without the churches, was to follow 'in his steps'. What was more ethical and final in the matter of personal purity than to be Christ-like? And could there be a more fitting place for Woodsworth's crisis of faith to come to an end than on the Mount of Olives during his last evening in Jerusalem?

I had my Bible and read in the gospels. It was one of the times that do not often come in one's life! I thought of many events in the life of Jesus but the one that stands out – 'Father, if thou be willing, remove this cup from me: nevertheless not my will, but thine be done. . . .' I could not but kneel for a moment and ask for strength to follow the Master. . . . A little way down the hill, where there was a fine view I sat down to rest and see and think. Glancing up I noticed on the wall an inscription in Latin – 'This is the place where Jesus saw the City and wept over it. . . .' The confused cries of the city came to me on the wind. I thought of the places I had visited . . . and the poor people. What must Jesus have thought during those last days? Was his mission a failure . . . ? He had come to the city and there came into contact and conflict with the established religion. And the leaders had hounded him to death. . . . Then in the dark I went on down the hill and . . . up through the gates of the city. In some such direction Jesus must have gone on the night of his betrayal. . . . Somewhere near here they crucified him. . . . I shall remember the view from the Mount of Olives with the glow over the city. . . . Before dinner I wrote and posted a letter declining the invitation to Revelstoke.

Now for home![67]

But he was soon to discover that although he was eager, there was no one willing to crucify him.

Woodsworth took the job in Revelstoke. It was, after all, only temporary. He sent a carefully prepared statement of resignation to the Manitoba Conference, which met in June of 1907 in Winnipeg, Woodsworth in attendance. His argument was that he could not agree with parts of the church's Discipline, which as a minister he was bound to accept and preach. Then, going beyond this legalistic argument, he denied that he had experienced conversion:

In this matter of personal experience lies the root of the difficulty. My experience has not been what among Methodists is considered normal. . . . My experience has determined my theology, and my theology my attitude toward the Discipline. And all three, according to our standards, are un-Methodistical. . . . With me, it was not a case of entering the church. I was born and brought up in the Methodist Church and easily found my way into its ministry. It was not difficult to give an assent to the doctrines of the Church as a whole. . . . But, during the past year, I have had the opportunity of viewing the situation with a certain detachment. . . . I have come to realize that my position in the church is an impossible one.[68]

A committee of men from Woodsworth's district in the Conference was struck to deal with the matter. This committee consisted of Woodsworth's own Professor of Ethics, Principal Sparling of Wesley; Dr William Sparling, who had replaced Bowles at Grace Church; and Professor S.P. Rose of

Wesley College. The composition of this committee leaves no doubt that the reputation of Wesley College (and that of Woodsworth's father) was at issue.

The three wise men met with Woodsworth in his home, 'long talk – they didn't ask anything much about my views – took for granted that I ought to stay – urged me to withdraw my resignation – this I refused to do.' The committee reported failure in urging Woodsworth to reconsider and was forced to pass the matter on to the larger Manitoba Conference. Some wished him 'to resign without giving any reasons. But I refused to do this.'

'As soon as the matter came up in Conf.', Dr James Elliot, the President, appointed another committee of three, including himself. There was another long meeting, during which 'I insisted on reading to them my statement and explaining my position'. Then, to Woodsworth's astonishment, the Committee reported to the Conference as follows: 'Having had a full and frank conversation with Bro. James S. Woodsworth re. the cause of his resignation, we find that there is nothing in his doctrinal beliefs and adhesion to our discipline to warrant his separation from the ministry of the Methodist Church, and therefore recommend that his resignation be not accepted and that his character be now passed.'[69] They called for a vote, 'there was no discussion – passed I should judge almost unanimously'. They would not let him out.

Woodsworth was bewildered and uncertain about what to do. 'I would gladly away to the mountains.' But at this point he was subjected to more 'father treatment'. The Stationing Committee, on which his father sat *primus inter pares*, appointed him to the All People's Mission, managed on behalf of the Conference by 'a representative Board. (Father is Chairman of the Board).' It had been decided to mount a church programme of social service for immigrants through the Mission, and 'Father says my work will be to organise and help formulate a policy'. Woodsworth recognised 'the opportunity of working along lines that I have long been thinking about', and so he accepted, though not as if he had much choice in the matter. As in the past, 'Father' had found the solution serving everyone's interests. 'After I was appointed Father said "You have your opportunity".'[70]

In 1902 Woodsworth had accepted Grace Church to stay

in the ministry. In 1907 the church and his father gave him All People's to keep him in. The point to be recognised is that both Woodsworth and the leaders of the church joined hands in finding a place for his unorthodoxy, and this led inevitably to the practical work of church-supported social service. The true story of J.S. Woodsworth's ministerial career has little to do with an emergent social conscience and a lot to do with an emergent unbelief which, given his father's prominence, had to be contained. All People's Mission, the institution through which the church appropriated the secular, provided sufficient flexibility to keep an apostate in the ministry. As for Woodsworth himself, social Christianity provided a way out of his theological-ethical dilemma, which was how to be holy in a profoundly religious sense when he no longer believed in traditional Christianity. He adopted a social gospel, which became synonymous with his name in Canada, as much because of his unbelief as of his belief. What Woodsworth wanted was exceedingly Methodistical – personal purity, sanctification, and knowledge of the truth. His crisis of faith, which was his conversion experience, came in the realisation that he could not find these things in orthodox Christianity, and this realisation drove him into socialised religion. When he discovered 'almost too late that to minister effectively to the poor . . . one must work outside organized church activities',[71] his only recourse was socialism and pacifism. Woodsworth could not live without religion, and his search for its truest form, which led in secular directions, was an escape from irreligion.

> Twenty years ago, I made a pilgrimage to the Holy Land. As, from a vantage point on the Mount of Olives I looked across to Jerusalem and tried to readjust my beliefs and manner of life in accordance with realities, there came to me with a new force the words of Robertson of Brighton – the 'sacrifice of Jesus must be completed and repeated in the life of each true follower.'
>
> The very heart of the teaching of Jesus was the setting up of the Kingdom of God on earth. The vision splendid has sent forth an increasing group to attempt the task of 'Christianizing the Social Order.' Some of us whose study of history and economics and social conditions has driven

us to the socialist position find it easy to associate the Ideal Kingdom of Jesus with the co-operative commonwealth of socialism.[72]

Social Christianity, in the notable case of James Shaver Woodsworth, was not a direct religious response to social problems. It was an attempt to protect faith from a loss of belief.

NOTES

1. Charles H. Hopkins, *The Rise of the Social Gospel in American Protestantism, 1865–1915* (New Haven, Conn., 1940); Henry F. May, *Protestant Churches and Industrial America* (New York, 1949); Paul Carter, *The Decline and Revival of the Social Gospel* (Ithaca, 1956); R.M. Miller, *American Protestantism and Social Issues* (Chapel Hill, NC, 1958); Stephen Mayor, *The Churches and the Labour Movement* (London, 1947); K.S. Inglis, *The Churches and the Working Classes in Victorian England* (London, 1963); Jeffery Cox, *The English Churches in a Secular Society* (Oxford, 1982). For a different view, close to my own, see Ramsay Cook, *The Regenerators* (Toronto, 1988).
2. Timothy L. Smith, *Revivalism and Social Reform* (New York, 1957); Donald B. Meyer, *The Protestant Search for Political Realism, 1919–1941* (Berkeley, Calif., 1960); Richard Allen, *The Social Gospel in Canada* (Ottawa, 1975).
3. Richard Allen, *The Social Passion* (Toronto, 1971); Robert T. Handy, *A Christian America* (Oxford, 1971); George N. Emery, 'Methodism on the Canadian Prairies, 1896–1914' (PhD diss., University of British Columbia, 1970).
4. Cox, *The English Churches*, 90–128.
5. Josiah Strong, *The New Era* (New York, 1893) 240.
6. Hopkins, *The Rise of the Social Gospel*, 3.
7. Kenneth McNaught, *A Prophet in Politics* (Toronto, 1959) 35.
8. Marilyn Barber, 'An Introduction', to J.S. Woodsworth, *Strangers within Our Gates* (Toronto, 1972) vii; emphasis mine. A re-issue of the original edition of 1904.
9. *Co-operative Commonwealth Federation Programme, Adopted at First National Convention Held at Regina, Sask., July 1933*, 1. See McNaught, *A Prophet in Politics*, 321–30.
10. Bruce Hutchinson, *The Unknown Country* (Toronto, 1943) 92.
11. Grace MacInnis, *J.S. Woodsworth: A Man to Remember* (Toronto, 1953) 37–8, 49, 59, 113; McNaught, *A Prophet in Politics*, 36, 57.
12. *The Spires*, 5, no. 3 (Fall 1979); MacInnis, *J.S. Woodsworth*, 57.
13. *Winnipeg Free Press*, 26 January and 3 February 1917.
14. Emery, 'Methodism on the Canadian Prairies', 129–45.
15. *The Christian Guardian*, 30 May 1917, 12.

16. Unsigned tribute in United Church Archives (UCA) biographical file on James Woodsworth.
17. MacInnis, *J.S. Woodsworth*, 57.
18. Tribute by Burton Richardson (UCA file on J.W. Sparling).
19. ibid.; J.W. Sparling, 'A Trinity of Testimony', *Canadian Methodist Quarterly*, 2, no. 3 (July 1890) 300.
20. UCA File on A. Stewart. See also Richard Allan, 'Children of Prophecy: Wesley College Students in an Age of Reform', *Red River Valley Historian*, 6 (Summer 1974) 15–20; A.G. Bedford, *The University of Winnipeg* (Toronto, 1976) 22–70.
21. *Vox Wesleyana*, 7, no. 4 (January 1903) 69.
22. ibid., 7, no. 5 (February 1903) 90.
23. Woodsworth Papers (Public Archives of Canada): J.S. Woodsworth, Diary 1896–8, 15 March 1897.
24. Woodsworth Papers (PAC): J.S. Woodsworth, Sermon Notebook 1903–6, 'The Christian Ideal', 9.
25. Nathanael Burwash, *Wesley's Doctrinal Standards* (Toronto, 1891) 71.
26. Woodsworth, Diary 1896–8, 27 February 1897.
27. ibid., 1 September 1897, 11 and 27 August 1896, 10 and 12 January 1897, 4 October 1896.
28. McNaught, *A Prophet in Politics*, 8; MacInnis, *J.S. Woodsworth*, 25.
29. Woodsworth, Diary 1896–8, 16 September and 2 October 1896.
30. Nathanael Burwash, *History of Victoria College* (Toronto, 1927) 530; Albert Carman, 'The Church of God and the Education of the People', *Acta Victoriana* (1898–9) 10.
31. McNaught, *A Prophet in Politics*, 9.
32. *The Mail and Empire*, 20 March 1900.
33. Woodsworth to his mother, 6 May 1900; emphasis mine.
34. Woodsworth to Burwash, 14 January 1902.
35. As Woodsworth's own 'New Evangel' promoted the entrance of the churches into the realm of social service. The outward-looking liberal theology known as the 'New Evangelicalism', which swept the larger Protestant denominations in both England and North America during the 1870s and 1880s, contributed to the rise of the social gospel. The church must 'go outside of its elegant sanctuaries, leave its padlocked pews, forsake its gentility and fastidiousness, and go forth to meet mankind' (Hopkins, *The Rise of the Social Gospel*, 45). See Mark D. Johnson, *The Dissolution of Dissent, 1850–1918*' (New York, 1987) ch. 1.
36. Johnson, *Dissolution*, ch. iv.
37. R.M. Irwin, *John Fletcher McLaughlin: Scholar Pilgrim* (Toronto, n.d.) 47.
38. Woodsworth to his mother, 25 October 1899; to his father, 19 May 1900.
39. Woodsworth Papers (PAC): J.S. Woodsworth, Oxford Notebook 1899–1900, 32–4; emphasis mine.
40. Woodsworth to his father, 25 October 1899.
41. Woodsworth to his sister, 6 November 1899, 11 December 1900;

Oxford Notebook 1899–1900, 35.
42. *C.C.F. News*, 13 December 1950, 3.
43. Woodsworth to his mother, 11 and 17 December 1899.
44. ibid., 25 December 1899.
45. ibid., 12 January 1900.
46. Woodsworth to his brother, 22 March 1900.
47. Woodsworth to his father, 4 February 1900.
48. ibid., 12 January 1900.
49. Oxford Notebook 1899–1900, 35; McNaught, *A Prophet in Politics*, 14–15.
50. Woodsworth to his father, 27 January 1900.
51. ibid., 22 March 1900.
52. ibid., 15 February 1900.
53. Woodsworth to Burwash, 5 March 1906; Oxford Notebook 1899–1900, 98.
54. Oxford Notebook 1899–1900, 99.
55. Woodsworth to Burwash, 14 January 1902.
56. Unpublished address given in honour of his father, 21 September 1930 (PAC Microfilm C9160); Woodsworth to C.B. Sissons, 17 February, 27 March, 10 April 1902.
57. Woodsworth to Sissons, 27 May, 17 June 1902.
58. ibid., 21 August 1902, 15 January, 14 December 1903.
59. ibid., 21 July 1904.
60. *Christian Guardian*, 23 February 1910, 8.
61. Naught, *A Prophet in Politics*, 24–7.
62. Woodsworth to Sissons, 21 July 1904.
63. Sermon Notebook 1903–6, 253–62.
64. Woodsworth to Sissons, 20 December 1905, 20 January, 24 May 1906; to Burwash, 5 March 1906.
65. Woodsworth Papers (PAC): J.S. Woodsworth, 1906 Journal of Travel, 3: 112, 123, 128.
66. ibid., 185, 190, 195, 201.
67. ibid., 205, 255–6.
68. J.S. Woodsworth, *Following the Gleam* (Ottawa, 1926) 5–8.
69. Woodsworth to Sissons, 13 June 1907.
70. ibid., 19 June, 12 July 1907.
71. *Christian Guardian*, 2 September 1914, 1041.
72. Woodsworth, *Following the Gleam*, 18.

Index